The Definitive
BANKIM CHANDRA CHATTERJEE

The Definitive
BANKIM CHANDRA CHATTERJEE

RUPA

Published by
Rupa Publications India Pvt. Ltd 2018
7/16, Ansari Road, Daryaganj
New Delhi 110002

Sales Centres:
Allahabad Bengaluru Chennai
Hyderabad Jaipur Kathmandu
Kolkata Mumbai

Copyright © Rupa Publications India Pvt. Ltd 2018

The views and opinions expressed in this book are the author's own and the facts are as reported by him which have been verified to the extent possible, and the publishers are not in any way liable for the same.

All rights reserved.
No part of this publication may be reproduced, transmitted, or stored in a retrieval system, in any form or by any means, electronic, mechanical, photocopying, recording or otherwise, without the prior permission of the publisher.

ISBN: 978-93-5304-357-5

First impression 2018

10 9 8 7 6 5 4 3 2 1

Printed at Parksons Graphics Pvt. Ltd., Mumbai

This book is sold subject to the condition that it shall not, by way of trade or otherwise, be lent, resold, hired out, or otherwise circulated, without the publisher's prior consent, in any form of binding or cover other than that in which it is published.

CONTENTS

VANDE MATARAM

1. Mother, I Bow to Thee ! 3

THE POISON TREE
A TALE OF HINDU LIFE IN BENGAL

1. Nagendra's Journey by Boat 7
2. Coming Events Cast Their Shadows Before 12
3. Of Many Subjects 16
4. Tara Charan 20
5. OH! Lotus-Eyed, Who Art Thou? 23
6. The Reader has Cause for Great Displeasure 28
7. Haridasi Boisnavi 30
8. The Babu 36
9. Surja Mukhi's Letter 40
10. The Sprout 43
11. Caught at Last 49
12. Hira 52
13. No! 55
14. Like to Like 59
15. The Forlorn One 63
16. Hira's Envy 68
17. Hira's Quarrel the Bud of the Poison Tree 72
18. The Caged Bird 77
19. Descent 81
20. Good News 84
21. Surja Mukhi and Kamal Mani 89
22. What is the Poison Tree? 93
23. The Search 95
24. Every Sort of Happiness is Fleeting 98

25.	The Fruit of the Poison Tree	100
26.	The Signs of Love	103
27.	By the Roadside	107
28.	Is There Hope?	110
29.	Hira's Poison Tree has Blossomed	114
30.	News of Surja Mukhi	116
31.	Though All Else Dies, Suffering Dies Not	121
32.	The Fruit of Hira's Poison Tree	126
33.	Hira's Grandmother	128
34.	A Dark House: A Dark Life	131
35.	The Return	133
36.	Explanation	139
37.	The Simpleton and the Serpent	141
38.	The Catastrophe	144
39.	Kunda's Tongue is Loosened	146
40.	The End	148
	Glossary	150

RAJMOHAN'S WIFE: A NOVEL

1.	The Drawers of Water	155
2.	The Two Cousins	160
3.	The Truant's Return Home	163
4.	The Rise and Progress of a Zemindar Family	166
5.	A Letter—A Visit to the Zenana	173
6.	Midnight Plotting	178
7.	Love Can Conquer Fear	184
8.	Forewarned and Forearmed	191
9.	We Meet to Part	197
10.	The Return	201
11.	When Thieves Fall Out	205
12.	The Friends and the Stranger	210
13.	The Protectress	214
14.	Between Rival Chambers	219

15.	Consultations and Council	226
16.	What Befell Our Hero	231
17.	The Vigilance of Love	234
18.	Captors and Captive	238
19.	Madhav and Tara	245
20.	Some Women are the Equals of Some Men	250
21.	The Last Chapter in Life's Book—And in This	253
	Conclusion	256

DURGESHNANDINI OR THE CHIEFTAIN'S DAUGHTER
PART 1

1.	The Temple	261
2.	Acquaintance	265
3.	The Mogal and The Pathan	269
4.	The Youthful General	272
5.	Garmandaran	275
6.	Abhiram Swami's Counsel	279
7.	Carelessness	282
8.	Bimala's Consultation	286
9.	The Luminary of the Race	288
10.	Preparation After Consultation	291
11.	Ashmani's Embassy	295
12.	Ashmani's Rendezvous	298
13.	Ashmani's Amour	302
14.	Abduction of Diggaja	305
15.	Diggaja's Courage	308
16.	In Presence of Saileshwara	313
17.	Vira Panchami	317
18.	The Clever Person and Her Foil	322
19.	The Lover and His Lass	327
20.	From Room to Room	331
21.	The Rencounter	334

PART II

1. Aesha — 341
2. The Flower-Embosomed Stone — 345
3. Aren't You Tilottama? — 348
4. The Lady of the Veil — 351
5. The Widow — 355
6. Bimala's Letter — 358
7. Bimala's Letter (Concluded) — 362
8. The Recovery — 368
9. Diggaja's Tidings — 373
10. Sweet Image, Away! — 377
11. Changing the Room — 381
12. The Singular Ornament — 386
13. Presenting the Ring — 391
14. The Trance — 395
15. The Declaration — 398
16. Your Slave's at Your Feet, Lord — 403
17. The Last Moments — 407
18. Hostility — 410
19. Aesha's Letter — 414
20. The Flickering Lamp — 416
21. The Consequence the Dream Belies — 420
22. The Conclusion — 423

KAPALKUNDALA
PART I

1. At the Estuary of the Ganges — 431
2. On the Coast — 435
3. In Solitude — 438
4. On the Top of a Sand-hill — 441
5. On the sea-side — 444
6. In the Kapalik's Company — 448
7. In Quest — 453
8. In Shelter — 454
9. In the Holy Shrine — 461

PART II

1.	On the Highway	465
2.	At the Inn	468
3.	Meeting with the Beautiful Woman	472
4.	In the Palanquin	475
5.	In His Native Land	476
6.	In Domestic Seclusion	479

PART III

1.	In the Long Past	487
2.	At the Parting of Ways	492
3.	In Her Rival's House	495
4.	In the Palace	500
5.	In Her Own Apartments	503
6.	Down at the Feet	506
7.	On the Outskirt of the City	510

PART IV

1.	In Bedchamber	515
2.	In the Wood	519
3.	In Dream	524
4.	At the Tryst	527
5.	On the Doorstep	529
6.	In Conversation	532
7.	Greeting with Co-wife	534
8.	Homeward	539
9.	Where Last Rites are Paid to the Departed Humanity	542

VANDE MATARAM

MOTHER, I BOW TO THEE!

Mother, I bow to thee!
Rich with thy hurrying streams,
Bright with orchard gleams,
Cool with thy winds of delight,
Dark fields waving Mother of might,
Mother free.

Glory of moonlight dreams,
Over thy branches and lordly streams,
Clad in thy blossoming trees,
Mother, giver of ease
Laughing low and sweet!
Mother I kiss thy feet,
Speaker sweet and low!
Mother, to thee I bow.

Who hath said thou art weak in thy lands,
When the sword flesh out in the seventy million hands
And seventy million voices roar
Thy dreadful name from shore to shore?
With many strengths who art mighty and stored,
To thee I call Mother and Lord!
Thou who savest, arise and save!
To her I cry who ever her foe man drove
Back from plain and sea
And shook herself free.

Thou art wisdom, thou art law,
Thou art heart, our soul, our breath
Thou art love divine, the awe
In our hearts that conquers death.

Thine the strength that nerves the arm,
Thine the beauty, thine the charm.
Every image made divine
In our temples is but thine.

Thou art Durga, Lady and Queen,
With her hands that strike and her swords of sheen,
Thou art Lakshmi lotus-throned,
And the Muse a hundred-toned,
Pure and perfect without peer,
Mother lend thine ear,
Rich with thy hurrying streams,
Bright with thy orchard gleams,
Dark of hue O candid-fair.

In thy soul, with jewelled hair
And thy glorious smile divine,
Loveliest of all earthly lands,
Showering wealth from well-stored hands!
Mother, mother mine!
Mother sweet, I bow to thee,
Mother great and free!

Translated by Sri Aurobindo

THE POISON TREE
A Tale of Hindu Life in Bengal

1

NAGENDRA'S JOURNEY BY BOAT

Nagendra Natha Datta is about to travel by boat. It is the month 'Joisto' (May–June), the time of storms. His wife, Surja Mukhi, had adjured him, saying, 'Be careful; if a storm arises be sure you fasten the boat to the shore. Do not remain in the boat.' Nagendra had consented to this, otherwise Surja Mukhi would not have permitted him to leave home; and unless he went to Calcutta his suits in the Courts would not prosper.

Nagendra Natha was a young man, about thirty years of age, a wealthy 'zemindar' (landholder) in Zillah Govindpur. He dwelt in a small village which we shall call Haripur. He was travelling in his own boat. The first day or two passed without obstacle. The river flowed smoothly on—leaped, danced, cried out, restless, unending, playful. On shore, herdsmen were grazing their oxen—one sitting under a tree singing, another smoking, some fighting, others eating. Inland, husbandmen were driving the plough, beating the oxen, lavishing abuse upon them, in which the owner shared. The wives of the husbandmen, bearing vessels of water, some carrying a torn quilt, or a dirty mat, wearing a silver amulet round the neck, a ring in the nose, bracelets of brass on the arm, with unwashed garments, their skins blacker than ink, their hair unkempt, formed a chattering crowd. Among them one beauty was rubbing her head with mud, another beating a child, a third speaking with a neighbour in abuse of some nameless person, a fourth beating clothes on a plank. Further on, ladies from respectable villages adorned the 'ghâts' (landing steps) with their appearance—the elders conversing, the middle-aged worshipping 'Siva', the younger covering their faces and plunging into the water; the boys and girls screaming, playing with mud, stealing the flowers offered in worship, swimming, throwing water over every one, sometimes stepping up to a lady, snatching away the image of 'Siva' from her, and running off with it. The Brahmans, good tranquil men, recited the praises of 'Ganga' (the sacred river Ganges) and performed their worship, sometimes, as they wiped their streaming hair, casting glances at the younger women.

In the sky, the white clouds float in the heated air. Below them fly the birds, like black dots. In the coconut trees, kites, like ministers of state, look around to see on what they can pounce; the cranes, being only small fry, stand raking in the mud; the 'dahuk' (coloured herons), merry creatures, dive in the water; other birds of a lighter kind merely fly about. Market boats sail along at good speed on their own behalf; ferry boats creep along at elephantine pace to serve the needs of others only: cargo boats make no progress at all—that is the owners' concern.

On the third day of Nagendra's journey clouds arose and gradually covered the sky. The river became black, the treetops drooped, the paddy birds flew aloft, the water became motionless. Nagendra ordered the 'manji' (boatman) to run the boat in shore and make it fast. At that moment the steersman, Rahamat Mullah, was saying his prayers, so he made no answer. Rahamat knew nothing of his business. His mother's father's sister was the daughter of a boatman; on that plea he had become a hanger-on of boatmen, and accident favoured his wishes; but he learned nothing, his work was done as fate willed. Rahamat was not backward in speech, and when his prayers were ended he turned to the Babu and said, 'Do not be alarmed, sir, there is no cause for fear.' Rahamat was thus brave because the shore was close at hand, and could be reached without delay, and in a few minutes the boat was secured.

Surely the gods must have had a quarrel with Rahamat Mullah, for a great storm came up quickly. First came the wind; then the wind, having wrestled for some moments with the boughs of the trees, called to its brother the rain, and the two began a fine game. Brother Rain, mounting on brother Wind's shoulders, flew along. The two together, seizing the treetops, bent them down, broke the boughs, tore off the creepers, washed away the flowers, cast up the river in great waves, and made a general tumult. One brother flew off with Rahamat Mullah's headgear; the other made a fountain of his beard. The boatmen lowered the sail, the Babu closed the windows, and the servants put the furniture under shelter.

Nagendra was in a great strait. If, in fear of the storm, he should leave the boat, the men would think him a coward; if he remained he would break his word to Surja Mukhi. Some may ask, What harm if he did? We know not, but Nagendra thought it harm. At this moment Rahamat Mullah said, 'Sir, the rope is old; I do not know what may happen. The storm has much increased; it will be well to leave the boat.' Accordingly Nagendra got out.

No one can stand on the river bank without shelter in a heavy storm of rain. There was no sign of abatement; therefore Nagendra, thinking it necessary to seek shelter, set out to walk to the village, which was at some distance from the river, through miry paths. Presently the rain ceased, the wind abated slightly, but the sky was still thickly covered with clouds; therefore both wind and rain might be expected at night. Nagendra went on, not turning back.

Though it was early in the evening, there was thick darkness, because of the clouds. There was no sign of village, house, plain, road, or river; but the trees, being surrounded by myriads of fireflies, looked like artificial trees studded with diamonds. The lightning goddess also still sent quick flashes through the now silent black and white clouds. A woman's anger does not die away suddenly. The assembled frogs, rejoicing in the newly fallen rain, held high festival; and if you listened attentively the voice of the cricket might be heard, like the undying crackle of Ravana's funeral pyre. Amid the sounds might be distinguished the fall of the raindrops on the leaves of the trees, and that of the leaves into the pools beneath; the noise of jackals' feet on the wet paths, occasionally that of the birds on the trees shaking the water from their drenched feathers, and now and then the moaning of the almost subdued wind. Presently Nagendra saw a light in the distance. Traversing the flooded earth, drenched by the drippings from the trees, and frightening away the jackals, he approached the light; and on nearing it with much difficulty, saw that it proceeded from an old brick-built house, the door of which was open. Leaving his servant outside, Nagendra entered the house, which he found in a frightful condition.

It was not quite an ordinary house, but it had no sign of prosperity.

The doorframes were broken and dirty; there was no trace of human occupation—only owls, mice, reptiles, and insects gathered there. The light came only from one side. Nagendra saw some articles of furniture for human use; but everything indicated poverty. One or two cooking vessels, a broken oven, three or four brass dishes—these were the sole ornaments of the place. The walls were black; spiders' webs hung in the corners; cockroaches, spiders, lizards, and mice, scampered about everywhere. On a dilapidated bedstead lay an old man who seemed to be at death's door; his eyes were sunken, his breath hurried, his lips trembling. By the side of his bed stood an earthen lamp upon a fragment of brick taken from the ruins of the house. In it the oil was deficient; so also was it in the body of the man. Another lamp shone by the bedside—a girl of faultlessly fair face, of soft, starry beauty.

Whether because the light from the oil-less lamp was dim, or because the two occupants of the house were absorbed in thinking of their approaching separation, Nagendra's entrance was unseen. Standing in the doorway, he heard the last sorrowful words that issued from the mouth of the old man. These two, the old man and the young girl, were friendless in this densely-peopled world. Once they had had wealth, relatives, men and maidservants—abundance of all kinds; but by the fickleness of fortune, one after another, all had gone. The mother of the family, seeing the faces of her son and daughter daily fading like the dew-drenched lotus from the pinch of poverty, had early sunk upon the bed of death. All the other stars had been extinguished with that moon. The support of the race, the jewel of his mother's eye, the hope of his father's age, even he had been laid on the pyre before his father's eyes. No one remained save the old man and this enchanting girl. They dwelt in this ruined, deserted house in the midst of the forest. Each was to the other the only helper.

Kunda Nandini was of marriageable age; but she was the staff of her father's blindness, his only bond to this world. While he lived he could give her up to no one. 'There are but a few more days; if I give away Kunda where can I abide?' were the old man's thoughts when the question of giving her in marriage arose in his mind. Had it never occurred to him to ask himself what would become of Kunda when his summons came? Now the messenger of death stood at his bedside; he was about to leave the world; where would Kunda be on the morrow?

The deep, indescribable suffering of this thought expressed itself in every failing breath. Tears streamed from his eyes, ever restlessly closing and opening, while at his head sat the thirteen-year-old girl, like a stone figure, firmly looking into her father's face, covered with the shadows of death. Forgetting herself, forgetting to think where she would go on the morrow, she gazed only on the face of her departing parent. Gradually the old man's utterance became obscure, the breath left the throat, the eyes lost their light, the suffering soul obtained release from pain. In that dark place, by that glimmering lamp, the solitary Kunda Nandini, drawing her father's dead body on to her lap, remained sitting. The night was extremely dark; even now raindrops fell, the leaves of the trees rustled, the wind moaned, the windows of the ruined house flapped noisily. In the house, the fitful light of the lamp flickered momentarily on the face of the dead, and again left it in darkness. The lamp had long been exhausted of oil; now, after two or three flashes, it went out. Then Nagendra, with noiseless steps, went forth from the doorway.

2

COMING EVENTS CAST THEIR SHADOWS BEFORE

It was night. In the ruined house Kunda Nandini sat by her father's corpse. She called 'Father!' No one made reply. At one moment Kunda thought her father slept, again that he was dead, but she could not bring that thought clearly into her mind. At length she could no longer call, no longer think. The fan still moved in her hand in the direction where her father's once living body now lay dead. At length she resolved that he slept, for if he were dead what would become of her?

After days and nights of watching amid such sorrow, sleep fell upon her. In that exposed, bitterly cold house, the palm-leaf fan in her hand, Kunda Nandini rested her head upon her arm, more beauteous than the lotus-stalk, and slept; and in her sleep she saw a vision. It seemed as if the night were bright and clear, the sky of a pure blue—that glorious blue when the moon is encircled by a halo. Kunda had never seen the halo so large as it seemed in her vision. The light was splendid, and refreshing to the eyes. But in the midst of that magnificent halo there was no moon; in its place Kunda saw the figure of a goddess of unparalleled brilliance. It seemed as if this brilliant goddess-ruled halo left the upper sky and descended gradually lower, throwing out a thousand rays of light, until it stood over Kunda's head. Then she saw that the central beauty, crowned with golden hair, and decked with jewels, had the form of a woman. The beautiful, compassionate face had a loving smile upon its lips. Kunda recognized, with mingled joy and fear, in this compassionate being the features of her long-dead mother. The shining, loving being, raising Kunda from the earth, took her into her bosom, and the orphan girl could for a long period do nought but utter the sweet word 'Mother!'

Then the shining figure, kissing Kunda's face, said to her: 'Child, thou hast suffered much, and I know thou hast yet more to suffer; thou so young, thy tender frame cannot endure such sorrow. Therefore abide not here; leave the earth and come with me.'

Kunda seemed to reply: 'Whither shall I go?'

Then the mother, with uplifted finger indicating the shining constellations, answered, 'There!'

Kunda seemed, in her dream, to gaze into the timeless, shoreless ocean of stars, and to say, 'I have no strength; I cannot go so far.'

Hearing this, the mother's kind and cheerful but somewhat grave face saddened, her brows knitted a little, as she said in grave, sweet tones:

'Child, follow thy own will, but it would be well for thee to go with me. The day will come when thou wilt gaze upon the stars, and long bitterly to go thither. I will once more appear to thee; when, bowed to the dust with affliction, thou rememberest me, and weepest to come to me, I will return. Then do thou come. But now do thou, looking on the horizon, follow the design of my finger. I will show thee two human figures. These two beings are in this world the arbiters of thy destiny. If possible, when thou meetest them turn away as from venomous snakes. In their paths walk thou not.'

Then the shining figure pointed to the opposite sky. Kunda, following the indication, saw traced on the blue vault the figure of a man more beautiful than a god. Beholding his high, capacious forehead, his sincere kindly glance, his swan-like neck a little bent, and other traits of a fine man, no one would have believed that from him there was anything to be feared.

Then the figure dissolving as a cloud in the sky, the mother said—

'Forget not this god-like form. Though benevolent, he will be the cause of thy misery; therefore avoid him as a snake.'

Again pointing to the heavens she continued—

'Look hither.'

Kunda, looking, saw a second figure sketched before her, not this time that of a man, but a young woman of bright complexion and lotus-shaped eyes. At this sight she felt no fear; but the mother said—

'This dark figure in a woman's dress is a 'Rakshasi'. When thou seest her, flee from her.'

As she thus spoke the heavens suddenly became dark, the halo disappeared from the sky, and with it the bright figure in its midst.

Then Kunda awoke from her sleep.

Nagendra went to the village, the name of which he heard was Jhunjhunpur. At his recommendation and expense, some of the villagers performed the necessary rites for the dead, one of the female neighbours remaining with the bereaved girl. When Kunda saw that they had taken her father away, she became convinced of his death, and gave way to ceaseless weeping.

In the morning the neighbour returned to her own house, but sent her daughter Champa to comfort Kunda Nandini.

Champa was of the same age as Kunda, and her friend. She strove to divert her mind by talking of various matters, but she saw that Kunda did not attend. She wept constantly, looking up every now and then into the sky as though in expectation.

Champa jestingly asked, 'What do you see that you look into the sky a hundred times?'

Kunda replied, 'My mother appeared to me yesterday, and bade me go with her, but I feared to do so; now I mourn that I did not. If she came again I would go: therefore I look constantly into the sky.'

Champa said, 'How can the dead return?'

To which Kunda replied by relating her vision.

Greatly astonished, Champa asked, 'Are you acquainted with the man and woman whose forms you saw in the sky?'

'No, I had never seen them. There cannot be anywhere a man so handsome; I never saw such beauty.'

On rising in the morning, Nagendra inquired of the people in the village what would become of the dead man's daughter, where she would live, and whether she had any relatives. He was told that there was no dwelling place for her, and that she had no relatives.

Then Nagendra said, 'Will not some of you receive her and give her in marriage? I will pay the expense, and so long as she remains amongst you I will pay so much a month for her board and lodging.'

If he had offered ready money many would have consented to his proposal; but after he had gone away Kunda would have been reduced to servitude, or turned out of the house. Nagendra did not act in so foolish a manner; therefore, money not being forthcoming, no one consented to his suggestion.

At length one, seeing him at the end of his resources, observed: 'A sister of her mother's lives at Sham Bazar; Binod Ghosh is the husband's name. You are on your way to Calcutta; if you take her with you and place her with her aunt, then this 'Kaystha' girl will be cared for, and you will have done your duty to your caste.'

Seeing no other plan, Nagendra adopted this suggestion, and sent for Kunda to acquaint her with the arrangement.

Champa accompanied Kunda. As they were coming, Kunda, seeing Nagendra from afar, suddenly stood still like one stunned. Her feet refused to move; she stood looking at him with eyes full of astonishment.

Champa asked, 'Why do you stand thus?'

Kunda, pointing with her finger, said, 'It is he!'

'He! Who?' said Champa.

'He whom last night my mother pictured in the heavens.'

Then Champa also stood frightened and astonished. Seeing that the girls shrank from approaching, Nagendra came near and explained everything. Kunda was unable to reply; she could only gaze with eyes full of surprise.

3

OF MANY SUBJECTS

Reluctantly did Nagendra Natha take Kunda with him to Calcutta. On arriving there he made much search for her aunt's husband, but he found no one in Sham Bazar named Binod Ghosh. He found a Binod Das, who admitted no relationship. Thus Kunda remained as a burthen upon Nagendra.

Nagendra had one sister, younger than himself, named Kamal Mani, whose father-in-law's house was in Calcutta. Her husband's name was Srish Chandra Mittra. Srish Babu was accountant in the house of Plunder, Fairly, and Co. It was a great house, and Srish Chandra was wealthy. He was much attached to his brother-in-law. Nagendra took Kunda Nandini thither, and imparted her story to Kamal Mani.

Kamal was about eighteen years of age. In features she resembled Nagendra; both brother and sister were very handsome. But, in addition to her beauty, Kamal was famed for her learning. Nagendra's father, engaging an English teacher, had had Kamal Mani and Surja Mukhi well instructed. Kamal's mother-in-law was living, but she dwelt in Srish Chandra's ancestral home. In Calcutta Kamal Mani was housemistress.

When he had finished the story of Kunda Nandini, Nagendra said, 'Unless you will keep her here, there is no place for her. Later, when I return home, I will take her to Govindpur with me.'

Kamal was very mischievous. When Nagendra had turned away, she snatched up Kunda in her arms and ran off with her. A tub of not very hot water stood in an adjoining room, and suddenly Kamal threw Kunda into it. Kunda was quite frightened. Then Kamal, laughing, took some scented soap and proceeded to wash Kunda. An attendant, seeing Kamal thus employed, bustled up, saying, 'I will do it! I will do it!' but Kamal, sprinkling some of the hot water over the woman, sent her running away. Kamal having bathed and rubbed Kunda, she appeared like a dew-washed lotus. Then Kamal, having robed her in a beautiful white garment, dressed her hair with scented oil, and decorated her with ornaments, said to her: 'Now go and salute the 'Dada Babu' (elder brother), and return, but mind you do not thus to the master of the house: if he should see you he will want to marry you.'

Nagendra Natha wrote Kunda's history to Surja Mukhi. Also when writing to an intimate friend of his living at a distance, named Hara Deb Ghosal, he spoke of Kunda in the following terms:

'Tell me what you consider to be the age of beauty in woman. You will say after forty, because your Brahmini is a year or two more than that. The girl Kunda, whose history I have given you, is thirteen. On looking at her, it seems as if that were the age of beauty. The sweetness and simplicity that precede the budding-time of youth are never seen afterwards. This Kunda's simplicity is astonishing; she understands nothing. Today she even wished to run into the streets to play with the boys. On being forbidden, she was much frightened, and desisted. Kamal is teaching her, and says she shows much aptitude in learning, but she does not understand other things. For instance, her large blue eyes—eyes swimming ever like the autumn lotus in clear water—these two eyes may be fixed upon my face, but they say nothing. I lose my senses gazing on them; I cannot explain better. You will laugh at this history of my mental stability; but if I could place you in front of those eyes, I should see what your firmness is worth. Up to this time I have been unable to determine what those eyes are like. I have not seen them look twice the same; I think there are no other such eyes in the world, they seem as if they scarcely saw the things of earth, but were ever seeking something in space. It is not that Kunda is faultlessly beautiful. Her features, if compared with those of many others, would not be highly praised; yet I think I never saw such rare beauty. It is as if there were in Kunda Nandini something not of this world, as though she were not made of flesh and blood, but of moonbeams and the scent of flowers. Nothing presents itself to my mind at this moment to which to liken her. Incomparable being! her whole person seems to breathe peace. If in some clear pool you have observed the sheen produced by the rays of the autumn moon, you have seen something resembling her. I can think of no other simile.'

Surja Mukhi's reply to Nagendra's letter came in a few days. It was after this manner:

'I know not what fault your servant has committed. If it is necessary you should stay so long in Calcutta, why am I not with you to attend upon you? This is my earnest wish; the moment I receive your consent, I will set out.

'In picking up a little girl, have you forgotten me? Many unripe things are esteemed. People like green guavas, and green cucumbers; green coconuts are cooling. This low-born female is also, I think, very young, else in meeting with her why should you forget me? Joking apart, have you given up all right over this girl? if not, I beg her from you. It is my business to arrange for her. In whatever becomes yours I have the right to share, but in this case I see your sister has entire possession. Still, I shall not vex myself much if Kamal usurps my rights.

'Do you ask what do I want with the girl? I wish to give her in marriage with Tara Charan. You know how much I have sought for a suitable wife for him. If Providence has sent us a good girl, do not disappoint me. If Kamal will give her up, bring Kunda Nandini with you when you come. I have written to Kamal also recommending this. I am having ornaments fashioned, and am making other preparations for the marriage. Do not linger in Calcutta. Is it not true that if a man stays six months in that city he becomes quite stupid? If you design to marry Kunda, bring her with you, and I will give her to you. Only say that you propose to marry her, and I will arrange the marriage-basket.'

Who Tara Charan was will be explained later. Whoever he was, both Nagendra and Kamal Mani consented to Surja Mukhi's proposal. Therefore it was resolved that when Nagendra went home Kunda Nandini should accompany him. Every one consented with delight, and Kamal also prepared some ornaments. How blind is man to the future! Some years later there came a day when Nagendra and Kamal Mani bowed to the dust, and, striking their foreheads in grief, murmured: 'In how evil a moment did we find Kunda Nandini! in how evil an hour did we agree to Surja Mukhi's letter!' Now Kamal Mani, Surja Mukhi, and Nagendra, together have sowed the poison seed; later they will all repent it with wailing.

Causing his boat to be got ready, Nagendra returned to Govindpur with Kunda Nandini. Kunda had almost forgotten her dream; while journeying with Nagendra it recurred to her memory, but thinking of his benevolent face and kindly character, Kunda could not believe that any harm would come to her from him. In like manner there are many insects who, seeing a destructive flame, enter therein.

4

TARA CHARAN

The Poet Kalidas was supplied with flowers by a Malini (flower-girl). He, being a poor Brahmin, could not pay for the flowers, but in place of that he used to read some of his own verses to the Malini. One day there bloomed in the Malini's tank a lily of unparalleled beauty. Plucking it, the Malini offered it to Kalidas. As a reward the poet read to her some verses from the Megha Duta (Cloud Messenger). That poem is an ocean of wit, but every one knows that its opening lines are tasteless. The Malini did not relish them, and being annoyed she rose to go.

The poet asked: 'Oh! friend "Malini", are you going?'

'Your verses have no flavour,' replied the 'Malini'.

'"Malini"! you will never reach heaven.'

'Why so?'

'There is a staircase to heaven. By ascending millions of steps heaven is reached. My poem has also a staircase; these tasteless verses are the steps. If you can't climb these few steps, how will you ascend the heavenly ladder?'

The 'Malini' then, in fear of losing heaven through the Brahmin's curse, listened to the 'Megha Duta' from beginning to end. She admired the poem; and next day, binding a wreath of flowers in the name of Cupid, she crowned the poet's temples therewith.

This ordinary poem of mine is not heaven; neither has it a staircase of a million steps. Its flavour is faint and the steps are few. These few tasteless chapters are the staircase. If among my readers there is one of the 'Malini's' disposition, I warn him that without climbing these steps he will not arrive at the pith of the story.

Surja Mukhi's father's house was in Konnagar. Her father was a 'Kaystha' of good position. He was cashier in some house at Calcutta. Surja Mukhi was his only child. In her infancy a 'Kaystha' widow named

Srimati lived in her father's house as a servant, and looked after Surja Mukhi. Srimati had one child named Tara Charan, of the same age as Surja Mukhi. With him Surja Mukhi had played, and on account of this childish association she felt towards him the affection of a sister.

Srimati was a beautiful woman, and therefore soon fell into trouble. A wealthy man of the village, of evil character, having cast his eyes upon her, she forsook the house of Surja Mukhi's father. Whither she went no one exactly knew, but she did not return. Tara Charan, forsaken by his mother, remained in the house of Surja Mukhi's father, who was a very kind-hearted man, and brought up this deserted boy as his own child; not keeping him in slavery as an unpaid servant, but having him taught to read and write. Tara Charan learned English at a free mission school. Afterwards Surja Mukhi was married, and some years later her father died. By this time Tara Charan had learned English after a clumsy fashion, but he was not qualified for any business. Rendered homeless by the death of Surja Mukhi's father, he went to her house. At her instigation Nagendra opened a school in the village, and Tara Charan was appointed master. Nowadays, by means of the grant-in-aid system in many villages, sleek-haired, song-singing, harmless Master Babus appear; but at that time such a being as a Master Babu was scarcely to be seen. Consequently, Tara Charan appeared as one of the village gods; especially as it was known in the bazaar that he had read the *Citizen of the World*, the *Spectator*, and three books of Euclid. On account of these gifts he was received into the Brahmo Samaj of Debendra Babu, the zemindar of Debipur, and reckoned as one of that Babu's retinue.

Tara Charan wrote many essays on widow remarriage, on the education of women, and against idol worship; read them weekly in the Samaj, and delivered many discourses beginning with 'Oh, most merciful God!' Some of these he took from the Tattwa Bodhini, and some he caused to be written for him by the school pandit. He was forever preaching: 'Abandon idol worship, give choice in marriage, give women education; why do you keep them shut up in a cage? let women come out.' There was a special cause for this liberality on the subject of women, inasmuch as in his own house there was no woman. Up to this time he had not married. Surja Mukhi had made great efforts to get him married, but as his mother's story was known in Govindpur, no respectable Kaystha consented to give him his daughter. Many a common, disreputable Kaystha girl he might have had; but Surja Mukhi, regarding Tara Charan as a brother, would not give her consent, since she did not choose to call such a girl sister-in-law. While she was seeking for a respectable 'Kaystha' girl, Nagendra's letter came, describing Kunda Nandini's gifts and beauty. She resolved to give her to Tara Charan in marriage.

5

OH! LOTUS-EYED, WHO ART THOU?

Kunda arrived safely with Nagendra at Govindpur. At the sight of Nagendra's dwelling she became speechless with wonder, for she had never seen one so grand. There were three divisions without and three within. Each division was a large city. The outer 'mahal' (division) was entered by an iron gate, and was surrounded on all sides by a handsome lofty iron railing. From the gate a broad, red, well-metalled path extended, on each side of which were beds of fresh grass that would have formed a paradise for cows. In the midst of each plat was a circle of shrubs, all blooming with variously coloured flowers. In front rose the lofty demi-upper-roomed 'boita khana' (reception-hall), approached by a broad flight of steps, the verandah of which was supported by massive fluted pillars. The floor of the lower part of this house was of marble. Above the parapet, in its centre, an enormous clay lion, with dependent mane, hung out its red tongue. This was Nagendra's 'boita khana'. To left and right of the grass plats stood a row of one-storied buildings, containing on one side the daftar 'khana' (accountant's office) and 'kacheri' (courthouse); on the other the storehouse, treasury, and servants' dwellings. On both sides of the gate were the doorkeepers' lodges. This first mahal was named the 'kacheri bari' (house of business); the next to it was the 'puja mahal' (division for worship). The large hall of worship formed one side of the 'puja mahal'; on the other three sides were two-storied houses. No one lived in this 'mahal'. At the festival of Durga it was thronged; but now grass sprouted between the tiles of the court, pigeons frequented the halls, the houses were full of furniture, and the doors were kept locked. Beside this was the 'thakur bari' (room assigned to the family deity): in it on one side was the temple of the gods, the handsome stone-built dancing hall; on the remaining sides, the kitchen for the gods, the dwelling rooms of the priests, and a guest house. In this 'mahal' there was no lack of people. The tribe of priests, with garlands on their necks and sandalwood marks on their foreheads; a troop of cooks; people bearing baskets of flowers for the altars; some bathing the gods, some ringing bells, chattering, pounding sandalwood, cooking; men and women servants bearing water, cleaning floors, washing rice, quarrelling with the cooks. In the guest house an ascetic, with ash-smeared, loose hair, is lying sleeping; one with upraised arm (stiffened thus through years) is distributing drugs and charms to the servants of the house; a white-bearded, red-robed 'Brahmachari', swinging his chaplet of beads, is reading from a manuscript copy of the 'Bhagavat-gita' in the 'Nagari' character; holy mendicants are quarrelling for their share of 'ghi' and flour. Here a company of emaciated 'Boiragis', with wreaths of 'tulsi' (a sacred plant) round their necks and the marks of their religion painted on their foreheads, the bead fastened into the knot of hair on their heads shaking with each movement, are beating the drums as they sing:

> 'I could not get the opportunity to speak,
> The elder brother Dolai was with me.'

The wives of the 'Boiragis', their hair braided in a manner pleasing to their husbands, are singing the tune of 'Govinda Adhi Kari' to the accompaniment of the tambourine. Young 'Boisnavis' singing with elder women of the same class, the middle-aged trying to bring their voices into unison with those of the old. In the midst of the courtyard idle boys fighting, and abusing each other's parents.

These three were the outer 'mahals'. Behind these came the three inner ones. The inner 'mahal' behind the 'kacheri bari' was for Nagendra's private use. In that only himself, his wife, and their personal attendants were allowed; also the furniture for their use. This place was new, built by Nagendra himself, and very well arranged. Next to it, and behind the 'puja bari', came another 'mahal'; this was old, ill-built, the rooms low, small, and dirty. Here was a whole city—full of female relations, mother's sister and mother's cousin, father's sister and cousin; mother's widowed sister, mother's married sister; father's sister's son's wife, mother's sister's son's daughter. All these female relatives cawing day and night like a set of crows in a banian tree; at every moment screams, laughter, quarrelling, bad reasoning, gossip, reproach, the scuffling of boys, the crying of girls. 'Bring water!' 'Give the clothes!' 'Cook the rice!' 'The child does not eat!' 'Where is the milk?' etc., is heard as an ocean of confused sounds. Next to it, behind the 'Thakur bari', was the cookhouse. Here a woman, having placed the rice pot on the fire, gathering up her feet, sits gossiping with her neighbour on the details of her son's marriage. Another, endeavouring to light a fire with green wood, her eyes smarting with the smoke, is abusing the 'gomashta' (factor), and producing abundant proof that he has supplied this wet wood to pocket part of the price. Another beauty, throwing fish into the hot oil, closes her eyes and twists her ten fingers, making a grimace, for oil leaping forth has burnt her skin. One having bathed her long hair, plentifully besmeared with oil, braiding it in a curve on the temples and fastening it in a knot on the top of her head, stirs the pulse cooking in an earthen pot, like Krishna prodding the cows with a stick. Here Bami, Kaymi, Gopal's mother, Nipal's mother, are shredding with a big knife vegetable pumpkins, brinjals, the sound of the cutting steel mingling with abuse of the neighbours, of the masters, of everybody: that Golapi has become a widow very young; that Chandi's husband is a great drunkard; that Koylash's husband has secured a fine appointment as writer to the 'Darogah'; that there could not be in the world such a flying journey as that of Gopal, nor such a wicked child as Parvati's; how the English must be of the race of 'Ravan' (the ten-headed king of Ceylon); how 'Bhagirati' had brought 'Ganga'; how Sham Biswas was the lover of the daughter of the Bhattacharjyas; with many other subjects. A dark, stout-bodied woman, placing a large 'bonti' (a fish-cutter) on a heap of ashes in the court, is cutting fish; the kites, frightened at her gigantic size and her quick-handedness, keeping away, yet now and again darting forward to peck at the fish. Here a white-haired woman is bringing water; there one with powerful hand is grinding spices. Here, in the storehouse, a servant, a cook, and the store keeper are quarrelling together; the store keeper maintaining, 'The "ghi" (clarified butter) I have given is the right quantity;' the cook disputing it; the servant saying, 'We could manage with the quantity you give if you left the storehouse unlocked.' In the hope of receiving doles of rice, many children and beggars with their dogs are sitting waiting. The cats do not flatter any one; they watch their opportunity, steal in, and help themselves. Here a cow without an owner is feasting with closed eyes upon the husks of pumpkins, other vegetables, and fruit.

Behind these three inner 'mahals' is the flower garden; and further yet a broad tank, blue as the sky. This tank is walled in. The inner house (the women's) has three divisions, and in the flower garden is a private path, and at each end of the path two doors; these doors are private, they give entrance to the three 'mahals' of the inner house. Outside the house are the stables, the elephant house, the kennels, the cowhouse, the aviaries, etc.

Kunda Nandini, full of astonishment at Nagendra's unbounded wealth, was borne in a palanquin to the inner apartments, where she saluted Surja Mukhi, who received her with a blessing.

Having recognized in Nagendra the likeness of the man she had seen in her dream, Kunda Nandini doubted whether his wife would not resemble the female figure she had seen later; but the sight of Surja Mukhi removed this doubt. Surja Mukhi was of a warm, golden colour, like the full moon; the figure in the dream was dark. Surja Mukhi's eyes were beautiful, but not like those in the dream. They were long deer-eyes, extending to the side hair; the eyebrows joined in a beautiful curve over the dilated, densely black pupils, full but steady. The eyes of the dark woman in the dream were not so enchanting. Then Surja Mukhi's features were not similar. The dream figure was dwarfish; Surja Mukhi rather tall, her figure swaying with the beauty of the honeysuckle creeper. The dream figure was beautiful, but Surja Mukhi was a hundredfold more so. The dream figure was not more than twenty years of age; Surja Mukhi was nearly twenty-six. Kunda saw clearly that there was no resemblance between the two. Surja Mukhi conversed pleasantly with Kunda, and summoned the attendants, to the chief among whom she said, 'This is Kunda with whom I shall give Tara Charan in marriage; therefore see that you treat her as my brother's wife.'

The servant expressed her assent, and took Kunda aside with her to another place. At sight of her Kunda's flesh crept; a cold moisture came over her from head to foot. The female figure which Kunda in her dream had seen her mother's fingers trace upon the heavens, this servant was that lotus-eyed, dark-complexioned woman.

Kunda, agitated with fear, breathing with difficulty, asked, 'Who are you?'

The servant answered, 'My name is Hira.'

6

THE READER HAS CAUSE FOR GREAT DISPLEASURE

At this point the reader will be much annoyed. It is a custom with novelists to conclude with a wedding, but we are about to begin with the marriage of Kunda Nandini. By another custom that has existed from ancient times, whoever shall marry the heroine must be extremely handsome, adorned with all virtues, himself a hero, and devoted to his mistress. Poor Tara Charan possessed no such advantages; his beauty consisted in a copper-tinted complexion and a snub nose; his heroism found exercise only in the schoolroom; and as for his love, I cannot say how much he had for Kunda Nandini, but he had some for a pet monkey.

However that may be, soon after Kunda Nandini's arrival at the house of Nagendra she was married to Tara Charan. Tara Charan took home his beautiful wife; but in marrying a beautiful wife he brought himself into a difficulty.

The reader will remember that Tara Charan had delivered some essays in the house of Debendra Babu on the subjects of women's education and the opening of the zenana. In the discussions that ensued, the Master Babu had said vauntingly: 'Should the opportunity ever be given me, I will be the first to set an example of reform in these matters. Should I marry, I will bring my wife out into society.'

Now he was married, and the fame of Kunda's beauty had spread through the district. All the neighbours now, quoting an old song, said, 'Where now is his pledge?' Debendra said, 'What, are you now also in the troop of old fools? Why do you not introduce us to your wife?'

Tara Charan was covered with shame; he could not escape from Debendra's banter and taunts. He consented to allow Debendra to make the acquaintance of his wife. Then fear arose lest Surja Mukhi should be displeased. A year passed in evasion and procrastination; when, seeing that this could be carried on no longer, he made an excuse that his house was in need of repair, and sent Kunda Nandini to Nagendra's house. When the repairs of the house were completed, Kunda Nandini returned home. A few days after, Debendra, with some of his friends, called upon Tara Charan, and jeered him for his false boasting. Driven thus, as it were, into a corner, Tara Charan persuaded Kunda Nandini to dress in suitable style, and brought her forth to converse with Debendra Babu. How could she do so? She remained standing veiled before him for a few seconds, then fled weeping. But Debendra was enchanted with her youthful grace and beauty. He never forgot it.

Soon after that, some kind of festival was held in Debendra's house, and a little girl was sent thence to Kunda to invite her attendance. But Surja Mukhi hearing of this, forbade her to accept the invitation, and she did not go. Later, Debendra again going to Tara Charan's house, had an interview with Kunda. Surja Mukhi hearing of this through others, gave to Tara Charan such a scolding, that from that time Debendra's visits were stopped.

In this manner three years passed after the marriage; then Kunda Nandini became a widow. Tara Charan died of fever. Surja Mukhi took Kunda to live with her, and selling the house she had given to Tara Charan, gave the proceeds in Government paper to Kunda.

The reader is no doubt much displeased, but in fact the tale is only begun. Of the poison tree the seed only has thus far been sown.

7

HARIDASI BOISNAVI

The widow Kunda Nandini passed some time in Nagendra's house. One afternoon the whole household of ladies were sitting together in the other division of the house, all occupied according to their tastes in the simple employment of village women. All ages were there, from the youngest girl to the grey-haired woman. One was binding another's hair, the other suffering it to be bound; one submitting to have her white hairs extracted, another extracting them by the aid of a grain of rice; one beauty sewing together shreds of cloth into a quilt for her boy, another suckling her child; one lovely being dressing the plaits of her hair; another beating her child, who now cried aloud, now quietly sobbed, by turns. Here one is sewing carpet work, another leaning over it in admiring examination. There one of artistic taste, thinking of some one's marriage, is drawing a design on the wooden seats to be used by the bridal pair. One learned lady is reading Dasu Rai's poetry. An old woman is delighting the ears of her neighbours with complaints of her son; a humorous young one, in a voice half bursting with laughter, relates in the ears of her companions whose husbands are absent some jocose story of her husband's, to beguile the pain of separation. Some are reproaching the 'Grihini' (housemistress), some the 'Korta' (master), some the neighbours; some reciting their own praises. She who may have received a gentle scolding in the morning from Surja Mukhi on account of her stupidity, is bringing forward many examples of her remarkable acuteness of understanding. She in whose cooking the flavours can never be depended upon, is dilating at great length upon her proficiency in the art. She whose husband is proverbial in the village for his ignorance, is astounding her companions by her praises of his superhuman learning. She whose children are dark and repulsive-looking, is pluming herself on having given birth to jewels of beauty. Surja Mukhi was not of the company. She was a little proud, and did not sit much with these people; if she came amongst them her presence was a restraint upon the enjoyment of the rest. All feared her somewhat, and were reserved towards her. Kunda Nandini associated with them; she was amongst them now, teaching a little boy his letters at his mother's request. During the lesson the pupil's eyes were fixed upon the sweetmeat in another child's hand, consequently his progress was not great. At this moment there appeared amongst them a 'Boisnavi' (female mendicant), exclaiming, 'Jai Radhika!'

A constant stream of guests was served in Nagendra's 'Thakur bari', and every Sunday quantities of rice were distributed in the same place, but neither 'Boisnavis' nor others were allowed to come to the women's apartments to beg; accordingly, on hearing the cry 'Jai Radha!' in these forbidden precincts, one of the inmates exclaimed: 'What, woman! Do you venture to intrude here? Go to the "Thakur bari." But even as she spoke, turning to look at the 'Boisnavi', she could not finish her speech, but said instead: 'Oh, ma, what "Boisnavi" are you?'

Looking up, all saw with astonishment that the 'Boisnavi' was young and of exceeding beauty; in that group of beautiful women there was none, excepting Kunda Nandini, so beautiful as she. Her trembling lips, well-formed nose, large lotus-eyes, pencilled brows, smooth, well-shaped forehead, arms like the lotus-stalk, and complexion like the champak flower, were rare among women. But had there been present any critic of loveliness, he would have said there was a want of sweetness in her beauty, while in her walk and in her movements there was a masculine character.

The sandal mark on the 'Boisnavi's' nose was long and fine, her hair was braided, she wore a sari with a coloured border, and carried a small tambourine in her hand. She wore brass bracelets, and over them others made of black glass.

One of the elder women addressed her saying, 'Who are you?'

The 'Boisnavi' replied, 'My name is Haridasi. Will the ladies like a song?'

The cry, 'Yes, yes! sing!' sounded on all sides from old and young. Raising her tambourine, the 'Boisnavi' seated herself near the ladies, where Kunda was teaching the little boy. Kunda was very fond of music; on hearing that the 'Boisnavi' would sing she came nearer.

Her pupil seized the opportunity to snatch the sweetmeat from the other child's hand, and eat it himself.

The 'Boisnavi' asking what she should sing, the listeners gave a number of different orders. One called for the strains of 'Govinda Adhikari', another 'Gopale Ure'. She who was reading Dasu Rai's poem desired to have it sung. Two or three asked for the old stories about Krishna; they were divided as to whether they would hear about the companions or about the separation. Some wanted to hear of his herding the cows in his youth. One shameless girl called out, 'If you do not sing such and such a passage I will not listen.' One mere child, by way of teaching the 'Boisnavi', sang some nonsensical syllables. The 'Boisnavi', listening to the different demands, gave a momentary glance at Kunda, saying: 'Have you no commands to give?'

Kunda, ashamed, bent her head smiling, but did not speak aloud; she whispered in the ear of a companion, 'Mention some hymn.'

The companion said, 'Kunda desires that you will sing a hymn.' The 'Boisnavi' then began a hymn. Kunda, seeing that the 'Boisnavi' had neglected all other commands to obey hers, was much abashed. Haridasi, striking gently on her tambourine as if in sport, recited in a gentle voice some few notes like the murmuring of a bee in early spring, or a bashful bride's first loving speech to her husband. Then suddenly she produced from that insignificant tambourine, as though with the fingers of a powerful musician, sounds like the crashing of the clouds in thunder, making the frames of her hearers shrink within them as she sang in tones more melodious than those of the 'Apsharas' (celestial singing women).

The ladies, astonished and enchanted, heard the 'Boisnavi's' unequalled voice filling the court with sound that ascended to the skies. What could secluded women understand of the method of that singing? An intelligent person would have comprehended that this perfect singing was not due to natural gifts alone. The 'Boisnavi', whoever she might be, had received a thorough scientific training in music, and, though young, she was very proficient.

The 'Boisnavi', having finished her song, was urged by the ladies to sing again. Haridasi, looking with thirsty eyes at Kunda, sang the following song from Krishna's address to Radhika:

THE BOISNAVI'S SONG

*'To see thy beauteous lily face
I come expectant to this place;
Let me, oh Rai! thy feet embrace.
To deprecate thy sullen ire,
Therefore I come in strange attire;
Revive me, Radha, kindness speak,
Clasping thy feet my home I'd seek.
Of thy fair form to catch a ray
From door to door with flute I stray;
When thy soft name it murmurs low
Mine eyes with sudden tears o'erflow.
If thou wilt not my pardon speak
The banks of Jumna's stream I'll seek,
Will break my flute and yield my life;
Oh! cease thy wrath, and end the strife.
The joys of Braj I've cast aside
A slave before thy feet t' abide;
Thine anklets round my neck I'll bind,
In Jumna's stream I'll refuge find.'*

The song over, the 'Boisnavi', looking at Kunda, said, 'Singing has made me thirsty; give me some water.'

Kunda brought water in a vessel; but the 'Boisnavi' said, 'I will not touch your vessel; come near and pour some water into my hands. I was not born a 'Boisnavi.' By this she gave it to be understood that she was formerly of some unholy caste, and had since become a 'Boisnavi.

In reply to her words, Kunda went behind her so as to pour the water into her hands. They were at such a distance from the rest that words spoken gently could not be heard by any of them. Kunda poured the water, and the 'Boisnavi' washed her hands and face.

While thus engaged the latter murmured, 'Are you not Kunda?'
In astonishment Kunda replied, 'Why do you ask?'
'Have you ever seen your mother-in-law?'
'No.'
Kunda had heard that her mother-in-law, having lost her good

name, had left the place.

Then said the 'Boisnavi': 'Your mother-in-law is here now. She is in my house, and is crying bitterly to be allowed to see you for once. She dare not show her face to the mistress of this house. Why should you not go with me to see her? Notwithstanding her fault, she is still your mother-in-law.'

Although Kunda was simple, she understood quite well that she should not acknowledge any connection with such a relation. Therefore she merely shook her head at the 'Boisnavi's words and refused her assent. But the 'Boisnavi' would not take a refusal; again she urged the matter.

Kunda replied, 'I cannot go without the "Grihini's" permission.'

This Haridasi forbade. 'You must not speak to the housemistress, she will not let you go; it may be she will send for your "Sasuri" (mother-in-law). In that case your mother-in-law would flee the country.'

The more the 'Boisnavi' insisted, the more Kunda refused to go without the 'Grihini's' permission.

Haridasi having no other resource, said: 'Very well, put the thing nicely to the "Grihini"; I will come another day and take you. Mind you put it prudently, and shed some tears also, else she will not consent.'

Even to this Kunda did not consent; she would not say either 'yes' or 'no.'

Haridasi, having finished purifying her face and hands, turned to the ladies and asked for contributions. At this moment Surja Mukhi came amongst them, the desultory talk ceased, and the younger women, all pretending some occupation, sat down.

Surja Mukhi, examining the 'Boisnavi' from head to foot, inquired, 'Who are you?'

An aunt of Nagendra's explained: 'She is a "Boisnavi" who came to sing. I never heard such beautiful singing! Will you let her sing for you? Sing something about the goddesses.'

Haridasi, having sung a beautiful piece about Sham, Surja Mukhi, enchanted, dismissed her with a handsome present. The 'Boisnavi', making a profound salute, cast one more glance at Kunda and went away. Once out of the range of Surja Mukhi's eyes, she made a few gentle taps on the tambourine, singing softly—

'Ah, my darling!
I'll give you honey to eat, golden robes to wear;
I'll fill your flask with "attar",
And your jar with water of rose,
Your box with spice prepared by my own hand.'

The 'Boisnavi' being gone, the women could talk of nothing else for some time. First they praised her highly, then began to point out her defects.

Biraj said, 'She is beautiful, but her nose is somewhat flat.'
Bama remarked, 'Her complexion is too pale.'
Chandra Mukhi added, 'Her hair is like tow.'
Kapal said, 'Her forehead is too high.'
Kamala said, 'Her lips are thick.'
Harani observed, 'Her figure is very wooden.'
Pramada added, 'The woman's bust is like that of a play actor, it has no grace.'

In this manner it soon appeared that the beautiful 'Boisnavi' was of unparalleled ugliness.

Then Lalita said, 'Whatever her looks may be, she sings beautifully.'

But even this was not admitted. Chandra Mukhi said the singing was coarse; Mukta Keshi confirmed this criticism.

Ananga said, 'The woman does not know any songs; she could not even give us one of Dasu Rai's songs.'

Kanak said, 'She does not understand time.'

Thus it appeared that Haridasi 'Boisnavi' was not only extremely ugly, but that her singing was of the worst description.

8

THE BABU

Haridasi 'Boisnavi', having left the house of the Datta family, went to Debipur. At this place there is a flower garden surrounded by painted iron railings. It is well stocked with fruit trees and flowering shrubs. In the centre is a tank, upon the edge of which stands a garden house. Entering a private room in this house, Haridasi threw off her dress. Suddenly that dense mass of hair fell from the head; the locks were borrowed. The bust also fell away; it was made of cloth. After putting on suitable apparel and removing the 'Boisnavi' garments, there stood forth a strikingly handsome young man of about five and twenty years of age. Having no hair on his face he looked quite a youth; in feature he was very handsome. This young man was Debendra Babu, of whom we have before had some slight knowledge.

Debendra and Nagendra were sprung from the same family, but between the two branches there had been feud for successive generations, so that the members of the Debipur family were not on speaking terms with those of Govindpur. From generation to generation there had been lawsuits between the two houses. At length, in an important suit, the grandfather of Nagendra had defeated the grandfather of Debendra, and since that time the Debipur family had been powerless. All their money was swallowed up in law expenses, and the Govindpur house had bought up all their estates. From that time the position of the Debipur family had declined, that of the other increased, the two branches no longer united.

Debendra's father had sought in one way to restore the fallen fortunes of his house. Another zemindar, named Ganesh, dwelt in the Haripur district; he had one unmarried daughter, Hembati, who was given to Debendra in marriage. Hembati had many virtues; she was ugly, ill-tempered, unamiable, selfish. Up to the time of his marriage with her, Debendra's character had been without stain. He had been very studious, and was by nature steady and truth-loving. But that marriage had been fatal to him. When Debendra came to years of discretion he perceived that on account of his wife's disposition there was no hope of domestic happiness for him. With manhood there arose in him a love for beauty, but in his own house this was denied to him; with manhood there came a desire for conjugal affection, but the mere sight of the unamiable Hembati quenched the desire. Putting happiness out of the question, Debendra perceived that it would be difficult to stay in the house to endure the venom of Hembati's tongue. One day Hembati poured forth abuse on her husband; he had endured much, he could endure no more, he dragged Hembati by the hair and kicked her. From that day, deserting his home, he went to Calcutta, leaving orders that a small house should be built for him in the garden. Before this occurred the father of Debendra had died, therefore he was independent. In Calcutta he plunged into vicious pursuits to allay his unsatisfied desires, and then strove to wash away his heart's reproaches in wine; after that he ceased to feel any remorse, he took delight in vice. When he had learned what Calcutta could teach him in regard to luxury, Debendra returned to his native place, and, taking up his abode in the garden house, gave himself up to the indulgence of his recently acquired tastes. Debendra had learned many peculiar fashions in Calcutta; on returning to Debipur he called himself a Reformer. First he established a 'Brahmo Samaj'; many such Brahmos as Tara Charan were attracted to it, and to the speech-making there was no limit. He also thought of opening a female school; but this required too much effort, he could not do it. About widow remarriage he was very zealous. One or two such marriages had been arranged, the widows being of low caste; but the credit of these was due, not to him, but to the contracting parties. He had been of one mind with Tara Charan about breaking the chains of the zenana; both had said, 'Let women come out.' In this matter Debendra was very successful, but then this emancipation had in his mind a special meaning.

When Debendra, on his return from Govindpur, had thrown off his disguise and resumed his natural appearance, he took his seat in the next room. His servant, having prepared the pain-relieving 'huka', placed the snake in front of him. Debendra spent some time in the service of that fatigue-destroying goddess, Tobacco. He is not worthy to be called a man who does not know the luxury of tobacco. Oh, satisfier of the hearts of all! Oh, world enchantress! May we ever be devoted to thee! Your vehicles, the 'huka', the pipe, let them ever remain before us. At the mere sight of them we shall obtain heavenly delight. Oh, 'huka'! Thou that sendest forth volumes of curling smoke, that hast a winding tube shaming the serpent! Oh, bowl that beautifies thy top! How graceful are the chains of thy turban; how great is the beauty of thy curved mouthpiece; how sonorous the murmur of the ice-cool water in thy depths! Oh, world enchantress! Oh, soother of the fatigues of man, employer of the idle, comforter of the henpecked husband's heart, encourager of timid dependents, who can know thy glory! Soother of the sorrowing! Thou givest courage to the timid, intellect to the stupid, peace to the angry! Oh, bestower of blessings, giver of all happiness, appear in undiminished power in my room! Let your sweet scent increase daily, let your cool waters continue to rumble in your depths, let your mouthpiece ever be glued to my lips!

Pleasure-loving Debendra enjoyed the favour of this great goddess as long as he would, but yet he was not satisfied; he proceeded to worship another great power. In the hand of his servant was displayed a number of straw-covered bottles. Then on that white, soft, spacious bed, a gold-coloured mat being laid, a spirit-stand was placed thereon, and the sunset-coloured liquid goddess poured into the power-giving decanter. A cut-glass tumbler and plated jug served as utensils for worship. From the kitchen a black, ugly priest came, bearing hot dishes of roast mutton and cutlets to take the place of the sacred flowers. Then Debendra, as a devoted worshipper, sat down to perform the rites.

Then came a troop of singers and musicians, and concluded the ceremonies with their music and songs.

At length a young man of about Debendra's age, of a placid countenance, came and sat with him. This was his cousin, Surendra. Surendra was in every respect the opposite of Debendra, yet the latter was much attached to his cousin; he heeded no one in the world but him. Every night Surendra came to see him, but, fearing the wine, he would only sit a few minutes.

When all were gone, Surendra asked Debendra, 'How are you today?'

'The body,' replied Debendra, 'is the temple of disease.'

'Yours is, especially,' said his cousin, 'Have you fever today?'

'No.'

'Is your liver out of order?'

'It is as before.'

'Would it not be better to refrain from these excesses?'

'What, drinking? How often will you speak of that? Wine is my constant companion,' said Debendra.

'But why should it be?' replied Surendra. 'Wine was not born with you; you can't take it away with you. Many give it up, why should not you do so?'

'What have I to gain by giving it up? Those who do so have some happiness in prospect, and therefore give it up. For me there is no happiness.'

'Then to save your life give it up.'

'Those to whom life brings happiness may give up wine; but what have I to gain by living?'

Surendra's eyes filled with tears. Full of love for his friend, he urged:

'Then for my sake give it up.'

Tears came into the eyes of Debendra as he said: 'No one but yourself urges me to walk in virtuous paths. If I ever do give it up it will be for your sake, and—'

'And what?'

'If ever I hear that my wife is dead I will give up drink. Otherwise, whether I live or die, I care not.'

Surendra, with moist eyes, mentally anathematising Hembati, took his leave.

9

SURJA MUKHI'S LETTER

'Dearest Srimati Kamal Mani Dasi, long may you live!

'I am ashamed to address you any longer with a blessing. You have become a woman, and the mistress of a house. Still I cannot think of you otherwise than as my younger sister. I have brought you up to womanhood, I taught you your letters; but now when I see your writing I am ashamed to send this scrawl. But of what use to be ashamed? My day is over; were it not so how should I be in this condition? What condition?—it is a thing I cannot speak of to any one; should I do so there will be sorrow and shame; yet if I do not tell some one of my heart's trouble I cannot endure it. To whom can I speak? You are my beloved sister; except you no one loves me. Also it concerns your brother. I can speak of it to no one but you.

'I have prepared my own funeral pyre. If I had not cared for Kunda Nandini, and she had died, would that have been any loss to me? God cares for so many others—would He not have cared for her? Why did I bring her home to my own destruction! When you saw that unfortunate being she was a child, now she is seventeen or eighteen. I admit she is beautiful; her beauty is fatal to me. If I have any happiness on earth it is in my husband; if I care about anything in this world it is for my husband; if there is any wealth belonging to me it is my husband: this husband Kunda Nandini is snatching from me. If I have a desire on earth it is for my husband's love: of that love Kunda Nandini is cheating me. Do not think evil of your brother; I am not reproaching him. He is virtuous, not even his enemies can find a fault in him. I can see daily that he tries to subdue his heart. Wherever Kunda Nandini may happen to be, from that spot, if possible, he averts his eyes; unless there is absolute necessity he does not speak her name. He is even harsh towards her; I have heard him scold her when she has committed no fault. Then why am I writing all this trash? Should a man ask this question it would be difficult to make him understand, but you being a woman will comprehend. If Kunda Nandini is in his eyes but as other women, why is he so careful not to look towards her? why take such pains to avoid speaking her name? He is conscious of guilt towards Kunda Nandini, therefore he scolds her without cause; that anger is not with her, but with himself; that scolding is not for her, but for himself. This I can understand. I who have been so long devoted to him, who within and without see only him, if I but see his shadow I can tell his thoughts. What can he hide from me? Occasionally when his mind is absent his eyes wander hither and thither; do I not know what they are seeking? If he meets it, again becoming troubled he withdraws his eyes; can I not understand that? For whose voice is he listening at mealtimes when he pauses in the act of carrying food to his mouth? and when Kunda's tones reach his ear, and he fastens to eat his meal, can one not understand that? My beloved always had a gracious countenance; why is he now always so absent-minded? If one speaks to him he does not hear, but gives an absent answer. If, becoming angry, I say, 'May I die?' paying no attention he answers, 'Yes.' If I ask where his thoughts are, he says with his lawsuits; but I know they have no place in his mind; when he speaks of his lawsuits he is always merry. Another point. One day the old women of the neighbourhood were speaking of Kunda Nandini, pitying her young widowhood, her unprotected condition. Your brother came up; from within I saw his eyes fill with tears; he turned away and left them quickly. The other day I engaged a new servant; her name is Kumuda. Sometimes the Babu calls Kumuda; when so doing he often slips out the name Kunda instead of Kumuda, then how confused he is—why should he be confused? I cannot say he is neglectful of me, or unaffectionate; rather he is more attentive than before, more affectionate. The reason of this I fully understand: he is conscious of fault towards me; but I know that I have no longer a place in his heart. Attention is one thing, love quite another; the difference between these two we women can easily understand.

'There is another amusing matter. A learned "pandit" in Calcutta, named Iswara Chandra Bidya Sagar, has published a book on the marriage of widows. If he who would establish the custom of marrying widows is a pandit , then who can be called a dunce? Just now, the Brahman Bhattacharjya bringing the book into the 'boita khana', there was a great discussion.

'After much talk in favour of widow remarriage, the Brahman, taking ten rupees from the Babu for the repairs of the 'Tote', went his way. On the following day Sharbabhoum Thakur replied on the same subject. I had some golden bracelets made for his daughter's wedding. No one else was in favour of widow remarriage.

'I have taken up much time in wearying you with my sorrows. Do I not know how vexed you will be? but what can I do, sister? If I do not tell you my sorrows, to whom shall I tell them? I have not said all yet, but hoping for some relief from you has calmed me a little. Say nothing of this to anyone; above all, I conjure you, show not this letter to your husband. Will you not come and see me? if you will come now your presence will heal many of my troubles. Send me quickly news of your husband and of your child.

'SURJA MUKHI.

'P.S.—Another word. If I can get rid of this girl I may be happy once more; but how to get rid of her? Can you take her? Would you not fear to do so?'

Kamal Mani replied—

'You have become quite foolish, else how can you doubt your husband's heart? Do not lose faith in him; if you really cannot trust him you had better drown yourself. I, Kamal Mani, tell you you had better drown yourself. She who can no longer trust her husband had better die.'

10

THE SPROUT

On the course of a short time Nagendra's whole nature was changed. As at eventime, in the hot season, the clear sky becomes suddenly veiled in cloud, so Nagendra's mind became clouded. Surja Mukhi wept secretly.

She thought to herself, 'I will take Kamal Mani's advice. Why should I doubt my husband's heart? His heart is firm as the hills. I am under a delusion. Perhaps he is suffering in health.' Alas! Surja Mukhi was building a bridge of sand.

In the house there dwelt a sort of doctor. Surja Mukhi was the housemistress. Sitting behind the 'purdah' (a half-transparent screen) she held converse with everyone, the person addressed remaining in the verandah. Calling the doctor, Surja Mukhi said—

'The Babu is not well; why do you not give him medicine?'

'Is he ill? I did not know of it; I have heard nothing.'

'Has not the Babu told you?'

'No; what is the matter?'

'What is the matter? Are you a doctor, and do you ask that? Do I know?'

The doctor was nonplussed, and saying, 'I will go and inquire,' he was about to leave; but Surja Mukhi, calling him back, said, 'Do not ask the Babu about it; give him some medicine.'

The doctor thought this a peculiar sort of treatment; but there was no lack of medicine in the house, and going to the dispensary, he composed a draught of soda, port wine, and some simple drugs, and, filling a bottle, labelled it, 'To be taken twice a day.'

Surja Mukhi took the physic to her husband, and requested him to drink it. Nagendra, taking the bottle, read the inscription, and, hurling it away, struck a cat with it. The cat fled, her tail drenched with the physic.

Surja Mukhi said: 'If you will not take the medicine, at least tell me what is your complaint.'

Nagendra, annoyed, said, 'What complaint have I?'

'Look at yourself,' replied Surja Mukhi, 'and see how thin you have become,' and she held a mirror before him.

Nagendra, taking the mirror from her, threw it down and smashed it to atoms.

Surja Mukhi began to weep. With an angry look Nagendra went away. Meeting a servant in the outer room, the Babu struck him for no fault. Surja Mukhi felt as if 'she' had received the blow. Formerly Nagendra had been of a very calm temper; now the least thing made him angry. Nor was this all. One night, the hour for the meal being already past,

Nagendra had not come in. Surja Mukhi sat expecting him. At length, when he appeared, she was astonished at his looks. His face and eyes were inflamed—he had been drinking, and as he had never been given to drinking before his wife was shocked. From that time it became a daily custom.

One day Surja Mukhi, casting herself at his feet, choking down the sobs in her throat, with much humility entreated, 'For my sake give this up.'

Nagendra asked angrily, 'What is my fault?'

Surja Mukhi said: 'If you do not know what is the fault, how can I? I only beg that for my sake you will give it up.'

Nagendra replied: 'Surja Mukhi, I am a drunkard! If devotion should be paid to a drunkard, pay it to me; otherwise it is not called for.'

Surja Mukhi left the room to conceal her tears, since her weeping irritated her husband, and led him to strike the servants.

Soon after, the 'Dewan' sent word to the mistress that the estate was going to ruin.

She asked, 'Why?'

'Because the Babu will not see to things. The people on the estates do just as they please. Since the 'Karta' is so careless, no one heeds what I say.'

Surja Mukhi answered: 'If the owner looks after the estate, it will be preserved; if not, let it go to ruin. I shall be thankful if I can only save my own property' (meaning her husband).

Formerly Nagendra had carefully looked after all his affairs.

One day some hundreds of his 'ryots' came to the 'kacheri', and with joined palms stood at the door. 'Give us justice,' they said, 'O your highness; we cannot survive the tyranny of the 'naib' (a law officer) and the 'gomashta'. We are being robbed of everything. If you do not save us, to whom shall we go?'

Nagendra gave orders to drive them away.

Formerly, when one of his 'gomashtas' had beaten a 'ryot' and taken a rupee from him, Nagendra had cut ten rupees from the 'gomashta's' pay and given it to the 'ryot'.

Hara Deb Ghosal wrote to Nagendra: 'What has happened to you? I cannot imagine what you are doing. I receive no letters from you, or, if I do, they contain but two or three lines without any meaning. Have you taken offence with me? If so, why do you not tell me? Have you lost your lawsuit? Then why not say so? If you do not tell me anything else, at least give me news of your health.'

Nagendra replied: 'Do not be angry with me. I am going to destruction.'

Hara Deb was very wise. On reading this letter he thought to himself: 'What is this? Anxiety about money? A quarrel with some friend? Debendra Datta? Nothing of the kind. Is this love?'

Kamal Mani received another letter from Surja Mukhi. It concluded thus: 'Come, Kamal Mani, sister; except you I have no friend. Come to me.'

Kamal Mani was agitated; she could contain herself no longer. She felt that she must consult her husband.

Srish Chandra, sitting in the inner apartments, was looking over the office account books. Beside him on the bed, Satish Chandra, a child of a year old, was rejoicing in the possession of an English newspaper. He had first tried to eat it; but, failing in that, had spread it out and was now sitting upon it. Kamal Mani, approaching her husband, brought the end of her 'sari' round her neck, threw herself down, bending her forehead to the floor, and, folding her hands, said, 'I pay my devotions to you, O great king.' Just before this time, a play had been performed in the house, from whence she borrowed this inflated speech.

Srish said, laughing, 'Have the cucumbers been stolen again?'

'Neither cucumbers nor melons; this time a most valuable thing has been stolen.'

'Where is the robbery?' asked Srish.

'The robbery took place at Govindpur. My elder brother had a broken shell in a golden box. Some one has stolen it.'

Srish, not understanding the metaphor, said 'Your brother's golden casket is Surja Mukhi. What is the broken shell?'

'Surja Mukhi's wits,' replied Kamal.

'People say if one has a mind to play he can do so, though the shells are broken' (referring to a game played with shells). 'If Surja Mukhi's understanding is defective, yet with it she gained your brother's heart, and with all your wisdom, you could not bring him over to your side. Who has stolen the broken shell?'

'That I know not; but, from reading her letter, I perceive it is gone—else how could a woman write such a letter?'

'May I see the letter?' asked Srish.

Kamal Mani placed the letter in her husband's hand, saying: 'Surja Mukhi forbade my telling you all this; but while I keep it from you I am quite uneasy. I can neither sleep nor eat, and I fear I may lose my senses.'

'If you have been forbidden to tell me of the matter I cannot read this letter, nor do I wish to hear its contents. Tell me what has to be done.'

'This is what must be done,' replied Kamal. 'Surja Mukhi's wits are scattered, and must be restored. There is no one that can do this except Satish Babu. His aunt has written requesting that he may be sent to Govindpur.'

Satish Babu had in the meantime upset a vase of flowers, and was now aiming at the inkstand. Watching him, Srish Chandra said: 'Yes; he is well fitted to act as physician. I understand now. He is invited to his aunt's house; if he goes, his mother must go also. Surja Mukhi's wits must be lost, or she could not have sent such an invitation.' 'Not Satish Babu only; we are all invited.'

'Why am I invited?' asked Srish.

'Can I go alone?' replied Kamal. 'Who will look after the luggage?'

'It is very unreasonable in Surja Mukhi if she wants her husband's brother-in-law only that he may look after the luggage. I can find some one else to perform that office for a couple of days.' Kamal Mani was angry; she frowned, mocked at Srish Chandra, and, snatching the paper on which he was writing out of his hand, tore it to pieces.

Srish Chandra, smiling, said, 'It serves you right.'

Kamal, affecting anger, said, 'I will speak in that way if I wish!'

Srish, in the same tone, replied, 'And I shall speak as I choose!'

Then a playful scuffle ensued; Kamal pretended to strike her husband, who in return pulled down her hair; whereupon she threw away his ink. Then they exchanged angry kisses. Satish Babu was delighted at this performance; he knew that kisses were his special property, so when he saw them scattered in this lavish manner he stood up, supporting himself by his mother's dress, to claim his royal share, crowing joyously. How sweetly that laugh fell on the ears of Kamal Mani! She took him in her lap, and showered kisses upon him. Srish Chandra followed her example. Then Satish Babu, having received his dues, got down and made for his father's brightly coloured pencil, which soon found its way into his mouth.

In the battle between the 'Kurus' and 'Pandus' there was a great struggle between Bhagadatta and Arjuna. In this fight, Bhagadatta being invincible, and Arjuna vulnerable, the latter called Krishna to his aid, who, receiving the charge of Bhagadatta on his breast, blunted the force of the weapons. In like manner, Satish Chandra having received these attacks on his face, peace was restored. But their peace and war was like the dropping of clouds, fitful.

Then Srish asked, 'Must you really go to Govindpur? What am I to do alone?'

'Do you think I can go alone?' answered his wife. 'We must both go. Arrange matters in the morning when you go to business, and come home quickly. If you are long, Satish and I will sit crying for you.'

'I cannot go,' replied Srish. 'This is the season for buying linseed. You must go without me.'

'Come, Satish,' was Kamal's reply; 'we two will go and weep.'

At the sound of his mother's voice Satish ceased to gnaw the pencil, and raised another shout of joyous laughter. So Kamal's cry did not come off this time; in place of it the kissing performance was gone through as before.

At its close Kamal said, 'Now what are your orders?'

Srish repeated that she must go without him, as he could not leave; whereupon she sat down sulking. Srish went behind her and began to mark her forehead with the ink from his pen.

Then with a laugh she embraced him, saying, 'Oh, dearer than life, how I love you!'

He was obliged to return the embrace, when the ink transferred itself from her face to his.

The quarrel thus ended, Kamal said, 'If you really will not go, then make arrangements for me.'

'When will you come back?'

'Need you ask?' said Kamal; 'if you don't go, can I stay there long?'

Srish Chandra sent Kamal Mani to Govindpur, but it is certain that Srish Chandra's employers did not do much in linseed at that time. The other clerks have privately informed us that this was the fault of Srish Chandra, who did not give his mind to it, but sat at home in meditation.

Srish hearing himself thus accused, remarked, 'It may be so, my wife was absent at that time.'

The hearers shook their heads, saying, 'He is under petticoat government!' which so delighted Srish Chandra that he called to his servant, 'Prepare dinner; these gentlemen will dine with me today.'

11

CAUGHT AT LAST

It was as though a flower had bloomed in the family house at Govindpur. The sight of Kamal Mani's smiling face dried the tears in the eyes of Surja Mukhi. The moment she set foot in the house Kamal took in hand the dressing of her sister-in-law's hair, for Surja Mukhi had neglected herself lately.

Kamal said, 'Shall I put in a flower or two?'

Surja Mukhi pinched her cheek, and forbade it.

So Kamal Mani did it slily. When people came in she said, 'Do you see the old woman wearing flowers in her hair?'

But even Kamal's bright face did not dispel the dark clouds from that of Nagendra. When he met her he only said, 'Where do you come from, Kamal?'

She bent before him, saying bashfully, 'Baby has brought me.'

'Indeed! I'll beat the rascal,' replied Nagendra, taking the child in his arms, and spending an hour in play with him, in return for which the grateful child made free with his moustache.

Kamal Mani playfully accosted Kunda with the words, 'Ha, Kundi, Kundi! Nundi, Dundi! Are you quite well, Kundi?'

The girl was silent in astonishment, but presently she said, 'I am well.'

'Call me "Didi" (elder sister); if you do not I will burn your hair when you are asleep, or else I will give your body to the cockroaches.'

Kunda obeyed. When she had been in Calcutta she had not addressed Kamal by any name; indeed she had rarely spoken; but seeing that Kamal was very loving-hearted, she had become fond of her. In the years that had intervened without a meeting she had a little forgotten Kamal; but now, both being amiable, their affection was born afresh, and became very close.

When Kamal Mani talked of returning home, Surja Mukhi said,

'Nay, sister, stay a little longer. I shall be wretched when you are gone. It relieves me to talk to you of my trouble.'

'I shall not go without arranging your affairs.'

'What affairs?' said Surja Mukhi.

'Your "Shradda" (funeral ceremonies),' replied Kamal; but mentally she said, 'Extracting the thorns from your path.'

When Kunda heard that Kamal talked of going, she went to her room and wept. Kamal going quietly after her found her with her head on the pillow, weeping. Kamal sat down to dress Kunda's hair, an occupation of which she was very fond. When she had finished she drew Kunda's head on to her lap, and wiped away the tears. Then she said, 'Kunda, why do you weep?'

'Why do you go away?' was the reply.

'Why should you weep for that?'

'Because you love me.'

'Does no one else love you?'

Kunda did not reply; and Kamal went on: 'Does not the "Bou" (Surja Mukhi) love you? No? Don't hide it from me.' (Still no answer.) 'Does not my brother love you?' (Still silence.) 'Since I love you and you love me, shall we not go together?' (Yet Kunda spoke not.) 'Will you go?'

Kunda shook her head, saying, 'I will not go.'

Kamal's joyous face became grave; she thought, 'This does not sound well. The girl has the same complaint as my brother, but he suffers the more deeply. My husband is not here, with whom can I take counsel?' Then Kamal Mani drew Kunda's head lovingly on her breast, and taking hold of her face caressingly, said, 'Kunda, will you tell me the truth?'

'About what?' said the girl.

'About what I shall ask thee. I am thy elder, I love thee as a sister; do not hide it from me, I will tell no one.' In her mind she thought, 'If I tell any one it will be my husband and my baby.'

After a pause Kunda asked, 'What shall I tell you?'

'You love my brother dearly, don't you?'

Kunda gave no answer.

Kamal Mani wept in her heart; aloud she said: 'I understand. It is so. Well that does not hurt you, but many others suffer from it.'

Kunda Nandini, raising her head, fixed a steadfast look on the face of Kamal Mani.

Kamal, understanding the silent question, replied, 'Ah, unhappy one! dost thou not see that my brother loves thee?'

Kunda's head again sank on Kamal's breast, which she watered with her tears. Both wept silently for many minutes.

What the passion of love is the golden Kamal Mani knew very well. In her innermost heart she sympathized with Kunda, both in her joy and in her sorrow. Wiping Kunda's eyes she said again, 'Kunda, will you go with me?'

Kunda's eyes again filled with tears.

More earnestly, Kamal said: 'If you are out of sight my brother will forget you, and you will forget him; otherwise, you will be lost, my brother will be lost and his wife—the house will go to ruin.'

Kunda continued weeping.

Again Kamal asked, 'Will you go? Only consider my brother's condition, his wife's.'

Kunda, after a long interval, wiped her eyes, sat up, and said, 'I will go.'

Why this consent after so long an interval? Kamal understood that Kunda had offered up her own life on the temple of the household peace. Her own peace? Kamal felt that Kunda did not comprehend what was for her own peace.

12

HIRA

On this occasion, Haridasi Boisnavi entering, sang—
'I went into the thorny forest to pluck a soiled flower—
Yes, my friend, a soiled flower;
I wore it twined about my head, I hung it in my ears—
Friends, a soiled flower.'
This day Surja Mukhi was present. She sent to call Kamal to hear the singing. Kamal came, bringing Kunda Nandini with her. The Boisnavi sang—

'I would die for this blooming thorn,
I will steal its honied sweets,
I go to seek where it doth bloom,
This fresh young bud.'

Kamal Mani frowned, and said: '"Boisnavi" Didi, may ashes be thrown on your face! Can you not sing something else?'
Haridasi asked, 'Why?'
Kamal, more angrily, said: 'Why? Bring a bough of the babla tree, and show her how pleasant it is to be pierced by thorns.'
Surja Mukhi said gently: 'We do not like songs of that sort; sing something suitable for the home circle.'
The Boisnavi, saying 'Very well,' began to sing—

'By clasping the Pandit's feet, I shall become learned in the Shastras;
Learning thus the holy Shastras, who will dare speak ill of me?'

Kamal, frowning, said: 'Listen to this singing if it pleases you, sister. I shall go away.'
She went, and Surja Mukhi also left, with a displeased countenance. Of the rest of the women, those who relished the song remained, the others left; Kunda Nandini stayed. She did not understand the hidden

meaning of the songs, she scarcely even heard them. Her thoughts were absent, so she remained where she was seated. Haridasi sang no more, but talked on trivial subjects. Seeing that there would be no more singing, all left except Kunda Nandini, whose feet seemed as though they would not move. Thus, finding herself alone with Kunda, the 'Boisnavi' talked much to her. Kunda heard something of her talk, but not all.

Surja Mukhi saw all this from a distance, and when the two showed signs of being deep in conversation she called Kamal and pointed them out to her.

Kamal said: 'What of that? They are only talking. She is a woman, not a man.'

'Who knows?' said Surja. 'I think it is a man in disguise; but I will soon find out. How wicked Kunda must be!'

'Stay a moment,' said Kamal, 'I will fetch a "babla" branch, and let her feel its thorns.'

Thus saying, Kamal went in search of a bough. On the way she saw Satish, who had got possession of his aunt's vermilion, and was seated, daubing neck, nose, chin, and breast with the red powder. At this sight Kamal forgot the 'Boisnavi,' the bough, Kunda Nandini, and everything else.

Surja Mukhi sent for the servant Hira.

Hira's name has been mentioned once; it is now needful to give a particular account of her. Nagendra and his father always took special care that the female servants of the household should be of good character. With this design they offered good wages, and sought to engage servants of a superior class. The women servants of the house dwelt in happiness and esteem, therefore many respectable women of small means took service with them. Amongst these Hira was the principal. Many maidservants are of the Kaystha caste. Hira was a Kaystha. Her grandmother had first been engaged as a servant, and Hira, being then a child, had come with her. When Hira became capable the old woman gave up service, built herself a house out of her savings, and dwelt in Govindpur. Hira entered the service of the Datta family. She was then about twenty years of age, younger than most of the other servants, but in intelligence and in mental qualities their superior. Hira had been known in Govindpur from childhood as a widow, but no one had ever heard anything of her husband, neither had any one heard of any stain upon her character. She was something of a shrew. She dressed and adorned herself as one whose husband is living. She was beautiful, of brilliant complexion, lotus-eyed, short in stature, her face like the moon covered with clouds, her hair raised in front like a snake-hood.

Hira was sitting alone singing. She made quarrels among the maids for her own amusement. She would frighten the cook in the dark, incite the boys to tease their parents to give them in marriage; if she saw any one sleeping she would paint the face with lime and ink. Truly she had many faults, as will appear by degrees. At present I will only add that if she saw attar or rosewater she would steal it.

Surja Mukhi, calling Hira, said, 'Do you know that "Boisnavi"?'

'No,' replied Hira. 'I was never out of the neighbourhood, how should I know a "Boisnavi" beggarman. Ask the women of the "Thakur bari"; Karuna or Sitala may know her.'

'This is not a "Thakur bari Boisnavi". I want to know who she is, where her home is, and why she talks so much with Kunda. If you find all this out for me I will give you a new Benares "sari", and send you to see the play.'

At this offer Hira became very zealous, and asked, 'When may I go to make inquiry?'

'When you like; but if you do not follow her now you will not be able to trace her. Be careful that neither the "Boisnavi" nor any one else suspects you.'

At this moment Kamal returned, and, approving of Surja Mukhi's design, said to Hira, 'And if you can, prick her with "babla" thorns.'

Hira said: 'I will do all, but only a Benares "sari" will not content me.'

'What do you want?' asked Surja.

'She wants a husband,' said Kamal. 'Give her in marriage.'

'Very well,' said Surja. 'Would you like to have the "Thakur Jamai"? Say so, and Kamal will arrange it.'

'Then I will see,' said Hira; 'but there is already in the house a husband suited to my mind.'

'Who is it?' asked Surja.

'Death,' was Hira's reply.

13

NO!

On the evening of that day, Kunda was sitting near the 'talao' in the middle of the garden. The 'talao' was broad; its water pure and always blue. The reader will remember that behind this 'talao' was a flower garden, in the midst of which stood a white marble house covered with creepers. In front, a flight of steps led down to the water. The steps were built of brick to resemble stone, very broad and clean. On either side grew an aged bakul tree. Beneath these trees sat Kunda Nandini, alone in the darkening evening, gazing at the reflection of the sky and stars in the clear water. Here and there lotus flowers could be dimly seen. On the other three sides of the 'talao', mango, jak, plum, orange, lichi, coconut, kul, bel, and other fruit trees grew thickly in rows, looking in the darkness like a wall with an uneven top. Occasionally the harsh voice of a bird in the branches broke the silence. The cool wind blowing over the 'talao' caused the water slightly to wet the lotus flowers, gave the reflected sky an appearance of trembling, and murmured in the leaves above Kunda Nandini's head. The scent of the flowers of the 'bakul' tree pervaded the air, mingled with that of jasmine and other blossoms. Everywhere fireflies flew in the darkness over the clear water, dancing, sparkling, becoming extinguished. Flying foxes talked to each other; jackals howled to keep off other animals. A few clouds having lost their way wandered over the sky; one or two stars fell as though overwhelmed with grief. Kunda Nandini sat brooding over her troubles. Thus ran her thoughts: 'All my family is gone. My mother, my brother, my father, all died. Why did I not die? If I could not die, why did I come here? Does the good man become a star when he dies?' Kunda no longer remembered the vision she had seen on the night of her father's death. It did not recur to her mind even now. Only a faint memory of the scene came to her with the idea that, since she had seen her mother in vision, that mother must have become a star. So she asked herself: 'Do the good become stars after death? and if so, are all I loved become stars? Then which are they among those hosts? how can I determine? Can they see me—I who have wept so much? Let them go, I will think of them no more. It makes me weep; what is the use of weeping? Is it my fate to weep? If not, my mother—again these thoughts! let them go. Would it not be well to die? How to do it?

'Shall I drown myself? Should I become a star if I did that? Should I see? Should I see every day—whom? Can I not say whom? why can I not pronounce the name? there is no one here who could hear it. Shall I please myself by uttering it for once? only in thought can I say it—Nagendra, my Nagendra! Oh, what do I say? my Nagendra! What am I?

'Surja Mukhi's Nagendra. How often have I uttered this name, and what is the use? If he could have married me instead of Surja Mukhi! Let it go! I shall drown myself. If I were to do that what would happen?

'Tomorrow I should float on the water; all would hear of it.

'Nagendra—again I say it, Nagendra; if Nagendra heard of it what would he say? It will not do to drown myself; my body would swell, I should look ugly if he should see me! Can I take poison? What poison? Where should I get it? Who would bring it for me? Could I take it? I could, but not today. Let me please myself with the thought that he loves me. Is it true? Kamal Didi said so; but how can she know it? my conscience will not let me ask. Does he love me? How does he love me?

'What does he love—my beauty or me? Beauty? let me see.' She went to examine the reflection of her face in the water, but, failing to see anything, returned to her former place. 'It cannot be; why do I think of that? Surja Mukhi is more beautiful than I. Haro Mani, Bishu, Mukta, Chandra, Prasunna, Bama, Pramada, are all more beautiful. Even Hira is more beautiful; yes, notwithstanding her dark complexion, her face is more beautiful. Then if it is not beauty, is it disposition? Let me think. I can't find any attraction in myself. Kamal said it to satisfy me. Why should he love me? Yet why should Kamal try to flatter me? Who knows? But I will not die; I will think of that. Though it is false I will ponder over it; I will think that true which is false.

'But I cannot go to Calcutta; I should not see him. I cannot, cannot go; yet if not, what shall I do? If Kamal's words are true, then those who have done so much for me are being made to suffer through me. I can see that there is something in Surja Mukhi's mind. True or false I will have to go; but I cannot! Then I must drown myself. If I must die I will die! Oh, my father! did you leave me here to such a fate?'

Then Kunda, putting her hands to her face, gave way to weeping. Suddenly the vision flashed into her mind; she started as if at a flash of lightning. 'I had forgotten it all,' she exclaimed. 'Why had I forgotten it? My mother showed me my destiny, and bade me evade it by ascending to the stars. Why did I not go? Why did I not die? Why do I delay now? I will delay no longer.' So saying, she began slowly to descend the steps. Kunda was but a woman, timid and cowardly; at each step she feared, at each step she shivered. Nevertheless she proceeded slowly with unshaken purpose to obey her mother's command. At this moment some one from behind touched her very gently on the shoulder. Some one said, 'Kunda!' Kunda looked round. In the darkness she at once recognized Nagendra. Kunda thought no more that day of dying.

And Nagendra, is this the stainless character you have preserved so long? Is this the return for your Surja Mukhi's devotion? Shame! shame! you are a thief; you are worse than a thief. What could a thief have done to Surja Mukhi? He might have stolen her ornaments, her wealth, but you have come to destroy her heart. Surja Mukhi never bestowed anything upon the thief, therefore if he stole, he was but a thief. But to you Surja Mukhi gave her all; therefore you are committing the worst of thefts. Nagendra, it were better for you to die. If you have the courage, drown yourself.

Shame! shame! Kunda Nandini; why do you tremble at the touch of a thief? Why are the words of a thief as a thorn in the flesh? See, Kunda Nandini! the water is pure, cool, pleasant; will you plunge into it? will you not die?

Kunda Nandini did not wish to die.

The robber said: 'Kunda, will you go tomorrow to Calcutta? Do you go willingly?'

Willingly—alas! alas! Kunda wiped her eyes, but did not speak.

'Kunda, why do you weep? Listen. With much difficulty I have endured so long; I cannot bear it longer. I cannot say how I have lived through it. Though I have struggled so hard, yet see how degraded I am. I have become a drunkard. I can struggle no longer; I cannot let you go. Listen, Kunda. Now widow marriage is allowed I will marry you, if you consent.'

This time Kunda spoke; she said 'No.'

'Why, Kunda? Do you think widow marriage unholy?'

'No.'

'Then why not? Say, say, will you be my wife or not? Will you love me or no?'

'No.'

Then Nagendra, as though he had a thousand tongues, entreated her with heart-piercing words. Still Kunda said 'No.'

Nagendra looked at the pure, cold water, and asked himself, 'Can I lie there?'

To herself Kunda said: 'No, widow marriage is allowed in the Shastras; it is not on that account.'

Why, then, did she not seek the water?

14

LIKE TO LIKE

Haridasi Boisnavi, returning to the garden house, suddenly became Debendra Babu, and sat down and smoked his huka, drinking brandy freely at intervals until he became intoxicated.

Then Surendra entered, sat down by Debendra, and after inquiring after his health, said, 'Where have you been today again?'

'Have you heard of this so soon?' said Debendra.

'This is another mistake of yours. You imagine that what you do is hidden, that no one can know anything about it; but it is known all over the place.'

'I have no desire to hide anything,' said Debendra.

'It reflects no credit upon you. So long as you show the least shame we have some hope of you. If you had any shame left, would you expose yourself in the village as a Boisnavi?'

Said Debendra, laughing, 'What a jolly Boisnavi I was! Were you not charmed with my get-up?'

'I did not see you in that base disguise,' replied Surendra, 'or I would have given you a taste of the whip.' Then snatching the glass from Debendra's hand, he said, 'Now do listen seriously while you are in your senses; after that, drink if you will.'

'Speak, brother,' said Debendra; 'why are you angry today? I think the atmosphere of Hembati has corrupted you.'

Surendra, lending no ear to his evil words, said, 'Whose destruction are you seeking to compass by assuming this disguise?'

'Do you not know?' was the reply. 'Don't you remember the schoolmaster's marriage to a goddess? This goddess is now a widow, and lives with the Datta family in that village. I went to see her.'

'Have you not gone far enough in vice? Are you not satisfied yet, that you wish to ruin that unprotected girl? See, Debendra, you are so sinful, so cruel, so destructive, that we can hardly associate with you any longer.'

Surendra said this with so much firmness that Debendra was quite stunned. Then he said, seriously: 'Do not be angry with me; my heart is not under my own control. I can give up everything else but the hope of possessing this woman. Since the day I first saw her in Tara Charan's house I have been under the power of her beauty. In my eyes there is no such beauty anywhere. As in fever the patient is burned with thirst, from that day my passion for her has burned within me. I cannot relate the many attempts I have made to see her. Until now I had not succeeded. By means of this Boisnavi dress I have accomplished my desire. There is no cause for you to fear. She is a virtuous woman.'

'Then why do you go?' asked his friend.

'Only to see her. I cannot describe what satisfaction I have found in seeing her, talking with her, singing to her.'

'I am speaking seriously, not jesting. If you do not abandon this evil purpose, then our intercourse must end. More than that, I shall become your enemy.'

'You are my only friend,' said Debendra; 'I would lose half of what I possess rather than lose you. Still, I confess I would rather lose you than give up the hope of seeing Kunda Nandini.'

'Then it must be so. I can no longer associate with you.'

Thus saying, Surendra departed with a sorrowful heart.

Debendra, greatly afflicted at losing his one friend, sat some time in repentant thought. At length he said: 'Let it go! in this world who cares for any one? Each for himself!'

Then filling his glass he drank, and under the influence of the liquor his heart quickly became joyous. Closing his eyes, he began to sing some doggerel beginning—

'My name is Hira, the flower girl.'

Presently a voice answered from without—

'My name is Hira Malini.

He is talking in his cups; I can't bear to see it.'

Debendra, hearing the voice, called out noisily, 'Who are you—a male or female spirit?'

Then, jingling her bangles, the spirit entered and sat down by

Debendra. The spirit was covered with a sari, bracelets on her arms, on her neck a charm, ornaments in her ears, silver chain round her waist, on her ankles rings. She was scented with attar.

Debendra held a light near to the face of the spirit. He did not know her.

Gently he said, 'Who are you? and from whence do you come?' Then holding the light in another direction, he asked, 'Whose spirit are you?' At last, finding he could not steady himself, he said, 'Go for today; I will worship you with cakes and flesh of goat on the night of the dark moon.'

Then the spirit, laughing, said, 'Are you well, Boisnavi Didi?'

'Good heavens!' said the tipsy one, 'are you a spirit from the Datta family?' Thus saying, he again held the lamp near her face; moving it hither and thither all round, he gravely examined the woman. At last, throwing down the lamp, he began to sing, 'Who are you? Surely I know you. Where have I seen you?'

The woman replied, 'I am Hira.'

'Hurrah! Three cheers for Hira!' Exclaiming thus, the drunken man began to jump about. Then, falling flat on the floor, he saluted Hira, and with glass in hand began to sing in her praise.

Hira had discovered during the day that Haridasi Boisnavi and Debendra Babu were one and the same person. But with what design Debendra had entered the house of the Dattas it was not so easy to discover. To find this out, Hira had come to Debendra's house; only Hira would have had courage for such a deed. She now said:

'What is my purpose? Today a thief entered the Datta's house and committed a robbery—I have come to seize the robber.'

Hearing this, the Babu said: 'It is true I went to steal; but, Hira, I went not to steal jewels or pearls, but to seek flowers and fruits.'

'What flower? Kunda?'

'Hurrah! Yes, Kunda. Three cheers for Kunda Nandini! I adore her.'

'I have come from Kunda Nandini.'

'Hurrah! Speak! speak! What has she sent you to say? Yes, I remember; why should it not be? For three years we have loved each other.'

Hira was astonished, but wishing to hear more, she said: 'I did not know you had loved so long. How did you first make love to her?'

'There is no difficulty in that. From my friendship with Tara Charan, I asked him to introduce me to his wife. He did so, and from that time I have loved her.'

'After that what happened?' asked Hira.

'After that, because of your mistress's anger, I did not see Kunda for many days. Then I entered the house as a Boisnavi. The girl is very timid, she will not speak; but the way in which I coaxed her today is sure to take effect. Why should it not succeed? Am I not Debendra? Learn well, oh lover! the art of winning hearts!'

Then Hira said: 'It has become very late; now good bye,' and smiling gently she arose and departed.

Debendra fell into a drunken sleep.

Early the next morning Hira related to Surja Mukhi all that she had heard from Debendra—his three years' passion, and his present attempt to play the lover to Kunda Nandini in the disguise of a Boisnavi.

Then Surja Mukhi's blue eyes grew inflamed with anger, the crimson veins on her temples stood out. Kamal also heard it all.

Surja Mukhi sent for Kunda Nandini, and when she came said to her—

'Kunda, we have learned who Haridasi Boisnavi is. We know that he is your paramour. I now know your true character. We give no place in our house to such a woman. Take yourself away from here, otherwise Hira shall drive you away with a broom.'

Kunda trembled. Kamal saw that she was about to fall, and led her away to her own chamber. Remaining there, she comforted Kunda as well as she could, saying, 'Let the Bou (wife) say what she will, I do not believe a word of it.'

15

THE FORLORN ONE

In the depth of night, when all were sleeping, Kunda Nandini opened the door of her chamber and went forth. With but one dress, the seventeen-year-old girl left the house of Surja Mukhi, and leaped alone into the ocean of the world. Kunda had never set foot outside the house; she could not tell in which direction to go.

The dark body of the large house loomed against the sky. Kunda wandered for some time in the dark; then she remembered that a light was usually to be seen from Nagendra's room. She knew how to reach the spot; and thinking that she would refresh her eyes by seeking that light, she went to that side of the house. The shutters were open, the sash closed. In the darkness three lights gleamed; insects were hovering near trying to reach the light, but the glass repelled them. Kunda in her heart sympathized with these insects. Her infatuated eyes dwelt upon the light; she could not bring herself to leave it. She sat beneath some casuarina trees near the window, every now and then watching the fireflies dancing in the trees. In the sky black clouds chased each other, only a star or two being visible at intervals. All round the house rows of casuarina trees raising their heads into the clouds, stood like apparitions of the night. At the touch of the wind these giant-faced apparitions whispered in their ghost language over Kunda Nandini's head. The very ghosts, in their fear of the terrible night, spoke in low voices. Occasionally the open shutters of the window flapped against the walls. Black owls hooted as they sat upon the house; sometimes a dog seeing another animal rushed after it; sometimes a twig or a fruit fell to the ground. In the distance the coconut palms waved their heads, the rustling of the leaves of the fan palm reached the ear. Over all the light streamed, and the insect troop came and went. Kunda sat there gazing.

A sash is gently opened; the figure of a man appears against the light.

Alas! it is Nagendra's figure. Nagendra, what if you should discover the flower, Kunda, under the trees? What if, seeing you in the window, the sound of her beating heart should make itself heard? What if, hearing this sound, she should know that if you move and become invisible her happiness will be gone? Nagendra, you are standing out of the light; move it so that she can see you. Kunda is very wretched; stand there that the clear water of the pool with the stars reflected in it may not recur to her mind. Listen! the black owl hoots! Should you move, Kunda will be terrified by the lightning. See there! the black clouds, pressed by the wind, meet as though in battle. There will be a rainstorm: who will shelter Kunda? See there! you have opened the sash, swarms of insects are rushing into your room. Kunda thinks, 'If I am virtuous, shall I be born again as an insect?' Kunda thinks she would like to share the fate of the insects. 'I have scorched myself, why do I not die?'

Nagendra, shutting the sash, moves away. Cruel! what harm you have done. You have no business waking in the night; go to sleep. Kunda Nandini is dying; let her die!—she would gladly do so to save you a headache. Now the lightened window has become dark. Looking—looking—wiping her eyes, Kunda Nandini arose and took the path before her. The ghost-like shrubs, murmuring, asked, 'Whither goest thou?' the fan palms rustled, 'Whither dost thou go?' the owl's deep voice asked the same question. The window said, 'Let her go— no more will I show to her Nagendra.' Then foolish Kunda Nandini gazed once more in that direction.

Oh, iron-hearted Surja Mukhi, arise! think what you have done. Make the forlorn one return.

Kunda went on, on, on; again the clouds clashed, the sky became as night, the lightning flashed, the wind moaned, the clouds thundered. Kunda! Kunda! whither goest thou? The storm came—first the sound, then clouds of dust, then leaves torn from the trees borne by the wind; at last, plash, plash, the rain. Kunda, with thy one garment, whither goest thou?

By the flashes of lightning Kunda saw a hut: its walls were of mud, supporting a low roof. She sat down within the doorway, resting against the door. In doing this she made some noise. The house owner being awake heard the noise, but thought it was made by the storm; but a dog, who slept within near the door, barking loudly, alarmed the householder, who timidly opened the door, and seeing only a desolate woman, asked, 'Who is there?' No reply. 'Who are you, woman?'

Kunda said, 'I am standing here because of the storm.'

'What? What? Speak again.'

Kunda repeated her words.

The householder recognizing the voice, drew Kunda indoors, and, making a fire, discovered herself to be Hira. She comforted Kunda, saying, 'I understand—you have run away from the scolding; have no fear, I will tell no one. You shall stay with me for a couple of days.'

Hira's dwelling was surrounded by a wall. Inside were a couple of clean mud-built huts. The walls of the rooms were decorated with figures of flowers, birds, and gods. In the courtyard grew red-leaved vegetables, and near them jasmine and roses. The gardener from the Babu's house had planted them. If Hira had wished, he would have given her anything from the Babu's garden. His profit in this was that Hira with her own hand prepared his huka and handed it to him.

In one of the huts Hira slept; in the other her grandmother. Hira made up a bed for Kunda beside her own. Kunda lay there, but did not sleep. Kunda desired to remain hidden, and therefore consented to be locked in the room on the following day when Hira went to her work, so that she should not be seen by the grandmother. At noon, when the grandmother went to bathe, Hira, coming home, permitted Kunda to bathe and eat. After this meal Kunda was again locked in, and Hira returned to her work till night, when she again made up the beds as before.

Creak, creak, creak—the sound of the chain of the outer door gently shaken. Hira was astonished. One person only, the gatekeeper, sometimes shook the chain to give warning at night. But in his hand the chain did not speak so sweetly; it spoke threateningly, as though to say, 'If you do not open, I will break the door.' Now it seemed to say, 'How are you, my Hira? Arise, my jewel of a Hira!' Hira arose, and opening the outer door saw a woman. At first she was puzzled, but in a moment, recognizing the visitor, she exclaimed, 'Oh, Ganga jal! how fortunate I am!'

Hira's Ganga jal was Malati the milkwoman, whose home was at Debipur, near Debendra Babu's house. She was a merry woman, from thirty to thirty-two years of age, dressed in a sari and wearing shell bracelets, her lips red from the spices she ate; her complexion was almost fair, with red spots on her cheeks; her nose flat, her temples tattooed, a quid of tobacco in her cheek. Malati was not a servant of Debendra's, not even a dependent, but yet a follower; the services that others refused to perform, he obtained from her.

At sight of this woman the cunning Hira said: 'Sister Ganga jal! May I meet you at my last moment; but why have you come now?'

Malati whispered, 'Debendra Babu wants you.'

Hira, with a laugh: 'Are you not to get anything?'

Malati answered, 'You best know what you mean. Come at once.'

As Hira desired to go, she told Kunda that she was called to her master's house, and must go to see what was wanted. Then extinguishing the light, she put on her dress and ornaments, and accompanied Ganga jal, the two singing as they went some love song.

Hira went alone into Debendra's boita khana. He had been drinking, but not heavily; he was quite sensible. His manner to Hira was altogether changed; he paid her no compliments, but said: 'I had taken so much that evening that I did not understand what you said. Why did you come that night? it is to know this that I have sent for you. You told me Kunda Nandini sent you, but you did not give her message. I suppose that was because you found me so much overcome; but you can tell me now.'

'Kunda Nandini did not send me to say anything.'

'Then why did you come?' replied Debendra.

'I only came to see you.'

Debendra laughed. 'You are very intelligent. Nagendra Babu is fortunate in possessing such a servant. I thought the talk about Kunda Nandini was a mere pretence. You came to inquire after Haridasi Boisnavi. You came to know my design in wearing the Boisnavi garb; why I went to the Datta house: this you came to learn, and in part you accomplished your purpose. I do not seek to hide the matter. You did your master's work, and have received your reward from him, no doubt. I have a commission for you; do it, and I also will reward you.'

It would be an unpleasant task to relate in detail the speech of a man so deeply sunk in vice. Debendra, promising Hira an abundant reward, proposed to buy Kunda Nandini.

At his words Hira's eyes reddened, her ears became like fire. When he had finished she rose and said—

'Sir, addressing me as a servant, you have said this to me. It is not for me to reply. I will tell my master, and he will give you a suitable answer.' Then she went quickly out.

For some moments Debendra sat puzzled and cowed. Then to revive himself he returned to the brandy, and the songs in which he usually indulged.

16

HIRA'S ENVY

Rising in the morning, Hira went to her work. For the past two days there had been a great tumult in the Datta house, because Kunda Nandini was not to be found. It was known to all the household that she had gone away in anger. It was also known to some of the neighbours. Nagendra heard that Kunda had gone, but no one told him the reason. He thought to himself, 'Kunda has left because she does not think it right to remain in the house after what I said to her. If so, why does she not go with Kamal?' Nagendra's brow was clouded. No one ventured to come near him. He knew not what fault Surja Mukhi had committed, yet he held no intercourse with her, but sent a female spy into the neighbourhood to make search for Kunda Nandini.

Surja Mukhi was much distressed on hearing of Kunda's flight, especially as Kamal Mani had assured her that what Debendra had said was not worthy of credit: for if she had had any bond with Debendra during three years, it could not have remained unknown; and Kunda's disposition gave no reason for suspicion of such a thing. Debendra was a drunkard, and in his cups he spoke falsely. Thinking over this, Surja Mukhi's distress increased. In addition to that, her husband's displeasure hurt her severely. A hundred times she abused Kunda—a thousand times she blamed herself. She also sent people in search of Kunda.

Kamal postponed her departure for Calcutta. She abused no one. She did not use a word of scolding to Surja Mukhi. Loosening her necklace from her throat, she showed it to all the household, saying, 'I will give this to whomsoever will bring Kunda back.'

The guilty Hira heard and saw all this, but said nothing. Seeing the necklace she coveted it, but repressed her desire. On the second day, arranging her work, she went at noon, at which hour her grandmother would be bathing, to give Kunda her meal. At night the two made their bed, and laid down together. Neither Hira nor Kunda slept: Kunda was kept awake by her sorrow; Hira by the mingled happiness and trouble of her thoughts. But whatever her thoughts were she did not give them words—they remained hidden.

Oh, Hira! Hira! You have not an evil countenance, you too are young; why this vice in your heart? Why did the Creator betray her? Because the Creator betrayed her, does she therefore wish to betray others? If Hira were in Surja Mukhi's place, would she be so deceitful? Hira says 'No!' But sitting in Hira's place she speaks as Hira. People say all evil that occurs is brought about by the wicked. Wicked people say, 'I should have been virtuous, but through the faults of others have become evil.' Some say, 'Why has not five become seven?' Five says, 'I would have been seven, but two and five make seven. If the Creator or the Creator's creatures had given me two more, I should have been seven.' So thought Hira.

Hira said to herself: 'Now what shall I do? Since the Creator has given me the opportunity, why should I lose it through my own fault? On the one side, if I take Kunda home to the Dattas, Kamal will give me the necklace, and the Grihini also will give me something. Shall I spare the Babu? On the other hand, if I give Kunda to Debendra Babu, I shall get a large sum of money at once. But I can't do that. Why does Debendra think Kunda so beautiful? If I had good food, dressed well, took my ease like a fine lady in a picture, I could be the same.

So simple a creature as Kunda can never understand the merits of Debendra Babu. If there were no mud there would be no lotus, and Kunda is the only woman who can excite love in Debendra Babu. Every one to their destiny! But why am I angry? Why should I trouble myself? I used to jest at love—I used to say it is mere talk, a mere story. Now I laugh no longer. I used to say, 'If anyone loves let him love; I shall never love any one.' Fate said, 'Wait, you will see by and by.' In trying to seize the robber of other's wealth, I have lost my own heart. What a face! what a neck! what a figure! is there another man like him? That the fellow should tell me to bring Kunda to him!

Could he set no one else this task? I could have struck him in the face! I have come to love him so dearly, I could even find pleasure in striking him. But let that pass. In that path there is danger; I must not think of it. I have long ceased to look for joy or sorrow in this life. Nevertheless, I cannot give Kunda into Debendra's hand; the thought of it torments me. Rather I will so manage that she shall not fall in his way. How shall I effect that? I will place Kunda where she was before, thus she will escape him. Whether he dress as Boisnavi or Vasudeva, he will not obtain admission into that house; therefore it will be well to take Kunda back there. But she will not go! Her face is set against the house. But if all coax her she must go. Another design I have in my mind; will God permit me to carry it out? Why am I so angry with Surja Mukhi? She never did me any harm; on the contrary, she loves me and is kind to me. Why, then, am I angry? Because Surja Mukhi is happy, and I am miserable; she is great, I am mean; she is mistress, I am servant; therefore my anger against her is strong. If, you say, God made her great, how is that her fault? Why should I hurt her? I reply, God has done me harm. Is that my fault? I do not wish to hurt her, but if hurting her benefits me, why should I not do it? Who does not seek his own advantage? Now I want money; I can't endure servitude any longer. Where will money come from? From the Datta house—where else? To get the Datta money, then, must be my object. Every one knows that Nagendra Babu's eyes have fallen on Kunda; the Babu worships her. What great people wish, they can accomplish. The only obstacle is Surja Mukhi. If the two should quarrel, then the great Surja Mukhi's wish will no longer be regarded. Now, let me see if I cannot bring about a quarrel. If that is done, the Babu will be free to worship Kunda. At present Kunda is but an innocent, but I will make her wise; I will soon bring her into subjection. She can be of much assistance to me. If I give my mind to it, I can make her do what I will. If the Babu devotes himself to Kunda, he will do what she bids him; and she shall do what I bid her.

So shall I receive the fruits of his devotion. If I am not to serve longer, this is the way it must be brought about. I will give Kunda Nandini to Nagendra, but not suddenly. I will hide her for a few days and see what happens. Love is deepened by separation. If I keep them apart the Babu's love will ripen. Then I will bring out Kunda and give her to him. Then if Surja Mukhi's fate is not broken, it must be a very strong fate. In the meantime I will mould Kunda to my will. But, first, I must send my grandmother to Kamarghat, else I cannot keep Kunda hidden.'

With this design, Hira set about her arrangements. On some pretext she induced her grandmother to go to the house of a relative in the village of Kamarghat, and kept Kunda closely concealed in her own house. Kunda, seeing all her zeal and care, thought to herself, 'There is no one living so good as Hira. Even Kamal does not love me so much.'

17

HIRA'S QUARREL
THE BUD OF THE POISON TREE

'Yes, that will do. Kunda shall submit. But if we do not make Surja Mukhi appear as poison in the eyes of Nagendra, nothing can be accomplished.'

So Hira set herself to divide the hearts hitherto undivided.

One morning early, the wicked Hira came into her mistress's house ready for work. There was a servant in the Datta household named Kousalya, who hated Hira because she was head servant and enjoyed the favour of the mistress. Hira said to her: 'Sister Kushi, I feel very strange today; will you do my work for me?'

Kousalya feared Hira, therefore she said: 'Of course I will do it; we are all subject to illness, and all the subjects of one mistress.'

It had been Hira's wish that Kousalya should give no reply, and she would make that a pretext for a quarrel. So, shaking her head, she said: 'You presume so far as to abuse me?'

Astonished, Kousalya said: 'When did I abuse any one?'

'What!' said Hira, angrily, 'you deny it? Why did you speak of my illness? Do you think I am going to die? You hope that I am ill that you may show people how good you are to me. May you be ill yourself.'

'Be it so! Why are you angry, sister? You must die some day; Death will not forget you, nor will he forget me.'

'May Death never forget you! You envy me! May you die of envy! May your life be short! Go to destruction! May blindness seize upon you!'

Kousalya could bear no more. She began to return these good wishes in similar terms. In the act of quarrelling Kousalya was the superior.

Therefore Hira got her deserts.

Then Hira went to complain to her mistress. If any one could have looked at her as she went, they would have seen no signs of anger on her face, but rather a smile on her lips. But when she reached her mistress, her face expressed great anger, and she began by using the weapon given by God to woman—that is to say, she shed a flood of tears.

Surja Mukhi inquired into the cause. On hearing the complaint, she judged that Hira was in fault. Nevertheless, for her sake, she scolded Kousalya slightly.

Not being satisfied with that, Hira said: 'You must dismiss that woman, or I will not remain.'

Then Surja Mukhi was much vexed with Hira, and said: 'You are very encroaching, Hira; you began the quarrel, the fault was entirely yours, and now you want me to dismiss the woman. I will do nothing so unjust. Go, if you will. I will not bid you stay.'

This was just what Hira wanted. Saying 'Very well, I go,' her eyes streaming with tears, she presented herself before the Babu in the outer apartments.

The Babu was alone in the boita khana—he was usually alone now. Seeing Hira weeping, he asked, 'Why do you weep, Hira?'

'I have been told to come for my wages.'

Nagendra, astonished, asked: 'What has happened?'

'I am dismissed. Ma Thakurani (the mistress) has dismissed me.'

'What have you done?' asked Nagendra.

'Kushi abused me; I complained: the mistress believes her account and dismisses me.'

Nagendra, shaking his head and laughing, said: 'That is not a likely story, Hira; tell the truth.'

Hira then, speaking plainly, said: 'The truth is I will not stay.'

'Why?'

'The mistress has become quite altered. One never knows what to expect from her.'

Nagendra, frowning, said in a sharp voice: 'What does that mean?'

Hira now brought in the fact she had wished to report.

'What did she not say that day to Kunda Nandini Thakurani? On hearing it, Kunda left the house. Our fear is that some day something of the same kind should be said to us. We could not endure that, therefore I chose to anticipate it.'

'What are you talking about?' asked Nagendra.

'I cannot tell you for shame.'

Nagendra's brow became dark. He said: 'Go home for today; I will call you tomorrow.'

Hira's desire was accomplished. With this design she had quarrelled with Kousalya.

Nagendra rose and went to Surja Mukhi. Stepping lightly, Hira followed him.

Taking Surja Mukhi aside, he asked, 'Have you dismissed Hira?'

Surja Mukhi replied, 'Yes,' and then related the particulars.

On hearing them, Nagendra said: 'Let her go. What did you say to Kunda Nandini?'

Nagendra saw that Surja Mukhi turned pale.

'What did I say to her?' she stammered.

'Yes; what evil words did you use to her?'

Surja Mukhi remained silent some moments. Then she said—

'You are my all, my present and my future; why should I hide anything from you? I did speak harshly to Kunda; then, fearing you would be angry, I said nothing to you about it. Forgive me that offence; I am telling you all.'

Then she related the whole matter frankly, from the discovery of the Boisnavi Haridasi to the reproof she had given to Kunda. At the end she said—

'I am deeply sorrowful that I have driven Kunda Nandini away. I have sent everywhere in search of her. If I had found her, I would have brought her back.'

Nagendra said—

'Your fault is not great. Could any respectable man's wife, hearing of such a stain, give refuge to the guilty person? But would it not have been well to think a little whether the charge was true? Did you not know of the talk about Tara Charan's house? Had you not heard that Debendra had been introduced to Kunda three years before? Why did you believe a drunkard's words?'

'I did not think of that at the time. Now I do. My mind was

wandering.' As she spoke the faithful wife sank at Nagendra's feet, and clasping them with her hands, wetted them with her tears. Then raising her face, she said: 'Oh, dearer than life, I will conceal nothing that is in my mind.'

Nagendra said: 'You need not speak; I know that you suspect me of feeling love for Kunda Nandini.'

Surja Mukhi, hiding her face at the feet of her husband, wept. Again raising her face, sad and tearful as the dew-drenched lily, and looking into the face of him who could remove all her sorrows, she said: 'What can I say? Can I tell you what I have suffered? Only lest my death might increase your sorrow, I do not die. Otherwise, when I knew that another shared your heart, I wished to die. But people cannot die by wishing to do so.'

Nagendra remained long silent; then, with a heavy sigh, he said—

'Surja Mukhi, the fault is entirely mine, not yours at all. I have indeed been unfaithful to you; in truth, forgetting you, my heart has gone out towards Kunda Nandini. What I have suffered, what I do suffer, how can I tell you? You think I have not tried to conquer it; but you must not think so. You could never reproach me so bitterly as I have reproached myself. I am sinful; I cannot rule my own heart.'

Surja Mukhi could endure no more. With clasped hands, she entreated bitterly—

'Tell me no more; keep it to yourself. Every word you say pierces my breast like a dart. What was written in my destiny has befallen me. I wish to hear no more; it is not fit for me to hear.'

'Not so, Surja Mukhi,' replied Nagendra; 'you must listen. Let me speak what I have long striven to say. I will leave this house; I will not die, but I will go elsewhere. Home and family no longer give me happiness. I have no pleasure with you. I am not fit to be your husband. I will trouble you no longer. I will find Kunda Nandini, and will go with her to another place. Do you remain mistress of this house. Regard yourself as a widow—since your husband is so base, are you not a widow? But, base as I am, I will not deceive you. Now I go: if I am able to forget Kunda, I will come again; if not, this is my last hour with you.'

What could Surja Mukhi say to these heart-piercing words? For some moments she stood like a statue, gazing on the ground. Then she cast herself down, hid her face, and wept.

As the murderous tiger gazes at the dying agonies of his prey, Nagendra stood calmly looking on. He was thinking, 'She will die today or tomorrow, as God may will. What can I do? If I willed it, could I die instead of her? I might die; but would that save Surja Mukhi?'

No, Nagendra, your dying would not save Surja Mukhi; but it would be well for you to die.

After a time Surja Mukhi sat up; again clasping her husband's feet, she said: 'Grant me one boon.'

'What is it?'

'Remain one month longer at home. If in that time we do not find Kunda Nandini, then go; I will not keep you.'

Nagendra went out without reply. Mentally he consented to remain for a month; Surja Mukhi understood that. She stood looking after his departing figure, thinking within herself: 'My darling, I would give my life to extract the thorns from your feet. You would leave your home on account of this wretched Surja Mukhi. Are you or I the greater?'

18

THE CAGED BIRD

Hira had lost her place, but her relation with the Datta family was not ended. Ever greedy for news from that house, whenever she met any one belonging to it Hira entered into a gossip. In this way she endeavoured to ascertain the disposition of Nagendra towards Surja Mukhi. If she met no one she found some pretext for going to the house, where, in the servants' quarters, while talking of all sorts of matters, she would learn what she wished and depart. Thus some time passed; but one day an unpleasant event occurred. After Hira's interview with Debendra, Malati the milkwoman became a constant visitor at Hira's dwelling. Malati perceived that Hira was not pleased at this; also that one room remained constantly closed. The door was secured by a chain and padlock on the outside; but Malati coming in unexpectedly, perceived that the padlock was absent. Malati removed the chain and pushed the door, but it was fastened inside, and she guessed that someone must be in the room. She asked herself who it could be? At first she thought of a lover; but then, whose lover? Malati knew everything that went on, so she dismissed this idea. Then the thought flashed across her that it might be Kunda, of whose expulsion from the house of Nagendra she had heard. She speedily determined upon a means of resolving her doubt.

Hira had brought from Nagendra's house a young deer, which, because of its restlessness, she kept tied up. Malati, pretending to feed the creature, loosened the fastening, and it instantly bounded away. Hira ran after it.

Seizing the opportunity of Hira's absence, Malati began to call out in a voice of distress: 'Hira! Hira! What has happened to my Hira?' Then rapping at Kunda's door, she exclaimed: 'Kunda Thakurun, come out quickly; something has happened to Hira!'

In alarm Kunda opened the door; whereupon Malati, with a laugh of triumph, ran away. Kunda again shut herself in. She did not say anything of the circumstance to Hira, lest she should be scolded. Malati went with her news to Debendra, who resolved to visit Hira's house on the following day, and bring the matter to a conclusion.

Kunda was now a caged bird, ever restless. Two currents uniting become a powerful stream. So it was in Kunda's heart. On one side shame, insult, expulsion by Surja Mukhi; on the other, passion for Nagendra. By the union of these two streams that of passion was increased, the smaller was swallowed up in the larger. The pain of the taunts and the insults began to fade; Surja Mukhi no longer found place in Kunda's mind, Nagendra occupied it entirely. She began to think, 'Why was I so hasty in leaving the house? What harm did a few words do to me? I used to see Nagendra, now I never see him. Could I go back there? if she would not drive me away I would go.' Day and night Kunda revolved these thoughts; she soon determined that she must return to the Datta house or she would die; that even if Surja Mukhi should again drive her away, she must make the attempt. Yet on what pretext could she present herself in the courtyard of the house? She would be ashamed to go thither alone. If Hira would accompany her she might venture; but she was ashamed to open her mouth to Hira.

Her heart could no longer endure not to see its lord. One morning, about four o'clock, while Hira was still sleeping, Kunda Nandini arose, and opening the door noiselessly, stepped out of the house. The dark fortnight being ended, the slender moon floated in the sky like a beautiful maiden on the ocean. Darkness lurked in masses amid the trees. The air was so still that the lotus in the weed-covered pool bordering the road did not shed its seed; the dogs were sleeping by the wayside; nature was full of sweet pensiveness. Kunda, guessing the road, went with doubtful steps to the front of the Datta house; she had no design in going, except that she might by a happy chance see Nagendra. Her return to his house might come about; let it occur when it would, what harm was there in the meantime in trying to see him secretly? While she remained shut up in Hira's house she had no chance of doing so. Now, as she walked, she thought, 'I will go round the house; I may see him at the window, in the palace, in the garden, or in the path.' Nagendra was accustomed to rise early; it was possible Kunda might obtain a glimpse of him, after which she meant to return to Hira's dwelling. But when she arrived at the house she saw nothing of Nagendra, neither in the path, nor on the roof, nor at the window. Kunda thought, 'He has not risen yet, it is not time; I will sit down.' She sat waiting amid the darkness under the trees; a fruit or a twig might be heard, in the silence, loosening itself with a slight cracking sound and falling to the earth. The birds in the boughs shook their wings overhead, and occasionally the sound of the watchmen knocking at the doors and giving their warning cry was to be heard. At length the cool wind blew, forerunner of the dawn, and the papiya (a bird) filled the air with its musical voice. Presently the cuckoo uttered his cry, and at length all the birds uniting raised a chorus of song. Then Kunda's hope was extinguished; she could no longer sit under the trees, for the dawn had come and she might be seen by any one. She rose to return. One hope had been strong in her mind. There was a flower garden attached to the inner apartments, where sometimes Nagendra took the air. He might be walking there now; Kunda could not go away without seeing if it were so. But the garden was walled in, and unless the inner door was open there was no entrance. Going thither, Kunda found the door open, and, stepping boldly in, hid herself within the boughs of a bakul tree growing in the midst. Thickly-planted rows of creeper-covered trees decked the garden, between which were fine stone-made paths, and here and there flowering shrubs of various hues—red, white, blue, and yellow. Above them hovered troops of insects, coveting the morning honey, now poising, now flying, humming as they went; and, following the example of man, settling in flocks on some specially attractive flower. Many-coloured birds of small size, flower-like themselves, hovered over the blossoms, sipping the sweet juices and pouring forth a flood of melody. The flower-weighted branches swayed in the gentle breeze, the flowerless boughs remaining still, having nothing to weigh them down. The cuckoo, proud bird, concealing his dark colour in the tufts of the bakul tree, triumphed over every one with his song.

In the middle of the garden stood a creeper-covered arbour of white stone, surrounded by flowering shrubs. Kunda Nandini, looking forth from the bakul tree, saw not Nagendra's tall and god-like form. She saw someone lying on the floor of the arbour, and concluded that it was he. She went forward to obtain a better new. Unfortunately the person arose and came out, and poor Kunda saw that it was not Nagendra, but Surja Mukhi. Frightened, Kunda stood still, she could neither advance nor recede. She saw that Surja Mukhi was walking about gathering flowers. Gradually Nagendra's wife approaching the bakul tree, saw someone lurking within its branches. Not recognizing Kunda, Surja Mukhi said, 'Who are you?'

Kunda could not speak for fear; her feet refused to move.

At length Surja Mukhi saw who it was, and exclaimed, 'Is it not Kunda?'

Kunda could not answer; but Surja Mukhi, seizing her hand, said, 'Come, sister, I will not say anything more to you!' and took her indoors.

19

DESCENT

On the night of that day, Debendra Datta, alone, in disguise, excited by wine, went to Hira's house in search of Kunda Nandini. He looked in the two huts, but Kunda was not there. Hira, covering her face with her sari, laughed at his discomfiture. Annoyed, Debendra said, 'Why do you laugh?'

'At your disappointment. The bird has fled; should you search my premises you will not find it.'

Then, in reply to Debendra's questions, Hira told all she knew, concluding with the words, 'When I missed her in the morning I sought her everywhere, and at last found her in the Babu's house receiving much kindness.'

Debendra's hopes thus destroyed, he had nothing to detain him; but the doubt in his mind was not dispelled, he wished to sit a little and obtain further information. Noting a cloud or two in the sky he moved restlessly, saying, 'I think it is going to rain.'

It was Hira's wish that he should sit awhile; but she was a woman, living alone; it was night, she could not bid him stay, if she did she would be taking another step in the downward course. Yet that was in her destiny.

Debendra said, 'Have you an umbrella?' There was no such thing in Hira's house. Then he asked, 'Will it cause remark if I sit here until the rain is past?'

'People will remark upon it, certainly; but the mischief has been done already in your coming to my house at night.'

'Then I may sit down?'

Hira did not answer, but made a comfortable seat for him on the bench, took a silver-mounted huka from a chest, prepared it for use and handed it to him.

Debendra drew a flask of brandy from his pocket, and drank

some of it undiluted. Under the influence of this spirit he perceived that Hira's eyes were beautiful. In truth they were so—large, dark, brilliant, and seductive. He said, 'Your eyes are heavenly!' Hira smiled. Debendra saw in a corner a broken violin. Humming a tune, he took the violin and touched it with the bow. 'Where did you get this instrument?' he asked.

'I bought it of a beggar.'

Debendra made it perform a sort of accompaniment to his voice, as he sang some song in accordance with his mood.

Hira's eyes shone yet more brilliantly. For a few moments she forgot self, forgot Debendra's position and her own. She thought, 'He is the husband, I am the wife; the Creator, making us for each other, designed long ago to bring us together, that we might both enjoy happiness.' The thoughts of the infatuated Hira found expression in speech. Debendra discovered from her half-spoken words that she had given her heart to him. The words were hardly uttered when Hira recovered consciousness. Then, with the wild look of a frantic creature, she exclaimed, 'Go from my house!'

Astonished, Debendra said, 'What is the matter, Hira?'

'You must go at once, or I shall.'

'Why do you drive me away?' said Debendra.

'Go, go, else I will call someone. Why should you destroy me?'

'Is this woman's nature?' asked Debendra.

Hira, enraged, answered: 'The nature of woman is not evil. The nature of such a man as you is very evil. You have no religion, you care nothing for the fate of others; you go about seeking only your own delight, thinking only what woman you can destroy. Otherwise, why are you sitting in my house? Was it not your design to compass my destruction? You thought me to be a courtesan, else you would not have had the boldness to sit down here. But I am not a courtesan; I am a poor woman, and live by my labour. I have no leisure for such evil doings. If I had been a rich man's wife, I can't say how it would have been.'

Debendra frowned.

Then Hira softened; she looked full at Debendra and said: 'The sight of your beauty and your gifts has made me foolish, but you are not to think of me as a courtesan. The sight of you makes me happy, and on that account I wished you to stay. I could not forbid you; but I am a woman. If I were too weak to forbid you, ought you to have sat down?

You are very wicked; you entered my house in order to destroy me. Now leave the place!'

Debendra, taking another draught of brandy, said: 'Well done, Hira! you have made a capital speech. Will you give a lecture in our Brahmo Samaj?'

Stung to the quick by this mockery, Hira said, bitterly: 'I am not to be made a jest of by you. Even if I loved so base a man as you, such love would be no fit subject for a jest. I am not virtuous; I don't understand virtue; my mind is not turned in that direction. The reason I told you I was not a courtesan is because I am resolved not to bring a stain upon my character in the hope of winning your love. If you had a spark of love for me, I would have made no such pledge to myself. I am not speaking of virtue; I should think nothing of infamy compared with the treasure of your love; but you do not love me. For what reward should I incur ill-fame? For what gain should I give up my independence? If a young woman falls into your hands, you will not let her go. If I were to give you my worship, you would accept it; but tomorrow you would forget me, or, if you remembered, it would be to jest over my words with your companions. Why, then, should I become subject to you? Should the day come when you can love me, I will be your devoted servant.'

In this manner Debendra discovered Hira's affection for himself. He thought: 'Now I know you, I can make you dance to my measure, and whenever I please effect my designs through you.'

With these thoughts in his mind, he departed. But Debendra did not yet know Hira.

20

GOOD NEWS

It is midday. Srish Babu is at office. The people in his house are all taking the noon siesta after their meal. The boita khana is locked. A mongrel terrier is sleeping on the doormat outside, his head between his paws. A couple of servants are seizing the opportunity to chat together in whispers.

Kamal Mani is sitting in her sleeping chamber at her ease, needle in hand, sewing at some canvas work, her hair all loose; no one about but Satish Babu, indulging in many noises. Satish Babu at first tried to snatch away his mother's wool; but finding it securely guarded, he gave his mind to sucking the head of a clay tiger. In the distance a cat with outstretched paws sits watching them both. Her disposition was grave, her face indicated much wisdom and a heart void of fickleness. She is thinking: 'The condition of human creatures is frightful; their minds are ever given to sewing canvas, playing with dolls, or some such silly employment. Their thoughts are not turned to good works, nor to providing suitable food for cats. What will become of them hereafter?' Elsewhere, a lizard on the wall with upraised face is watching a fly. No doubt he is pondering the evil disposition of flies. A butterfly is flying about. In the spot where Satish Babu sits eating sweets, the flies collect in swarms; the ants also do their share towards removing the sweet food. In a few moments the lizard, not being able to catch the fly, moves elsewhere. The cat also, seeing no means by which she could improve the disposition of mankind, heaving a sigh, slowly departs. The butterfly wings its way out of the room. Kamal Mani, tired of her work, puts it down, and turns to talk with Satish Babu.

'Oh, Satu Babu, can you tell me why men go to office?'

'Sli—li—bli,' was the child's only answer.

'Satu Babu,' said his mother, 'mind you never go to office.'

'Hama,' said Satu.

'What do you mean by Hama? You must not go to office to do hama. Do not go at all. If you do, the Bou will sit crying at home before the day is half done.'

Satish Babu understood the word Bou, because Kamal Mani kept him in order by saying that the Bou would come and beat him; so he said, 'Bou will beat.'

'Remember that, then; if you go to office, the Bou will beat you.'

How long this sort of conversation would have continued does not appear, for at that moment a maidservant entered, rubbing her sleepy eyes, and gave a letter to Kamal Mani. Kamal saw it was from Surja Mukhi; she read it twice through, then sat silent and dejected. This was the letter:

'Dearest,—Since you returned to Calcutta you have forgotten me; else why have I had only one letter from you? Do you not know that I always long for news of you? You ask for news of Kunda. You will be delighted to hear that she is found. Besides that, I have another piece of good news for you. My husband is about to be married to Kunda. I have arranged this marriage. Widow remarriage is allowed in the Shastras, so what fault can be found with it? The wedding will take place in a couple of days; but you will not be able to attend, otherwise I would have invited you. Come, if you can, in time for the ceremony of Phul Saja. I have a great desire to see you.'

Kamal could not understand the meaning of this letter. She proceeded to take counsel with Satish Babu, who sat in front of her nibbling at the corners of a book. Kamal read the letter to him and said—

'Now, Satish Babu, tell me the meaning of this.'

Satish understood the joke; he stood up ready to cover his mother with kisses.

Then for some moments Kamal forgot Surja Mukhi; but presently she returned to the letter, reflecting—

'This work is beyond Satish Babu, it needs the help of my minister; will he never come in? Come, baby, we are very angry.'

In due time Srish Chandra returned from office and changed his dress. Kamal Mani attended to his wants and then threw herself on the couch in a fume, the baby by her side. Srish Chandra, seeing the state of things, smiled, and seated himself, with his huka, on a distant couch. Invoking the huka as a witness he said—

'O huka! thou hast cool water in thy belly but a fire in thy head, be thou a witness. Let her who is angry with me talk to me, else I will sit smoking for hours.'

At this Kamal Mani sat up, and in gentle anger turning to him her blue lotus eyes, said—

'It is no use speaking to you while you smoke; you will not attend.'

Then she rose from the couch and took away the huka.

Kamal Mani's fit of sulking thus broken through, she gave Surja Mukhi's letter to be read, by way of explanation saying—

'Tell me the meaning of this, or I shall cut your pay.'

'Rather give me next month's pay in advance, then I will explain.'

Kamal Mani brought her mouth close to that of Srish Chandra, who took the coin he wished. After reading the letter he said—

'This is a joke!'

'What is? your words, or the letter?'

'The letter.'

'I shall discharge you today. Have you not a spark of understanding? Is this a matter a woman could jest about?'

'It is impossible it can be meant in earnest.'

'I fear it is true.'

'Nonsense! How can it be true?'

'I fear my brother is forcing on this marriage.'

Srish Chandra mused a while; then said, 'I cannot understand this at all. What do you say? Shall I write to Nagendra?'

Kamal Mani assented. Srish made a grimace, but he wrote the letter. Nagendra's reply was as follows:—

'Do not despise me, brother. Yet what is the use of such a petition; the despicable must be despised. I must effect this marriage. Should all the world abandon me I must do it, otherwise I shall go mad: I am not far short of it now. After this there seems nothing more to be said. You will perceive it is useless to try to turn me from it; but if you have anything to say I am ready to argue with you. If any one says that widow remarriage is contrary to religion, I will give him Vidya Sagar's essay to read. When so learned a teacher affirms that widow remarriage is approved by the Shastras, who can contradict? And if you say that though allowed by the Shastras it is not countenanced by society, that if I carry out this marriage I shall be excluded from society, the answer is, 'Who in Govindpur can exclude me from society?

In a place where I constitute society, who is there to banish me?' Nevertheless, for your sakes I will effect the marriage secretly; no one shall know anything about it. You will not make the foregoing objections; you will say a double marriage is contrary to morals. Brother, how do you know that it is opposed to morality? You have learned this from the English; it was not held so in India formerly. Are the English infallible? They have taken this idea from the law of Moses; but we do not hold Moses' law to be the word of God, therefore why should we say that for a man to marry two wives is immoral? You will say if a man may marry two wives why should not a woman have two husbands? The answer is, if a woman had two husbands certain evils would follow which would not result from a man's having two wives. If a woman has two husbands the children have no protector; should there be uncertainty about the father, society would be much disordered; but no such uncertainty arises when a man has two wives. Many other such objections might be pointed out. Whatever is injurious to the many is contrary to morals. If you think a man's having two wives opposed to morality, point out in what way it is injurious to the majority. You will instance to me discord in the family. I will give you a reason: I am childless. If I die my family name will become extinct; if I marry I may expect children: is this unreasonable? The final objection—Surja Mukhi: Why do I distress a loving wife with a rival? The answer is, Surja Mukhi is not troubled by this marriage: she herself suggested it; she prepared me for it; she is zealous for it. What objection then remains? and why should I be blamed?'

Kamal Mani having read the letter, said—

'In what respect he is to blame God knows; but what delusions he cherishes! I think men understand nothing. Be that as it may, arrange your affairs, husband; we must go to Govindpur.'

'But,' replied Srish, 'can you stop the marriage?'

'If not, I will die at my brother's feet.'

'Nay, you can't do that; but we may bring the new wife away.

Let us try.'

Then both prepared for the journey to Govindpur. Early the next day they started by boat, and arrived there in due time. Before entering the house they met the women servants and some neighbours, who had come to bring Kamal Mani from the ghat. Both she and her husband were extremely anxious to know if the marriage had taken place, but neither could put a single question. How could they speak to strangers of such a shameful subject?

Hurriedly Kamal Mani entered the women's apartments; she even forgot Satish Babu, who remained lingering behind. Indistinctly, and dreading the answer, she asked the servants—

'Where is Surja Mukhi?'

She feared lest they should say the marriage was accomplished, or that Surja Mukhi was dead. The women replied that their mistress was in her bedroom. Kamal Mani darted thither. For a minute or two she searched hither and thither, finding no one. At last she saw a woman sitting near a window, her head bowed down. Kamal Mani could not see her face, but she knew it was Surja Mukhi, who, now hearing footsteps, arose and came forward. Not even yet could Kamal ask if the marriage had taken place. Surja Mukhi had lost flesh; her figure, formerly straight as a pine, had become bent like a bow; her laughing eyes were sunk; her lily face had lost its roundness.

Kamal Mani comprehended that the marriage was accomplished. She inquired, 'When was it?'

Surja Mukhi answered, 'Yesterday.'

Then the two sat down together, neither speaking. Surja Mukhi hid her face in the other's lap, and wept. Kamal Mani's tears fell on Surja Mukhi's unbound hair.

Of what was Nagendra thinking at that time as he sat in the boita khana? His thoughts said: 'Kunda Nandini! Kunda is mine; Kunda is my wife! Kunda! Kunda! she is mine!'

Srish Chandra sat down beside him, but Nagendra could say little; he could think only, 'Surja Mukhi herself hastened to give Kunda to me in marriage; who then can object to my enjoying this happiness?'

21

SURJA MUKHI AND KAMAL MANI

When, in the evening, the two gained self-control to talk together, Surja Mukhi related the affair of the marriage from beginning to end.

Astonished, Kamal Mani said—

'This marriage has been brought about by your exertions! Why have you thus sacrificed yourself?'

Surja Mukhi smiled, a faint smile indeed, like the pale flashes of lightning after rain; then answered—

'What am I? Look upon your brother's face, radiant with happiness, then you will know what joy is his. If I have been able with my own eyes to see him so happy, has not my life answered its purpose? What joy could I hope for in denying happiness to him? He for whom I would die rather than see him unhappy for a single hour; him I saw day and night suffering anguish, ready to abandon all joys and become a wanderer—what happiness would have remained to me? I said to him, "My lord, your joy is my joy! Do you marry Kunda; I shall be happy." And so he married her.'

'And are you happy?' asked Kamal.

'Why do you still ask about me? what am I? If I had ever seen my husband hurt his foot by walking on a stony path, I should have reproached myself that I had not laid my body down over the stones that he might have stepped upon me.'

Surja Mukhi remained some moments silent, her dress drenched with her tears. Suddenly raising her face, she asked—

'Kamal, in what country are females destroyed at birth?'

Kamal understanding her thought, replied—

'What does it matter in what country it happens? it is according to destiny.'

'Whose destiny could be better than mine was? Who so fortunate as myself? Who ever had such a husband? Beauty, wealth, these are small matters; but in virtues, whose husband equals mine? Mine was a splendid destiny; how has it changed thus?'

'That also is destiny,' said Kamal.

'Then why do I suffer on this account?'

'But just now you said you were happy in the sight of your husband's joyous face; yet you speak of suffering so much. Can both be true?'

'Both are true. I am happy in his joy. But that he should thrust me away; that he has thrust me away, and yet is so glad—'

Surja could say no more, she was choking. But Kamal, understanding the meaning of her unfinished sentence, said—

'Because of that your heart burns within you; then why do you say, 'What am I?' With half of your heart you still think of your own rights; else why, having sacrificed yourself, do you repent?'

'I do not repent,' replied Surja. 'That I have done right I do not doubt; but in dying there is suffering. I felt that I must give way, and I did so voluntarily. Still, may I not weep over that suffering with you?'

Kamal Mani drew Surja Mukhi's head on to her breast; their thoughts were not expressed by words, but they conversed in their hearts. Kamal Mani understood the wretchedness of Surja Mukhi; Surja Mukhi comprehended that Kamal appreciated her suffering. They checked their sobs and ceased to weep.

Surja Mukhi, setting her own affairs on one side, spoke of others, desired that Satish Babu should be brought, and talked to him. With Kamal she spoke long of Srish Chandra and of Satish, of the education of Satish and of his marriage. Thus they talked until far in the night, when Surja Mukhi embraced Kamal with much affection, and taking Satish into her lap kissed him lovingly.

When they came to part, Surja Mukhi was again drowned in tears. She blessed Satish, saying—

'I wish that thou mayst be rich in the imperishable virtues of thy mother's brother; I know no greater blessing than this.'

Surja Mukhi spoke in her natural, gentle voice; nevertheless Kamal was astonished at its broken accents. 'Bon!!' she exclaimed, 'what is in your mind? tell me.'

'Nothing,' replied Surja.

'Do not hide it from me,' said Kamal.

'I have nothing to conceal,' said Surja.

Pacified, Kamal went to her room. But Surja Mukhi had a purpose to conceal. This Kamal learned in the morning. At dawn she went to Surja Mukhi's room in search of her; Surja Mukhi was not there, but upon the undisturbed bed there lay a letter. At the sight of it Kamal became dizzy; she could not read it. Without doing so she understood all, understood that Surja Mukhi had fled. She had no desire to read the letter, but crushed it in her hand. Striking her forehead, she sat down upon the bed, exclaiming: 'I am a fool! how could I allow myself to be put off last night when parting from her?'

Satish Babu, standing near, joined his tears with his mother's.

The first passion of grief having spent itself, Kamal Mani opened and read the letter. It was addressed to herself, and ran as follows:

'On the day on which I heard from my husband's mouth that he no longer had any pleasure in me, that for Kunda Nandini he was losing his senses or must die—on that day I resolved, if I could find Kunda Nandini, to give her to my husband and to make him happy; and that when I had done so I would leave my home, for I am not able to endure to see my husband become Kunda Nandini's. Now I have done these things.

'I wished to have gone on the night of the wedding day, but I had a desire to see my husband's happiness, to give him which I had sacrificed myself; also, I desired to see you once more. Now these desires are fulfilled, and I have left.

'When you receive this letter I shall be far distant. My reason for not telling you beforehand is that you would not have allowed me to go. Now I beg this boon from you, that you will make no search for me. I have no hope that I shall ever see you again. While Kunda Nandini remains I shall not return to this place, and should I be sought for I shall not be found. I am now a poor wanderer. In the garb of a beggar I shall go from place to place. In begging I shall pass my life; who will know me? I might have brought some money with me, but I was not willing. I have left my husband—would I take his money?

'Do one thing for me. Make a million salutations in my name at my husband's feet. I strove to write to him, but I could not; I could not see to write for tears, the paper was spoilt. Tearing it up, I wrote again and again, but in vain; what I have to say I could not write in any letter. Break the intelligence to him in any manner you think proper. Make him understand that I have not left him in anger; I am not angry, am never angry, shall never be angry with him. Could I be angry with him whom it is my joy to think upon? To him whom I love so devotedly, I remain constant so long as I remain on earth. Why not? since I cannot forget his thousand graces. No one has so many graces as he. If I could forget his numerous virtues on account of one fault, I should not be worthy to be his wife. I have taken a last farewell of him. In doing this I have given up all I possess.

'From you also I have taken a last farewell, wishing you the blessing that your husband and son may live long. May you long be happy! Another blessing I wish you—that on the day you lose your husband's love your life may end. No one has conferred this blessing on me.'

22

WHAT IS THE POISON TREE?

The poison tree, the narrative of whose growth we have given from the sowing of the seed to the production of its fruit, is to be found in every house. Its seed is sown in every field. There is no human being, however wise, whose heart is not touched by the passions of anger, envy, and desire. Some are able to subdue their passions as they arise; these are great men. Others have not this power, and here the poison tree springs up. The want of self-control is the germ of the poison tree, and also the cause of its growth. This tree is very vigorous; once nourished it cannot be destroyed. Its appearance is very pleasant to the eye; from a distance its variegated leaves and opening buds charm the sight. But its fruit is poisonous; who eats it dies.

In different soils the poison tree bears different fruits. In some natures it bears sickness, in some sorrow, and other fruits. To keep the passions in subjection will is needed, and also power. The power must be natural, the will must be educated. Nature also is influenced by education; therefore education is the root of self-control. I speak not of such education as the schoolmaster can give. The most effectual teacher of the heart is suffering.

Nagendra had never had this education. The Creator sent him into the world the possessor of every kind of happiness. Beauty of form, unlimited wealth, physical health, great learning, an amiable disposition, a devoted wife—all these seldom fall to the lot of one person; all had been bestowed on Nagendra. Most important of all, Nagendra was of a happy disposition: he was truthful and candid, yet agreeable: benevolent, yet just; generous, yet prudent; loving, yet firm in his duty. During the lifetime of his parents he was devoted to them. Attached to his wife, kind to his friends, considerate to his servants, a protector of his dependants, and peaceable towards his enemies, wise in counsel, trustworthy in act, gentle in conversation, ready at a jest. The natural reward of such a nature was unalloyed happiness. Since Nagendra's infancy it had been so: honour at home, fame abroad, devoted servants, an attached tenantry; from Surja Mukhi, unwavering, unbounded, unstained love. If so much happiness had not been allotted to him he could not have suffered so keenly. Had he not suffered he had not given way to his passion. Before he had cast the eyes of desire upon Kunda Nandini he had never fallen into this snare, because he had never known the want of love. Therefore he had never felt the necessity of putting a rein upon his inclinations.

Accordingly, when the need of self-control arose he had not the power to exercise it. Unqualified happiness is often the source of suffering; and unless there has been suffering, permanent happiness cannot exist. It cannot be said that Nagendra was faultless. His fault was very heavy. A severe expiation had begun.

23

THE SEARCH

It is needless to say that when the news of Surja Mukhi's flight had spread through the house, people were sent in great haste in search of her. Nagendra sent people in all directions, Srish Chandra sent, and Kamal Mani sent. The upper servants among the women threw down their water jars and started off; the Hindustani Durwans of the North-West Provinces, carrying bamboo staves, wearing cotton-quilted chintz coats, clattered along in shoes of undressed leather; the khansamahs, with towel on the shoulder and silver chain round the waist, went in search of the mistress. Some relatives drove in carriages along the public roads. The villagers searched the fields and gháts; some sat smoking in council under a tree; some went to the barowari puja house, to the verandah of Siva's temple, and to the schools of the professors of logic, and in other similar places sat and discussed the matter. Old and young women formed a small cause court on the gháts; to the boys of the place it was cause of great excitement; many of them hoped to escape going to school.

At first Srish Chandra and Kamal Mani comforted Nagendra, saying, 'She has never been accustomed to walk; how far can she go? Half a mile, or a mile at the most; hence she must be sitting somewhere near at hand, we shall find her immediately.'

But when two or three hours had passed without bringing news of Surja Mukhi, Nagendra himself went forth. After some stay in the broiling sun he said to himself, 'I am looking here, when no doubt she has been found by this time;' and he returned home. Then finding no news of her he went out again, again to return, and again to go forth. So the day passed.

In fact, Srish Chandra's words were true—Surja Mukhi had never walked; how far could she go? About a mile from the house she was lying in a mango garden at the edge of a tank. A khansamah who was accustomed to serve in the women's apartment came to that place in his search, and recognizing her, said, 'Will you not please to come home?'

Surja Mukhi made no answer.

Again he said, 'Pray come home, the whole household is anxious.'

Then, in an angry voice, Surja Mukhi said, 'Who are you to take me back?'

The khansamah was frightened; nevertheless he remained standing.

Then Surja Mukhi said, 'If you stay there I shall drown myself in the tank.'

The khansamah, finding he was unable to do anything, ran swiftly with the news to Nagendra. Nagendra came with a palanquin for her; but Surja Mukhi was no longer there. He searched all about, but found no trace.

Surja Mukhi had wandered thence into a wood. There she met an old woman who had come to gather sticks. She had heard of a reward being offered for finding Surja Mukhi, therefore on seeing her she asked—

'Are you not our mistress?'

'No, mother,' replied Surja Mukhi.

'Yes, you must be our mistress.'

'Who is your mistress?'

'The lady of the Babu's house.'

'Am I wearing any gold ornaments that I should be the lady of the Babu's house?'

The old woman thought, 'That is true,' and went further into the wood gathering sticks.

Thus the day passed vainly; the night brought no more success. The two following days brought no tidings, though nothing was neglected in the search. Of the male searchers, scarcely any one knew Surja Mukhi by sight; so they seized many poor women and brought them before Nagendra. At length the daughters of respectable people feared to walk along the roads or on the ghâts. If one was seen alone, the devoted Hindustani Durwans followed, calling out 'Ma Thakurani,' and, preventing them from bathing, brought a palki. Many of those who were not accustomed to travel in a palki seized the opportunity of doing so free of expense.

Srish Chandra could not remain longer. Returning to Calcutta, he began a search there. Kamal Mani, remaining in Govindpur, continued to look for the lost one.

24

EVERY SORT OF HAPPINESS IS FLEETING

The happiness for which Kunda Nandini had never ventured to hope was now hers; she had become the wife of Nagendra. On the marriage day she thought, 'This joy is boundless; it can never end!'

But after the flight of Surja Mukhi, repentance came to Kunda Nandini. She thought: 'Surja Mukhi rescued me in my time of distress, when but for her I should have been lost; now on my account she is an outcast. If I am not to be happy, it were better I had died.' She perceived that happiness has limits.

It is evening. Nagendra is lying on the couch; Kunda Nandini sits at his head fanning him. Both are silent. This is not a good sign. No one else is present, yet they do not speak. This was not like perfect happiness; but since the flight of Surja Mukhi, where had there been perfect happiness? Kunda's thoughts were constantly seeking some means by which things could be restored to their former state, and she now ventured to ask Nagendra what could be done.

Nagendra, somewhat disturbed, replied: 'Do you wish things to be as they were before? do you repent having married me?'

Kunda Nandini felt hurt. She said: 'I never hoped that you would make me happy by marrying me. I am not saying I repent it. I am asking what can be done to induce Surja Mukhi to return.'

'Never speak of that. To hear the name of Surja Mukhi from your lips gives me pain; on your account Surja Mukhi has abandoned me.'

This was known to Kunda, yet to hear Nagendra say it hurt her. She asked herself: 'Is this censure? How evil is my fate, yet I have committed no fault; Surja Mukhi brought about the marriage.' She did not utter these thoughts aloud, but continued fanning.

Noticing her silence, Nagendra said: 'Why do you not talk? Are you angry?'

'No,' she replied.

'Is a bare "no" all you can say? Do you no longer love me?'
'Do I not love you!'
'"Do I not love you!" Words to soothe a boy. Kunda, I believe you never loved me.'

'I have always loved you,' said Kunda, earnestly.

Wise as Nagendra was, he did not comprehend the difference between Surja Mukhi and Kunda Nandini. It was not that Kunda did not feel the love for him that Surja Mukhi felt, but that she knew not how to express it. She was a girl of a timid nature; she had not the gift of words. What more could she say? But Nagendra, not understanding this, said: 'Surja Mukhi always loved me. Why hang pearls on a monkey's neck? An iron chain were better.'

At this Kunda Nandini could not restrain her tears. Slowly rising, she went out of the room. There was no one now to whom she could look for sympathy. Kunda had not sought Kamal Mani since her arrival. Imagining herself the one chiefly to blame in the marriage, Kunda had not dared to show herself to Kamal Mani; but now, wounded to the quick, she longed to go to her compassionate, loving friend, who on a former occasion had soothed and shared her grief and wiped away her tears. But now things were altered. When Kamal saw Kunda Nandini approaching she was displeased, but she made no remark. Kunda, sitting down, began to weep; but Kamal did not inquire into the cause of her grief, so Kunda remained silent. Presently, Kamal Mani, saying 'I am busy,' went away. Kunda Nandini perceived that all joy is fleeting.

25

THE FRUIT OF THE POISON TREE

Nagendra's letter to Hara Deb Ghosal: 'You wrote that of all the acts I have done in my life, my marriage with Kunda Nandini is the most erroneous. I admit it. By doing this I have lost Surja Mukhi. I was very fortunate in obtaining Surja Mukhi for a wife. Every one digs for jewels, but only one finds the Koh-i-nur. Surja Mukhi is the Koh-i-nur. In no respect can Kunda Nandini fill her place. Why, then, did I install Kunda Nandini in her seat? Delusion, delusion; now I am sensible of it. I have woken up from my dream to realize my loss. Now where shall I find Surja Mukhi?

'Why did I marry Kunda Nandini? Did I love her? Certainly I loved her; I lost my senses for her; my life was leaving me. But now I know this was but the love of the eye; or else, when I have been only fifteen days married, why do I say, "Did I love her?" I love her still; but where is my Surja Mukhi?

'I meant to have written much more today; but I cannot, it is very difficult.'

Hara Deb Ghosal's reply:

'I understand your state of mind. It is not that you do not love Kunda Nandini; you do love her, but when you said it was the love of the eye only, you spoke the truth. Towards Surja Mukhi your love is deep, but for a couple of days it has been covered by the shadow of Kunda Nandini. Now you understand that you have lost Surja Mukhi. So long as the sun remains unclouded, we are warmed by his beams and we love the clouds; but when the sun is gone we know that he was the eye of the world. Not understanding your own heart, you have committed this great error. I will not reproach you more, because you fell into it under a delusion which it was very difficult to resist.

'The mind has many different affections; men call them all love, but only that condition of heart which is ready to sacrifice its own happiness to secure that of another is true love. The passion for beauty is not love. The unstable lust for beauty is no more love than the desire of the hungry for rice. True love is the offspring of reason. When the qualities of a lovable person are perceived by the understanding, the heart being charmed by these qualities is drawn towards the possessor; it desires union with that treasury of virtues and becomes devoted to it. The fruits of this love are expansion of the heart, self-forgetfulness, self-denial. This is true love. Shakespeare, Valmiki, Madame de Staël, are its poets; as Kalidas, Byron, Jayadeva are of the other species of love. The effect on the heart produced by the sight of beauty is dulled by repetition. But love caused by the good qualities of a person does not lose its charm, because beauty has but one appearance, because virtues display themselves anew in every fresh act. If beauty and virtues are found together, love is quickly generated; but if once the intelligence be the cause for love, it is of no importance whether beauty exists or not. Towards an ugly husband or an ugly wife love of this kind holds a firm place. The love produced by virtue as virtue is lasting certainly, but it takes time to know these virtues; therefore this love never becomes suddenly strong, it is of gradual growth. The infatuation for beauty springs into full force at first sight; its first strength is so uncontrollable that all other faculties are destroyed by it. Whether it be a lasting love there is no means of knowing. It thinks itself undying. So you have thought. In the first strength of this infatuation your enduring love for Surja Mukhi became invisible to your eyes. This delusion is inherent in man's nature; therefore I do not censure you, rather I counsel you to strive to be happy in this state.

'Do not despair; Surja Mukhi will certainly return. How long can she exist without seeing you? So long as she remains absent, do you cherish Kunda Nandini. So far as I understand your letters she is not without attractive qualities. When the infatuation for her beauty is lessened, there may remain something to create a lasting love; if that is so, you will be able to make yourself happy with her; and should you not again see your elder wife you may forget her, especially as the younger one loves you. Be not careless about love; for in love is man's only spotless and imperishable joy, the final means by which his nature can be elevated. Without love man could not dwell in this world that he has made so evil.'

Nagendra Natha's reply:

'I have not answered your letter until now because of the trouble of my mind. I understand all you have written, and I know your counsel is good. But I cannot resolve to stay at home. A month ago my Surja Mukhi left me, and I have had no news of her. I design to follow her; I will wander from place to place in search of her. If I find her I will bring her home, otherwise I shall not return. I cannot remain with Kunda Nandini; she has become a pain to my eyes. It is not her fault, it is mine, but I cannot endure to see her face. Formerly I said nothing to her, but now I am perpetually finding fault with her. She weeps—what can I do? I shall soon be with you.'

As Nagendra wrote so he acted. Placing the care of everything in the hands of the Dewan during his temporary absence, he set forth on his wanderings. Kamal Mani had previously gone to Calcutta; therefore of the people mentioned in this narrative, Kunda Nandini alone was left in the Datta mansion, and the servant Hira remained in attendance upon her.

Darkness fell on the large household. As a brilliantly lighted, densely crowded dancing hall, resounding with song and music, becomes dark, silent, and empty when the performance is over, so that immense household became when abandoned by Surja Mukhi and Nagendra Natha.

As a child, having played for a day with a gaily painted doll, breaks and throws it away, and by degrees, earth accumulating, grass springs over it, so Kunda Nandini, abandoned by Nagendra Natha, remained untended and alone amid the crowd of people in that vast house.

As when the forest is on fire the nests of young birds are consumed in the flames, and the mother-bird bringing food, and seeing neither tree, nor nest, nor young ones, with cries of anguish whirls in circles round the fire seeking her nest, so did Nagendra wander from place to place in search of Surja Mukhi.

As in the fathomless depths of the boundless ocean, a jewel having fallen cannot again be seen, so Surja Mukhi was lost to sight.

26

THE SIGNS OF LOVE

As a cotton rag placed near fire becomes burnt, so the heart of Hira became ever more inflamed by the remarkable beauty of Debendra. Many a time Hira's virtue and good name would have been endangered by passion, but that Debendra's character for sensuality without love came to her mind and proved a safeguard. Hira had great power of self-control, and it was through this power that she, though not very virtuous, had hitherto easily preserved her chastity. The more certainly to rule her heart, Hira determined to go again to service.

She felt that in daily work her mind would be distracted, and she would be able to forget this unfortunate passion which stung like the bite of a scorpion. Thus when Nagendra, leaving Kunda Nandini at Govindpur, was about to set forth, Hira, on the strength of past service, begged to be re-engaged, and Nagendra consented. There was another cause for Hira's resolve to resume service. In her greed for money, anticipating that Kunda would become the favourite of Nagendra, she had taken pains to bring her under her own sway. 'Nagendra's wealth,' she had reflected, 'will fall into Kunda's hands, and when it is Kunda's it will be Hira's.' Now Kunda had become the mistress of Nagendra's house, but she had not obtained possession of any special wealth. But at this time Hira's mind was not dwelling on this matter. Hira was not thinking of wealth; even had she done so, money obtained from Kunda would have been as poison to her.

Hira was able to endure the pain of her own unsatisfied passion, but she could not bear Debendra's passion for Kunda. When Hira heard that Nagendra was journeying abroad, and that Kunda would remain as grihini (housemistress), then, remembering Haridasi Boisnavi, she became much alarmed, and stationed herself as a sentinel to place obstacles in the path of Debendra. It was not from a desire to secure the welfare of Kunda Nandini that Hira conceived this design. Under the influence of jealousy Hira had become so enraged with Kunda, that far from wishing her well she would gladly have seen her go to destruction. But in jealous fear lest Debendra should gain access to Kunda, Hira constituted herself the guardian of Nagendra's wife.

Thus the servant Hira became the cause of suffering to Kunda, who saw that Hira's zeal and attention did not arise from affection. She perceived that Hira, though a servant, showed want of trust in her, and continually scolded and insulted her. Kunda was of a very peaceful disposition; though rendered ill by Hira's conduct she said nothing to her. Kunda's nature was calm, Hira's passionate. Thus Kunda, though the master's wife, submitted as if she were a dependant; Hira lorded it over her as if she were the mistress. Sometimes the other ladies of the house, seeing Kunda suffer, scolded Hira, but they could not stand before Hira's eloquence.

The Dewan hearing of her doings, said to Hira: 'Go away; I dismiss you.'

Hira replied, with flaming eyes: 'Who are you to dismiss me? I was placed here by the master, and except at his command I will not go. I have as much power to dismiss you as you have to dismiss me.'

The Dewan, fearing further insult, said not another word. Except Surja Mukhi, no one could rule Hira.

One day, after the departure of Nagendra, Hira was lying alone in the creeper-covered summerhouse in the flower garden near to the women's apartments. Since it had been abandoned by Surja Mukhi and Nagendra, Hira had taken possession of this summerhouse. It was evening, an almost full moon shone in the heavens. Her rays shining through the branches of the trees fell on the white marble, and danced upon the wind-moved waters of the talao close by. The air was filled with the intoxicating perfume of the scented shrubs. There is nothing in nature so intoxicating as flower-perfumed air. Hira suddenly perceived the figure of a man in a grove of trees; a second glance showed it to be Debendra. He was not disguised, but wore his own apparel.

Hira exclaimed in astonishment: 'You are very bold, sir; should you be discovered you will be beaten!'

'Where Hira is, what cause have I for fear?' Thus saying, Debendra sat down by Hira, who, after a little silent enjoyment this pleasure, said—

'Why have you come here? You will not be able to see her whom you hoped to see.'

'I have already attained my hope. I came to see you.'

Hira, not deceived by the sweet, flattering words she coveted, said with a laugh: 'I did not know I was destined to such pleasure; still, since it has befallen me, let us go where I can satisfy myself by beholding you without interruption. Here there are many obstacles.'

'Where shall we go?' said Debendra.

'Into that summerhouse; there we need fear nothing.'

'Do not fear for me.'

'If there is nothing to fear for you, there is for me. If I am seen with you what will be my position?'

Shrinking at this, Debendra said: 'Let us go. Would it not be well that I should renew acquaintance with your new grihini?'

The burning glance of hate cast on him by Hira at these words, Debendra failed to see in the uncertain light.

Hira said: 'How will you get to see her?'

'By your kindness it will be accomplished,' said Debendra.

'Then do you remain here on the watch; I will bring her to you.'

With these words Hira went out of the summerhouse. Proceeding some distance, she stopped beneath the shelter of a tree and gave way to a burst of sobbing: then went on into the house—not to Kunda Nandini, but to the darwans (gatekeepers), to whom she said—

'Come quickly; there is a thief in the garden.'

Then Dobe, Chobe, Paure, and Teowari, taking thick bamboo sticks in their hands, started off for the flower garden. Debendra, hearing from afar the sound of their clumsy, clattering shoes, and seeing their black, napkin-swathed chins, leaped from the summerhouse and fled in haste. Teowari and Co. ran some distance, but they could not catch him; yet he did not get off scot-free. We cannot certainly say whether he tasted the bamboo, but we have heard that he was pursued by some very abusive terms from the mouths of the darwans; and that his servant, having had a little of his brandy, in gossip the next day with a female friend remarked—

'Today, when I was rubbing the Babu with oil, I saw a bruise on his back.'

Returning home, Debendra made two resolutions: the first, that while Hira remained he would never again enter the Datta house; the second, that he would retaliate upon Hira. In the end he had a frightful revenge upon her. Hira's venial fault received a heavy punishment, so heavy that at sight of it even Debendra's stony heart was lacerated.

We will relate it briefly later.

27

BY THE ROADSIDE

It is one of the worst days of the rainy season; not once had the sun appeared, only a continuous downpour of rain. The well metalled road to Benares was a mass of slush. But one traveller was to be seen, his dress was that of a Brahmachari (an ascetic): yellow garments, a bead chaplet on his neck, the mark on the forehead, the bald crown surrounded by only a few white hairs, a palm leaf umbrella in one hand, in the other a brass drinking vessel. Thus the Brahmachari travelled in the soaking rain through the dark day, followed by a night as black as though the earth were full of ink. He could not distinguish between road and no road; nevertheless he continued his way, for he had renounced the world, he was a Brahmachari. To those who have given up worldly pleasures, light and darkness, a good and a bad road, are all one. It was now far on in the night; now and then it lightened; the darkness itself was preferable, was less frightful than those flashes of light.

'Friend!'

Plodding along in the darkness the Brahmachari heard suddenly in the pathway some such sound, followed by a long sigh. The sound was muffled, nevertheless it seemed to come from a human throat, from some one in pain. The Brahmachari stood waiting, the lightning flashed brightly; he saw something lying at the side of the road—was it a human being? Still he waited; the next flash convinced him that his conjecture was correct. He called out, 'Who are you lying by the roadside?' No one made reply. Again he asked. This time an indistinct sound of distress caught his ear. Then the Brahmachari laid his umbrella and drinking vessel on the ground, and extending his hands began to feel about. Ere long he touched a soft body; then as his hand came in contact with a knot of hair he exclaimed, 'Oh, Durga, it is a woman!'

Leaving umbrella and drinking vessel, he raised the dying or senseless woman in his arms, and, leaving the road, crossed the plain towards a village; he was familiar with the neighbourhood, and could make his way through the darkness. His frame was not powerful, yet he carried this dying creature like a child through this difficult path. Those who are strong in goodwill to others are not sensible of bodily weakness.

Bearing the unconscious woman in his arms, the Brahmachari stopped at the door of a leaf-thatched hut at the entrance of the village, and called to one within, 'Haro, child, are you at home?'

A woman replied, 'Do I hear the Thakur's voice? When did the Thakur come?'

'But now. Open the door quickly; I am in a great difficulty.'

Haro Mani opened the door. The Brahmachari, bidding her light a lamp, laid his burden on the floor of the hut. Haro lit the lamp, and bringing it near the dying woman, they both examined her carefully. They saw that she was not old, but in the condition of her body it was difficult to guess her age. She was extremely emaciated, and seemed struck with mortal illness. At one time she certainly must have had beauty, but she had none now. Her wet garments were greatly soiled, and torn in a hundred places; her wet, unbound hair was much tangled; her closed eyes deeply sunk. She breathed, but was not conscious; she seemed near death.

Haro Mani asked: 'Who is this? where did you find her?'

The Brahmachari explained, and added, 'I see she is near death, yet if we could but renew the warmth of her body she might live; do as I tell you and let us see.'

Then Haro Mani, following the Brahmachari's directions, changed the woman's wet clothes for dry garments, and dried her wet hair. Then lighting a fire, they endeavoured to warm her.

The Brahmachari said: 'Probably she has been long without food; if there is milk in the house, give her a little at a time.'

Haro Mani possessed a cow, and had milk at hand; warming some, she administered it slowly. After a while the woman opened her eyes; when Haro Mani said, 'Where have you come from, mother?'

Reviving, the woman asked, 'Where am I?'

The Brahmachari answered, 'Finding you dying by the roadside, I brought you hither. Where are you going?'

'Very far.'

Haro Mani said: 'You still wear your bracelet; is your husband living?'

The sick woman's brow darkened. Haro Mani was perplexed.

The Brahmachari asked 'What shall we call you? what is your name?'

The desolate creature, moving a little restlessly, replied, 'My name is Surja Mukhi.'

28

IS THERE HOPE?

There was apparently no hope of Surja Mukhi's life. The Brahmachari, not understanding her symptoms, next morning called in the village doctor. Ram Krishna Rai was very learned, particularly in medicine. He was renowned in the village for his skill. On seeing the symptoms, he said—

'This is consumption, and on this fever has set in. It is, I fear, a mortal sickness; still she may live.'

These words were not said in the presence of Surja Mukhi.

The doctor administered physic, and seeing the destitute condition of the woman he said nothing about fees. He was not an avaricious man.

Dismissing the physician, the Brahmachari sent Haro Mani about other work, and entered into conversation with Surja Mukhi, who said—

'Thakur, why have you taken so much trouble about me? There is no need to do so on my account.'

'What trouble have I taken?' replied the Brahmachari; 'this is my work. To assist others is my vocation; if I had not been occupied with you, someone else in similar circumstances would have required my services.'

'Then leave me, and attend to others. You can assist others, you cannot help me.'

'Wherefore?' asked the Brahmachari.

'To restore me to health will not help me. Death alone will give me peace. Last night, when I fell down by the roadside, I hoped that I should die. Why did you save me?'

'I knew not that you were in such deep trouble. But however deep it is, self-destruction is a great sin. Never be guilty of such an act. To kill one's self is as sinful as to kill another.'

'I have not tried to kill myself; death has approached voluntarily, therefore I hoped; but even in dying I have no joy.' Saying these words, Surja Mukhi's voice broke, and she began to weep.

The Brahmachari said: 'Whenever you speak of dying I see you weep; you wish to die. Mother, I am like a son to you; look upon me as such, and tell me your wish. If there is any remedy for your trouble, tell me, and I will bring it about. Wishing to say this, I have sent Haro Mani away, and am sitting alone with you. From your speech I infer that you belong to a very respectable family. That you are in a state of very great anxiety, I perceive. Why should you not tell me what it is? Consider me as your son, and speak.'

Surja Mukhi, with wet eyes, said: 'I am dying; why should I feel shame at such a time? I have no other trouble than this, that I am dying without seeing my husband's face. If I could but see him once I should die happy.'

The Brahmachari wiped his eyes also, and said:

'Where is your husband? It is impossible for you to go to him now; but if he, on receiving the news, could come here, I would let him know by letter.'

Surja Mukhi's wan face expanded into a smile; then again becoming dejected, she said: 'He could come, but I cannot tell if he would. I am guilty of a great offence against him, but he is full of kindness to me; he might forgive me, but he is far from here. Can I live till he comes?'

Finding, on further inquiry, that the Babu lived at Haripur Zillah, the Brahmachari brought pen and paper, and, taking Surja Mukhi's instructions, wrote as follows:

'SIR,—

I am a stranger to you. I am a Brahman, leading the life of a Brahmachari. I do not even know who you are; this only I know, that Srimati Surja Mukhi Dasi is your wife. She is lying in a dangerous state of illness in the house of the Boisnavi Haro Mani, in the village of Madhupur. She is under medical treatment, but it appears uncertain whether she will recover. Her last desire is to see you once more and die. If you are able to pardon her offence, whatever it may be, then pray come hither quickly. I address her as 'Mother.' As a son I write this letter by her direction. She has no strength to write herself. If you come, do so by way of Ranigunj. Inquire in Ranigunj for Sriman Madhab Chandra, and on mentioning my name he will send someone with you. In this way you will not have to search Madhupur for the house. If you come, come quickly, or it may be too late. Receive my blessing.

'(Signed)

SIVA PRASAD.'

The letter ended, the Brahmachari asked, 'What address shall I write?'

Surja Mukhi replied, 'When Haro Mani comes I will tell you.'

Haro Mani, having arrived, addressed the letter to Nagendra Natha Datta, and took it to the post-office. When the Brahmachari had gone, Surja Mukhi, with tearful eyes, joined hands, and upturned face, put up her petition to the Creator, saying, 'Oh, supreme God, if you are faithful, then, as I am a true wife, may this letter accomplish its end. I knew nothing during my life save the feet of my husband. I do not desire heaven as the reward of my devotion; this only I desire, that I may see my husband ere I die.'

But the letter did not reach Nagendra. He had left Govindpur long before it arrived there. The messenger gave the letter to the Dewan, and went away. Nagendra had said to the Dewan, 'When I stay at any place I shall write thence to you. When you receive my instructions, forward any letters that may have arrived for me.'

In due time Nagendra reached Benares, whence he wrote to the Dewan, who sent Siva Prasad's epistle with the rest of the letters. On receiving this letter Nagendra was struck to the heart, and, pressing his forehead, exclaimed in distress, 'Lord of all the world, preserve my senses for one moment!'

This prayer reached the ear of God, and for a time his senses were preserved. Calling his head servant, he said, 'I must go tonight to Ranigunj; make all arrangements.'

The man went to do his bidding; then Nagendra fell senseless on the floor.

That night Nagendra left Benares behind him. Oh, world-enchanting Benares! what happy man could have quitted thee on such an autumn night with satiated eyes? It is a moonless night. From the Ganges stream, in whatever direction you look you will see the sky studded with stars—from endless ages ever-burning stars, resting never. Below, a second sky reflected in the deep blue water; on shore, flights of steps, and tall houses showing a thousand lights; these again reflected in the river. Seeing this, Nagendra closed his eyes. Tonight he could not endure the beauty of earth. He knew that Siva Prasad's letter had been delayed many days. Where was Surja Mukhi now?

29

HIRA'S POISON TREE HAS BLOSSOMED

On the day when the durwans had driven out Debendra Babu with bamboos, Hira had laughed heartily within herself. But later she had felt much remorse. She thought, 'I have not done well to disgrace him; I know not how much I have angered him. Now I shall have no place in his thoughts; all my hopes are destroyed.'

Debendra also was occupied in devising a plan of vengeance upon Hira for the punishment she had caused to be inflicted on him. At last he sent for Hira, and after one or two days of doubt she came. Debendra showed no displeasure, and made no allusion to what had occurred. Avoiding that, he entered into pleasant conversation with her. As the spider spreads his net for the fly, so Debendra spread his net for Hira.

In the hope of obtaining her desire, Hira easily fell into the snare. Intoxicated with Debendra's sweet words, she was imposed upon by his crafty speech. She thought, 'Surely this is love! Debendra loves me.'

Hira was cunning, but now her cunning did not serve her. The power which the ancient poets describe as having been used to disturb the meditations of Siva, who had renounced passion—by that power Hira had lost her cunning.

Then Debendra took his guitar, and, stimulated by wine, began to sing. His rich and cultivated voice gave forth such honied waves of song, that Hira was as one enchanted. Her heart became restless, and melted with love of Debendra. Then in her eyes Debendra seemed the perfection of beauty, the essence of all that was adorable to a woman. Her eyes overflowed with tears springing from love.

Putting down his guitar, Debendra wiped away her tears. Hira shivered. Then Debendra began such pleasant jesting, mingled with loving speeches, and adorned his conversation with such ambiguous phrases, that Hira, entranced, thought, 'This is heavenly joy!' Never had she heard such words. If her senses had not been bewildered she would have thought, 'This is hell.'

Debendra had never known real love; but he was very learned in the love language of the old poets. Hearing from Debendra songs in praise of the inexpressible delights of love, Hira thought of giving herself up to him. She became steeped in love from head to foot. Then again Debendra sang with the voice of the first bird of spring. Hira, inspired by love, joined in with her feminine voice. Debendra urged her to sing. Hira, with sparkling eyes and smiling face, impelled by her happy feelings, sang a love song, a petition for love. Then, sitting in that evil room, with sinful hearts, the two, under the influence of evil desires, bound themselves to live in sin.

Hira knew how to subdue her heart, but having no inclination to do so she entered the flame as easily as an insect. Her belief that Debendra did not love her had been her protection until now. When her love for Debendra was but in the germ she smilingly confessed it to herself, but turned away from him without hesitation. When the full-grown passion pierced her heart she took service to distract her thoughts. But when she imagined he loved her she had no desire to resist. Therefore she now had to eat the fruit of the poison tree.

People say that you do not see sin punished in this world. Be that true or not, you may be sure that those who do not rule their own hearts will have to bear the consequences.

30

NEWS OF SURJA MUKHI

It is late autumn. The waters from the fields are drying up; the rice crop is ripening; the lotus flowers have disappeared from the tanks. At dawn, dew falls from the boughs of the trees; at evening, mist rises over the plains. One day at dawn a palanquin was borne along the Madhupur road. At this sight all the boys of the place assembled in a row; all the daughters and wives, old and young, resting their water vessels on the hip, stood awhile to gaze. The husbandmen, leaving the rice crop, sickle in hand and with turbaned heads, stood staring at the palanquin. The influential men of the village sat in committee. A booted foot was set down from the palanquin: the general opinion was that an English gentleman had arrived; the children thought it was Bogie.

When Nagendra Natha had descended from the palanquin, half a dozen people saluted him because he wore pantaloons and a smoking cap. Some thought he was the police inspector; others that he was a constable. Addressing an old man in the crowd, Nagendra inquired for Siva Prasad Brahmachari.

The person addressed felt certain that this must be a case of investigation into a murder, and that therefore it would not be well to give a truthful answer. He replied, 'Sir, I am but a child; I do not know as much as that.'

Nagendra perceived that unless he could meet with an educated man he would learn nothing. There were many in the village, therefore Nagendra went to a house of superior class. It proved to be that of Ram Kristo Rai, who, noticing the arrival of a strange gentleman, requested him to sit down. Nagendra, inquiring for Siva Prasad Brahmachari, was informed that he had left the place.

Much dejected, Nagendra asked, 'Where is he gone?'

'That I do not know; he never remains long in one place.'

'Does any one know when he will return?' asked Nagendra.

'I have some business with him, therefore I also made that inquiry, but no one can tell me.'

'How long is it since he left?'

'About a month.'

'Could any one show me the house of Haro Mani Boisnavi, of this village?'

'Haro Mani's house stood by the roadside; but it exists no longer, it has been destroyed by fire.'

Nagendra pressed his forehead. In a weak voice he asked, 'Where is Haro Mani?'

'No one can say. Since the night her house was burned she has fled somewhere. Some even say that she herself set fire to it.'

In a broken voice Nagendra asked, 'Did any other woman live in her house?'

'No. In the month Sraban a stranger, falling sick, stayed in her house. She was placed there by the Brahmachari. I heard her name was Surja Mukhi. She was ill of consumption; I attended her, had almost cured her. Now—'

Breathing hard, Nagendra repeated, 'Now?'

'In the destruction of Haro Mani's house the woman was burnt.'

Nagendra fell from his chair, striking his head severely. The blow stunned him. The doctor attended to his needs.

Who would live in a world so full of sorrow? The poison tree grows in every one's court. Who would love? to have one's heart torn in pieces.

Oh, Creator! why hast Thou not made this a happy world? Thou hadst the power if Thou hadst wished to make it a world of joy! Why is there so much sorrow in it?

When, at evening, Nagendra Natha left Madhupur in his palanquin, he said to himself—

'Now I have lost all. What is lost—happiness? that was lost on the day when Surja Mukhi left home. Then what is lost now—hope? So long as hope remains to man all is not lost; when hope dies, all dies.'

Now, therefore, he resolved to go to Govindpur, not with the purpose of remaining, but to arrange all his affairs and bid farewell to the house. The zemindari, the family house, and the rest of his landed property of his own acquiring, he would make over by deed to his nephew, Satish Chandra. The deed would need to be drawn up by a lawyer, or it would not stand. The movable wealth he would send to Kamal Mani in Calcutta, sending Kunda Nandini there also. A certain amount of money he would reserve for his own support in Government securities. The account books of the estate he would place in the hands of Srish Chandra.

He would not give Surja Mukhi's ornaments to his sister, but would keep them beside him wherever he went, and when his time came would die looking at them. After completing the needful arrangements he would leave home, revisit the spot where Surja Mukhi had died, and then resume his wandering life. So long as he should live he would hide in some corner of the earth.

Such were Nagendra's thoughts as he was borne on in his palanquin; its doors were open, the night was lightened by the October moon, stars shone in the sky. The telegraph wires by the wayside hummed in the wind; but on that night not even a star could seem beautiful in the eyes of Nagendra, even the moonlight seemed harsh. All things seemed to give pain. The earth was cruel. Why should everything that seemed beautiful in days of happiness seem today so ugly? Those long slender moonbeams by which the heart was wont to be refreshed, why did they now seem so glaring? The sky is today as blue, the clouds as white, the stars as bright, the wind as playful; the animal creation, as ever, rove at will. Man is as smiling and joyous, the earth pursues its endless course, family affairs follow their daily round. The world's hardness is unendurable. Why did not the earth open and swallow up Nagendra in his palanquin?

Thus thinking, Nagendra perceived that he was himself to blame for all. He had reached his thirty-third year only, yet he had lost all. God had given him everything that makes the happiness of man. Riches, greatness, prosperity, honour—all these he had received from the beginning in unwonted measure. Without intelligence these had been nothing, but God had given that also without stint. His education had not been neglected by his parents; who was so well instructed as himself? Beauty, strength, health, lovableness—these also nature had given to him with liberal hand. That gift which is priceless in the world, a loving, faithful wife, even this had been granted to him; who on this earth had possessed more of the elements of happiness? who was there on earth today more wretched? If by giving up everything, riches, honour, beauty, youth, learning, intelligence, he could have changed conditions with one of his palanquin-bearers, he would have considered it a heavenly happiness. 'Yet why a bearer?' thought he; 'is there a prisoner in the gaols of this country who is not more happy than I? not more holy than I? They have slain others; I have slain Surja Mukhi. If I had ruled my passions, would she have been brought to die such a death in a strange place? I am her murderer. What slayer of father, mother, or son, is a greater sinner than I? Was Surja Mukhi my wife only? She was my all. In relation a wife, in friendship a brother, in care a sister, abounding in hospitality, in love a mother, in devotion a daughter, in pleasure a friend, in counsel a teacher, in attendance a servant! My Surja Mukhi! who else possesses such a wife? A helper in domestic affairs, a fortune in the house, a religion in the heart, an ornament round the neck, the pupil of my eyes, the blood of my heart, the life of my body, the smile of my happiness, my comfort in dejection, the enlightener of my mind, my spur in work, the light of my eyes, the music of my ears, the breath of my life, the world to my touch! My present delight, the memory of my past, the hope of my future, my salvation in the next world! I am a swine—how should I recognize a pearl?'

Suddenly it occurred to him that he was being borne in a palanquin at his ease, while Surja Mukhi had worn herself out by travelling on foot. At this thought Nagendra leaped from the palanquin and proceeded on foot, his bearers carrying the empty vehicle in the rear. When he reached the bazaar where he had arrived in the morning he dismissed the men with their palanquin, resolving to finish his journey on foot.

'I will devote my life to expiating the death of Surja Mukhi. What expiation? All the joys of which Surja Mukhi was deprived in leaving her home, I will henceforth give up. Wealth, servants, friends, none of these will I retain. I will subject myself to all the sufferings she endured. From the day I leave Govindpur I will go on foot, live upon rice, sleep beneath a tree or in a hut. What further expiation?

Whenever I see a helpless woman I will serve her to the utmost of my power. Of the wealth I reserve to myself I will take only enough to sustain life; the rest I will devote to the service of helpless women. Even of that portion of my wealth that I give to Satish, I will direct that half of it shall be devoted during my life to the support of destitute women. Expiation! Sin may be expiated, sorrow cannot be. The only expiation for sorrow is death. In dying, sorrow leaves you: why do I not seek that expiation?'

Then covering his face with his hands, and remembering his Creator, Nagendra Natha put from him the desire to seek death.

31

THOUGH ALL ELSE DIES, SUFFERING DIES NOT

Srish Chandra was sitting alone in his boita khana one evening, when Nagendra entered, carpet bag in hand, and throwing the bag to a distance, silently took a seat. Srish Chandra, seeing his distressed and wearied condition, was alarmed, but knew not how to ask an explanation. He knew that Nagendra had received the Brahmachari's letter at Benares, and had gone thence to Madhupur. As he saw that Nagendra would not begin to speak, Srish Chandra took his hand and said—

'Brother Nagendra, I am distressed to see you thus silent. Did you not go to Madhupur?'

Nagendra only said, 'I went.'

'Did you not meet the Brahmachari?'

'No.'

'Did you find Surja Mukhi? Where is she?'

Pointing upwards with his finger, Nagendra said, 'In heaven.'

Both sat silent for some moments; then Nagendra, looking up, said, 'You do not believe in heaven. I do.'

Srish Chandra knew that formerly Nagendra had not believed in a heaven, and understood why he now did so—understood that this heaven was the creation of love.

Not being able to endure the thought that Surja Mukhi no longer existed, he said to himself, 'She is in heaven,' and in this thought found comfort.

Still they remained silent, for Srish Chandra felt that this was not the time to offer consolation; that words from others would be as poison, their society also. So he went away to prepare a chamber for Nagendra. He did not venture to ask him to eat; he would leave that task to Kamal.

But when Kamal Mani heard that Surja Mukhi was no more, she would undertake no duty. Leaving Satish Chandra, for that night she became invisible. The servants, seeing Kamal Mani bowed to the ground with hair unbound, left Satish and hurried to her. But Satish would not be left; he at first stood in silence by his weeping mother, and then, with his little finger under her chin, he tried to raise her face. Kamal looked up, but did not speak. Satish, wishing to comfort his mother, kissed her. Kamal caressed, but did not kiss him, nor did she speak. Satish put his hand on his mother's throat, crept into her lap, and began to cry. Except the Creator, who could enter into that child's heart and discern the cause of his crying?

The unfortunate Srish Chandra, left to his own resources, took some food to Nagendra, who said: 'I do not want food. Sit down, I have much to say to you; for that I came hither.' He then related all that he had heard from Ram Kristo Rai, and detailed his designs for the future.

After listening to the narration, Srish Chandra said: 'It is surprising that you should not have met the Brahmachari, as it is only yesterday he left Calcutta for Madhupur in search of you.'

'What?' said Nagendra; 'how did you meet with the Brahmachari?'

'He is a very noble person,' answered Srish. 'Not receiving a reply to his letter to you, he went to Govindpur in search of you. There he learned that his letter would be sent on to Benares. This satisfied him, and without remark to any one he went on his business to Purushuttam. Returning thence, he again went to Govindpur. Still hearing nothing of you, he was informed that I might have news. He came to me the next day, and I showed him your letter. Yesterday he started for Govindpur, expecting to meet you last night at Ranigunj.'

'I was not at Ranigunj last night,' said Nagendra. 'Did he tell you anything of Surja Mukhi?'

'I will tell you all that tomorrow,' said Srish.

'You think my suffering will be increased by hearing it. Tell me all,' entreated Nagendra.

Then Srish Chandra repeated what the Brahmachari had told him of his meeting Surja Mukhi by the roadside, her illness, medical treatment, and improvement in health. Omitting many painful details, he concluded with the words: 'Ram Kristo Kai did not relate all that Surja Mukhi had suffered.'

On hearing this, Nagendra rushed out of the house. Srish Chandra would have gone with him, but Nagendra would not allow it. The wretched man wandered up and down the road like a madman for hours. He wished to forget himself in the crowd, but at that time there was no crowd; and who can forget himself? Then he returned to the house, and sat down with Srish Chandra, to whom he said: 'The Brahmachari must have learned from her where she went, and what she did. Tell me all he said to you.'

'Why talk of it now?' said Srish; 'take some rest.'

Nagendra frowned, and commanded Srish Chandra to speak.

Srish perceived that Nagendra had become like a madman. His face was dark as a thunder-cloud. Afraid to oppose him, he consented to speak, and Nagendra's face relaxed. He began—

'Walking slowly from Govindpur, Surja Mukhi came first in this direction.'

'What distance did she walk daily?' interrupted Nagendra.

'Two or three miles.'

'She did not take a farthing from home; how did she live?'

'Some days fasting, some days begging—are you mad?' with these words Srish Chandra threatened Nagendra, who had clutched at his own throat as though to strangle himself, saying—

'If I die, shall I meet Surja Mukhi?'

Srish Chandra held the hands of Nagendra, who then desired him to continue his narrative.

'If you will not listen calmly, I will tell you no more,' said Srish.

But Nagendra heard no more; he had lost consciousness. With closed eyes he sought the form of the heaven-ascended Surja Mukhi; he saw her seated as a queen upon a jewelled throne. The perfumed wind played in her hair, all around flower-like birds sang with the voice of the lute; at her feet bloomed hundreds of red waterlilies; in the canopy of her throne a hundred moons were shining, surrounded by hundreds of stars. He saw himself in a place full of darkness, pain in all his limbs, demons inflicting blows upon him, Surja Mukhi forbidding them with her outstretched finger.

With much difficulty Srish Chandra restored Nagendra to consciousness; whereupon Nagendra cried loudly—

'Surja Mukhi, dearer to me than life, where art thou?'

At this cry, Srish Chandra, stupefied and frightened, sat down in silence.

At length, recovering his natural state, Nagendra said, 'Speak.'

'What can I say?' asked Srish.

'Speak!' said Nagendra. 'If you do not I shall die before your eyes.'

Then Srish said: 'Surja Mukhi did not endure this suffering many days. A wealthy Brahman, travelling with his family, had to come as far as Calcutta by boat, on his way to Benares. One day as Surja Mukhi was lying under a tree on the river's bank, the Brahman family came there to cook. The grihini entered into conversation with Surja Mukhi, and, pitying her condition, took her into the boat, as she had said that she also was going to Benares.'

'What is the name of that Brahman? where does he live?' asked Nagendra, thinking that by some means he would find out the man and reward him. He then bade Srish Chandra continue. 'Surja Mukhi,' continued Srish, 'travelled as one of the family as far as Barhi; to Calcutta by boat, to Raniganj by rail, from Raniganj by bullock train—so far Surja Mukhi proceeded in comfort.'

'After that did the Brahman dismiss her?' asked Nagendra.

'No,' replied Srish; 'Surja Mukhi herself took leave. She went no further than Benares. How many days could she go on without seeing you? With that purpose she returned from Barhi on foot.'

As Srish Chandra spoke tears came into his eyes, the sight of which was an infinite comfort to Nagendra, who rested his head on the shoulder of Srish and wept. Since entering the house Nagendra had not wept, his grief had been beyond tears; but now the stream of sorrow found free vent. He cried like a boy, and his suffering was much lessened thereby. The grief that cannot weep is the messenger of death!

As Nagendra became calmer, Srish Chandra said, 'We will speak no more of this today.'

'What more is there to say?' said Nagendra. 'The rest that happened I have seen with my own eyes. From Barhi she walked alone to Madhupur. From fatigue, fasting, sun, rain, despair, and grief, Surja Mukhi, seized by illness, fell to the ground ready to die.'

Srish Chandra was silent for a time; at length he said: 'Brother, why dwell upon this an longer? You are not in fault; you did nothing to oppose or vex her. There is no cause to repent of that which has come about without fault of our own.'

Nagendra did not understand. He knew himself to blame for all. Why had he not torn up the seed of the poison tree from his heart?

32

THE FRUIT OF HIRA'S POISON TREE

Hira has sold her precious jewel in exchange for a cowrie. Virtue may be preserved with much pains for a long time; yet a day's carelessness may lose it. So it was with Hira. The wealth to gain which she had sold her precious jewel was but a broken shell; for such love as Debendra's is like the bore in the river, as muddy as transient. In three days the flood subsided, and Hira was left in the mud. As the miser, or the man greedy of fame, having long preserved his treasure, at the marriage of a son, or some other festival, spends all in one day's enjoyment, Hira, who had so long preserved her chastity, had now lost it for a day's delight, and like the ruined miser was left standing in the path of endless regret.

Abandoned by Debendra, as a boy throws away an unripe mango not to his taste, Hira at first suffered frightfully. It was not only that she had been cast adrift by Debendra, but that, having been degraded and wounded by him, she had sunk to so low a position among women. It was this she found so unendurable. When, in her last interview, embracing Debendra's feet, she had said, 'Do not cast me off!' he had replied, 'It has only been in the hope of obtaining Kunda Nandini that I have honoured you so long. If you can secure me her society I will continue to live with you; otherwise not. I have given you the fitting reward of your pride; now, with the ink of this stain upon you, you may go home.'

Everything seemed dark around Hira in her anger. When her head ceased to swim she stood in front of Debendra, her brows knitted, her eyes inflamed, and as with a hundred tongues she gave vent to her temper. Abuse such as the foulest women use she poured upon him, till he, losing patience, kicked her out of the pleasure garden. Hira was a sinner; Debendra a sinner and a brute.

Thus ended the promise of eternal love.

Hira, thus abused, did not go home. In Govindpur there was a low-caste doctor who attended only low-caste people. He had no knowledge of treatment or of drugs; he knew only the poisonous pills by which life is destroyed. Hira knew that for the preparation of these pills he kept vegetable, mineral, snake, and other life-destroying poisons. That night she went to his house, and calling him aside said—

'I am troubled every day by a jackal who eats from my cooking vessels. Unless I can kill this jackal I cannot remain here. If I mix some poison with the rice today he will eat it and die. You keep many poisons; can you sell me one that will instantly destroy life?'

The Chandal (outcast) did not believe the jackal story. He said—

'I have what you want, but I cannot sell it. Should I be known to sell poison the police would seize me.'

'Be not anxious about that,' said Hira; 'no one shall know that you have sold it. I will swear to you by my patron deity, and by the Ganges, if you wish. Give me enough to kill two jackals, and I will pay you fifty rupees.'

The Chandal felt certain that a murder was intended, but he could not resist the fifty rupees, and consented to sell the poison.

Hira fetched the money from her house and gave it to him. The Chandal twisted up a pungent life-destroying poison in paper, and gave it to her.

In departing, Hira said, 'Mind you betray this to no one, else we shall both suffer.'

The Chandal answered, 'I do not even know you, mother.'

Thus freed from fear, Hira went home. When there she held the poison in her hand, weeping bitterly; then, wiping her eyes, she said—

'What fault have I committed that I should die? Why should I die without killing him who has struck me? I will not take this poison. He who has reduced me to this condition shall eat it, or, if not, I will give it to his beloved Kunda Nandini. After one of these two are dead, if necessary I also will take it.'

33

HIRA'S GRANDMOTHER

> 'Hira's old grandmother
> Walks about picking up
> A basket of cowdung.
> With her teeth cracking pebbles.
> Eating jak fruit by the hundred.'

Hira's grandmother hobbled along with the help of a stick, followed by boys reciting the above unrivalled verses, clapping their hands and dancing as they went. Whether any special taunt was meant by these verses is doubtful, but the old woman became furious, and desired the boys to go to destruction, wishing that their fathers might eat refuse (a common form of abuse). This was a daily occurrence.

Arriving at the door of Nagendra's house, the grandmother escaped from her enemies, who at sight of the fierce black moustaches of the durwans fled from the battlefield, one crying—

> 'Bama Charn Dobé
> Goes to bed early,
> And when the thief comes he runs away.'

Another—

> 'Ram Sing Paré
> With a stick marches boldly,
> But at sight of a thief he flies to the tank.'

A third—

> 'Lal Chand Sing
> Doth briskly dance and sing,
> Is death on the food,

But at work is no good.'

The boys fled, attacked by the durwans with a shower of words not to be found in any dictionary.

Hira's grandmother, plodding along, arrived at the dispensary attached to Nagendra's dwelling. Perceiving the doctor, she said, 'Oh, father, where is the doctor, father?'

'I am he.'

'Oh, father, I am getting blind. I am twenty-eight or eighty years old; how shall I speak of my troubles? I had a son; he is dead. I had a granddaughter; she also—' Here the old woman broke down, and began to whine like a cat.

The doctor asked, 'What has happened to you?'

Without answering this question, the woman began to relate the history of her life; and when, amid much crying, she had finished, the doctor again asked, 'What do you want now? What has happened to you?' Again she began the unequalled story of her life; but the doctor showing much impatience, she changed it for that of Hira, of Hira's mother, and Hira's husband.

With much difficulty the doctor at last arrived at her meaning, to which all this talking and crying was quite irrelevant. The old woman desired some medicine for Hira. Her complaint, she said, was a species of lunacy. Before Hira's birth, her mother had been mad, had continued so for some time, and had died in that condition. Hira had not hitherto shown any sign of her mother's disorder; but now the old woman felt some doubts about her. Hira would now laugh, now weep, now, closing the door, she would dance. Sometimes she screamed, and sometimes became unconscious. Therefore her grandmother wanted medicine for her. After some reflection the doctor said, 'Your daughter has hysteria.'

'Well, doctor, is there no medicine for that disease?'

'Certainly there is: keep her very warm; take this dose of castor oil, give it to her early tomorrow morning. Later I will come and give her another medicine.'

With the bottle of castor oil in her hand, the old woman hobbled forth. On the road she was met by a neighbour, who said, 'Oh, Hira's grandmother, what have you in your hand?'

The old woman answered, 'Hira has become hysterical; the doctor has given me some castor oil for her; do you think that will be good for hysterics?'

'It may be; castor oil is the god of all. But what has made your granddaughter so jolly lately?'

After much reflection the old woman said, 'It is the fault of her age;' whereupon the neighbour prescribed a remedy, and they parted.

On arriving at home, the old woman remembered that the doctor had said Hira must be kept warm; therefore she placed a pan of fire before her granddaughter.

'Fire!' exclaimed Hira. 'What is this for?'

'The doctor told me to keep you warm,' replied the old woman.

34

A DARK HOUSE: A DARK LIFE

In the absence of Nagendra and Surja Mukhi from their spacious home, all was darkness therein. The clerks sat in the office, and Kunda Nandini dwelt in the inner apartments with the poor relations. But how can stars dispel the darkness of a moonless night?

In the corners hung spiders' webs; in the rooms stood dust in heaps; pigeons built their nests in the cornices and sparrows in the beams. Heaps of withered leaves lay rotting in the garden; weeds grew over the tanks; the flower beds were hidden by jungle. There were jackals in the courtyard, and rats in the granary; mould and fungus were everywhere to be seen; musk rats and centipedes swarmed in the rooms; bats flew about night and day. Nearly all Surja Mukhi's pet birds had been eaten by cats; their soiled feathers lay scattered around. The ducks had been killed by the jackals, the peacocks had flown into the woods; the cows had become emaciated, and no longer gave milk. Nagendra's dogs had no spirit left in them, they neither played nor barked; they were never let loose; some had died, some had gone mad, some had escaped. The horses were diseased, or had become ill from want of work; the stables were littered with stubble, grass, and feathers. The horses were sometimes fed, sometimes neglected. The grooms were never to be found in the stables. The cornice of the house was broken in places, as were the sashes, the shutters, and the railings. The matting was soaked with rain; there was dust on the painted walls. Over the bookcases were the dwellings of insects; straws from the sparrows' nests on the glass of the chandeliers. In the house there was no mistress, and without a mistress paradise itself would be a ruin.

As in an untended garden overgrown with grass a single rose or lily will bloom, so in this house Kunda Nandini lived alone. Wherever a few joined in a meal Kunda partook of it. If any one addressed her as housemistress, Kunda thought, 'They are mocking me.' If the Dewan sent to ask her about anything her heart beat with fear. There was a reason for this. As Nagendra did not write to Kunda, she had been accustomed to send to the Dewan for the letters received by him. She did not return the letters, and she lived in fear that the Dewan would claim them; and in fact the man no longer sent them to her, but only suffered her to read them as he held them in his hand.

The suffering felt by Surja Mukhi was endured in equal measure by Kunda Nandini. Surja Mukhi loved her husband; did not Kunda love him? In that little heart there was inexhaustible love, and because it could find no expression, like obstructed breathing it wounded her heart. From childhood, before her first marriage, Kunda had loved Nagendra; she had told no one, no one knew it. She had had no desire to obtain Nagendra, no hope of doing so; her despair she had borne in silence. To have striven for it would have been like striving to reach the moon in the sky. Now where was that moon? For what fault had Nagendra thrust her from him? Kunda revolved these thoughts in her mind night and day; night and day she wept. Well! let Nagendra not love her. It was her good fortune to love him. Why might she not even see him? Nor that only: he regarded Kunda as the root of his troubles; every one considered her so. Kunda thought, 'Why should I be blamed for all this?'

In an evil moment Nagendra had married Kunda. As every one who sits under the upas tree must die, so every one who had been touched by the shadow of this marriage was ruined.

Then again Kunda thought, 'Surja Mukhi has come to this condition through me. Surja Mukhi protected me, loved me as a sister; I have made her a beggar by the roadside. Who is there more unfortunate than I? Why did I not die by the roadside? Why do I not die now? I will not die now; let him come, let me see him again. Will he not come?' Kunda had not received the news of Surja Mukhi's death, therefore she thought, 'What is the use of dying now? Should Surja Mukhi return, then I will die; I will no longer be a thorn in her path.'

35

THE RETURN

The work required to be done in Calcutta was finished. The deed of gift was drawn up. In it special rewards were indicated for the Brahmachari and the unknown Brahman. The deed would have to be registered at Haripur, therefore Nagendra went to Govindpur, taking it with him. He had instructed his brother-in-law to follow. Srish Chandra had striven to prevent his executing this deed, also to restrain him from making the journey on foot, but in vain. His efforts thus defeated, he followed by boat; and as Kamal Mani could not endure to be parted from her husband, she and Satish simply accompanied him without asking any questions.

When Kunda saw Kamal Mani she thought that once more a star had risen in the sky. Since the flight of Surja Mukhi, Kamal's anger against Kunda had been inflexible; she had always refused to see her. But now, at the sight of Kunda's emaciated figure, Kamal's anger departed. She endeavoured to cheer her with the news that Nagendra was coming, which brought a smile to the girl's face; but at the news of Surja Mukhi's death Kunda Nandini wept.

Many fair readers will smile at this, thinking, 'The cat weeps over the death of the fish.' But Kunda was very stupid; that she had cause to rejoice never entered her head: this silly woman actually cried over her rival's death.

Kamal Mani not only cheered Kunda, she herself felt comforted. She had already wept much, and now she began to think, 'What is the use of weeping? If I do, Srish Chandra will be miserable and Satish will cry. Weeping will not bring back Surja Mukhi.' So she gave up weeping, and became her natural self.

Kamal Mani said to Srish Chandra, 'The goddess of this paradise has abandoned it; when my brother comes he will have only a bed of straw to lie upon.' They resolved to put the place in order; so the coolies, the lamp cleaners, and the gardeners were set to work. Under Kamal Mani's vigorous treatment the musk rats, bats, and mice departed squeaking; the pigeons flew from cornice to cornice; the sparrows fled in distress. Where the windows were closed, the sparrows, taking them for open doorways, pecked at them with their beaks till they were ready to drop. The women servants, broom in hand, were victorious everywhere. Before long the place again wore a smiling appearance, and at length Nagendra arrived.

It was evening. As a river courses swiftly when at flood, but at ebb the deep water is calm, so Nagendra's violent grief was now changed into a quiet gravity. His sorrow was not lessened, but he was no longer restless. In a quiet manner he conversed with the household, making inquiries from each one. In the presence of none of them did he mention the name of Surja Mukhi, but all were grieved at the sorrow expressed by his grave countenance. The old servants, saluting him, went aside and wept. One person only did Nagendra wound. With the long-sorrowing Kunda he did not speak.

By the orders of Nagendra the servants prepared his bed in Surja Mukhi's room. At this order Kamal Mani shook her head. At midnight, when all the household had retired, Nagendra went to Surja Mukhi's chamber, not to lie down, but to weep. Surja Mukhi's room was spacious and beautiful; it was the temple of all Nagendra's joys, therefore he had adorned it with care. The room was wide and lofty, the floor inlaid with white and black marble, the walls painted in floral designs, blue, yellow, and red. Above the flowers hovered various birds. On one side stood a costly bedstead, beautifully carved and inlaid with ivory; elsewhere, seats in variously coloured coverings, a large mirror, and other suitable furniture. Some pictures, not English, hung upon the walls. Surja Mukhi and Nagendra together had chosen the subjects, and caused them to be painted by a native artist, who had been taught by an Englishman, and could draw well. Nagendra had framed the pictures handsomely, and hung them on the walls. One picture was taken from the Birth of Kartika: Siva, sunk in meditation, on the summit of the hill; Nandi at the door of the arbour. On the left Hembatra, finger on lip, is hushing the sounds of the garden. All is still, the bees hid among the leaves, the deer reposing. At this moment Madan (Cupid) enters to interrupt the meditation of Siva; with him comes Spring. In advance, Parvati, wreathed with flowers, has come to salute Siva. Uma's joyous face is bent in salutation, one knee resting on the earth. This is the position depicted in the painting. As she bends her head, one or two flowers escape from the wreaths fastened in her hair. In the distance Cupid, half hidden by the woods, one knee touching earth, his beauteous bow bent, is fitting to it the flower-wreathed arrow.

In another picture, Ram, returning from Lanka with Janaki, both sitting in a jewelled chariot, is coursing through the sky. Ram has one hand on the shoulders of Janaki, with the other is pointing out the beauties of the earth below. Around the chariot many-coloured clouds, blue, red, and white, sail past in purple waves. Below, the broad blue ocean heaves its billows, shining like heaps of diamonds in the sun's rays. In the distance, opal-crowned Lanka, its rows of palaces like golden peaks in the sun's light; the opposite shore beautiful with tamal and palm trees. In the mid distance flocks of swans are flying.

Another picture represents Subhadra with Arjuna in the chariot. Countless Yadav soldiers, their flags streaming out against the gloomy sky, are running after the chariot. Subhadra herself is driving, the horses grinding the clouds with their hoofs. Subhadra, proud of her skill, is looking round towards Arjuna, biting her lower lip with her ivory teeth, her hair streaming in the chariot-created wind; two or three braids moistened with perspiration lie in a curve on her temples.

In another, Sakuntala, with the desire of seeing Dushmanta, is pretending to take a thorn from her foot. Anasuya and Priamboda are smiling. Sakuntala, between anger and shame will not raise her face. She cannot look at Dushmanta, nor yet can she leave the spot.

In another, Prince Abhimaya, armed for battle, and, like the young lion, eager for glory, is taking leave of Uttora that he may go to the field. Uttora, saying that she will not let him go, is standing against the closed door weeping, with her hands over her eyes.

It was past twelve when Nagendra entered the room. The night was fearful. Late in the evening some rain had fallen; now the wind had risen and was blowing fiercely, the rain continuing at intervals. Wherever the shutters were not fastened they flapped to and fro with the noise of thunderclaps, the sashes rattling continuously. When Nagendra closed the door the noise was less noticeable. There was another door near the bedstead, but as the wind did not blow in that direction he left it open. Nagendra sat on the sofa, weeping bitterly. How often had he sat there with Surja Mukhi; what pleasant talks they had had! Again and again Nagendra embraced that senseless seat; then raising his face he looked at the pictures so dear to Surja Mukhi. In the fitful light of the lamp the figures in the pictures seemed to be alive; in each picture Nagendra saw Surja Mukhi. He remembered that one day she expressed a wish to be decked with flowers like Uma in the picture. He had gone forth, brought in flowers from the garden, and with them decked her person. What beauty decked with jewels had ever felt the pleasure felt by Surja Mukhi at that moment? Another day she had desired to drive Nagendra's carriage in imitation of Subhadra; whereupon he had brought a small carriage drawn by ponies to the inner garden. They both got in, Surja Mukhi taking the reins; like Subhadra, she turned her face towards Nagendra, biting her lower lip and laughing. The ponies, taking advantage of her inattention, went through an open gate into the road. Then Surja Mukhi, afraid of being seen by the people, drew her sari over her face, and Nagendra, seeing her distress, took the reins and brought the carriage back into the garden. They went into the chamber laughing over the adventure, and Surja Mukhi shook her fist at Subhadra in the picture, saying, 'You are the cause of this misfortune.'

How bitterly Nagendra wept over this remembrance! Unable longer to endure his suffering he walked about; but look where he would there were signs of Surja Mukhi. On the wall where the artist had drawn twining plants she had sketched a copy of one of them; the sketch remained there still. One day during the Dol festival she had thrown a ball of red powder at her husband; she had missed her aim and struck the wall, where still the stain was visible. When the room was finished, Surja Mukhi had written in one spot—

'In the year 1910 of Vikramaditya
    This room was prepared
For my Guardian Deity, my husband,
    By his servant

SURJA MUKHI.'

Nagendra read this inscription repeatedly. He could not satisfy his desire to read it. Though the tears filled his eyes so that he could not see, he would not desist. As he read he perceived the light becoming dim, and found the lamp ready to expire. With a sigh he laid down; but scarcely had he done so ere the wind began to rage furiously. The lamp, void of oil, was on the point of extinction, only a faint spark like that of a firefly remained. In that dim light a remarkable circumstance occurred. Astonished by the noise of the shutters, Nagendra looked towards the door near the bed. In that open doorway, shown by the dim light, a shadowy form appeared. The shape was that of a woman; but what he saw further made his hair stand on end, he trembled from head to foot. The woman's face had the features of Surja Mukhi! Nagendra started to his feet and hastened to the figure. But the light went out, the form became invisible; with a loud cry Nagendra fell senseless to the ground.

When Nagendra recovered consciousness thick darkness filled the room. By degrees he collected his senses. As he remembered what had caused the swoon, surprise was added to surprise. He had fallen senseless on the floor, then whence came the pillow on which his head was resting? Was it a pillow? or was it the lap of someone—of Kunda Nandini?

To solve his doubt he said, 'Who are you?' But the supporter of his head made no reply. Only a hot drop or two fell on his forehead, by which he understood that the person was weeping. He tried to identify the person by touch. Suddenly he became quite bewildered; he remained motionless for some moments, then with labouring breath raised his head and sat up. The rain had ceased, the clouds had disappeared, light began to peep into the room. Nagendra rose and seated himself. He perceived that the woman had also risen, and was slowly making towards the door. Then Nagendra guessed that it was not Kunda Nandini. There was not light enough to recognize any one, but something might be guessed from form and gait. Nagendra studied these for a moment, then falling at the feet of the standing figure, in troubled tones he said—

'Whether thou art a god or a human being, I am at thy feet; speak to me, or I shall die!'

What the woman said he could not understand, but no sooner had the sound of her voice entered his ear than he sprang to his feet and tried to grasp the form. But mind and body again became benumbed, and, like the creeper from the tree, he sank at the feet of the enchantress; he could not speak. Again the woman, sitting down, took his head upon her lap. When Nagendra once more recovered from stupor it was day. The birds were singing in the adjacent garden. The rays of the newly risen sun were shining into the room. Without raising his eyes Nagendra said—

'Kunda, when did you come? This whole night I have been dreaming of Surja Mukhi. In my dream I saw myself with my head on Surja Mukhi's lap. If you could be Surja Mukhi, how joyful it would be!'

The woman answered, 'If it would delight you so much to see that unhappy being, then I am she.'

Nagendra started up, wiped his eyes, sat holding his temples, again rubbed his eyes and gazed; then bowing his head, he said in a low voice—

'Am I demented, or is Surja Mukhi living? Is this the end of my destiny, that I should go mad?'

Then the woman, clasping his feet, wept over them, saying, 'Arise, arise, my all! I have suffered so much. Today all my sorrow is ended. I am not dead. Again I have come to serve you.'

Could delusion last longer? Nagendra embraced Surja Mukhi, and laid his head upon her breast. Together they wept; but how joyous was that weeping!

36

EXPLANATION

In due time Surja Mukhi satisfied Nagendra's inquiries, saying—

'I did not die. What the Kabiraj said of my dying was not true. He did not know. When I had become strong through his treatment, I was extremely anxious to come to Govindpur to see you. I teased the Brahmachari till he consented to take me. On arriving here, we learned you were not in the place. The Brahmachari took me to a spot six miles from here, placed me in the house of a Brahmin to attend on his daughter, and then went in search of you: first to Calcutta, where he had an interview with Srish Chandra, from whom he heard that you were gone to Madhupur. At that place he learned that on the day we left Haro Mani's house it was burned, and Haro Mani in it. In the morning people could not recognize the body. They reasoned that as of the two people in the house one was sick and one was well, that the former could not have escaped from want of strength; therefore that Haro Mani must have escaped and the dead person must be myself. What was at first a supposition became established by report. Ram Krishna heard the report, and repeated it to you. The Brahmachari heard all this, and also that you had been there, had heard of my death, and had come hither. He came after you, arriving last night at Protappur. I also heard that in a day or two you were expected home. In that belief I came here the day before yesterday. It does not trouble me now to walk a few miles. As you had not come I went back, saw the Brahmachari, and returned yesterday, arriving at one this morning. The window being open, I entered the house and hid under the stairs without being seen. When all slept I ascended; I thought you would certainly sleep in this room. I peeped in, and saw you sitting with your head in your hands. I longed to throw myself at your feet, but I feared you would not forgive my sin against you, so I refrained. From within the window I looked, thinking, "Now I will let him see me." I came in, but you fell senseless, and since then I have sat with your head on my lap. I knew not that such joy was in my destiny. But, fie! you love me not; when you put your hand upon me you did not recognize me! I should have known you by your breath.'

37

THE SIMPLETON AND THE SERPENT

While in the sleeping—chamber, bathed in a sea of joy, Nagendra and Surja Mukhi held loving converse, in another apartment of that same house a fatal dialogue was being held. Before relating it, it is necessary to record what occurred on the previous night. As we know, Nagendra had held no converse with Kunda Nandini on his return. In her own room, with her head on the pillow, Kunda had wept the whole night, not the easy tears of girlhood, but from a mortal wound. Whosoever in childhood has in all sincerity delivered the priceless treasure of her heart to any one, and has in exchange received only neglect, can imagine the piercing pain of that weeping. 'Why have I preserved my life,' she asked herself, 'with the desire to see my husband? Now what happiness remains to be hoped for?' With the dawn sleep came, and in that sleep, for the second time, a frightful vision. The bright figure assuming the form of her mother, which she had seen four years before by her dead father's bedside, now appeared above Kunda's head; but this time it was not surrounded by a shining halo, it descended upon a dense cloud ready to fall in rain. From the midst of the thick cloud another face smiled, while every now and then flashes of lightning broke forth. Kunda perceived with alarm that the incessantly smiling face resembled that of Hira, while her mother's compassionate countenance was very grave. The mother said: 'Kunda, when I came before you did not listen, you did not come with me; now you see what trouble has befallen you.' Kunda wept. The mother continued: 'I told you I would come once more, and here I am. If now you are satisfied with the joy that the world can give, come with me.'

'Take me with you, mother; I do not desire to stay here longer.'

The mother, much pleased, repeated, 'Come, then!' and vanished from sight.

Kunda woke, and, remembering her vision, desired of the gods that this time her dream might be fulfilled.

At dawn, when Hira entered the room to wait upon Kunda, she perceived that the girl was crying. Since the arrival of Kamal Mani, Hira had resumed a respectful demeanour towards Kunda, because she heard that Nagendra was returning. As though in atonement for her past behaviour, Hira became even more obedient and affectionate than formerly. Any one else would have easily penetrated this craftiness, but Kunda was unusually simple, and easily appeased. She felt no suspicion of this new affection; she imagined Hira to be sour-tempered, but not unfaithful. The woman said—

'Why do you weep, Ma Thakurani?'

Kunda did not speak, but only looked at Hira, who saw that her eyes were swollen and the pillow soaked.

'What is this? you have been crying all night. Has the Babu said anything to you?'

'Nothing,' said Kunda, sobbing with greater violence than before. Hira's heart swam with joy at the sight of Kunda's distress. With a melancholy face she asked—

'Has the Babu had any talk with you since he came home? I am only a servant, you need not mind telling me.'

'I have had no talk with him.'

'How is that, Ma? After so many days' absence has he nothing to say to you?'

'He has not been near me,' and with these words fresh tears burst forth.

Hira was delighted. She said, smiling, 'Ma, why do you weep in this way? Many people are over head and ears in trouble, yet you cry incessantly over one sorrow. If you had as much to bear as I have, you would have destroyed yourself before this time.'

Suicide! this disastrous word struck heavily on the ear of Kunda; shuddering, she sat down. During the night she had frequently contemplated this step, and these words from Hira's mouth seemed to confirm her purpose.

Hira continued: 'Now hear what my troubles are. I also loved a man more than my own life. He was not my husband, but why should

I hide my sin from my mistress? it is better to confess it plainly.'

These shameless words did not enter Kunda's ear; in it the word 'suicide' was repeating itself, as though a demon kept whispering, 'Would it not be better for you to destroy yourself than to endure this misery?'

Hira continued: 'He was not my husband, but I loved him better than the best husband. I knew he did not love me; he loved another sinner, a hundred times less attractive than I.' At this point, Hira cast a sharp, angry glance from under her eyelids at Kunda, then went on: 'Knowing this, I did not run after him, but one day we were both wicked.'

Beginning thus, Hira briefly related the terrible history. She mentioned no name, neither that of Debendra nor that of Kunda. She said nothing from which it could be inferred whom she had loved, or who was beloved by him. At length, after speaking of the abuse she had received, she said—

'Now what do you suppose I did?'

'What did you do?'

'I went to a Kabiraj. He has all sorts of poisons by which life can be destroyed.'

In low tones Kunda said, 'After that?'

'I intended to kill myself. I bought some poison, but afterwards I thought, 'Why should I die for another?' so I have kept the poison in a box.'

Hira brought from the corner of the room a box in which she kept the treasures received as rewards from her employers, and also what she got by less fair means. Opening it, she showed the poison to Kunda, who eyed it as a cat does cream. Then Hira, leaving the box open as though from absence of mind, began to console Kunda. At this moment, suddenly, in the early dawn, sounds of happiness and rejoicing were heard in the household. Hira darted forth in astonishment. The ill-fated Kunda Nandini seized the opportunity to steal the poison from the box.

38

THE CATASTROPHE

Hira could not at first understand the cause of the joyous sounds she heard. She saw in one of the large rooms all the women of the house, the boys and the girls surrounding someone and making a great noise. Of the person surrounded, Hira could see nothing but the hair, which Kousalya and the other attendants were dressing with scented oil and arranging becomingly. Of the bystanders encircling them some were laughing, some weeping, some talking, some uttering blessings. The girls and boys were dancing, singing, and clapping their hands. Kamal Mani was going round directing that shells should be blown and other joyous demonstrations, laughing, crying, and even dancing.

Hira was astonished. Stepping into the throng, she stretched her neck and peeped about. What were her feelings on beholding Surja Mukhi seated on the floor, a loving smile upon her lips; submitting to be decked with all her ornaments, so long laid aside, speaking kindly to all, a little shamefaced.

Hira could not all at once believe that Surja Mukhi who had died was now amongst them smiling so pleasantly. Stammeringly she asked one of the throng of women, 'Who is that?'

Kousalya heard the question, and answered, 'Don't you know? The goddess of our house, and your executioner.'

Kousalya had lived all this time in fear of Hira. Now in her day of triumph she vented her spleen.

The dressing being completed and all kindly greetings exchanged, Surja Mukhi said in a low voice to Kamal Mani, 'Let us go and see Kunda. She is not guilty of any fault towards me. I am not angry with her; she is now my younger sister.'

Only they two went. They were long away. At last Kamal Mani came out of Kunda's room with a countenance full of fear and distress, and in great haste sent for Nagendra.

On his arrival the ladies told him he was wanted in Kunda's room. At the door he met Surja Mukhi weeping.

'What has happened?' he asked.

'Destruction! I have long known I was destined not to have a single day of happiness, else how is it that in the first moment of joy this calamity comes upon me?'

'What has happened?'

'I brought up Kunda to womanhood, and now that I have come hither with the desire to cherish her as my little sister, my desire has turned to ashes: Kunda has taken poison!'

'What do you say?' 'Do you remain with her. I will go for a doctor.'

Surja Mukhi went on her errand, and Nagendra to Kunda's room alone. He found Kunda's face darkened, her eyes lustreless, her body relaxed.

39

KUNDA'S TONGUE IS LOOSENED

Kunda Nandini was seated on the floor, her head resting against the the bedpost. At sight of Nagendra the tears came into her eyes. As he stood beside her, Kunda, like a severed branch of a twining plant, laid her head at his feet. In a stifled voice he said—

'What is this, Kunda? for what fault are you leaving me?'

Kunda had not been used to answer her husband, but now, at her last hour, her tongue was loosened. She said, 'For what fault did you leave me?'

Silenced, Nagendra sat beside Kunda with bent head.

She went on: 'If on coming home yesterday you had called for me, if you had once come and sat by me in this way, I had not died. I have had you but a short time, even to day my desire to see you is not satisfied. I would not have died.'

At these loving, heart-piercing words, Nagendra let his head fall upon his knees, and remained speechless.

Then Kunda spoke again. Today she was eloquent, for it was her last day with her husband. She said, 'Fie! do not sit thus silent; if I see not your face smiling as I die, I shall not die happy.'

Surja Mukhi also had thus spoken. In death all are equal.

Struck to the heart, Nagendra said in troubled tones, 'Why have you done this? Why did you not send for me?'

Kunda, with many a smile transient as a flash of lightning, said, 'Think not of that; what I said, I said in the hurry of my mind. Before you came I had determined that after I had seen you I would die. I had resolved that if the Didi (Surja Mukhi) returned, I would leave you with her and die. I would no longer be a thorn in her path of happiness. I had determined to die, but on seeing you I was not willing.'

Nagendra made no answer. Today he was without reply to the formerly speechless Kunda Nandini. Kunda remained silent for some time; she was losing the power of speech, death was taking possession. Then Nagendra saw the death-shadowed face full of love. Its gentle light shining in her troubled face, remained stamped on Nagendra's heart to his latest day. After a rest, she said, with great difficulty—

'My thirst for speech has not been satisfied. I knew you to be a god; I never had the courage to speak, my desire was not extinguished. Death is approaching, my mouth is dry, my tongue falters, I have no more time.'

She rested her head upon Nagendra, closed her eyes, and remained speechless. The doctor came but he gave her no medicine. Seeing that there was no hope, he withdrew with a sad countenance. Feeling that the last hour was come, Kunda wished to see Surja Mukhi and Kamal Mani. Both came; Kunda took the dust from their feet, they weeping loudly. Then Kunda hid her face between her husband's feet. She spoke no more, consciousness gradually departed. Her face lying on her husband's feet, the youthful Kunda Nandini's spirit departed, the blooming flower died.

Surja Mukhi, checking her sobs, looked at her dead companion-wife, and said, 'May thy happy fate be mine; may I die thus, my head on my husband's feet.' Then taking her weeping husband's hand, she led him away.

Afterwards, Nagendra, recovering his firmness, took Kunda to the riverside, performed the last rites, and bade farewell to the lovely form.

40

THE END

After Kunda Nandini's death, people asked where she obtained the poison, and all began to suspect that it was Hira's work.

Nagendra directed that Hira should be called, but she was not to be found; since Kunda's death she had disappeared. From that time no one ever saw Hira in that part of the country; her name was no longer heard in Govindpur.

Once only, a year later, she showed herself to Debendra. The poison tree planted by Debendra had by that time borne fruit; he was seized with a malignant disease, and as he did not cease drinking, the disease became incurable. During the first year after Kunda's death, Debendra's summons came. Two or three days before his death, as he lay on his bed without power to rise, there suddenly arose a great noise at the door.

In answer to Debendra's inquiries, the servant said, 'A mad woman wants to see you, sir; she will not be forbidden.'

He gave orders that she should be admitted. The woman appeared. Debendra saw that she was reduced by want, but observed no sign of madness; he thought her a wretched beggar woman. She was young, and retained the signs of former beauty, but now she was a sight indeed. Her apparel soiled, ragged, patched, and so scanty that it barely reached her knees, while her back and head remained uncovered; her hair unkempt, dishevelled, covered with dust and matted together; her body never oiled, withered-looking, covered with mud. As she approached, she cast so wild a glance on Debendra that he saw the servants were right—she was truly a madwoman.

After gazing at him some time, she said, 'Do you not know me? I am Hira.'

Recognizing her, Debendra asked in astonishment, 'Who has brought you to this condition?'

Hira, with a glance full of rage, biting her lip and clenching her fist, approached to strike Debendra; but restraining herself she said, 'Ask again who has brought me to this condition: this is your doing. You don't know me now, but once you took your pleasure of me. You don't remember it, but one day you sang this song'—bursting forth into a love song.

In this manner reminding him of many things, she said: 'On the day you drove me out I became mad. I went to take poison. Then a thought of delight came to me; instead of taking it myself, I would cause either you or Kunda Nandini to do so. In that hope I hid my illness for a time; it comes and goes; when it was on me I stayed at home, when well I worked. Finally, having poisoned your Kunda, my trouble was soothed; but after seeing her death my illness increased. Finding that I could not hide it any longer, I left the place. Now I have no food. Who gives food to a madwoman? Since then I have begged. When well I beg; when the disease presses I stay under a tree. Hearing of your approaching death, I have come to delight myself in seeing you. I give you my blessing, that even hell may find no place for you.'

Thus saying, the madwoman uttered a loud laugh. Alarmed, Debendra moved to the other side of the bed; then Hira danced out of the house, singing the old love song.

From that time Debendra's bed of death was full of thorns. He died delirious, uttering words of the love song.

After his death the night watch heard with a beating heart the familiar strain from the madwoman in the garden.

The 'Poison Tree' is finished. We trust it will yield nectar in many a house.

GLOSSARY

Attar.	Commonly called in England Otto of Roses.
Bari.	The Hindu home.
Bhagirati.	A river, branch of the Ganges.
Boiragi.	A religious devotee.
Boisnavi.	A female mendicant; a votary of Vishnu.
Boroari.	A Hindu festival.
Boita khana.	The sitting room of the male members of the household, and their guests.
Bonti.	A fish knife.
Bou.	The wife.
Brahmachari.	A student of the Vedas.
Brahman.	An officiating Hindu priest
Brahmo Somaj.	The church of the Theistic sect or Brahmos.
Dada Babu.	Elder brother.
Dahuk.	A bird of the crane species.
Didi.	Elder sister.
Duftur Khana.	Accountant's office.
Durga.	A Hindu goddess.
Darwan.	A doorkeeper.
Ghat.	Landing steps to a river or tank.
Ghi.	Clarified butter.
Gomashta.	Factor or agent; a rent collector.
Grihini.	The housemistress.
Ganga.	The river Ganges.
Joisto.	The Hindu month corresponding to May–June.
Kabiraj.	A Hindu physician.
Kacheri.	Courthouse, or revenue office.
Kayasta.	The writer caste.
Khansamah.	A Mahommedan butler.
Korta.	The master of the house.
Ma Thakurani.	A title of respect to the mistress.

Mahal.	A division of a house.
Malini.	A flower girl.
Manji.	A boatman.
Naib.	A deputy, representing the Zemindar.
Pandit.	A learned Brahman.
Papiya.	A bird.
Puja.	Hindu worship.
Puja Mahal.	The division of the house devoted to worship.
Pardah.	A screen or curtain.
Ryot.	A tiller of the soil.
Sari.	A woman's garment.
Shastras.	Hindu sacred books.
Shradda.	An obsequial ceremony, in which food and water are offered to deceased ancestors.
Siva.	A Hindu god.
Sraban.	The Hindu months corresponding to July–August.
Talao.	A tank or enclosed pond
Thakur.	The Deity; sometimes applied as a title of honour to the master of the house.
Thakur Ban.	The chamber occupied by the family deity.
Tulsi.	A plant held sacred by the Hindus.
Zemindar.	A landholder.
Zillah.	A district or local division.

RAJMOHAN'S WIFE
A NOVEL

1

THE DRAWERS OF WATER

There is a small village on the river Madhumati. On account of its being the residence of wealthy zemindars it is regarded as a village of importance. One Chaitra afternoon the summer heat was gradually abating with the weakening of the once keen rays of the sun; a gentle breeze was blowing; it began to dry the perspiring brow of the peasant in the field and play with the moist locks of village women just risen from their siesta.

It was after such a siesta that a woman of about thirty was engaged in her toilet in a humble thatched cottage. She took very little time to finish the process usually so elaborate with womankind; a dish of water, a tin-framed looking glass three inches wide, and a comb matching it sufficed for the task. Then, a little vermilion adorned her forehead. Last of all some betel leaves dyed her lips. Thus armed, a formidable champion of the world-conquering sex set out with a pitcher in her arm and pushing open the wattled gate of a neighbouring house entered within it.

There were four huts in the house which she entered. They had mud floors and bamboo walls. There was no sign of poverty anywhere, everything was neat and tidy. The four huts stood on the four sides of a quadrangle. Of these three had entrances opening on the yard, the fourth opened outwards. This last was die reception room, while the others, screened on all sides, constituted the zenana. Some brinjals and salads were growing on the carefully tilled plot of land in front of die raised terrace before the outer room. The whole was enclosed by a reed fence with a bamboo gate. So the woman could easily make her way into the house.

It is superfluous to add that she went straight towards the zenana. I know not where the other inmates of the house had gone after their siesta, but at that time diere were only two persons there—one, a young woman of eighteen bent over her embroidery and a child of four immersed in play. His elder brother had wilfully left his inkpot behind when going to school. The child's eyes had fallen on it, and he was joyfully smearing his face with die ink. He seemed to be afraid of his brother coming back and snatching the inkpot away, and so he was emptying the pot. The newcomer sat down on the floor by the side of her who was working and asked, 'What are you doing?'

The other laughed and said, 'Oh, it's Didi. What kindness! Whose face was it that I first saw on getting up this morning?'

The guest laughed back and retorted, 'Who else but the person you see every morning?'

At this, the face of the younger woman clouded over for a moment, while the smile half-lingered on the lips of the other. Let us describe them both at this place.

It has already been mentioned that the visitor was thirty years of age. She was neither dark nor exactly olive; her face was not quite pretty yet there was no feature which displeased the eye; she had a sort of restless charm, and her smiling eyes heightened the effect of it. The ornaments on her person were not large in number, but constituted a fair load for a porter. The conch-shell worker who had made her shell bracelet was no doubt a descendant of Visvakarma himself. The woman adorned with these ornaments had only a coarse *sari* on her plump figure. There was evidently no love lost between the *sari* and the washerman, for it had not visited the laundry for a long time.

The dainty limbs of the woman of eighteen were not burdened with such abundance of ornaments, nor did her speech betray any trace of the East Bengal accent, which clearly showed that this perfect flower of beauty was no daughter of the banks of the Madhumati, but was born and brought up on the Bhagirathi in some place near the capital. Some sorrow or deep anxiety had dimmed the lustre of her fair complexion. Yet her bloom was as full of charm as that of the land lotus half-scorched and half-radiant under the noonday sun. Her long locks were tied up in a careless knot on her shoulder; but some loose tresses had thrown away that bondage and were straying over her forehead and cheeks. Her faultlessly drawn arched eyebrows were quivering with bashfulness under a full and wide forehead. The eyes were often only half-seen under their drooping lids. But when they were raised for a glance, lightning seemed to play in a summer cloud. Yet even those keen glances charged with the fire of youth betrayed anxiety. The small lips indicated the sorrow nursed in her heart. The beauty of her figure and limbs had been greatly spoilt by her physical or mental suffering. Yet no sculptor had ever created anything nearly as perfect as the form half revealed by the neat *sari* she wore. The well-shaped limbs were almost entirely bare of ornaments. There were only *churis* on the wrists and a small amulet on her arm. These too were elegant in shape.

The younger woman put away her needlework and began to talk with the visitor. The latter displayed great eloquence in describing her domestic tribulations, most of which unfortunately were imaginary. She put the fringe of her mud-stained *sari* again and again to her eyes, which were not in a condition to call for it. But in certain eventualities even the *Salagram* (god) dies. As often as the end of the *sari* touched her eyes they shed copious tears. After many such showers she was preparing for a full-dress outburst when her eyes suddenly fell on the ink-smeared face of the child who had emptied the inkpot and was standing with a darkened countenance. The bizarre sight converted the tears of the narrator of household misery into laughter; humour swept away pathos.

When the ceremony of tears ended at last, the sun was really sinking down to rest. At this the speaker invited the young woman to come with her to fetch water. She had in fact come there with a view to making that invitation. The younger woman refused, and when her companion began to press her, said, 'There are crocodiles in the Madhumati. They will drag me away.'

Her companion laughed out loudly at this, which showed her that her objection was not admitted. Yet she added, 'You should go now, Kanak. It's growing late.'

Kanak pointed to the sun which was still above the trees and said, 'It's still noon.'

At this the younger woman became grave and said, 'You know, Kanak Didi, I never fetch water.'

'That is why I am asking you to,' replied Kanak. 'Why should you remain in a cage all the day. Do not all other housewives draw water?'

The younger woman said disdainfully, 'That's a work for servant girls.'

'Why, who fetches water for you? Where are your servants?'

'Well, Thakurjhi fetches our water.'

'If the daughter can do servants' work, cannot the daughter-in-law?'

The young woman said firmly, 'I cannot argue about it, Kanak. You know my husband has forbidden me to fetch water, and you know him well.'

Kanakmayee did not reply off-hand. She quickly glanced round to see if anyone was coming. When she saw there was no one about, she stood with her eyes fixed on the face of her companion as if wanting to say something. But she repressed the impulse from fear and remained musing with downcast eyes. The younger girl asked, 'What are you thinking about?'

'If only you had eyes,' replied Kanak.

The younger woman would not, however, listen to her. She made a sign to Kanak to stop and said, 'Hush, hush, I understand your meaning.'

'If you have done so, what are you going to do now?' asked Kanak.

The younger girl remained silent for a while. Her quivering lips and reddening brow betrayed the preoccupation of her mind. A slight tremor in her limbs also showed how agitated she was. After some time she said, 'Let us go, but is it wrong?'

Kanak laughed and replied, 'Wrong! I am not a fat-bellied Bhattacharya. I have nothing to do with the Shastras. But I would have gone even if I had fifty men.'

'Oh! what bravery!' replied the other laughing as she went out to get her pitcher. 'Fifty! Do you really wish for as many?'

Kanak smiled sadly and said, 'It's sin even to say so. But if all the fifty were of the same sort as the one given me by Fate, it would hardly matter. If I meet none, I am a chaste and devoted wife even if married to a crore of men.'

'The Kulin girl's lot!' exclaimed the other and quickly got a tiny pitcher from the kitchen. The pitcher perfectly matched the carrier of water. Then they both marched off towards the river. Kanak laughed and said, 'Come now, my proud girl, let's go and show beauty's splendour to the gaping idiots.'

'Hang you, monkey!' cried the other and hid her blushing face in her veil.

2

THE TWO COUSINS

The rays of the setting sun had vanished from the tops of the coconut palms. But night had not yet descended on the earth. It was at this time that Kanak and her companion were returning home, each with a pitcher in her arm. By the roadside was a small garden, of a type rare in East Bengal. Numerous roses and *mallika* buds were caressing the eyes of the passersby from within the compound surrounded by a handsome iron fence. Walks covered with red brickdust had been laid down beside the old style square and oval beds. There was a tank in the middle of the gardens, whose banks were covered with soft turf. On one side was a row of brick-paved steps. Facing the steps was the reception room, in the front verandah of which two men were engaged in talk.

The older of the two would be above thirty. He was a tall and stout man. It was because he was too stout that he could not be said to possess a good figure. His complexion was dull and dark. There was no feature on his face which could give him the least claim to handsomeness. On the contrary, he had something positively unattractive about him. In fact, his was not a common face; at the same time it was difficult to define its peculiarity off-hand. He had a *dhoti* of Dacca manufacture on. A long and twisted Dacca *chudder* was tied round his head in the shape of turban which hid even the few wisps of hair that still remained there. His dark and corpulent body could be fully seen through the shirt of Dacca muslin he was wearing, and with it his gold amulet which peeped out off and on. But the thick gold chain which adorned his neck had actually intruded outside his shirt. The shirt had gold studs fastened with a gold chain; all the fingers had rings; and there was a huge bludgeon of peach in his hand. The two small feet were enclosed in English shoes.

This man's companion was a remarkably handsome young man of

about twenty-two. His clear placid complexion had turned a little dull either through want of exercise or too much comfort. His clothes were good but not very costly; a *dhoti*, a fine *chudder*, a cambric shirt and English shoes. There was a single ring on one finger, and no amulet or necklace. The elder man addressed the other, 'Well Madhav, you have turned to Calcutta again. Why this infatuation?'

'Infatuation?' replied Madhav, 'if my liking for Calcutta be an infatuation, why shouldn't yours for Radhaganj be called by the same name?'

Mathur asked, 'Why?'

Madhav: 'Why not? You have spent your life in the shade of the mango gardens of Radhaganj. You love Radhaganj. I have spent my life in the stench of Calcutta. I love Calcutta.'

Mathur: 'Stench only? The filth of the drains with rotten rats and cats thrown in. Surely a feast for the gods!'

Madhav smiled and said, 'It is not for these that I go to Calcutta. I have business, too.'

Mathur: 'Business indeed! New horses, new carriages, visiting all the sharks of the town, throwing away money, burning the oil, drinks for anglicized friends, and pleasures. What are you staring at that way? Have you never seen Kanak? Or has the girl with her just dropped from the sky? Ah, Yes! Who is it with her?'

Madhav flushed, but immediately changed the subject and said, 'What a girl Kanak is! She can laugh with so much sorrow eating into her heart.'

Mathur: 'Yes. But who is it she's got with her!'

Madhav: 'How can I say? I cannot see through clothes. You see she is veiled.'

It was in fact Kanak and her companion who were returning with their pitchers. Everybody knew Kanak. But such indescribable beauty radiated from every movement of the other woman that it charmed the eyes first of Madhav and then of Mathur. Their looks remained fixed on her and they were as fascinated by the sight as a deer is by the sound of the flute.

When the words last recorded came out of the mouth of Madhav, a sudden gust of wind passed over the heads of the women. The younger woman was then adjusting the pitcher in arms still unused to carrying water, and she had brought down her hand from the veil. The wind blew it away and revealed the face. Madhav raised his brows in surprise. Mathur said, 'There, you know her.'

'Yes.'

'You know her and I do not ? I have spent my life here and you are only a newcomer. Well, if you know her, who is she?'

'My sister-in-law.'

'Your sister-in-law? Rajmohan's wife!'

'Yes.'

'Rajmohan's wife, and I have not seen her!'

'How can you? She never leaves her house.'

'Why then has she today?'

'I don't know.'

'What sort of a woman is she?'

'You have seen her.—Very handsome.'

'Oh a thought-reader indeed! I am not asking that. Is she a good woman?'

'What do you mean by a 'good woman'?'

Mathur. 'Oh the college has done for you! It's impossible to talk with people who have once gone there and recited the jargon of the red-faced sahibs. What I mean is—has she—'

The stern frown of Madhav cut short the coarse speech forming on Mathur's lips.

Madhav said haughtily, 'You need not be so outspoken. You have no business to prattle about a respectable woman passing along the road.'

Mathur replied, 'Did I not say that a smattering of English converts our brethren into fiery sahibs! Well, if one is not to discuss one's sister-in-law, whom is one to discuss—his grandmother? Anyway, let it pass. Relax your scowling face, or the crows would begin to peck at it. What luck! That clown Rajmohan to have a wife like this!'

'Marriage is called a lottery,' said Madhav.

And after a few more words the two parted company.

3

THE TRUANT'S RETURN HOME

Kanakmayee and her companion silently pursued their way home. The latter was feeling extremely shy before men, and at her silence Kanak also had to remain silent. Kanak, however, felt the missed opportunity of wagging her tongue very keenly. The pathway was more lonely near their homes, and the younger woman began, 'How the wretched wind hustled me!'

'Why?' replied Kanak laughingly, 'has your brother-in-law never seen you before?'

'I am not thinking of him. But there was another man with him.'

'He is Mathur Babu. Have you never seen him?'

'No, indeed! Is he Mathur Babu, the cousin of my sister's husband?'

'Yes, who else?'

'What a shame! Please don't talk about it to anybody.'

'Oh no! I am going to tell people that you dropped your veil and showed your face when coming back from the river,' said Kanak and began to simper. The younger woman said angrily, 'Go to Jericho! How she goes on! I would never have come with you if I had known—'

Kanak laughed again.

'Leave your jokes alone—O horror! Durga save me!' cried out the young woman as she cast her eyes towards her house and began to tremble. They were at that time quite close to it. Kanak saw Rajmohan standing at the door with glaring eyes, the very image of Death, and whispered to her companion, 'There is trouble for you! Let me go in with you. I might be of some help.'

Rajmohan's wife replied in the same low tone, 'Oh no! I am quite used to it. It would probably be worse if you are there. You had better go home.'

At this Kanak went her way. Rajmohan did not speak to his wife when she entered the house. She went to the kitchen to put her pitcher down. He followed her silently there. When she had set it down, he said to her, 'Wait a moment,' and poured out all the water on the dust-heap. Rajmohan had an old aunt who used to do his cooking. She scolded Rajmohan for thus wasting the water, 'Why are you throwing the water away? You don't keep a score of servants to draw water.'

'Shut up, you old hag,' cried out Rajmohan and flung away the empty pitcher. Then he turned round to his wife and said in a softer but scathing tone, 'Well, queen, where have you been?' The woman firmly whispered back, 'I had gone to fetch water.' She was standing like a statue exactly on the spot where her husband had asked her to stop.

'To fetch water!' taunted Rajmohan, 'but with whose permission did you go out?'

'With nobody's permission.'

Rajmohan could restrain himself no longer. 'With nobody's permission!' he shouted, 'have I not forbidden you a thousand times!'

The woman replied in the same even tone, 'You have.'

'Then, wretched girl, why did you go?'

The woman proudly replied, 'I am your wife.' Her face reddened and her voice began to be choked. 'I had gone because I thought there was nothing wrong in it.'

At this display of boldness, Rajmohan absolutely blazed up. 'Have I not forbidden you a thousand times?' he shouted, and jumping on his wife who was standing stock-still, gripped her by the wrist, raising his other hand to strike her.

The helpless woman seemed to understand nothing. She did not move away one step from her assailant, but only looked at him with such pathetic eyes that his hand remained motionless as if spellbound. After a moment's silence Rajmohan dropped his wife's hand, but immediately shouted out, 'I'll kick you to death.'

Even then the chidden woman did not reply. Only tears were streaming down her face. At the sight of her silent suffering the cruel man softened a little. He no longer tried to beat her, but continued his abuse. It is unnecessary to try the patience of my readers by reproducing all of his Billingsgate. The patient woman bore it silently. When, at last, Rajmohan's anger ebbed away, his aunt gathered some courage. She took her nephew's wife by the hand and led her into a room, all the while scolding her nephew. Even that was done circumspectly. But when she saw at last that Rajmohan had almost cooled down she burst out in her turn and paid the nephew back in his own coin. Rajmohan was then nursing his own grievances. He could not quite appreciate the language of his aunt. At any rate there was no novelty in it, for he had heard it many times before. So they both parted. The aunt began to console the wife, and Rajmohan went out pondering whom to fall upon and smash up.

4

THE RISE AND PROGRESS OF A ZEMINDAR FAMILY

It is a notorious fact that many eminent zemindar families in Bengal owe their rise to some ignoble origin.

Bangshibadan Ghose lived as a menial servant with an old zemindar of East Bengal whose name and family are now extinct. The unfruitfulness of his first marriage induced the zemindar, late in life, to take another wife, but it had been preordained that he should live and die childless. He had, however, a blessing which next to a progeny he deemed the greatest good that could befall him in his old age—a young and beautiful wife. It is true indeed that discordance and broils between his two helpmates often interrupted his domestic felicity, for the elder lady always sturdily maintained that seniority constituted the indisputable rule by which favours should be bestowed, which indisputable rule, however, the old gentleman always presumed to dispute. Matters were getting to a hopeless state when interfered an umpire whose award brooked no question, and justly acknowledging the claims of her own indefeasible right of seniority removed the elder lady to another world. The old man and his youthful mate were now left in peace, but the former justly took warning by the occurrence and perceived that he himself might be called upon to follow at no distant day. Now hopeless of leaving a family, he reflected with bitterness that his ample estates must be left to the enjoyment of those who had been to him almost strangers, and that though they might remain in the possession of his wife during her lifetime, she could not, with her hands fettered by the law, be anything more than a pensioner on her own estate. Desirous of leaving it in a condition which should leave the young woman its complete mistress, and led into the same course by the advice and influence of his wife, whose perception of her own future prospects was wonderfully clear, he began to free his possessions of landed incumbrances and to convert his zemindaris into ready money and movables as often as he could advantageously do it, and so successful was his uxorious zeal that when he died his relict became the mistress of a splendid fortune of which landed property formed a very inconsiderable portion. Now Karunamayee was a decidedly sensible woman, and she judged it right that, mistress of her fortune and her person, she should enjoy both. Ram, the godhead, she argued, had, in the depth of his love and gratitude for his adored wife, consoled himself in the days of his bereavement by a metallic representative of Sita. Why then should not her immense love for her departed husband find expression under the same representative system? She also thought that it would be a decided improvement in the plan, if she made a human being instead of a metallic image represent the loved and lost one for whom she mourned, inasmuch as a human being is a nobler thing, and would bear a closer resemblance than metal, and also as such resemblance would by no means be confined to the external form alone. Thus fortified by reason and veneration for the departed as well as by the example of the gods, she lost no time in making her choice. Bangshibadan Ghose the menial servant was the happy mortal on whom it fell. This crafty person perceived his advantage too clearly to neglect it, and lord of his mistress's bosom, he saw no reason why he should not be the same of her fortune. It was an easy achievement and his progress from the rank of Khansama to that of Sadar Naib was rapid. A fever originally slight, but which from unintelligible or rather very intelligible causes, became fearfully violent, forced the anxious widow to part with her domestic and with the world before age had chilled her fires. A few days after, the distant and expectant relatives of her husband came to take possession of her estates, but found to their great mortification that they consisted only of a few wretched villages. Of movables, they were told, there were only a few and these she had given away to her servants.

Bangshibadan carried with him a splendid fortune to Radhaganj, the seat of his humble paternal abode. He very prudently made no display of his immense wealth, except so much as was necessary to a life of comfort. On his demise he left a splendid patrimony to each of his three sons. These, who deemed long possession had conferred security, were no longer restrained by the same prudential considerations as their father, purchased zemindaris, built fine houses, and assumed the state and style that belonged to their wealth. The eldest Ramkanta by dint of prudent and able management improved his share, and after having lived to a green old age bequeathed it to the equally able or abler hands of his only son, Mathur, with whom we have had the pleasure of making the reader acquainted. Ramkanta had viewed with eyes of jealousy the encroachments that were being made in the ancient manners and usages by the influence of western civilization and had steadily forborne to send his son to an English school, which he condemned as a thing not only useless but as positively mischievous. Mathur was early associated with his father in the management of the zemindari and proved an exceedingly apt scholar in the science of chicane, fraud and torture.

The fate of Ramkanai, the second son of Bangshibadan, was different. By nature indolent and extravagant, he soon managed to throw his affairs into disorder. His houses and gardens were the most magnificent, his estates the most unprofitable and the worst managed. Some wily hangers-on, too, played on his credulity and painted to him in alluring colours the chances which a certain mercantile scheme they propounded presented of retrieving his affairs. Ramkanai followed their advice and, placing himself under their guidance, took up his residence in Calcutta. It is needless to add that his advisers continued to fleece him of every farthing he had ventured in the speculation and eventually to bring his mismanaged and neglected estates to the hammer.

One good result however had followed Ramkanai's residence in the metropolis. Influenced by the example of the metropolitans, he had bestowed on his son Madhav as good an education as he could receive in Calcutta. He had also accomplished that great object of a Hindu father's love—the marriage of his son with a girl of remarkable beauty. A poor Kayastha dwelt in a small village in the vicinity of Calcutta, who boasted that the only good fortune that the heavens had conferred on him was perfect in its kind, and his two daughters had not their equal in beauty or in dutiful and amiable conduct.

But the same circumstances which often so cruelly match the fairest and tenderest of fair and tender Bengalis, consigned the eldest of his daughters, the noble and beautiful Matangini, to the arms of the brutal Rajmohan; yet, when the marriage took place, Matangini's father thought he had not chosen ill. Rajmohan had indeed then reached manhood and was therefore unsuited in age—but this was not minded much. He possessed no handsome person—but a handsome person was to be looked for in a boy bridegroom, not in a man. He lived in an adjoining village, and the prospect that no great distance would separate father and daughter served greatly to favour the match in the eyes of the former. His robust frame and vast strength were the envy and admiration of all who knew him. His spirit was active and energetic, ready in expedients, and as a natural consequence, though his father had left him no fortune and given him no education, he was never much in want. This circumstance which promised to rescue Matangini from the pinchings of poverty seemed to her father to be another and the greatest recommendation, and the marriage accordingly took place. The younger and more fortunate Hemangini became the bride of young Madhav.

The father of Madhav died a little before the latter completed his studies at college. He would have been left penniless but for a circumstance which nobody had foreseen.

Ramgopal the third son of Bangshibadan was neither so fortunate as the first, nor so unfortunate as the second. He died early and childless bequeathing nearly the whole of his property to his nephew Madhav on condition the latter maintained his relict as long as she lived in Madhav's household.

Madhav continued his studies till he finished them, his agents managing his estate for him during his absence and minority. After the expiration of the year, he prepared to leave the city for Radhaganj with his young and beautiful wife. Before going there he took her to her father's house in order to enable her to bid her parents farewell. Madhav's wife was beloved by her sister, and design or accident brought also Rajmohan and his wife to the house.

Madhav intended to make a short stay with his father-in-law; Hemangini incessantly wept at the prospect of parting with her parents and her sister, for how long she knew not. It was a far, far country whither she was going, and would she ever come back to the scene of her earliest affection? Would her parents ever visit her there? Her father said he would, but then her mother? her sister? Her mother and sister answered not, but wept with her in silence, and gave her their blessings.

Matangini took hold of her sister's hand and drew her aside. When they were alone, she said, 'Hem, I have something to ask of you.' Hemangini did not reply but gazed upon her sister with an enquiring look in her large black eyes.

'Hem,' Matangini resumed, 'we part tomorrow.'

Hemangini burst into tears. 'Weep not, sister,' said Matangini, calming her own agitated features with effort, 'weep not; the gods will bless you, and you have a husband, Hem, who will make you happy.' As she said this, warm tears ran down her cheeks and fell upon the lily hands that she held in her own.

'What were you going to ask of me?' inquired Hemangini, wiping her eyes.

'I am poor, Hem, very poor, but were it for me only I would never speak of it to you. But my husband, whatever he is, sister, Heaven made him so—he is my husband and I care for him. He has now nothing to do and is reduced to great straits. He has besought me to ask you to speak to my brother-in-law.'

'Yes, I will; but what shall I ask in his behalf?'

'An employment—some means of earning a livelihood.'

'I will,' promised Hem, and then the sisters conversed on other subjects.

Hemangini had in the ardour of her affection for her sister undertaken a task which she knew not how to execute. She was still of that tender age when wives in her country speak always timidly to their husbands, and hardly ever on such subjects. She mustered resolution, nevertheless, and when she saw her husband, related to him the conversation she had had with her sister. Her husband promised to do what he could. Rajmohan had, with the usual bashfulness of boors, chosen the indirect agency of *sari* Government, usually resorted to by poor relatives, instead of a direct and personal application to his brother-in-law. Madhav chose to reply in person, and the next morning drew Rajmohan into a conversation on the subject. He politely enquired what Rajmohan's present pursuits were, and desired to know if he wished to change them. Rajmohan, from foolish pride or shame or perhaps from design, made no avowal of distress, but said he, he had nothing particular to do at present. Madhav then informed him that he had need of the assistance of some able and trustworthy relative to overlook the management of a part of his zemindari, and if Rajmohan had no objection to a change of residence to Radhaganj, he would ask him to do this friendly office.

'That cannot be, sir,' replied Rajmohan; 'with whom can I leave my family?'

'I have thought of that,' replied Madhav, 'I shall provide them with a comfortable home at Radhaganj.'

Rajmohan darted an expression of fierce anger at his brother-in-law.

'At Radhaganj!' he exclaimed, 'never, I shall sooner die if necessary in prison.' Saying this, he walked away in great anger.

Madhav was surprised at this burst of temper but said nothing. Rajmohan however had scarcely a choice to make. For reasons which even his wife did not know, he had himself become anxious for a change of residence, though Radhaganj he had never thought of. He had made poverty the pretext of his application, but poverty seemed to be the least powerful cause which had led to it. And he also seemed to entertain the utmost repugnance to Madhav's proposal. Taking his *chudder* Rajmohan left the house. He ran rather than walked through the fields in the noonday sun, stopping nowhere and speaking to nobody. Hours and hours after he returned, with a gloomy and vexed countenance. He had decided on going to Radhaganj with his family, and informed Madhav of his determination in no very gracious terms. Madhav agreed to wait a few days more in Calcutta to allow him to make his preparations, which done they left the city together and reached Radhaganj in a few days.

Notwithstanding the churlish manner with which Rajmohan had accepted of his assistance, Madhav behaved very handsomely towards him. Aware of the unprincipled and unscrupulous character of his rude brother-in-law, but sincerely compassionating the unmerited fate of Matangini, he vested him with the nominal control of one single village but allowed him a handsome salary in return. He also built him a house, the one where this narrative opened, and gave him lands to cultivate by hired labourers if he chose. Indeed, this latter employment chiefly engaged Rajmohan's attention, as he had little or nothing to do with the zemindar's sherista.

But this liberality did not command much gratitude from its unworthy object. Ever since their arrival at Radhaganj he behaved with coldness, and perhaps with more than coldness towards his benefactor, and the benefactor and the benefited had little intercourse with each other. Madhav seemed not to notice his strange conduct or if he did, it was with indifference, though he never lessened his bounty to its ungrateful object. One painful effect of this feeling on both sides was that the sisters, who loved each other dearly, had very little of each other's company.

5

A LETTER—A VISIT TO THE ZENANA

When Madhav returned from his garden, where he had parted with his cousin, he found a messenger waiting for him with a letter which he said was '*Zaruri.*' Madhav tore it open with eagerness, and devoured its contents. It was from his lawyer at the Sadar station of his district. We will endeavour to give a literal translation of this epistle, interspersing it with the remarks Madhav made as he read.

'To sea of glory.'

'Your servant has been engaged in conducting your honour's lawsuits at this station, with great carefulness, and hopes that he will succeed in all of them.'—

'All of them' thought Madhav, 'aye, you may say so, lawyer, for my cases are all just. But it is not in the nature of our courts to be right in every case, so I fear, I must take my lawyer's dictum with some allowance. He is an able fellow, however, and manages cases excellently, I must confess.—I heartily wish all this mummery were at an end, but my neighbours must drag me to law. But what next?' The letter proceeded—

'It gives me great pain to have to inform you that this day, your aunt has by proxy instituted a suit against you in the principal Sadar Amin's Court, alleging that her husband's will is a forgery and claiming the whole estate with wasilut.'

'My aunt!' exlaimed Madhav in astonishment, the letter dropping from his hands, 'my aunt! she! Heavens! and for my whole fortune! I a forger. The wretch! I shall kick her out of the house!'

He stood musing for some moments, trembling with rage. But calming himself a little, he picked up the paper and proceeded with it.

'I do not know who gave her such counsels, but your servant has made many enquiries, knowing well that someone must have counselled it, and he has heard who it is. Great men are there at her back.'

'Counsellors indeed!' thought Madhav 'who can they be?' He tried to make a guess, first thought of one neighbouring zemindar, then of another, but no one seemed likely, and he resumed reading.

> 'But do not think your honour has anything to fear. The will is in truth real, as I know, and where there is virtue, there is victory. But it is necessary to be very cautious. It would be advisable to give vakalatnamas to Babus .... and ...., vakils of the Judge's Court, as well as to engage another from the Sadar Court on necessary occasions. Barristers from the Supreme Court need also be engaged when the parties join issue as well as at the final hearing. Your servant will do all in his power, and will try for the case even with his life. He waits your honour's orders.
>
> Obedient to orders,
Gokul Chandra Das.
>
> P.S.—A thousand rupees are at present required to meet necessary expenses.'

Madhav's first thought, after he had finished the perusal of the letter was to go and seek his aunt, and to hear what explanation she had to give of her strange proceeding. Madhav therefore immediately hurried into the inner apartments where he found it no very easy task to make himself heard in that busy hour of zenana life. There was a servant woman, black, rotund and eloquent, demanding the transmission to her hands of sundry articles of domestic use, without however making it at all intelligible to whom her demands were particularly addressed. There was another, who boasted similar blessed corporal dimensions, but who had thought it beneath her dignity to shelter them from view; and was busily employed, broomstick in hand, in demolishing the little mountains of the skins and stems of sundry culinary vegetables which decorated the floors, and against which the half-naked dame never aimed a blow but coupled it with a curse on those whose duty it had been to prepare the said vegetables for dressing.

A third had ensconced herself in that corner of the yard which formed the grand receptacle of household filth, and was employing all her energies in scouring some brass pots; and as her ancient arms whirled round in rapid evolutions the scarcely less active engine in her mouth hurled dire anathemas against the unfortunate cook, for the mighty reason, that the latter had put the said vessels to their legitimate use, and thus caused the labours which excited the worthy matron's ire. The cook herself, far removed from the scene where both her spiritual and her temporal prospects were being so fiercely dealt with by the excited scourer of the brass pots, was engaged in an angry discussion with an elderly lady, apparently the housewife and governess, the subject of debate being no less interesting and important than the quantity of ghee to be allowed her for the culinary purposes of the night. The honest manufacturer of rice and curry was anxious to secure only just double the quantity that was necessary, wisely deeming it advisable that half should be set apart in secret for her own special benefit and consumption. In another corner might be heard those sounds so suggestive of an agreeable supper, the huge *bunti* severing the bodies of fishes doomed to augment the labours of the conscientious cook aforesaid. Several elegant forms might be seen flitting, not often noiselessly but always gracefully, across the *daláns* and veranda with dirty earthen lamps lighted in their little hands, and occasionally sending forth the tinkling of the silver *mal* on their ankles or a summons to another in a voice which surpassed the silver in delicacy. A couple of urchins utterly naked and evidently excrescences in the household, thought the opportunity a fitting one for the display of their belligerent propensities and were making desperate attempts at tearing each other's hair. Some young girls were very clamorously engaged in playing at *Agdum Bagdum* in the corner of a terrace.

Madhav stood for some moments in utter hopelessness of ever making himself heard in this the veriest of Babels.

'Will you, you wenches,' he cried at length in a key creditable to his lungs, 'will you cease? Can I speak?'

The change this short exclamation produced was magical. The vociferations of the dame whose demands for nameless articles had been thitherto addressed to the air, ceased in the midst of a scream of more than ordinary power, and the black rotund form of the screamer was nowhere to be seen. She of the broomstick threw away the formidable weapon as if stung by an adder, and sought in precipitate flight to shelter her half-naked mass of flesh in the friendly cover of some dark corner. The anathematizing scourer of the brass vessels was cut short in the midst of a very sonorous curse; and both her tongue and her arm were suspended in the middle of half-performed evolutions. The destroyer of the finny tribe, also, experienced a momentary interruption, but though she mustered courage to resume her task, it was certainly executed with a far smaller expenditure of noise. The presiding divinity of the kitchen abruptly terminated her vocal exertions in favour of ghee and betook to her heels, carrying off in the precipitancy of her flight the entire ghee-pot, a bare moiety of which had just formed her demands. The flitting figures with the lit lamps disappeared in tumultuous flight, little caring that the tinkling of the ornaments in their feet betrayed the very presence they endeavoured to conceal. The combat of the sturdy little warriors who fought in nudity and darkness for victory suddenly terminated in flight on both sides, though the abler general of the two did not fail to fire a retiring shot in the shape of a hearty kick at the shins of his antagonist The little girls too, who had been so merrily playing, rose and followed the said general accompanying him with an ill-suppressed tittle of hilarity. The scene which had just exhibited an unparalleled confusion was suddenly changed into one of utter silence and solitude, and the grave housewife was the only being who stood unmoved and unchanged before the master of the house.

'Masi,' said Madhav, addressing the matron, 'how is this? My house is a very bazar.'

'Women, son, women,' replied the Masi with a benevolent and affectionate smile, 'it is woman's nature to be screaming.'

'Where is Khuri now, Masi?'

'That is what I was thinking of' was the reply, 'she has not been seen in the house since morning.'

'Not seen in the house since morning!' exclaimed Madhav in amazement, 'the thing is true then?'

'What is true, son?' replied the maternal aunt.

'Nothing; I will tell you afterwards. Where is she then? Has any one seen her anywhere?'

'Ambika, Srimati,' cried the matron, addressing the women who were engaged with the fish and the vessels respectively, 'have you seen her anywhere?'

'No,' replied each softly.

'Strange,' said the matron; then, as if addressing the walls, she enquired, 'has any one seen her?'

'I met her at the Elder House at bathing time,' replied a voice from behind the walls.

'There!' exclaimed the matron in surprise.

'There! in Mathur Dada's house,' exclaimed Madhav also, and then muttered between his teeth, a sudden light flashing upon him, 'cousin Mathur! can he be the instigator? No, no, it cannot be, I judge wrong.' Then speaking out he said, raising his voice, to one of the women present, 'Go to the Elder House, and see if my aunt is there; if she is, ask her to return, and in case she refuses, know her reasons.'

6

MIDNIGHT PLOTTING

All who have their eyes shut do not sleep. Mat walls like stone walls have ears.

Let us now return to Matangini. Led to her chamber by her aged aunt-in-law after the harsh treatment she had received from her husband, she shut herself up in anguish of spirit. Supper was prepared in due time by the old woman, but not all her requests and entreaties nor those of Kishori, her sister-in-law, could prevail upon her to come out to partake of it. They were obliged therefore to desist and leave her to her own melancholy reflections.

Matangini lay in her bed brooding over the sufferings she was doomed for ever to bear. Her husband, she knew, would not see her that night, as was his wont whenever he was offended with her. She, however, felt all the happier for it, and felt a pleasure too in being left alone to indulge in her reflections. The night advanced and one by one the inmates of the house retired to rest. A deep silence pervaded the household as well as all external nature. Matangini's chamber was without a light, and total darkness pervaded it, except where a bright moonbeam that crept through a slight crevice in the small window, streaked the cold mud-floor. With her head raised from the pillow and supported on her hand, her *anchal* thrown off from her bosom towards the waist on account of the sultry heat, Matangini gazed on the single ray of moonlight that recalled to her remembrance the days when she could sport beneath the evening beam with the gay and light heart of childhood. Childhood! That time when she used to lie in the open air, arm in arm with her beloved Hemangini, gazing on the silver orb that poured the sweet light and the interminable deep blue ocean on which she sailed! Many, many were the tales, such as childhood loves, which they then told to each other or heard from their affectionate grandmothers, and hearty was the mirth with which they listened. Eight years had wrought a change. The loud laugh was forgotten, the feces which she loved and whose pictures lay treasured in her heart, she never more could see. And then that smile and that tone of affection! Oh! she could give all she had now in the world again to see that smile, again to hear that tone of human voice. Her heart was a warm spring of inexhaustible love, but it found no vent, and the cold breath of unkindness congealed the celestial stream at its source. One painful remembrance, painful but too sweet in its painfulness not to be brooded over again and again, still con-nected her past happiness with her present lot. That she wished to forget; but she could not. There was but one human being near her who loved her, the good and guileless Kanak and she alone was mistress of her secret. Beyond this her life was continued misery, and Matangini wept as she thought it could be nothing more.

The sultry heat incident to the season became intolerable, and Matangini rose from her bed to open the window. She was about to open it when the sound of soft and cautious footsteps caught her ear. The sound evidently proceeded from outside the house, and from no distance from the window behind which she stood. The window was, as usual in mat-walled houses, very small, being not more than three feet by two and stood at a height of two feet above the floor. Matangini paused and tried to see through the chink, but could observe nothing beyond a cluster of trees and the far-off tops of others waving against the moonlit sky.

As no footpath lay close to the place whence the sounds of footsteps proceeded, Matangini's apprehensions were excited; she stood motionless, and listened with intense attention. The footsteps approached very close to her and at length ceased; and she could hear whispering voices. Her curiosity was still more strongly excited when she recognized in one of the voices that of her husband, who spoke a little louder than the other. As the mat wall alone divided them, Matangini could catch enough of the sounds though not all to be able to understand the meaning of the speaker.

'Why do you speak so loud?' said one of the whisperers, after a few words had been exchanged, 'people in your house may hear us.'

'None can be awake at this hour,' said Rajmohan, as Matangini guessed from the voice.

'Had we not better go a little further off from the wall? Should any one happen to be awake, she could not then overhear us,' observed the other.

'No,' returned Rajmohan, 'should any be awake as you fear, then we are best as we are, for here under the shadows of the wall and the eaves, no one can possibly see us from the house—neither through the chinks nor probably from outside, should people happen to be out at this hour.'

'True,' said the other, 'but who are in this room here?'

'Why should I tell you that?' Rajmohan said, but immediately addressed, 'there can be no harm in telling it, in my chamber there is nobody there but my wife.'

'Are you sure she is asleep?' demanded the other.

'I think so, but I will go round and see, you wait here.'

Matangini now heard steps receding, Softly and noiselessly she trod the floors and returned to her bed, on which she alighted still more gently and cautiously, so that the least rustling of clothes was not heard. She then threw herself into a posture of sleep, and shut her eyes.

Rajmohan came round to the door of his chamber and lightly tapped at it, nobody came to open it. He called gently to his wife to open the door, but with no better success. He now thought that his wife was really asleep, but thinking it not impossible that she would keep silence from resentment for which he had furnished ample cause, he determined to enter the room any how. Rajmohan went to the kitchen, struck a light, and returned with the kitchen lamp in his hand. Then laying it on the ground he applied one foot to one leaf of the door, and held fast the other with an arm. The slack hinges permitted a slight opening to be thus made between the leaves, and Rajmohan thrust a finger in to see if the large bar, the slight wooden bolt, and the little iron chain had all been fastened. He perceived that only the wooden bolt had been used, and rightly judged that his wife had left the door so slightly secured in order to permit him to open it from without if he chose to go in. He easily unfastened the slack bolt by thrusting two fingers in and drawing it aside, and entered the room with the lamp in his hand.

Rajmohan found the features of his wife composed in sleep. He called her several times by name, but so gently as not to awake her; spoke kindly, so that if his wife's silence proceeded from resentment or anger, it might vanish, but still finding her silent and breathing hard, and knowing no reason why she should counterfeit sleep, he was satisfied of its reality and went out, shutting the door after him by the same artifice that had helped him to open it. He then extinguished the lamp, and went round the whole house, tapping at each door and calling in a gentle voice to the slumberers, but finding none awake, rejoined his companion.

As the footsteps of her husband died away, Matangini left her bed and stealing with the same soft tread to the window overheard the following conversation.

After learning from Rajmohan that all was safe, his unknown companion began.

'Are you willing to assist us in this affair?'

'Not much I confess,' said Rajmohan. 'Not that I pretend to be honest so late, but though I don't like the man, he has done me some good.'

'Why then do you not like him?' ashed the shrewd stranger.

'Because if he has done me some good he has done me harm too, and perhaps more harm than good,' replied Rajmohan.

'Well, if so, why not assist us?'

'I will, if you give me what I demand. I am anxious to remove from his cursed neighbourhood, but I don't see how I can get food elsewhere without coming to trouble. I wish much therefore to get a sum that will make me care little where I go. If your affair will bring me such an amount of money, I will assist you.'

'Name your condition,' said the stranger.

'First let me know what I am required to do,' responded the other.

'You will do what you have done for us sometimes before this—help us to conceal the property. This time we mean to leave everything we get except cash on your hands, and that this very night.'

'I understand,' Rajmohan replied, 'you will do well not to conceal from me how much you stand in need of my aid. You are aware that a deed in such a big and wealthy house will be followed by too strict an enquiry and too hot a search for the property to render it convenient to you all to be enjoying your shares in quiet for some time, and you absolutely want somebody who can hold them in trust for you—which you well know none can do so well as I, specially as suspicion will not easily fall on me. Yes, I have an excellent hiding place for such things; but I shall demand too much I fear.'

'You see it—be moderate in your terms,' rejoined the dacoit, for such, the reader sees, he was.

'We won't haggle,' replied Rajmohan, 'I want one-fourth of what you may sell the things for.'

The dacoit knew Rajmohan too well to think he was endeavouring to bully him into a bad bargain. He was silent for a moment and then said:

'So far as I am concerned—agreed; but I must take the opinion of the others, though you know my word in such matters is their word also.'

'I have no doubt of that,' responded Rajmohan, 'but one word more. Before you take away these things, we will make a guesswork of what the things will sell for—and you will pay me down a fourth of it in cash. Of course I shall afterwards make up for anything that may fall short of expectation, and you will do the same to me ii you get more.'

'Certainly it will be so, but one word to you also. You are to do another service.'

'I will, if you name another price.'

'Yes, of course. We mean to carry off Madhav Ghose's property for ourselves; but we want to carry off something else for another.'

'What?' enquired Rajmohan with some show of curiosity.

'His uncle's will.'

'*Hoon*,' exclaimed Rajmohan starting slightly.

'Yes -and will be paid for it. Now we want to know from you where Madhav keeps that will.'

'I don't know it exactly myself. I have seen him take out his document from a certain box, but I don't know where that box is kept, whether he keeps it in another box or chest or almirah, I know nothing—but who pays you for the will?'

'I am bound not to tell.'
'Not even to me?'
'To none.'
'Is it Mathur Ghose?'
'May be or may not—but what sort of a box is it?'
'The terms?'
'What do you ask?'
'Two hundred in cash.'

'Rather too much for two, or three words. But we have too much to do'—the dacoit continued, speaking more to himself than to the other, 'to be searching for a bit of paper all night. The box must be in some iron chest in the bedroom; so we can find it easily if we only know what sort of box contains it. There is no jabbering with you—so be it as you say.'

'It is an ivory box' Rajmohan said, 'with three English letters written in gold on the lid. Those are the first letters of his name.'

'So now that it is arranged,' said the dacoit, 'come with me and let us see our men. We will appoint a place of rendezvous where you will wait for us. Come, there is no time to lose; the work must be commenced as soon as the moon sets, and summer nights are short.'

So saying the robber and his confederate softly stole from the shadow of the wall and took their way towards the woods at a distance from each other, soon to reunite in another dark spot. Matangini sank on the floor in astonishment and dismay.

7

LOVE CAN CONQUER FEAR

Every word that caught the ear of Matangini froze her with horror during the terrible dialogue she overheard. As long as it continued, the intense interest with which she listened sustained her trembling frame, but so soon as it was ended, she sank overpowered on the floor. For some moments she remained almost insensible from the stupor of fear and agony. By degrees she recovered composure enough to think on what she had heard. A new and terrible light had just been thrown on the life and character of her husband. She had hitherto known him as a man of mad heart and brutal temper, but she recoiled with horror at the recollection that the accomplice of robbers, himself a robber perhaps, had hitherto enjoyed her innocent bosom. And the future? Was it in her power, now that her eyes were opened, to tear herself from his disgusting embraces? No, no, she was for ever cursed!

Such thoughts would rend her bosom at one moment—at the next the daring crime to which he was going to lend a hand burst on her sight with fearful vividness. She trembled as she thought of this. And the victims of this horrible deed were to be her own Hemangini and her Madhav. Her hair stood on end, her blood tingled in her veins, and a sharp pang shot across her head. All thoughts of her own accursed future and degraded womanhood vanished as she thought of the beloved beings who were now sleeping in fancied security while utter poverty and misery, perhaps worse, yawned to engulf them in an hour. She felt she must save them if she could, even at the price of her life.

Her first thought was to alarm her own household. But the next moment she perceived the folly of the thought. Who in the household would believe it of Rajmohan? Would his aunt believe it? or would his sister? Most probably they would think her crazed, delirious or dreaming. And supposing they did believe, would they endanger

Rajmohan to save Madhav? And even if they would, could they save him? No, they dreaded too much their formidable relative to act in the slightest manner against his wishes. And should they not believe her, but in any manner let him know what she had uttered, her doom would be sealed.

She next thought of Kanak. Might not Kanak be sent to inform Madhav's household? Kanak's house was close by and Matangini might steal away from her chamber and awaken and impart to her so much of what she knew as would suffice to warn Madhav without endangering Rajmohan. But this course also appeared unpromising, if not impossible. She could not awaken Kanak without awakening Kanak's mother also, for both she knew, slept in the same room. Kanak might perhaps believe anything she said without asking for explanations, but Kanak's mother would not. To satisfy her it would be necessary to reveal everything and implicate her husband, but Matangini could not for all the world turn informer against the man to whom she had pledged her faith before God and man. Nor would it be possible to impart to Kanak alone the purpose of a midnight visit, and would Kanak's mother allow her daughter to leave her home at midnight, alone, or what she perhaps might think as bad, in the company of another young woman? Far from it, it was rather more likely that she would awaken Matangini's household in return, and deliver her over to their custody, fairly making it certain that Matangini had become either mad or dishonest. And even with her mother's consent, would Kanak have the courage to venture on such a journey at such an hour unattended or attended by only another woman, herself, specially when bands of dacoits were out, lurking on the wayside?

Matangini now perceived with despair that her only resource lay in herself. She must go herself. Her whole soul recoiled at the idea. She thought not of the danger, though the danger was great. At this hour of dread loneliness, a young woman would have to thread her way through a wild and jungly path. She was, naturally enough, superstitious and her rich imagination was stored with tales of unearthly haunters of the woods, and had fed on them since infancy. A band of desperate robbers were stationed somewhere in the vicinity, and should she fall into their hands, she shuddered to think what might be the consequence. If among these robbers she should meet her husband! Matangini shuddered again.

Matangini had a brave heart, and for her sister and her husband she felt she could risk her life.

As the appalling dangers rose before her mind, her noble love expanded and rose also, and she longed to sacrifice at its altar a life whose burden her crushed heart could not longer bear. But still another womanly feeling kept her back. To go to the house of Madhav at midnight and alone! Who would understand her? What would Madhav think! She pressed her brows and stood thinking in an unmoved attitude.

Undecided she heaved a deep sigh, and to relieve herself of the heat that oppressed her, she ventured to open the little window. The trees now cast shadows of huge length and the moon hung over the far horizon, shedding a waning light In an hour she would vanish, the loud shout of the robbers would be heard, 'and then,' thought Matangini, 'it will be too late to save them.' The near approach of certain danger banished her scruples, her love returned with tenfold energy, and she no longer hesitated.

Wrapping herself in a coarse piece of bedcloth from head to foot she gently opened the door, and issuing out of the chamber, closed it with the same care and drew the bolt after her in the same manner as Rajmohan had done. As she stood out in the open space and eyed the vast solitude of the blue heavens and the thick mass of the noiseless tops of the trees, her heart again misgave her and her feet refused their office. 'Gods, give me strength,' she uttered with her hands clasped on her bosom. Then summoning all her resolutions, she made rapid but noiseless steps. Her heart beat as she walked through the jungly path. The dreary silence and the dark shadows appalled her. The knotted trunks of huge trees showed like so many unearthly forms watching her progress in malignant silence. In each leafy bough that shot over her darkened path, she fancied there lurked a demon. In each dark recess she could see the skulking form and glistening eyes of a spectre or of a robber. All the wild tales she had heard of fierce visages and ghostly grins that had appalled to death the belated traveller, rushed to her imagination. The light crack of the falling leaf, the flapping wings of some frightened night bird as it changed its unseen seat among the dark branches, the slight rustle of crawling reptiles among the fallen leaves, even her own footsteps made her heart fainter and fainter. Still the resolute girl hurried on, taking the name of her patron goddess a thousand times within her heart, and now and then muttering a prayer. The darkest part of the path wound along a glade which lay between two plots of raised ground. On one side was a vast mango-*tope* enclosed by a high and impervious hedge of prickly vegetation. On the other side was the raised bank of a pool covered with underwood above which waved the vast foliage of three Bur trees, darkening the footpath which wound beneath their shadows. Matangini cast around her eyes in fear. From the middle of the mango-*tope* issued a strong glare of light, and she could even hear low discordant voices. All her worst fears were realized. There was the robber band. Matangini stood chained to the spot, unable to move a step. To add to her misfortune a dog which lay by the wayside rose up and began to bark loudly at the sight of a passenger at night. Immediately the voices in the garden were hushed. Matangini still retained presence of mind enough to see that the dacoits had taken the warning given by the animal, and that she was likely soon to be discovered. Danger again restored her energies. Darting with the fleetness and the lightness of the gazelle across the darkened bank of the pool, she as swiftly ascended to the edge of the water. Her position was now concealed by the bank from the view of any who might look for her in the footpath; but should the robbers think of looking about the bank on which the *Bur* trees stood, she was lost. No bush or thicket was near to afford her a shelter. Her energies had been roused and she did not lose a moment. The dog still barked. She hastily loosened a heavy clod of earth from the moist edge of the water, placed it in the coarse cloth in which she had wrapped herself, and tied it in a bundle, so that it might not float when thrown into the water. Thus prepared to free herself from an incumbrance which might betray her, for the light *sari* could be managed with ease, she stood ready for an emergency. Footsteps could now be distinctly heard and voices whispered on the other side of the bank. She gently sank the bundle in the water, taking care that the water might not splash. Then as gently gliding into die water at a spot where the spreading branches of the *Bur* cast a deep shadow, she sat down immersed to her chin, so that nothing but her head was visible, if indeed it could be seen where the dark water of die pool was made darker by the sombre shade of the tree. But still apprehensive lest the fair complexion of her lily face should betray her, she unloosed the knot of her hair and spread the dark luxuriant tresses on all sides of her head, so that not even die closest scrutiny could now distinguish from above the dark hair floating over the darkened pool.

Presently the footsteps and the whispering voices approached this side of the bank and descended half way. Matangini could hear this; but did not turn her head.

'It is strange,' said one of die voices within her hearing, 'I thought I saw through an opening in die hedge a figure wrapped in a chudder standing on the pathway.'

'You must have mistaken a tree for a man,' said the other, 'for could any have disappeared so soon? Besides, would any sane man wrap himself in a thick chudder as you say, in this season?'

'Yes, you may be right,' was the reply, 'or it might be an *apadevata* that I have seen.'

She too gave a last glance around them, without discovering, however, the timid intruder who formed the cause of their apprehension. They then walked away.

Matangini waited in the water for some minutes even after she had heard the last audible sound of their footsteps, and when she thought they had regained the mango grove, she came out of her watery shelter and gently squeezed the water out of her *sari*, abandoning to it the lost chudder. Without venturing again on the dangerous foot-path above, she took her way along the edge of the water, along a bank at right angles to the one she had left, casting looks of anxious fear behind her. She knew well the footpaths here, for though so strictly forbidden the Madhumati, she had permission to resort to this piece of water for her daily ablutions. From this bank the fair adventurer cut across a little footpath which she knew led through a dense mass of underwood to the one that she had been compelled to desert. It was at length gained, though not without repeated misgivings of the heart. There she stood at a distance from the mango grove and the animal which had caused her so much trouble. But a new difficulty threatened to check her further progress. Since her arrival at Radhaganj she had but twice visited her sister, and never on foot, but closed in a palki. As much of the way as she knew from hearsay she had passed, but now her footsteps rested at the intersecting point of cross-roads. Bewildered by her new difficulty, she turned her eyes on all directions and luckily caught sight of the tops of the tall *Devdaru* trees which she knew stood in front of Madhav's house. She immediately struck the path which led in that direction and soon got the huge edifice in view, towards the *khirki* or postern gate of which she turned her steps.

The last difficulty had yet to be overcome. All in the household were asleep at that hour, and it was after knocking a good many times that she succeeded in rousing Karuna, the maidservant of the house.

'Who knocks at this time of night?' enquired Karuna surlily.

'Oh hasten, hasten, Karuna, open the door' cried Matangini anxiously.

'But who are you that I shall open the door to you at this time of night?' again demanded Karuna in the same surly tone, indignant that the sweetness of her repose should be disturbed by an untimely intruder.

'Come, come soon—you will see,' said Matangini in a beseeching tone, unwilling to speak out who she was.

'But who are you,' cried Karuna more furiously than ever.

'I am a woman and no thief, come and see,' was the reply.

It struck the slowly opening senses of Karuna that a thief does not usually possess so sweet a voice as the one she heard. Without further parley, therefore, she came to the door and opened it.

'You, Thakurani!' exclaimed Karuna in utter astonishment at beholding Matangini.

'I want to see my sister,' said the latter, 'lead me to her.'

But Karuna's faculties had scarcely recovered from her surprise, and the worthy dame kept on asking questions.

'You here!' she repeated, 'and at midnight! What brings you here, mother? Your clothes are wet. What has happened?'

The impatient girl replied not to her questions, but said again in a commanding tone, 'Lead me to my sister.'

'She is asleep,' said Karuna, 'yet we will awaken her. But wait, first change your clothes.'

'Give me a *sari* soon if you can, or lead on.'

Karuna gave her a *sari* that was at hand, and Matangini changing her light apparel in a trice followed Karuna to the apartments above stairs.

8

FOREWARNED AND FOREARMED

Matangini stopped at an open veranda and desired Karuna to awaken her sister and bring her thither. In a few minutes Hemangini, who had not been asleep, came with utter astonishment depicted in her face and enquired in an eager tone the object of her unexpected and untimely visit.

'I come to warn,' said Matangini, 'there will be a dacoity in your house.'

'Dacoity!' half screamed, half muttered the astounded girl.

'*Hem!*' shrieked Karuna.

'Softly, Karuna' said Matangini, 'gently Hem; why stand you here? Go warn your husband and bid him be prepared.'

But Hemangini was then utterly unfit for the task. She stood pale and trembling, unable either to answer or move. Matangini was perplexed, she saw that her sister was lost in fear and time could not be spared. The loquacious zeal of Karuna, who could not for the world forego this opportunity of being the first to carry such dreadful tidings, as well as the salutary effect that had been produced upon her fears by the unexpected intelligence, relieved Matangini of her anxiety, and the mortal enemy of the finny tribe, big with the importance of being the messenger of evil, flew to Madhav's chamber to discharge the mission which legitimately belonged to Hemangini.

She soon returned and informed Matangini that Madhav did not feel disposed to give weight to her (Karuna's) words and seemed particularly incredulous when she said that Matangini was in the house and that it was she who had brought the intelligence. 'If she is here,' Madhav had said, 'I can hear the news from herself; bring her to me that I may learn from my sister-in-law how much there is to fear. Ask her to come hither.'

'Go Hem,' said Matangini to her sister, 'You go—tell your husband that I am here and that what I say is true. He will believe you.'

'No, no,' said the girl, 'you must go yourself. How can I answer all the questions that he may ask ? Go—answer all the questions that he may ask. Go and lose no time, for if it be as you say,—'

'I had better not go. Tell him that I say it, and that it is true.'

'No—you go,' again urged the reluctant girl with sweet childlike obstinacy.

'I *cannot* go, I must not,' said Matangini in the most serious tone and in an agitated voice.

'O Luck!' shouted Karuna laughingly, 'it is nothing then? Your sister wants to frighten you only, mother.'

'Ah! sister, do you want to frighten me only,' said Hemangini, her face brightening. 'I confess I am frightened—now tell me what is your errand.'

Matangini mused in deep silence for a minute; then taking her resolution, she said, 'Yes, I will go to him. You come with me, Hem.'

But the modest girl positively refused to appear before her husband in the presence of her sister, though she did not say as much in words. 'Stay then and speak not a word about me or my errand till I come back,' said Matangini and darted away through the veranda, for she saw the moon's disk sinking on the tops of the trees. But as Matangini neared the door of Madhav's apartment, her feet trembled more violently than even when she had stood eying the glaring light in the mango-grove. She drew her *sari* over her forehead and proceeded softly and with seeming reluctance. She receded, advanced, stopped short, pushed aside the door, stopped again, and at length entered. A single lamp illuminated the gaily decorated apartment and the young Babu reclined on a rich sofa. Matangini stationed herself close to a wall with downcast head as befitted the modesty of her sex and age, her face scarcely turned towards that of her brother-in-law. Madhav gave a start and then only half rose from his reclining posture.

Neither, however, spoke, although one was as anxious to impart the fearful tidings she bore as the other to receive them, and a silence ensued which evidently embarrassed both. At length Madhav spoke jestingly, as the connection between them authorized.

'I wish you were an English Memshahib, sister-in-law,' said he with a smile, 'that I might offer you a seat. But why not sit down on—on—'

Matangini relieved him from his embarrassment by saying almost in a whisper, 'Have you heard what I have to say?'

'Yes,' said Madhav seriously, 'is it true?'

'It is true,' she said in the same half audible tone.

'Tonight you say?'

'Tonight, even now they will make their attack as soon as the moon sinks and the moon will sink in half a *danda*.'

'Is it? Then I am lost But how do you know all this sister-in-law?'

'That,' replied Matangini in a more distinct voice, slightly lifting the cloth which covered her forehead, 'That you must not ask me.'

'You perplex me,' rejoined he, 'I scarcely know what to think.' Matangini now completely uncovered her face and looking steadily into his, spoke in a yet bolder tone. 'Do you not know me, Madhav? Can I deceive you? And do you think I would come to your house, at this hour, and unattended—'

'Sure—I was wrong,' he answered, 'wait here with your sister while I go and rouse my men.'

Matangini arrested him with a look as he was rising and asked him to give her one word more.

'What is it?' he asked.

'Where is your uncle's will—take care of it—they mean to carry it off.'

'Humph' ejaculated Madhav, a sudden light flashing upon him as he called to mind his aunt's lawsuit, 'They shall not have it.'

'Do you not keep it in an ivory box in this room?'

'Yes—how do you know it?' he enquired in fresh amazement.

'Why I? they know it,'—she replied.

'Now I see it!' he answered, 'you must be too well informed,' and he rose to depart.

'I have something to beg of you—will you grant it?'

'Ask it and it will be yours.'

'Then say not a word to a human being that I have been your informant or even that I have been here tonight; my life depends on it.'

'How your life ? Who dares threaten it?' exclaimed he with a flash of indignation.

'Hush!' said she.

'Yes, I forget!' said he checking himself, 'I promise you silence.'

'And impose the same on Karuna and my sister as you go.'

'With Karuna, it will be rather difficult, but I shall frighten the wench into dumbness. You stop with your sister, with closed doors and you will remain here unperceived by the household. When I come back I shall lead you to a place of greater security and privacy.'

So saying he passed by his wife and Karuna, each of whom he desired or commanded to be strictly silent regarding Matangini. Then darting swiftly into the outer department, he was at once in the midst of his darwans.

Madhav knew Matangini to be a woman of too clear a mind to have been greatly deceived, and he knew her also too well to think she would ever be at so much pains to deceive him. He therefore set himself to the work of preparation in earnest. Before total darkness had covered the face of the earth, the housetop might be seen full of human forms flitting against the sky. These were select men from the tenantry who lived close to the house and from among whom a little *lattial* force could be collected at any time at a moment's notice. These were mostly armed with *latties*, spears, bricks and other missiles ready to be hurled at the doomed invader that durst approach the walls or enter the house. We do not pretend to say that all these midnight warriors bore a heart as sturdy as the *latties* that they clasped in their hands, and many doubtless there were who thought this untimely interruption of their repose very unwelcome, and who would, have gladly beat a retreat did not the stern voice of their landlord, as it rolled forth command after command, convince them that it would be safer to stay and trust to chance than risk his displeasure. Most however felt secure in their position; there was but little in the house on the top, to tempt the steps of robbers, and with this comfortable assurance the bold defenders stood boldly by their posts. Five or six men of the sturdier race from the North-west protected the entrance, well accoutred with sword, shield, spear and musket. Four or five others could be seen walking round, with orders to be on the alert, and to give the warning when necessary to the rest. Inside the house, the boxes and chest which contained the most valuable things, jewels, cash, plate and other articles of small bulk and great value, as also the coveted ivory box, were nowhere to be seen. They were removed to obscure hiding places which among the endless apartments of the ample edifice could never be discovered by one who had never seen them, and it was not every one of the inmates of the house that had a knowledge of their existence. Madhav was everywhere mild and easily yielding by nature under ordinary circumstances; his energy and activity in the moment of excitement was feverish and held in awe the timid and the hesitating. Nevertheless not few were the women, who dragging naked children in one arm and holding large wallets under the other, stealthily left the threatened house to seek shelter in the neighbouring huts, Whose humble pretensions protected them from the chance of spoliation. Among the fleetest and foremost might be, seen the conscientious cook who had signalized herself by victory in the preceding evening, and who now conducted a most dexterous retreat with bag and baggage, not forgetting the famous ghee-pot which formed the glorious trophy of her evening triumph.

The hum and bustle of preparation subsided as all was completed and the expectant crowd awaited the issue in silence. The moon had already set and Madhav began half to doubt the truth of Matangini's suspicions. Just as his thoughts were taking that direction a darwan came up to him and informed him in Hindi that one of the men appointed to keep a look out, had seen a light in the direction of the 'old garden' (as the mango-grove where Matangini had nearly encountered the robbers was called) and that venturing in that direction very close to the grove he had observed several armed men assembled in that place. 'What is your command,' asked the man, 'shall we go and attack them?'

'Hurry not, Bhup Singh,' replied Madhav, 'it is unnecessary, and besides if you go in insufficient numbers, you will be overpowered, but if on the other hand many of you go, you leave the house unprotected, and who knows but there may be another company?'

'Is it Maharaj's pleasure, then, we remain as we are?' asked the darwan.

'Yes—but set up a shout all of you together, and let the rascals perceive how well prepared we are.'

No sooner had he spoken than a long loud shout rent the midnight air. The females trembled in their apartments as they listened in awe and thought the danger near. A dismal silence succeeded the noise.

'Another shout—once more.' Said Madhav.

Again a similar sound shook the night. No sooner had its echoes died away, than out rose a terrific yell from the wilderness, as if uttered by midnight demons who revelled in the dark. The blood ran cold in the veins of the listeners as the horrible sound fell on their ears.

'Again, again, my men, once more raise your voices, and louder than ever,' shouted Madhav, apprehensive lest the appalling sound chilled the courage of his retainers. Again was the order obeyed with zeal and promptness, and again arose a responsive cry from the direction of the 'old garden.' But this time it was the cooing cry known among robbers as the signal of retreat.

'They fly; they fly; they fly;' shouted several voices, 'that is the cry of flight.'

'Yes, but do not be too sure,' said Madhav, 'it may have been uttered to deceive you. Remain as you are.'

Long did Madhav and his men wait, but nothing occurred. After another injunction to his retainers not to relax their vigilance and to keep up all night, Madhav turned his steps towards the inner apartments to thank the brave woman who had saved him from imminent danger.

9

WE MEET TO PART

'Can I ever forget what you have done for me?' said Madhav to Matangini, after he had rejoined his wife and his sister-in-law. The former, as soon as her heart was relieved of its load of apprehensions, lightly tripped out of the room leaving her sister alone with him. 'Can I ever forget what you have done?' said Madhav looking more gratitude than he expressed in words.

'If you cannot, let it be for Hem's sake that you remember it. Should she ever fall under your displeasure, which Heavens forbid! may the memory of her sister's sufferings obtain her pardon! As for myself, I could not do otherwise than I have done it—I will take leave of you.'

'Why, sister-in-law?' returned Madhav, 'your sister has not seen you long—she will be overjoyed to be with you for a few hours more. When it is day, my *pálki* will convey you to your home, if you cannot longer remain. Why depart tonight and on foot?'

'Fate rules it otherwise. That happiness I must forego,' returned she sadly; 'I must go.'

'Why sister-in-law, why so?' asked Madhav again, 'cannot your sister's husband know the reason?'

'*He!*' said she, as much with shame as with sorrow. 'You know *him* well. He will be angry if I remain.'

'Angry if you remain with your sister?' again inquired Madhav, 'did you promise him to return so soon? Does he know where you are?'

'No,' said she, 'I did not promise him anything, nor does he know where I am.'

'Strange,' said Madhav 'I don't understand how then you could come. Was he at home when you left?'

'Ask not such questions,' replied she.

A dark suspicion crossed Madhav's mind at this reply, but he soon abandoned it as groundless. He sat musing in deep silence for moments during which Matangini kept fixed on him her large, blue, sorrowful eyes.

'Why do I linger?' she said at length, 'I go; Karuna will go with me. Farewell,' added she sadly, her voice growing thick, 'Fare you well! Be you happy, Madhav.' Madhav looked up to her face—it was wet. Matangini was weeping! 'and be my Hem happy with you.'

'You weep!' said Madhav, 'you are unhappy.'

Matangini replied not, but sobbed. Then, as if under the influence of a maddening agony of soul, she grasped his hands in her own and bending over them her lily face so that Madhav trembled under the thrilling touch of the delicate curls that fringed her spotless brow, she bathed them in a flood of warm and gushing tears.

'Ah, hate me not, despise me not,' cried she with an intensity of feeling which shook her delicate frame. 'Spurn me not for this last weakness; this, Madhav, this, may be our last meeting; it must be so, and too, too deeply have I loved you—too deeply do I love you still, to part with you for ever without a struggle.'

Did Madhav chide her? Ah, no! He covered his eyes with his palm and his palm became wet with tears. There was a deep silence for some moments, but their hearts beat loud. Matangini, recovering her presence of mind as speedily as she had lost it, first broke the heart-rending silence.

The distant and reserved demeanour, the air of dejection and broken-heartedness which had marked her from the first had disappeared; the impetuosity and fervour of the first burst of a deep and burning love had subsided; and Matangini now stood calm and serene, her usually melancholy features beaming with the light of an unutterable feeling. A sweet and sober pensiveness still mantled her tender features, but it was not the pensiveness of deep-felt enjoyment, for the wild current of passion had hurried her to that region where naught but the present was visible, and in which all knowledge of right and wrong is whirled and merged in the vortex of intense present felicity. Was not Matangini now in Madhav's presence? And had not her long pent-up tears fallen on his hands? Had he not wept with her? That was all Matangini remembered, and for a moment the memory of duty, virtue, principle ceased to fling its sombre shadow on the brightness of the impure felicity in which her heart revelled. There was a fire in that voluptuous eye,—there was a flow on that moonbeam brow, and as she stood leaning with her well-rounded arm on the damask-covered back of the sofa, her beautiful head resting on the palm of her hand over which, as over the heaving bosom, strayed the luxuriant tresses of raven hue;—as thus she stood, Madhav might well have felt sure earth had not to show a more dazzling vision of female loveliness.

'I had thought,' she cried at length in a voice which trembled from emotion, 'I had thought that never again would human ears, not even your own, hear from my lips the language I breathed tonight, ah! I know not what I felt.'

'Matangini,' said Madhav, speaking for the first time since the storm of passion had burst, 'I too had thought we could part without a struggle, but you have—you see what you have done. But,' continued he, his eyes again suffused with tears, 'you have made many sacrifices, make one last sacrifice. Root out the feeling from a heart on which no impurity should leave a spot. Forget.'

'Blame me not,' she said, and then interrupting herself, she bent down her head to hide the tear that gushed again with the current of feeling. 'Yes, reproach me, Madhav,' she continued, 'censure me, teach me, for I have been sinful; sinful in the eyes of my God, and I must say it, Madhav, of my God on earth, of yourself. But you cannot hate me more than I hate myself. Heaven alone knows what I have felt—felt for the long long years that have past, could I rip open this heart you could then and then only know how it beats.'

Madhav wept again. 'Matangini dear, beloved Matangini,'—he began, but his voice thickened, and he could not proceed.

'Oh say again, again say those words, words that my heart has yearned to hear—say Madhav, do you then love me still? Oh! say but once again and tonight I shall meet death with happiness.'

'Listen to me, Matangini,' replied Madhav, scarcely cool himself, 'listen and spare both of us this sore affliction. At your father's house the flame was kindled which seems fated to consume us both and which then we were too young to quench by desperate efforts, but if even then we never flinched from the path of duty, shall we not, now that years of affliction have schooled our hearts, eradicate from them the evil which corrodes and blisters them? Oh! Matangini, let us forget each other. Let us separate.' And Madhav heaved a sigh.

Matangini rose and stood erect in the splendour of new flushed beauty. 'Yes,' said she with desperate effort, 'if the human mind can be taught to forget, I will forget you. We part now and for ever,' and there was desperate calmness in her voice.

Pulling her veil over her face to hide the stream that again welled forth from her eyes in spite of her efforts, Matangini hurriedly left the room.

10

THE RETURN

It wanted an hour to the first streaks of daybreak, when Matangini with sad heart and heavy steps again threaded the wild foot-path. Karuna silently followed her homeward footsteps. The paling blue of the starry heavens was now half covered by numbers of driving clouds, while one dense and settled mass of black hovered over the distant horizon and shed a sombre grey over the dimly seen outlines of the far-off treetops on its verge. A wild and fitful breeze occasionally moaned over the dark woods with an ominous sound and a few drops of pattering rain fell on the earth, on the leafy trees and on the luxuriant shrubbery. Matangini was too deeply absorbed in her own thoughts to heed the appearance of external nature, though lowering and gloomy looked the scene around her. The remembrance of the forbidden and fond interview she had just stolen, engrossed all her soul; not even the thoughts of the reception which might await her at home, not even the risk and danger of discovery by her husband, obliterated the faintest tint of the vivid picture which memory of fancy successfully traced before her mental view, now in the darkest, now in the most radiant colours. She had promised to forget; the first thing she did after leaving Madhav was to remember; to remember and hang with rapture on each word he had uttered,—on each tear he had shed; and often would the rapture vanish and be succeeded by the thought that god and man abhorred her impurity of heart.

A part of their journey had been accomplished when the growing blackness of the skies announced that a storm was near.

'Thakuran, hasten your footsteps,' said Karuna, breaking the long silence; 'there will be a storm; let us reach your house before it commences.'

'Yes,' said Matangini unconsciously, 'go on.'

Karuna increased her speed and Matangini imitated her, more from example than from any sense of necessity.

'There—hear,—bigger drops are falling on the leaves,' said Karuna speaking once more.

'Yes?' said Matangini, then awaking for the first time from her abstraction, and, stopping to listen, continued, 'Ah it is not the sound of rain-drops—it seems to be—what? perhaps the sound of human feet treading over the leaves and stumps of trees.'

'Is it so, Thakuran?' ejaculated Karuna and increased her speed, apprehensive lest she should fall into the hands of some loiterer from among the dacoit band.

But they had not proceeded far when the wind rose in fury, the lightning flashed, the thunder growled, and big drops of rain poured down too unmistakably.

'We shall be drenched to death,' said Karuna, 'can we not shelter ourselves beneath this tree?'

'Come then,' said Matangini, as she led the way to the covert afforded by the overspreading boughs of a large tamarind. Just then a sudden flash of light illuminated the earth and revealed by its momentary gleam a human figure standing at the foot of the tree, within speaking distance of themselves.

'Fly, O fly!' shrieked Karuna, and waiting not for an answer, ran with all her might, dragging the nerveless Matangini after her as she sped away. 'Fly, fly, fly,' she kept on crying and ran on amidst the storm and rain and stopped not to take breath till she had reached the house which fortunately was nigh.

'Stay here not,' said Matangini after they had arrived there, 'although it is cruel to turn you out at this hour—it will be more dangerous for you to stay, cross over to Kanak's and remain there in the veranda; when the storm abates a little and the daylight comes you can leave the house before the family arise from their beds.

So saying, Matangini proceeded to open the door of her sleeping apartment, and Karuna left the house. Matangini found the door still shut, and unbarring it by the same artifice which Rajmohan had used a few hours before, she gently entered the apartment. She was in the act of shutting the door again when another figure glided into the room after her and drew the massive bar. The very sound of the tread of his feet told Matangini that it was her dreaded husband.

Rajmohan said nothing, but by feeling in the dark he brought out a tinder box and with flint and steel struck a light and placed it on its accustomed seat. Still he spoke not but sat on the *taktapos* or bedstead eying his wife with a savage glance. Matangini read her fate in his looks and stood, not pale and trembling but firmly and proudly, with all the dignity and courage which had that very evening awed into silence the fury of her brutal oppressor. The howling of the wind and the clatter of the rain without, and the angry growl in the clouds above were the only sounds that disturbed the appalling silence.

At length Rajmohan spoke, 'Accursed woman,' he said in a bitter tone which had in it nothing of the unusual savage impetuosity of his temper, 'did you not go to your paramour?' Matangini did not answer. 'Speak,' he said in a low voice of fearful imperiousness, stamping his foot on the ground.

'I shall not answer to questions which I ought not to be asked,' replied the half guilty and half innocent woman.

'Wretch,' exclaimed Rajmohan, gnashing his teeth and growing furious; but again assuming a forced calmness, he added, 'Did you or did you not go to Madhav Ghose's home this night?'

'Yes, I did,' she said, suddenly excited beyond herself by the sound of the name, 'I did—to save him from the robbery you had planned.'

Rajmohan sprang from the bed with clenched fists.

'Woman,' he said fiercely, 'deceive me not. Canst thou? Thou little knowest how I have watched thee; how from the earliest day that thy beauty became thy curse, I have followed every footstep of thine— caught every look that shot from thine eyes. Brute though I be,' continued he again becoming gentle, 'I was proud of my beautiful wife and as the tigress watches over her whelp, I watched over thee. Did I not perceive how before thou wert a woman, thou didst already become fond of that cursed wretch? Did I not see how time ripened thy fondness into sin? Doubt thou what I say? Know then that this very afternoon, when won by the poisoned words of that harlot, thy friend, thou didst leave the house unbidden, thou didst not leave unwatched. Then too I was behind thee—I was behind thee—deny it woman, if thou canst, when before the garden thou didst wilfully, yea most wickedly—most treacherously, let go thy veil, why? that your eyes might meet—and be blasted! Once and once only I missed thee—and I rue the hour when I did so. But returning at night to my untenanted chamber could I not guess the serpent's hole into which the vile worm had crept? I did and watched thee again at his *khirki* gate. Knowest not that in the moaning wind and amidst the howling storm I have dogged thy steps even but now?—knowest thou, harlot, why I have whetted my knife tonight? You answer not and I ask not for answer. I will kill you.' He ceased and his eyes darted fire as he cast a last glance of scrutiny over her petrified features. A momentary pause ensued during which the howling storm without was alone heard. At length Matangini spoke and desperate calmness was in her voice.

'You are right,' she said. 'I love him—deeply do I love him; long loved I and I love him so. I will also tell you that words have I uttered which, but for the uncontrolled—uncontrollable madness of a love you cannot understand, would never have passed these lips. But beyond this I have not been guilty to you. Do you believe me?'

'No,' said he, rising from his seat, 'I will kill you.' And he unsheathed a small dagger that hung from his waist concealed in his clothes.

'My mother, O mother! and you father! where are you now?' were the only sounds that escaped the lips of the doomed girl, as she sunk about lifeless on the floor. The ruthless weapon gleamed high, as it was about to descend on the lovely bosom of the trembling victim, when the purpose was suddenly arrested by a violent noise at the window. Rajmohan turned round to see the cause of the unexpected noise. The *jhamp* flew open and two dark and athletic forms sprang one after another into the chamber, dripping with rain and bespattered with mud, but shooting sparks of fire from their red and fierce glances.

11

WHEN THIEVES FALL OUT

In which is discussed the physical possibility of a robber being robbed and an assassin assassinated.

'YOU think of killing your wife, ruffian?' said one of the newcomers, who, however, had not come with any peaceful intentions himself as his heavy arms and gleaming dagger showed.

'Who are you?' roared Rajmohan, turning all his fury towards the intruders, and brandishing his knife with fearful rapidity. 'Burglary in my house!'

'Softly, the inmates in the other rooms will be aroused. No thieves, friend. Look well and possibly you may recognize me,' responded one of the newcomers with a contemptuous smile. 'Lass,' continued he addressing Matangini, 'bring that lamp here that your husband may have a look at the face of a friend.'

But Matangini, though not absolutely senseless, had fallen into a stupor—so bewildering had been the attack on her life and so strange the scarcely less fearful interruption that followed it.

'Friend or foe,' said Rajmohan, 'go out of my house.'

'That you may murder your wife in quiet?' said the intrepid stranger with a sarcastic laugh.

'And who will prevent me from doing it if I choose?' exclaimed the furious husband, and dagger in hand rushed to plunge it in the audacious visitor's breast. But quick as lightning the latter parried the blow, and then with one stroke of his own gleaming sabre he made that tiny weapon in Rajmohan's hand fly off to a distance of several feet. Losing not a moment, he seized Rajmohan's arms in an iron grasp. 'Now Bhiku,' said he to his hitherto silent companion, 'will you hold the lamp and let this fellow see my face. It is a moon face,

Raju, and will please you as much as your golden moon of a wife there.' Bhiku brought the lamp and as bid held it close to his face.

'Sardar!' exclaimed Rajmohan in amazement, as he recognized his fellow-plotter of the night.

'Yes, sardar,' replied the other, 'I see you recognized me; friends never forget each other so soon.'

'What brings you here?' said he in the same angry tone as before; 'what do you want by breaking into my house?'

'First tell me,' replied the other 'what were you going to murder your wife for.'

'That concerns you not,' returned Rajmohan, 'leave me alone, or sardar or no sardar I will kick you out of the house.'

'Ah! Let me see your kick, prisoner as you are,' said the other sneeringly.

'My legs are free yet,' roared Rajmohan, dealing a tremendous kick at his antagonist beneath which even the sturdy frame of the robber chief staggered some paces back, involuntarily letting go his hold of the agile antagonist's arms.

'Pin him, Bhiku, pin him down,' roared the bandit as he saw Rajmohan running to regain his lost dagger; and before the sounds were uttered the vigorous arm of the second robber felled their opponent to the ground.

The sardar now sprang to the fallen man's breast with the agility and fierceness of a tiger, and while he thus held him down, the other bound Rajmohan's hands and feet with a piece of rope which, fastened to two bamboo sticks on two of the walls, had formed a sort of rude clothstand for Matangini.

'Now, traitor!' said the sardar, 'you are at our mercy.'

'Yes, because you are two to one—but what have I done,' asked Rajmohan, 'that you should do thus to me?'

'What have you done? You have been a traitor, know that! Did you not send warning to the house and save your brother-in-law? You, hypocrite, you,' he added fiercely, his eyes gleaming in rage, 'you did it, you deserve to die.'

'I! I give notice to him! I would sooner tear open his eyes,' returned Rajmohan gnashing his teeth.

'Have done with your hypocrisy,' said the sardar threateningly, 'Fool that I was to believe that you would serve us against your own brother-in-law. Yet such a rascally tongue is yours, so deeply and smoothly does it lie—so often have you cursed him in our presence, that I thought I could trust you.'

'I tell you, sardar, it was not I,' returned Rajmohan with vehemence as he began to grow apprehensive for his life, for he knew well the desperate character he had to deal with. 'I tell you it was not I. Do you not remember that I left the house in your company and, till your purpose failed, have been in your company only? Have I left you for the twinkling of an eye since we went?'

'Ah! don't hope to deceive me again; no snatching of a child's sweetmeat with me. You knew your wife was awake when you brought me to your mat wall here; perhaps when you came round under the pretence of assuring yourself that she was asleep, you gave her a hint of what to do. Deny that if you can. If it was not she, can you tell me who else in the world did it?'

'*She* did it, I confess, but I can swear to you it was without my knowledge. When I came round I assure you I found her asleep. Propose the oath and I will swear that it was so.'

'You have lived long,' said the other sternly, 'it is useless now. We know you now. Do you think I would mistake the meaning of the haste with which you left as soon as the shouts from the house told us that your end had been gained? Believe me, comrade, I am too old a sinner to be deceived so easily. Prepare then to die.'

'For Heaven's sake descend from my bosom,' said Rajmohan, gasping for breath. The heavy burden of the bandit's body was pressing on his chest and at length became unsupportable even to his strength and iron frame. 'Release me. I swear to you by my patron God it was not so. I swear to you by my mother I did not know it.'

'How did your wife do it then?' enquired the bandit chief in the same tone as before.

With this question he alighted from the breast of the other, but kept a hold on his throat by a light grasp prepared to tighten at the least hostile movement from his prisoner.

'Could it not be' said Rajmohan, now breathing free, 'that she had only counterfeited sleep when I saw her?'

'Ha! ha! you take me for a fool' said the sardar with a gurgling laugh, 'I wanted to stand off from the wall, you made me come to the wall; why was that? Why, but for this treachery? You have betrayed us to Madhav Ghose; who can say you will not betray us to the police also, for that man will protect you? You must die or there is no safety for us. You gave us the slip very smartly or you would not live till now.'

'And what?' exclaimed Rajmohan with a sudden vehemence, 'what did you see when you came in? Was I not going to murder the very woman whom you say I employed as my agent? But for your interference she would have been a corpse now.'

'*Han*' exclaimed the sardar in an altered voice, as he gazed steadily on his silent comrade as if to ask what he thought of the matter.

'Yes, sardar, he speaks truth,' said Bhiku, breaking silence for the first time, 'why else should he kill the woman.'

'I was going to kill her,' said Rajmohan with a shudder, 'for having done the very deed you charge me with.'

'The woman! the woman! Kill the woman,' said the sardar as he sprang to the spot where he had seen Rajmohan's wife sink at her husband's uplifted blade.

He alighted on a heap of clothes which he had mistaken for his intended victim in the dim light of the expiring lamp.

'Wretch' muttered he, 'you need not escape me—don't think a sardar can't hunt you out in this little room.'

'Stop,' said Rajmohan, recovering the accustomed energy of his voice, 'none but myself touches my wife; unbind me.'

'Unbind him, Bhiku, while I drag her out by her hair,' said the sardar as he jumped to another corner where he saw something white again. Bhiku quickly cut Rajmohan's bandages with his sword. 'Het! clothes again!' muttered the robber as again he struck the hilt of his sword at a cane *petara*. 'Out! Out! Wicked woman,' said he highly exasperated and struck his weapon here and there on the bedstead. There was no Matangini on the bedstead.

'Here, Bhiku, bring the lamp here,' roared the sardar once more, 'the woman has hid herself beneath the *taktaposh*.' Bhiku brought the lamp, trimming it well. Rajmohan followed; all then bent down to look beneath the *taktaposh* for the affrighted fugitive, when lo! nobody was there.

Lifting the lamp high they could see by its improved light every corner and angle of the room, but Matangini was nowhere.

'The door! the door!' exclaimed Rajmohan, 'look! it is unbarred. I had barred it when I entered. She has fled.'

Matangini had indeed fled. Profiting by the mutual quarrel of the robbers who were too deeply engaged in their own life and death struggle to remember her whom less brutal hearts could never forget, Matangini had stolen away unperceived to the door, which she had quietly unbarred, and it is to be doubted if far more clamorous proceedings on her part would have attracted the attention of combatants so busily engaged.

'Run, run after her,' said the sardar, 'she will ruin us.'

'Yes, run' said Rajmohan. 'But hark you, none but I lift a finger against my wife. I will kill her when she is found, or if I do not, kill me as you proposed. But no one else must touch her. Haste, I will precede you.'

The three rushed out. The skies were still murky and continued drizzling. The fair fugitive was searched for in every direction. Day was now dawning fast, and little time was left for the search.

Rajmohan's first thought was to peep at Kanak's house. He and the sardar stealthily approached the hut and ascending to the level of the floor, slightly removed the *jhamp* which closed it. There they beheld in the faint gray light admitted by the opening thus made the sleeping forms of mother and daughter only. They looked over the neighbouring bushes, but with the same ill-success. A bright and ruddy morning was now following the wet and murky dawn too fast to render the search safe for the dacoits any longer. They then separated for the present, appointing a place of rendezvous at night, the sardar uttering an obscene threat to ensure the attendance of the suspected Rajmohan.

12

THE FRIENDS AND THE STRANGER

The recent shower had lent to the morning a delightful and invigorating freshness. Leaving the mass of floating clouds behind, the sun advanced and careered on the vast blue plain that shone above; and every housetop and every treetop, the cocoa palm and the date palm, the mango and the acacia received the flood of splendid light and rejoiced. The still-lingering water drops on the leaves of trees and creepers glittered and shone like a thousand radiant gems as they received the slanting rays of the luminary. Through the openings in the thick-knit boughs of the groves glanced the mild ray on the moistened grass beneath. The newly awakened and joyous birds raised their thousand dissonant voices, while at intervals the *papia* sent forth its rich thrilling notes into the trembling air. Light fleecy clouds of white wandered in the solitude of the now purified blue of the heavens, which were fanned by a light breeze that had sprung up to shake the pattering drops from the pendant and wooing boughs.

The reader will now follow us to the pool which had been the scene of Matangini's temporary danger and escape on the previous night. The sun had run a two hours' course in the heavens. Beneath a young tamarind tree, where the surrounding underwood lent a sort of cover, Matangini sat on the moist grass. Her clothes were wet; her *sari* had been soiled by mud, her usually curly tresses, washed by the drizzling rain, now fell in straight and loosely-flowing bands on her neck and arms; and her head was slightly bent to permit the sunbeams to play on that raven hair, darker than any cloud which had ever opposed their progress through the atmosphere. Close by her was to be seen the rather full and developed figure of Kanak shining with recently rubbed oil. A dirty napkin thrown over her neck, the brass *kalsi* maintaining its capacious but as yet empty bulk close by its mistress, and the blue *mishi* which had recently been called upon to lend its hue to her teeth, showed that the morning ablutions had drawn Kanak out of her home, but that important business had not been hitherto performed. The friends were evidently engaged in an earnest and interesting conversation. The reader need not be informed that with much of the subject of this interesting dialogue, he is already acquainted. Matangini was pouring cautiously and in whispers a narrative of the occurrences of the eventful night into the faithful and discreet ears of her only friend. The concluding part of this conversation we shall, with the reader's leave, place before him for his gratification.

'*Ma gow!*' said Kanak with a shudder, after having listened for some time in silent and mute astonishment. 'Ah! were it I, I would have been dead through fear. But you are a brave woman. But do you think of returning to your husband's house?'

'Where else can I go?' replied Matangini with a deep drawn sigh.

'Ah, do not, do not return, I beseech you,' returned Kanak vehemently, 'they will kill you.'

'I know my death is inevitable, but who can help fate? Who will tell me how I can find a shelter elsewhere?' and Matangini wept.

'My house will be no shelter for you, I know well,' replied Kanak, her eyes brimming over with tears in sympathy for the affliction of her friend. 'But you must not return home. Why will you not go to your sister?'

Matangini's features changed; she dashed the teardrops from her eyes, and assuming the same energy of voice in which she had bidden Madhav farewell, said, 'Never! never again while life lasts.'

Matangini's manner silenced all contradiction. Kanak covered her face with her *anchal* and wept.

'Ah, mothers!' interrupted a voice from behind 'What are you speaking of in secret? Ah, you are weeping I see; why, what is the matter?'

The new speaker who stood by the startled friends, was a middle-aged woman of dark complexion. Her hair had turned partly grey and her countenance was fast becoming wrinkled. She was dressed in a coarse *thenthe*, rather clean; her freshly oiled face, the dirty napkin on her shoulder, as well as the empty *kalsi* on her waist, betokened the nature of her visit to the waterside.

'Why, it is Suki's mother,' said Kanak, forgetting her tears and laughing and smiling in an instant, 'why, Suki's mother, why this unusual visit to the Phulpukur today?'

'I rose late this morning,' replied Suki's mother with benignant civility, 'and so, hasty of going to work direct, I thought of washing myself first. But what has happened, child? Why are you both weeping?'

'Ah, Suki's mother!' said Kanak, her eyes again moistening, 'how shall I speak of this poor woman's misfortunes?' A quiet but significant glance from Matangini's eye, which meant that her misfortunes were such as should not meet strangers' ears, warned Kanak against indiscreet disclosures; but Kanak, replying by a glance as full of meaning, seemed to imply that her secrets were safe.

'Talk not of her misfortunes,' said Kanak to the newcomer. 'The wretched woman has been turned out of her house by her husband and she knows not where to seek a shelter.'

'Oh fie,' exclaimed Suki's mother, 'is that a thing to weep for? Husbands and wives quarrel in the morning and become reconciled in the evening—who does not know that! He is angry now—will entreat you to go home as soon his anger is gone. Fie, mother, why do you weep for that? Ah, Kanak, when my son-in-law comes to see us, there is not a night when he does not quarrel with my daughter. But what of that? He loves my daughter as no one eke loves his wife. Even last Wednesday, he came and brought her a handsome gold *noth*—and such a *noth*, Kanak!' Kanak cut short the happy mother's description of her son-in-law's amiable disposition by observing, 'True, Suki's mother, but Raju da wants to marry another girl—the match that came from Junglebariah; you know well now why he treats her after this fashion, often and often; she will not go home again, Suki's mother, no woman ought to go. She will never trust herself again to that house to receive insults and reproaches. But alas, poor woman, whither else can she go! Is her father's hut close by to give her shelter?'

'Ah what a hard fate!' said the good dame, sympathizing, 'No no, if she be worthy of the name of woman, she cannot return home. Marry again! Why, where could he get a more beautiful wife? And will the little child he will bring home be a housewife like her? No, mother, do not return but go to your sister and see what he will do.' 'Alas! Suki's mother, she cannot go to her sister even,' responded Kanak, Matangini silently eyeing the ground from shame and confusion. 'She has quarrelled with her sister because Madhav Babu did not invite her husband at the late *shradh*. I could indeed give her shelter, but we are poor, Suki's mother, and I cannot take her there to starve.'

'My death; but what a simpler-hearted woman is she,' replied Suki's mother. 'She quarrelled with her sister on behalf of such a husband! The man does not deserve such a wife. Were he my son-in-law, I would have scolded not only him but his mother and his father too; but come, mother,' said she, turning to the silent and confused Matangini, 'come with me and live with my mistress as long as you choose; the elder Thakurani likes you so much that she will be overjoyed to see you. There, when your husband forgets his anger, and entreats you to go,—for soon he will—you can return to your own house. But do not listen to him too soon; first see that tears flow from his eyes—and that he takes the straw between his teeth.'

'Ah! yes, yes!' exclaimed Kanak joyfully, 'you have spoken well, Suki's mother. She will go with you now; what say you, sister? Will it not be the best thing to go with Suki's mother? The elder Thakurani, I am sure, loves you; you must be quite welcome to her. Why do you not speak?' Matangini frowned, but without heeding her, her loquacious friend went on glibly. 'Yes, yes, she will go; go, bathe yourself, Suki's mother, and when you return she will follow you. Go then, delay not.'

Suki's mother hastened to perform her morning ablutions. When the friends were alone, Matangini spoke. 'To what a depth am I fallen, Kanak!' said she.

Kanak returned with an impressive energy of manner, 'Oh! Do not say nay—drink my blood if you do. Go—go now; in the evening I will see you—Be silent.'

Kanak waited not for a reply, but taking her *kalsi* up in haste, she ran to the waterside to join Suki's mother and to perform her morning ablutions.

13

THE PROTECTRESS

The house of Mathur Ghose was a genuine specimen of mofussil magnificence united with mofussil want of cleanliness.

From the far-off paddy fields you could descry through the intervening foliage, its high palisades and blackened walls. On a nearer view might be seen pieces of plaster of venerable antiquity prepared to bid farewell to their old and weather-beaten tenement. Some rude and unpainted shutter hanging by a single hinge whose companion had left the precincts years before, while in others both hinge and plank had left little trace of their existence and had been supplanted by the less pretentious tribe of *tát* screens. But a small portion of the huge edifice had ever been plastered on the outside. On the favoured region which boasted such decoration, and which no doubt composed the sanctum sanctorum of some great man in the house, if not Mathur Ghose himself, you might descry a few apologies for Venetians, but window panes the giant house had eschewed as too frail a substance to be permitted to ornament its limbs. By far the greater part of the exterior was unplastered, and the dried slime and soot reposed on the mass of bricks in murky grandeur. Not unfrequently a young shoot of a *Bur* or a less noble vegetable had struck its roots in the crevices between the layers of bricks, realizing, rather on an humble scale, the Persian monarch's dream of a hanging garden.

The house was divided into four distinct sections. In front you entered through a pair of massive iron-plated and tar-coloured doors into a spacious courtyard, three sides of which were faced by double-storied verandas of no very respectable height. Opposite the portal arose the lofty and spacious hall of five arches. All around was well plastered, but the return of many a rainy season had variegated the white with streaks of dark, particularly in those regions which were surmounted by spouts for drawing off the water from the top. A mazy suite of dark and damp apartments led from a corner of this part of the building to the inner *mahal*, another quadrangle, on all four sides of which towered double-storied verandas as before. These had indeed a plastering of sand and lime, but few were the pillars which wore these decorations entire, decay aided by the manipulations of idle children having stripped most of them of their coverings. The walls of all the chambers above and below were well striped with numerous streaks of red, white, black, green, all colours of the rainbow, caused by the spittles of such as had found their mouths too much encumbered with *pán* or by some improvident woman servant who had broken the *Gola handi* while it was full of its muddy contents, most frequently by the fingers of her whose pleasant task it had been to prepare the betel leaves, and who had cleverly impressed the walls into her service and had made them act as substitutes for towels. Numerous sketches in charcoal, which showed, we fear, nothing of the conception of Angelo or the tinting of Guido, attested the art or idleness of the wicked boys and ingenious girls who had contrived to while away hungry hours by essays in the arts of designing and of defacing wall. The courtyard, devoid of brick or tile, exposed mother earth in all her vegetable glories. The said vegetable glories, however, were gathered at the four corners leaving in the centre paths in several directions for entrance and exit. Household filth and water had left thick crusts of slime which reposed for ages in unmitigated blackness. A narrow passage, terminated by a small thick door, led you to the third section of the house. This was the kitchen of the household; it had two suites of one-storied apartments on two sides of a vast courtyard where vegetation was much more rank than in the other. Here might be always seen the traces of the havoc daily made on vegetables of the earth, and the fishes of the water by the good dames in charge of this useful department, and here too might be seen the empire of soot in all the majesty of darkness. The fourth department lay behind the kitchen, but apparently all access to it was barred from this side and few were the females of the household who had ever set their feet on it.

A thick and massive door led to the 'godown,' as the *mahal* was called by the males, directly from outside. Bare but high walls, the summits of which were secured against the invasion of human feet by broken fragments of bottles enclosed it on three sides. On the fourth stood the single row of one-storied apartments which it contained. The walls of the apartments were all of unusual thickness, the doors small and plated with iron, and not a window was to be seen. The use to which these 'godowns' were put was known to be that of storehouses for all sorts of things. A vast garden of *Supari* trees interspersed with *Bakul*, stood on one side of the building, and being enclosed on all sides by brick walls and containing a well-filled tank in the middle, composed the *khirki* of the household. The passage to it lay through the precincts of the cook, from which a small door opened on the garden.

The reader will be good enough to ascend in our company, through a flight of dark and narrow stairs of solid brickwork to the upper story of the *andarmahal*, properly so called, that which formed the second section of the large edifice a view of which we have placed before him. We invite him to enter a no less unapproached and unapproachable region than the bedchamber of Mathur Ghose himself. The polished plastering of the walls was clean enough, though not unfrequently could stains and scratches be seen defacing its purity. A little towards one end of the room stood a massive and high cot of teak wood on the uncovered floor over which loosely hung a striped gauge curtain, rather disproportioned to the wooden frame. A few huge almirahs and chest of drawers of the same material, the varnish of which had considerably been soiled by time and rough usage, lined the foot of the walls opposite to the cot. One or two escritoirs, as well as some common country boxes and chests decorated with enormous brass plates across their lids and on the edges, and ornamented with semi-lunes of *Chandan*, completed the wooden furniture of the room. Two paintings of the largest size, from one of which lowered the grim black figure of Kali, and on the other of which was displayed the crab-like form of Durga, faced each other from high position on two opposite walls.

On the two remaining walls, and placed lower than the terrific Kali and the gorgeous Durga, might be seen arrayed a few specimens of European art, and the exquisite conception of the Virgin and Child might itself be seen adorning the chamber the inmates of which had little knowledge what the artist's genius and engraver's skill had strove to represent. A female of about twenty-eight years of age sat on a window sill. Her face and figure were still handsome. Her complexion was that of a brunette and her eyes were large, dark, and shone with a mild and almost benignant lustre. Beyond this there was nothing particularly remarkable in her countenance, unless it was the expression of sweetness and amiability that never abandoned it. A clean *sari* covered her rounded limbs and frame, but not her head, which was now uncovered; and the crisp and shining tresses of hair, rendered still more so by recent ablution, fell loosened on the back, scattered and uncombed, but still beautiful from their irregular luxuriance. Golden ornaments of great value but rather of lighter make than usual, graced her ears, her neck, her bosom and arms and wrists. For some reason or other the fine and delicate circumference of the *noth* was absent from her nostril and cheek, but the tinkling *malls* maintained their place in her ankles. A few long ringlets of human hair tied to the window grating furnished occupation to her little fingers as she tried to weave them into mat oft-coveted object of young girls, the hair string. A child of about ten years in whose exquisitely handsome features might be discerned a likeness to the elder female, sat by her and proved by the interest she took in the occupation of the latter that it was to tie in bondage her own wild locks that the product of her mother's delicate labours was destined. A little removed from them, modest, confused, melancholy, sat another woman who however needs no introduction. Suki's mother—the mother-in-law of whose felicity the reader has had her own description—had redeemed her promise by leading the reluctant Matangini to the presence of Mathur's first or eldest wife—the female who was weaving the hair strings for her daughter.

A dialogue was being carried on between Mathur's wife and Matangini in a low voice, while Suki's mother was pouring on a loose prattle without any apprehensions of interrupting either. We need not detain the reader with a detail of either the dialogue or the prattle, as of their purport we will do him the justice to presume he has already some conception. Suki's mother had rendered her mistress acquainted with the unfortunate position of the refugee, so far as she had gathered them from the rather unfaithful version of Kanak, embellishing the narrative with a good many interpolations of her own, and a few observations on connubial felicity as exemplified by the lot of her own happy daughter. The good dame rightly judged that such embellishments and interpolations would do no harm to the interests of her protegée; while at the same time they would afford a varied field for the display of her own powers of harangue. Matangini had not the heart to disclose the real circumstances of her misfortune, especially in the presence of the servant. She therefore unwillingly passed over most points in the good woman's narrative in silence, intending to undeceive her new friend, should it be necessary for her to trespass long on her kindness, on a future occasion, and with so much reserve as might be necessary to conceal the depth to which her husband had fallen. Mathur's wife gave her the warmest and most cordial welcome, rendering it apparent by an intuitive generosity of heart wholly dissimilar to acquired polish of manners, that she rather pressed an invitation than afforded shelter. One step, however, was indispensable before Matangini could be enrolled a member of the household; Mathur Ghose's permission had to be obtained. With the intention of requesting it, she deputed the still eloquent parent of the happy daughter to the *sadar* to request her husband to step inside for a moment, without, however, mentioning her object before Matangini. After a few minutes, her husband entered the chamber, the wife drew her cloth over her head, and Matangini, as etiquette required, stepped out, not however without meeting a fixed gaze of recognition and wonder from the eyes of the master of the house.

14

BETWEEN RIVAL CHAMBERS

Containing a dissertation on connubial warfare.—A siege and a dubious capitulation.

Mathur Ghose, as our reader had no doubt guessed in the course of the previous chapter, had the good fortune or misfortune of being blessed or incommoded by double ties of matrimony and was the master or slave or both of his two wives. Tara, the eldest, has already been introduced; Champak, the younger, was Tara's junior by not less than eight years. She possessed decided superiority over her rival in the regularity of her features and in the blooming fairness of her complexion. To this, nature had added a witchery of coquettish grace that marked the movements of this proud and insolent beauty which won for her the envied distinction of the proudest damsel in the vicinity. Proud and imperious, Champak ever ruled the household with the authority of its sole mistress. The household approached her with fear and perhaps with a secret feeling of dislike, for often it was that her naughty temper made them feel that every fair face is not the reflector of a generous heart. And, in spite of the rival and superior claims of Tara, she was the real as well as the apparent mistress of the house. Mathur Ghose was not perhaps formed by nature to love and be loved; affection was not certainly the ruling passion of his heart, but the power of woman and her beauty have their influence upon all, and Mathur Ghose was fond of his wife. Sensibility and refinement of the heart lend to the passion of love the form of a fervent and etherialized feeling which finds its gratification in the communings of heart with heart; while, in grosser natures, it degenerates into the yearnings of desire or perhaps into a blind obedience to the mystic power of female loveliness; but the strength of the passion can be equally great in either case. It was not strange therefore that Mathur loved Champak, or if we may not use the word love, was fond of her blindly and ardently. The master who bent with an iron will the interest of all who surrounded him to Subserve his own—was but a slave to the will of this coquette. To Tara, whose sweetness and patience put it beyond his power to be offended—he was indifferent, too much so perhaps to be ever unkind.

Tara had procured an easy assent from her husband to her proposal that the wife of Rajmohan should find a shelter in their house. 'Food and clothing,' Mathur said in reply, 'are not scarce in my house, under the blessing of the gods and the Brahmans, and if the woman is as you say of good character, let her remain here as long as she chooses.' But Tara's simple heart had not reckoned upon an opposition which certainly was powerful enough to counteract her benevolence. Champak liked not that it should be under the auspices of her rival that the stranger should obtain a footing in the household.

The sun was shedding its mellowed parting beams on the house of Mathur Ghose, and the day which had been ushered in amidst the gloomy deeds which threatened the fate of Matangini was hastening to a close. The slanting rays fell at intervals on an open veranda, on the second floor. Tara was seated on the bare ground and was employed in tying the hair of her daughter into a *khompa* the knots and bends of which however satisfied neither herself nor the child. Matangini sat close by answering with reserve to some very provoking and impertinent questions, which Champak, employed in painting her little feet with the lac-dye, by the aid of a barber's garrulous wife, was pouring upon her, without the consciousness that a refugee to whom her husband had afforded shelter from mere compassion and whom she herself could turn out any moment, could ever entertain reluctance to answer questions coming from herself direct. Matangini was answering with meekness and reserve, which however had merely the effect of provoking further impertinence from the haughty beauty. Tara saw the vexation of her protégée and delicately interfered by drawing off the attention of both.

'I can't tie this child's *khompa*, though you see I have been trying my hand at it since noon,' said she addressing Matangini, 'you can do it better perhaps. If you will only show me how to turn this *binuni*,

I think I can do the rest.' Matangini asked to be permitted to tie the braids for the day herself.

'I do not think I can do it well,' she said, 'but I will do what I can.'

Matangini took her position behind the child and taking up the braids in her hands, began to untie them and form new ones.

'Aha!' said Champak, 'I fear our sister will make only one of her Western country *khompas*. It is best as it is.'

'If I succeed in tying a *khompa* as they do in our part of the country, returned Matangini, 'this beautiful child will look twice more beautiful.'

'No, no—you must not do it,' rejoined Champak, 'that is the way in which disreputable females dress their hair—it does not look seemly in good people's children.'

'Oh fie!' interposed Tara, 'Is beauty ever disdained because sometimes a bad woman is beautiful? At that rate, sister, you should have disfigured your own fine countenance long before this. No, no, because bad woman may have a fine knot of hair, that is no reason why a good woman should have none. Tie the knot as you please, sister,' concluded she, addressing Matangini.

Champak replied not, but it was evident from the sullen looks she assumed that Tara's compliment had not been enough to make her forget that she was refused her own way. The tread of heavy slipshod feet was just then heard downstairs, and Mathur Ghose soon appeared in the veranda. Champak drew her cloth over her face down to the very chin and lightly tripped to her own chamber, her *malls* tinkling as she ran; Tara drew her cloth over her face also but not to the same depth, and slowly rose to retire; Matangini covered herself also, and stood aside. Mathur Ghose stopped to speak with his daughter to whom he addressed a few ordinary questions. Champak who was watching him from behind the door observed, and jealous wife as she was, observed it with dismay, that though he addressed the child alone his eyes occasionally wandered with an eager glance towards the veiled form of the stranger. Mathur Ghose passed on to the apartment of his younger wife, and the interrupted females resumed their occupations with the exception of Champak whom her husband found in the apartment.

Champak well knew that the steps of her husband would seek her there, and she herself sought an interview. But to avoid the appearance of having sought her room in the expectation of meeting him, she hastily opened a box as soon as she saw him leave the veranda, and busied herself in taking out of it some choice spices used in preparing the betel leaf for mastication. Mathur Ghose saw the floor strewed with many a silver, horn, or wooden *kauta* without end or aim, and his wife little inclined to take any notice of his entrance. Her face was still partly covered with her cloth, her back was turned towards her husband and the work of strewing the floor with little boxes of cardamoms, cinnamon, cloves, almonds, went on bravely progressing. After waiting for a few moments in silence, Mathur observed, 'What is the matter now? Some storm brewing I suppose?'

Champak answered not, but went on strewing the floor with *kautas* after *kautas*.

'Aha, I see it,' said Mathur, 'now tell me for what offence I have to pay the penalty.'

But still Champak did not reply. She now began to gather up the *kautas* as if she had found what she sought, and having replaced them in the box and locked them up she turned towards the door to go out.

'That won't do, my life!' said Mathur as he arrested her progress by catching her by the arm, 'this cursed *ghomta* has no business here' and he pushed back the cloth from her face.

'Why do you detain me?' asked Champak, casting on him a look of high displeasure.

'Tell me, my life, what have I done that you wear this look?'

'Let me go,' she said, though of course no entreaty was needed to obtain her release as her husband held her arm by a light and loving grasp, and she could have had her pleasure if only she were so minded, 'Let me go, I have business.'

'You have business, my lily face? What can this business be?' enquired Mathur, laughing.

'I have to prepare *pán*,' responded she with the same irritable look.

'Do it then here and let me have some,' said he.

'Let me go,' said she again.

'Why, what is it?' said Mathur fondly, 'Name but my offence to you and I promise you expiation.'

'Offence to me,' said she in the same pettish manner, 'what offence can you be guilty of towards me? What am I that I can be offended with you? You can do what you please without offending anybody—and I am nobody.'

'*Sabash*,' said he, 'this is anger indeed! But tell me, queen of my life, what is that I must undo, and I will undo it immediately.'

'Go to the wife you love,' she said 'and she may tell you if there is anything to undo, and undo it then.—What matters to you this wishes of a poor woman who no further trespasses on your bounty than to live in your household which even strangers are permitted to do?'

'Oh! can it be *that*?' asked Mathur, now comprehending how matters stood—'are you angry that I have taken the poor woman to my household at the'—he would have added—'at the intercession of your rival,'—but he forebore and stopped short.

'It is your house', returned she, still with apparent displeasure, but now glad at heart that he had divined the cause of her displeasure, 'you can admit anybody you please.'

'But seriously,' he added with earnestness of manner, 'Let go womanishness now and tell me truly how you can object to my affording temporary shelter to such a forlorn creature.'

'Forlorn creature?' returned Champak, 'why if she has done ill, she has deserved to be turned out.'

'And how do you know she has done ill?'

'Why, do you think she would be turned out for nothing? Do people turn out their wives from caprice?'

'Yes—it may be she was wrong—it may also be her husband was wrong. But still it cannot be wrong to give her shelter in the house in any case.'

'You can do your pleasure,' she returned sulkily again. 'Why do you ask my opinion about it at all?'

'There again! Fie, a woman should be more kind.'

'Yes, kind to those who deserve kindness. But is it right to be kind to all alike, be she good or bad?'

'But still you cannot be sure she has not been more unfortunate than anything else, and report speaks very favourably of her conduct.'

'Report!' said Champak with a contemptuous swing of her large fine *noth*, 'you have picked up all your information on the point from Suki's mother's little gossip and you dignify her garrulous lies with the name of *report*.'

'Why, have you heard any one speak otherwise than well of her?' inquired Mathur rather surprised.

'Women always hear more of each other than men,' said she.

'What have you heard?' Mathur again inquired.

'What propriety is this in you,' replied she a little archly now, 'to enquire about the secrets of woman.'

Mathur Ghose felt vexed. From whatever motives, he evidently desired that Matangini should enjoy the benefit of his protection, and he felt vexed, as we have said, at this unexpected resistance from one who, he was aware, was pretty well accustomed to have her own will.

'At least you will admit,' he added after musing for some time, 'you will admit that it looks very bad to turn out a kinswoman from the house, for you know she is a kinswoman of ours. Has she not a claim upon us?'

'She is our kinswoman through another kinswoman' was the ready reply. 'Why has she not sought shelter with her sister? Are we nearer or dearer to her than her sister? She dares not perhaps to seek shelter with those who know her well.'

'You are very ungenerous,' returned Mathur in vexation of spirit, 'what can you have to object to an unfriended woman ? Is there want of food or raiment in my house?'

'No,' returned she proudly, 'at least I shall not claim my share if she become welcome to them. Send me to my father's house and let her live here. My father is not one who will be pleased to see his daughter the inmate of a house in which such a woman lives.'

'What is all this again?' Mathur said, becoming irritated.

'Send me to my father's house,' she replied.

'You know I cannot part with you. Leave off childishness' returned he, softening.

'Then part with that woman,' was the reply.

'Part with that woman; why, what is she to me that there is any difficulty in my parting with her? Well, I will think of it.'

With these words Mathur left the room, resolved to prevaricate and deceive his wife till her mind should change.

That evening when he again returned to the chamber, an extraordinary spectacle presented itself to his eyes. In a corner of the room, far apart from his bedstead, another bed had been neatly prepared on an humble couch which had been pitched up from the room for service.

'What is that for?' asked Mathur, as the additional bed caught his eye. Champak spoke not, but throwing herself on it, went to sleep without deigning a reply.

Our readers will guess what a night the uxorious Mathur Ghose passed. When he rose next morning and went out to his *baithak khana*, he observed a visitor waiting for him, who said he was Rajmohan Ghose. He explained to Mathur the object of his visit to be that having obtained intelligence that his wife who had left his house on pretence of a quarrel was here, he had come over to request that she be made to return. Mathur could not well refuse to restore a wife to her husband, a course which, he had been taught, was become necessary to him to pursue on other considerations, if he had any relish for domestic peace and the smiles of Champak.

When Matangini was informed that she must depart, her blood froze within her as she reflected on the fate that awaited her. More dead than alive, she followed the steps of Suki's mother, who was entrusted with the duty of escorting her home. Tara accompanied her as far as the postern gate and would gladly have gone further if she could. She bade her farewell with sorrow and heartily wished her peace and oblivion of past disagreements with her husband.

15

CONSULTATIONS AND COUNCIL

The wild and lovely shores of the Madhumati are covered even in the vicinity of well-inhabited villages by a tall rank grass almost impervious to human feet. Such a spot of peculiar and almost frightful solitude lay a little to the south of Radhaganj. There the impervious grass was intermixed with an equally high and impervious range of cane-bushes and other underwood which extended far into the land from the margin of the river. Were there a site in the vicinity which commanded an unbroken view of the whole area covered by the interminable underwood, not a single interruption could have been discerned to its luxuriant uniformity. One narrow footpath seemed to present the only evidence that human footsteps had ever disturbed this dark habitation of venomous reptiles. But even this footpath could be discerned upon the closest observation and for a short distance only, and then every trace of its further progress was lost. To the practised eye of those, however, who were wont to thread its maze, it presented the only guidance to a little hovel of straw which stood in the very heart of the jungle. The roof of the hovel, a little elevated above the general height of the bushes, was carefully concealed from the view of curious eyes outside by so drawing off and arranging the twigs of adjacent boughs that the whole thatch wore the appearance of the top of a bush higher than the rest. The inside of this small and wretched habitation, if such it could be called, was gloomy and damp. The walls were of bamboo and *darmá*, and two or three *darmás* were spread over the humid floor. Blackened pots and cooking utensils were stowed in one corner of the hovel, though apparently they were not often put to use. It was still early in the morning and the streaks of sunbeams that had penetrated inside through crevices had the length that slanting rays alone could possess. Its only inhabitants were men of a deep black complexion and of a stature and muscular formation that promised vast strength. A short and coarse cloth of small width lightly covered the waist of each, but their legs and thighs and the rest of their dark bodies were completely naked. *Latties* and swords lay scattered beside them and betokened that their profession was anything but peaceful. The noxious fume of *ganja* which was being smoked by the two by turns, filled the whole cabin. They were engaged in conversing with each other in a guarded tone which the secluded locality made little necessary.

'What will the business bring?' asked one in whom the reader will recognize Bhiku.

'A large sum,' responded his companion who was no other than the sardar, 'full five thousand rupees. It is as good as a night's affair, nay better, for we go shares with nobody.'

'Bosh' ejaculated Bhiku, his dull eyes glistening with joy, 'but why will you not attempt it on the road when that lawyer carries it with him? How else can you get hold of it elsewhere!'

'Because you know that accursed wench, Rajmohan's wife, had overheard me talking to her husband about it,' replied the sardar, 'and has informed Madhav that we wanted it. He has warning and means to send the paper under good escort. And we are only two. Do you now understand, you monkey?'

'But how can we get at it otherwise?' observed the other. 'Two of us cannot force the house.'

'Leave that to me, leave that to me. Wit will succeed where strength fails.'

Bhiku pulled a long puff at his *chillum* and then leisurely sent out the smoke in curls before him. Then shaking his head he observed, 'No, no, sardar, I don't see how it can be done. I tell you one thing, will not our employer advance us one of the five thousands he has promised? It will be a more profitable business then; he cannot find us out when we leave this place.'

'Do you think him such a fool?' replied the sardar. 'Do hear what conditions the sharp bargainer has proposed. He gives us one thousand when we can show him the paper to be in our possession; we receive three thousands in all when we deliver it to his hands. And only when the suit is won, which will surely be if the will is destroyed, will we get the other two thousands.'

'But, then, tell me how we are to rob it.'

'No, no, no! you will spoil the business if you know it beforehand. Cunning Rajmohan may make you give it out to him. Follow me as my shadow and rest assured we will succeed.'

'Rajmohan cheat me that way!' exclaimed Bhiku with some enthusiasm, but immediately lowering his voice he said, 'Hush I hear footsteps approaching.'

A cry like that of screech owls but evidently uttered in a human voice, was heard from within the jungle.

'It is only Rajmohan,' observed the sardar and responded by a similar cry. Rajmohan soon made his appearance at the hovel.

'What news, Raj?' asked the sardar.

'All is well,' replied Rajmohan, 'I have got back my wife.'

'Indeed! how was it? Where was she?' asked he with some show of satisfaction.

'Well it is rather strange,' said Rajmohan. 'Instead of going to her sister where did she go, think you?'

'Where?' enquired both the banditti.

'Why, did not I think she would go there? The house of Mathur Ghose himself.'

'Indeed, and what has she been saying?'

'I believe, nothing, so far as I could gather. I had some talk with the domestics on purpose, but I believe they had no suspicion of anything.'

'Still,' said the sardar, lowering his eyes while a fierce glance shot therefrom, 'we must get rid of her.'

'Why, consider,' said Rajmohan, 'consider if she may not be spared.'

'Ah! was I right when I said you were—'

'Hear me sardar, hear me out,' interrupted Rajmohan with vehemence. 'I hate that wretched woman more than you can ever do. Had I found her out that morning, you would have seen I am no lover. But I confess now that my blood has cooled, I have not the courage and cruelty to do such a deed. Besides, what we feared she had not done; she neither went to Madhav Ghose's house, nor made a noise of last night's affair. If she has not done it today, what reason is there that she will do it tomorrow.'

'Well,' said the sardar, musing, 'I have a place and it may suit both your mind and ours.'

'What is it?' inquired Rajmohan.

'Pack up, take your beautiful wife with you, and come and live with us at Mitguntie.'

'And lead the life of a robber?'

'Yes. Are you not one?'

'Perhaps, but it is impossible for me to be one by reputation.'

'You decline to go?'

'Yes, I have others to take care of, besides this wretched wife. Can I lead the life of a robber with such a family?'

'Have we not our families there?'

'Yes—but then mine must not know that they live with—'

'Peace!' exclaimed the sardar, interrupting him authoritatively, 'If you want to join us you can easily send off your sister and her children to her husband,—poor husband or rich husband, it is no look-out of yours; and as to your aunt, she is the aunt of many others like yourself and can shift for herself.'

Rajmohan still hesitated. A long debate ensued, but the threats of the sardar joined to his own wish to leave the neighbourhood of Madhav Ghose for ever, at length prevailed on Rajmohan, and he consented.

It was yet wanting to noon when Rajmohan returned home to bathe himself and break his fast.

The first person who met his eyes was his sister Kishori.

'Kishori,' he said to her, 'tell the wretched woman to come before me. I shall teach her how to run away again from my house.'

'Whom do you mean, brother?' enquired Kishori.

'Whom? why, your sister-in-law,' exclaimed Rajmohan, irritated at the question. 'Where can your senses be gone?'

'My sister-in-law is not here, you know,' replied Kishori.

'Not here!' ejaculated Rajmohan in surprise. 'Has she not returned in the morning?'

'You said you would send her here from the 'Elder House',' returned Kishori, 'but you have not done so.'

Rajmohan started up in anger and surprise. 'It is false!' he cried,

'I myself saw her coming in that woman Suki's mother's company.'

'That's strange,' replied Kishori, 'but she has not returned. Ask anybody here—none has seen her.' Rajmohan flew like a tiger round the house and ransacked every part of it, but could not find Matangini skulking anywhere.

'Run,' he cried to his sister, 'run to her sister's house; the wretch has sheltered herself there no doubt. Stop—ask aunt to go over to Kanak's house and look for her there. She may be there probably. I shall keep watch for her here.'

Both Kishori and her aunt started on their errands, but both returned unsuccessfully. Vexation, rage, and surprise bewildered the disappointed husband. With angry words and gestures he again compelled his sister to undertake another fatiguing journey in the midday to learn by inquiry in Mathur Ghose's household if Matangini had not returned. The obedient Kishori executed her commission with patience and fidelity, but could not succeed in bringing any news of her sister-in-law.

16

WHAT BEFELL OUR HERO

Three days had elapsed since the occurrences of the last chapter. The night was dark, and the brilliant and trembling light in Madhav's room, which could be seen from afar, showed in rich contrast with the impenetrable gloom beyond. Madhav Ghose was alone. He sat reclining on a mahogany couch covered with satin. A single, but well-fed light illumined the chamber. Some two or three English books were scattered over the couch, and one of these Madhav held in his hand but he hardly read it. He sat with his abstracted gaze fixed on the dark but star-besprinkled heavens which were visible through the open windows. His pensive thoughts rambled over a variety of subjects. He feared the uncertain result of his lawsuit, and he was aware that there was everything to fear from the unprincipled agency employed by cunning and clever antagonists, whom he had neither the will nor the power to fight with their own weapons. And should they succeed what was to be the future? Then again he thought of the strange and unknown fate of Matangini. He had been informed of her retreat to Mathur Ghose's house, her return thence, and of her sudden disappearance. He was ignorant of the events which had driven her to seek shelter under a stranger's roof, except of what rumour gave, but Madhav knew Matangini too well to suspect that a light cause could have driven this brave-hearted girl to a step which published her own unhappiness and her failure to evince the patience of a woman and a wife. He well understood and appreciated the reasons which had deterred her from seeking shelter in her sister's house when shelter had become necessary to her. But he was unable to account for her leaving home, and still less for her sudden and strange disappearance. That Matangini had come to know of the conspiracy formed against his property by dacoits and that she had given the timely warning which frustrated their purpose, drove Madhav into a thousand torturing conjectures as to her fate, but each surmise he rejected as wild and unreasonable. Certain he was, so well did he know her character, that whatever might have been her misfortune, she had not been guilty of a dishonourable desertion of her household. Assured, therefore, in his mind that she had come by some misfortune, his heart underwent excruciating torments. The deep and tender feeling which he had stifled in his breast at such cost, seemed to burn with redoubled fervour. His thoughts long dwelt on the remembrance of that parting scene; he recalled every word that she had uttered, and tears rushed to his eyes. Long did he muse and weep in silence. At length he rose from his seat and, as if to forget his reflections in the touch of the balmy air that blew outside, he went out to the veranda. His reflections pursued him there. Leaning against the balustrade, his head supported on the palm of his hand, his eye fixed on the starry heavens and the range of tall *Devdaru* trees that stood in bold relief against the blue vault, he again lost himself in a melancholy reverie. As he gazed and gazed, a curious object caught his attention. A protuberance on the trunk of a *Devdaru* which stood out in relief against the sky, and on which he for some time fixed his listless gaze, seemed suddenly to vanish. It is a singular trait in the human mind that when most intensely employed in brooding over its own gloomy feelings, the most indifferent circumstance will sometimes arrest its attention. The disappearance of the protruding object on the circumference of the tree, struck Madhav as singular. He was sure that the remnant of the stem of a lopped off branch, or a knotted protuberance on the wood, was no longer where he had seen it against the sky. Not attaching however any importance to the circumstance at the moment, and too busy with his own thoughts, he again resumed the subject which lay nearest his heart. A few moments after, however, his eyes again wandered to the same tree, and now he thought he could see the object once more where it was. His curiosity being now slightly awakened, he looked at it for some time with more care than before. Suddenly again the object disappeared. It distinctly exhibited motion in its disappearance. 'What can it be?' he thought. Perhaps, he surmised, it was an owl or other night-bird sleeping on its perch among twigs invisible to him in darkness and distance. Again, however, the object reappeared. Madhav could not distinguish in its form the outlines of that of either bat or bird, and it rather seemed to possess more of the shape and size of a human head than of anything else. The outlines could be clearly discerned against the sky, and he even fancied he saw part of the neck protruding from behind the tree. It appeared however on a height in the tree to which it was not usual for men to ascend. As the object appeared and disappeared again and again, his curiosity or apprehension or both, were excited. He thought of going to examine. Usually led on by first impulses, the thought no sooner struck him, than he decided on going himself to see who lurked behind the tree, if any did lurk. He armed himself with a small silver-handled sword that hung in his parlour, and descended the stairs. He again closely looked at the tree from his front gate, as the row of the *Devdarus* lay very near it, but could see nothing there where he had before perceived the strange object. He looked around but without meeting with what he sought. It was therefore necessary to go to the foot of the tree. Scarcely had he reached it when a wild shriek like that of a screech owl startled him, and at the same moment his sword was wrested from him by a vigorous blow. Before he could turn to see who and where was this sudden assailant, the large and rough palm of a vigorous hand was laid upon his mouth. At the same instant a heavy body fell upon the earth from the tree, and Madhav Ghose saw before him a tall and sombre figure, vigorous and well-armed.

'Bind him, this is unexpected,' said the man in a whisper to the one who had disarmed Madhav, 'gag him first.'

The other man took out a napkin and some rope from his waist, and, gagging Madhav well with the napkin, proceeded to bind his limbs, while he who had descended from the tree, held him down. Madhav who saw the uselessness of struggling, and was powerless to call for help, quietly submitted.

'Now, take him up in your arms; you can singly carry him away,' said the latter comer in the same low tone.

The other took up Madhav in his large arms and bore off the unfortunate young man without much difficulty. The other followed, and the two left the spot without having given the smallest alarm to the household.

17

THE VIGILANCE OF LOVE

At the hour when this strange turn of fortune overtook the hero of our tale, for such we believe the reader thinks Madhav, Mathur Ghose was resting, or, to be more accurate, endeavouring to rest in Tara's chamber. Tara was seated on the couch close by his reclining form, with a little delicate straw punkha in her hand, with which she patiently and affectionately endeavoured to lull to sleep the disturbed spirit of her husband. Her efforts however did not seem successful, for though Mathur was silent and his eyes closed, an occasional sigh which now and then escaped him, betrayed an anxiety of mind proceeding from some cause unknown to Tara. She at length broke silence and spoke.

'You do not sleep,' said she.

'No I cannot; this you see is not my hour to sleep.'

'Then why come to sleep at all? I fear to speak, but will you forgive me if I am bold?'

'What have you to say?'

'You are unhappy; may one who sincerely loves you learn the cause?'

Mathur gave a start. Then checking himself he answered with an assumed lightness of air which was too transparent to deceive the eyes of affection, 'Why, who told you that? What have I to grieve for?'

'Do not try to deceive me, love,' returned Tara in a tone of earnest but affectionate remonstrance. 'I know you care little for me or my love, but to a woman, her husband is—I cannot say what he is not. Deceive the world, but you cannot deceive me.'

'You are surely mad to think me wretched,' said Mathur, in a tone that most significantly contradicted his words, 'What put that fancy in you?'

'Yourself' replied she. 'Listen: you have manythings to think of; your *taluqs*, your lawsuits, your rents, your *kacharis*, your houses, gardens, servants, family, and of much more: I have nothing to care for, but my husband and my daughter. Do you wonder then that for the last three days I have noted before others, that your step had lost its wonted pride? That your eyes wandered and had a strange look; that you spoke less often, and that when you smiled, your smile came not from your heart; nay, can you suppose that a mother's eye would forget to note that her child met not from its father his former warm embrace? Yes, often during these three days has Bindu held your finger, and played round your knee, and you have not spoken to her; and even my sister,' here an arch smile, which passed off as soon as it came, momentarily interrupted the earnestness of Tara's manner, 'and even my sister has pouted and stormed, and you have not listened with your wonted courtesy: and that sigh! Nay, can you longer deny that something troubles you?'

Mathur did not reply.

'Do you not think me worthy of sharing your griefs?' continued Tara, seeing that her husband did not reply. 'I know you do not love me.' Tara hesitated. Mathur still continued silent. He gazed steadfastly on the angel purity of his affectionate wife's countenance; his bosom slowly heaved, and a sigh escaped him.

'You are unhappy; conceal it not, deceive me not,' sobbed rather than uttered Tara, with an intensity of agony in the stifled tones of her voice beyond the power of language, 'Deceive not, conceal not, tell me all. If my life will purchase your happiness, you can yet be happy.'

Mathur still continued mute.

He no longer jested, prevaricated, or denied, but maintained a sombre and determined silence, and the look of cold and hypocritical levity with which he was presently attempting to evade the questions of his wife, had given place to a serious earnest gaze which seemed to seek and yet repel sympathy. Tears rolled down the cheek of Tara as she perceived, with a woman's sensitiveness and a woman's depth of feeling, this unusual change in the expression of her husband's face.

'Cursed be the hour of my birth!' burst from the lips of the mortified wife. 'Not even *this*! I would lay down my life to make you happy, but cursed be the hour when I was born! I cannot even know what it is that makes you unhappy.'

Mathur was touched. 'It is useless now to conceal from you that

I am unhappy,' he confessed at last, 'but do not grieve that I confide not my troubles to you. Human ears will not hear them.'

As Tara heard these words, a fleeting expression of intense pain shot across her pallid but noble features, but the next moment she stood calm and apparently without emotion.

'Give me one poor request then,' said she now calmly, 'will you promise?' A wild and hollow shriek like that of a screech owl interrupted her words. Her husband started to his feet at the sound.

'Why do you start?' enquired his wife. 'It is a screech owl only, though certainly the sound was fearful to hear.'

The sound came borne once again in still more fearful notes upon the wind. Before Tara could speak, Mathur bounded out of the room.

Tara was surprised. She was certain the shriek was from a screech owl, or if not, of nothing more fearful, and to her mind, there was nothing in it to apprehend except as a sound of ill omen, which however people daily hear and tolerate. She had also some perception that the sound they had heard, rather bore a resemblance to that of the night-bird that presented its unmistakable notes in their reality. Her curiosity was awakened, and she came out of her apartment. Finding that her husband had gone downstairs, she ascended the staircase which led to the terrace overhead in order to see what had so much startled him. Looking earnestly and long in the direction whence the sound had proceeded, she could discern nothing. Thinking therefore that the sound could have been nothing more than what it had appeared to be, and that the bird itself perhaps sat concealed in some leafy branch or invisible cornice, and also that her husband had left her in that abrupt manner only perhaps to avoid yielding to the emotion which she had seen rising palpably in his bosom, she thought the matter unworthy of further attention, and was in the act of returning, when the unusual sight of a human figure, evidently that of a man too, and not of a female inmate of the house, issuing out of the postern gate, caught her eyes. A second glance convinced Tara that it was her husband, making swiftly towards the jungles. She was staggered. A cold tremor seized her limbs, and she felt overpowered and ready to faint. A thousand vague fears and harrowing suspicions swept over her mind. She loved her unworthy husband too well to think him the agent in some dark or unhallowed purpose, but gloomy conjectures of approaching dangers and of some fearful risk which her husband ran, rushed through her mind. She stood rivetted to the spot. Bending over the low parapet, which surrounded the edges of the terrace, she gazed and gazed and followed his motions with distracted eyes. Suddenly she lost all view of him. She still gazed and turned her eyes on all sides, but could no longer perceive his vigorous form gliding amid the darkness. Her fears increased tenfold. Long, long did she gaze in this attitude, silent and unmoved like a marble-formed ornament of the huge edifice. She was on the point of giving up the search in despair when a last and sweeping glance met the object of her solicitude as he lightly leaped into the small iron-door which opened outside from that tenantless part of the house already known to the reader as the *godown mahal*.

Tara's heart felt greatly relieved when she saw her husband within the shelter of his own roof. Still her apprehensions were not entirely quieted. This nocturnal and clandestine walk outside and a visit at such an hour to a part of the house rarely visited by any, coupled with his previous anxiety and loss of spirits and the ominous sound of the night-bird which still rung in Tara's ears, spoke some approaching misfortune. Tara did not leave her watch but continued anxiously waiting for the reappearance of her husband. But again she watched in vain. More than half an hour elapsed, still her husband did not repass through the secret gate. She felt tired with standing and as she was more sure of her husband's personal safety, she at last for the present descended and returned to her apartment.

A sudden light had flashed upon her. Would not this furnish a clue to her husband's secret? Her resolution was now formed.

In the course of a few moments, her husband re-entered the room. His manner was restless and uneasy, but there was exultation in his eyes. Tara spoke not a word to him of what she had seen.

18

CAPTORS AND CAPTIVE

Let us shift the scene. A solitary and feeble lamp lighted a gloomy and low-roofed room, whose sombre and massive walls looked more grim in the dim light. The room was as small in area as it was low in altitude, and altogether wore the appearance more of a habitation destined for the reception of criminals than of an ordinary residence of any who could find another shelter. A low small thick door of iron shut the only entrance to this gloomy apartment, and was furnished with bolts and bars of a proportionately massive character. As if still suspicious of the character of the security of this cell, the architect had taken the unusual precaution of plating the very walls with a coat of iron. The black metal frowned by the dim and flickering light as if it inclosed a living grave. There was another passage or resemblance of a passage from this room besides the iron door already mentioned. It was another door, precisely of the same character, placed in one of the corners and leading apparently to a sideroom; but it was even of smaller dimensions, so much so that a child had to creep through it. The gloomy apartment was without a single article of furniture. It was totally empty. One solitary individual, the sole occupant, was pacing it in the dim and fitful light of the single lamp. It was Madhav Ghose.

Our readers need not be apprised that this was the place where Madhav had been deposited by his captors. But his captors were not there. The hour was about deep midnight. The bolts were drawn outside; and Madhav Ghose for the present at least was shut up in a living grave. Still his mien was not stricken down or dejected or hopeless. Resentment more than any other feeling was foremost in his mind; and as he continued unceasingly to pace the silent chamber with a lofty step, he gathered resolution to meet the worst he had to expect from the desperate character of his captors.

At length a sound was heard of a key turning in the lock which closed the door outside. Next followed the sound of the bolt and bar and chain being cautiously unfastened, the massive doors slowly creaked on their hinges, and his two savage captors silently entered the room, shutting the door after them with the same carefulness.

Madhav cast a glance of unbounded resentment but, without taking any other notice of their entrance, continued pacing the chamber as before. The sardar and Bhiku seated themselves by the lamp, and taking out a little *ganja* from a bag which the latter carried in his waist, as well as a small and almost headless *kalika*, began pounding the drug on his palm by the strong pressure of his thumb, preparatory to its ignition. The sardar trimmed the lamp and, while thus employed, observed sarcastically, 'The Baboo seems particularly submissive tonight.'

Madhav stopped short in his walk, and faced the miscreant; his features worked as if he would reply, but he suddenly turned without saying anything and resumed his previous employment of pacing the chamber. The *ganja* was now ready for the *kalika*, and it being duly ignited, the robbers commenced smoking. The silent contempt of the prisoner now began to irritate his captors, who had hitherto been restrained from offering needless insult by that habitual awe and respect which compels even the most reckless among the vulgar to observe a proper distance to those entitled to deference. The sardar was no vulgar ruffian, as our readers have doubtless perceived, but the lofty mien and stern deportment of the prisoner had restrained even his petulance. But now the fumes of the *ganja* loosened his spirits.

'Baboo,' said he with a malicious smile on his lips, 'will you deign a pull at the *kalika*? It is done exactly to a millionaire's taste, I can promise you.'

Madhav again disdained replying, and the discomfited sardar went on smoking, carrying on a horribly obscene conversation with his associate.

'Will you tell me what your master intends doing with me?' at length inquired Madhav, speaking for the first time.

'We have no master,' answered the sardar gruffly, without further interruption to the smoking and the obscene dialogue.

'Your employer then?' asked Madhav again.

'We have no employer,' said the sardar in the same tone, and went on pulling at the *kalika*.

'He who bade you do this deed?' said Madhav.

'No one bade us,' said the sardar.

'No one? Have you seized and confined me for play?'

'Not for play,' retorted the sardar. 'We have seized and confined you for money.' The cool and collected demeanour of Madhav Ghose and the imperious tone of his language had mortified the ruffianly pride of the bandit, who piqued himself upon being the scourge and humiliator of the rich and the great, and he was resolved to be as mortifying in his answers.

'And who gives you this money?' enquired Madhav.

'Guess,' said the sardar.

'I need not.'

A deep and hollow sound interrupted the speaker and his auditors.

'What's that?' ejaculated Bhiku in amazement.

'What's that?' ejaculated the sardar in his turn.

All three remained silent for a few moments.

'Can there be another in the room? That would be a fine affair indeed,' said the sardar. 'Let me see.'

Although the whole room was visible with the distinctness that the faint light would permit from the place where they sat, the sardar nevertheless got up and scrutinized every corner, but of course with little success.

'It is strange,' he observed as he resumed his place, 'but let it go. You were speaking of my employer, sir; who do you think he is?'

The presuming tone of the question highly irritated Madhav Ghose, but suppressing his resentment he briefly answered, 'I know he is Mathur Ghose; now tell me what are your instructions.'

Bhiku gaped in surprise, and leering towards the sardar, observed, 'How is it that he knows it already?'

'Fool!' said the sardar 'do you gape at this, who else in Radhaganj has an iron-walled dungeon to cage his prisoners in?'

But he returned no answer to Madhav's question, true to his determination of humbling the yet lofty pride of his captive and perhaps to mould him to that state of mind which would facilitate his object. But Bhiku was getting impudent, and warmed by the fumes of the *ganja*, his usual taciturnity was fast giving place to an uncontrollable propensity to chatter.

'In truth,' said he, 'what are we to do with our booty: booty of flesh and blood I mean?'

'Eat him up, I suppose,' said the sardar.

Bhiku broke out into a hoarse laugh at this sally of his chief. But his rude laugh was suddenly checked by another plaintive groan which seemed to issue this time from the ceiling.

'Again!' ejaculated the startled sardar.

Bhiku sat aghast, superstitious fears now coming over him. Madhav also felt uneasy though from other causes.

'This place has been long untenanted,' observed Bhiku speaking in a whisper, 'who knows what beings may have made this room their abode.'

Though, of course, equally given to superstition, the much stronger mind of the sardar did not so easily yield to such influences. Generally, their lawless and terrible profession renders people of this class habitually conversant with those scenes which are best calculated to give rise to fears of a superhuman character, and though they as firmly believe as other ignorant people in the existence of superhuman agencies, habit renders them less liable to their impressions.

'Or somebody may be lurking somewhere,' said the sardar, 'this must be looked to; you watch our friend here.'

The sardar tore up an edge from his small *dhoti* and rolling it up into a wick, dipped it in the oil of the lamp, and ignited it in its flame. Thus furnished with a light, he cautiously opened the door. He then proceeded to examine every creek and corner of the veranda which lined the single row of rooms, of which the one now occupied by Madhav and his watchers was the middle one. Not finding anything in the veranda to explain the cause of his alarm he proceeded to search the open ground in front, which was enclosed by the walls already mentioned. But there also the search proved equally fruitless, and he returned vexed and doubtful. Bhiku was now really frightened and, in his anxiety to get rid of the place, gave a hard and significant pinch under the elbow of his chief to hasten negotiations. The sardar complied.

'It is getting late,' he said, addressing Madhav, 'and this is no place for us to sleep in. If you will comply with our conditions you can regain your liberty.'

'What are they?' inquired Madhav with indifference, for he saw his advantage.

'Deliver up to us your uncle's will.'

'It is not with me here,' said he laconically, and turned round to resume his walk.

'Remain here then,' said the sardar with equal brevity; 'we go with the keys.'

'And suppose I am inclined to give up the paper, how am I to get at it from here?'

The bandit in his turn perceived his advantage, and replied, 'That is your own concern. Devise the best means in your power. If I were you I would think of sending a note by one of my captors to a friend at home, asking him to send me the paper by the bearer.'

'And if my friend asks you where is the writer of the note, what answer will you give?'

Again the same unearthly sound burst upon their ears. This time it was a low stifled shriek, such as no human being could utter. Again the sound seemed to proceed from the ceiling.

The robbers started to their feet; even Madhav himself was shaken.

'Is there an upper story?' said he.

'No, no,' answered both the robbers at once.

'Stop; I will go up to the roof and see again,' said the sardar.

It was easy for such a practised dacoit as the sardar to scale the no great elevation of the rooms. When up, however, his search proved as fruitless as before.

Bending over the edge of the roof he gazed intently on the ground on the back of the building, but here also his search proved equally unsuccessful. He returned once more, vexed and troubled.

A sudden light broke upon Madhav. 'Are there not two other rooms, similar to this, in the row?'

'Yes,' said the sardar, 'it seems so.'

'Did you bring any other captives to these dungeons?'

'No.'

'Perhaps then others did; some unfortunate victim of this wretch's cupidity is undergoing a horrible fate in one of these cells,' said he, more as speaking to himself. 'Can you go and see if there are any there?'

'You say right,' replied the sardar, musingly. 'Probably in that case, these doors are locked; but I can speak, and the prisoner, if any there is, will doubtless reply.' The sardar again made a wick and proceeded to examine. To his great disappointment the doors of both the rooms were open and the rooms entirely empty.

Utter amazement now seized on Madhav, who clearly saw that every possible existing source had been enquired into, while the robber chief now began seriously to give way to superstitious apprehensions.

Bhiku cowered with fear and crouched near the sardar.

'We have no heart to stay any longer,' said the sardar to Madhav, 'the ways of gods are known to themselves. Give your answer at once, or we shut you up and go.'

Madhav saw that his only chance lay in compliance. If they left him shut up, he could not guess how or when he could expect release. If he complied, it was probable that his note would cause enquiry and afford a clue to his friends by which they would trace out his place of confinement. Still he was determined to make a last effort.

'You expect money,' he said to the sardar, 'if you get the will from me; name the sum and I will double it, if you will let me go without giving up the paper.'

'We are satisfied with what has been promised to us. Who can be fool enough to think that you, once free, would give us the money you promise now. The note, or we go.'

Clothes rustled somewhere in the rooms. The dacoits looked at each other, as if ready to fly without waiting further. Madhav understood the look and inquired if they had pen and paper, to which they replied that they had come 'provided with them Madhav took the pen and paper, and commenced writing a note to his chief *amlá* at home.

'I will dictate,' said the sardar, 'so that I may be neither doubted nor entrapped, nor your retreat found out. I could once read and write like you.'

Madhav looked up in surprise, but signified his assent and the sardar began to dictate, though from the supernatural fears which agitated him, he was far from being cool enough for the purpose.

Madhav began to write.

At that moment a heavy clanking of chains, followed by a tremendous clattering sound, came thundering on the already frightened party, and then again issued the same unearthly moan, more loud and piercing. At one bound Bhiku cleared the veranda, and ran out of the house with a scream. The sardar also rose startled and leaped into the veranda. He was petrified with the vision that there met his eyes and, without turning back even to lock the door, precipitately ran out of the house, leaving Madhav entirely free.

But Madhav himself was just then too much bewildered by the mysterious sounds and the sudden impetuous flight of his captors, to be able fully to comprehend his position. For a moment he remained motionless and undecided. But he was soon ashamed of himself and shaking off unmanly apprehensions jumped into the veranda. Nothing was to be seen. He looked and looked and perceived a small streak of light creeping through a crevice which opened from the veranda into the open ground. Bounding in that direction he found that the door was not locked, and throwing it open saw a female figure standing it that lonely spot. A small lantern was on the ground. Eagerly holding it up for closer examination, he was staggered at what he saw.

'Tara!' escaped from his lips.

'Madhav!' murmured Tara, speechless with astonishment.

But again came the plaintive cry from above.

19

MADHAV AND TARA

Madhav and Tara had known each other from their infancy. Tara's father and Madhav's maternal grandfather were residents of the same village, and in Madhav's constant visits to the place during his boyhood, Tara had been his playmate. They were distantly related to each other on this side, a circumstance which was the means of their coming so frequently in contact with each other in their early age as to be each other's play-fellow. Although Tara was Madhav's senior by a few years, they had always called each other 'Tara' and 'Madhav' respectively. Tara's marriage with Mathur did not to any great extent interfere to banish the feeling in the mind of each towards the other, generated by the familiar and unrestrained intercourse of infancy. For, before Mathur evinced his grasping avarice by the secret but not unperceived aid he rendered to his aunt in her lawsuit, friendly intercourse, apparently cordial on both sides, had subsisted between the cousins, and necessarily Madhav's visits to Mathur's household were frequent. By so many years the junior of Mathur, zenana etiquette did not stand in the way of his holding frequent conversations with Tara on these occasions, and Madhav always availed himself of every such opportunity. Such an intercourse was equally gratifying to both, for each had a high esteem for the other. But their mutual fondness, and such the feeling might suitably be termed, was far removed from all impurity of the heart. Their attachment to each other springing in childhood, and nurtured by a daily growing appreciation of the moral beauty of each other's heart, had ripened into an affection that was akin to the love of brother and sister.

Nevertheless, when Tara and Madhav found themselves face to face in the godown *mahal*, their situation was sufficiently embarrassing. Surprise at this strange and, to both, inexplicable meeting, was the first feeling that predominated in their minds. When its effects had subsided, they began to feel the embarrassing character of their situation, and for some time neither spoke. Tara first broke the silence. 'You here, Madhav!'

Madhav could not well retort the interrogatory on Tara, but remained silent, hardly knowing how to answer. Tara felt all the novelty and embarrassment of the situation; but in such cases women, perhaps, are better able to get over the difficulty than men. Tara, confident in the integrity of her own character and feeling secure from misapprehension on the part of the other, in the esteem she knew Madhav entertained for her, as well as sensible of the necessity of coming to an explanation, proceeded to bring matters to an issue.

'First, tell me, *Thakurpo*, who could be the two *Jamadut*-like men who just now ran away from here? I wonder what business you could have had with people of that description, and here in our house too? One of them gazed at me fixedly when I stood there in the veranda, and perhaps taking me for a ghost fled precipitately.'

'Was it you then who opened this door and clanked the chains?'

'Yes, I opened the door, and was making towards the room from which you came out, but the appearance of these *Jamaduts* frightened me, and I was returning.'

'And whence came the sounds?'

'What sounds?'

'Have you heard nothing strange?'

'Yes, a freezing shriek of woe; but I thought it was coming from your room.'

'No.'

'No? You frighten me. I shall return.'

'Without hearing, hearing why I am here?'

'I must hear it, and I must also tell you why I came here. Be quick then.'

'Gladly,' replied Madhav, 'but I must take some precautions from interruption which you will by and by understand.'

Madhav went out, and drew the massive bar of the door which led from the godown *mahal* at once out of the house. He then re-entered the apartment which had so lately been his prison, and beckoning to Tara to follow, sat down to narrate the history of his capture. He neither concealed nor extenuated any circumstance, speaking as he did in the bitterness of resentment, as well as from a consciousness that however affectionately Tara might love her husband, she was too pure-minded herself to sympathize with his crooked policy. Tara felt sorely grieved as well as disappointed.

'You are not then what I seek,' she said; 'you have arrived only this evening, while I believe my suspicions were roused two days ago.'

Tara related in her turn the purpose of her visit. That need not be detailed to the reader. He has already seen with what solicitude this affectionate wife had watched the change in her husband; how she had racked her mind with fruitless conjectures for its cause; how at last she had importuned her husband for a disclosure, and how disappointed she had been in her wishes; how at last the strange and secret walk her husband had taken that night, and his clandestine and mysterious entry into the godowns, had raised suspicion in her mind that the mysterious cause of her solicitude lay concealed in that apartment; how she determined to wrest the secret at all hazards and to visit the godowns that night, to know what misfortune lay hid beneath its roof; and lastly, how she had secured the keys from her husband while he slept, from beneath his pillow.

'How many fears, what tremor, what anxiety,' continued Tara 'assailed me as, possessed of the stolen keys I threaded my dark way beneath these sombre walls, you can better conceive than I describe. But I felt myself acting under a supernatural impulse and came on. I could have died if my death would have removed his unhappiness. Judge then what impression your presence here, made on me. I at once connected your presence here, with the cause of his unhappiness. But you say you are here only from this evening. You cannot then be what I seek.'

'You will not perhaps be disappointed,' said Madhav in reply, shuddering as he spoke. 'Those sounds—did you not hear them? There is a mystery yet to solve.'

Tara turned pale.

'Do not be frightened,' said Madhav 'I believe there is nothing to fear, I will relate what I have just heard and seen. I will do so, however, only if you give me a promise not to indulge in a woman's fears. Do you promise?'

It was with difficulty that she gasped out the words, 'Speak on.' Madhav then gave her an account of the strange sounds that had interrupted his interview with the dacoits, relieving her by the tone of his narrative as much of supernatural fears, as the nature of the subject admitted.

Tara's feelings were most painful. Fear, natural in women whom philosophy never taught to disbelieve in supernatural beings, predominated. Mingled with it, was curiosity, such as danger excites, and an intense regret that her search should be attended with so much terror. She now almost repented having undertaken it, and asked Madhav to see her safe to the interior of the house.

'Will you give up your search so easily? I assure you there is no danger,' said Madhav with some vehemence, for his curiosity and interest had been intensely awakened, and he had forgotten his own precarious, and with Tara in his company, delicate situation, for its gratification.

Tara remained silent for some moments. Mustering resolution at last, she replied, 'Where can we search? Have not the robbers searched everywhere?'

'Yes, but I see now that one thing escaped them. There is a door,' he said, pointing to the little iron door we have described before, 'which remained to be opened.'

'It evidently leads to the other room: did not they examine that other room also?'

At this moment, again came the hollow agony-bespeaking sound, clearer, more distinct than ever. The listeners started; its touching and startling tones thrilled them in every nerve.

A short pang shot across Madhav's brain. A dark and agonizing thought seized him. Wrenching almost with violence the bunch of keys from Tara's hand, he madly sprung towards the little door, knelt down, and pushed a key into the keyhole. It did not turn. With the same vehemence of movement he tried a second and a third key, but with the same ill-success. Maddened with vexation, and the torture of suspense, he would have torn open the ponderous metal, had he the strength. Happily for his self-command, the fourth key he tried turned in the lock, and away flew the heavy door as though it were a feather.

'Tara! Tara! hesitate not, but follow,' he said, with compressed energy, and crept in, bruising his sides.

Led by the contagion of impulse, Tara followed with the light. Joy and surprise held Madhav mute when they discerned a staircase of brick, narrow and deep, and filled with spiders' webs. Without stopping to speak Madhav bounded up, and Tara lost in amazement, mechanically continued to follow. The staircase led to a small door of apparently an upper-storied room. A glance at the very small height of this room sufficed to convince Madhav of the art with which it had been so made as to be concealed from every other part of the building. He saw that the height of the two rooms, upper and lower together, made up the height of the side rooms and the veranda, and being destitute of windows the existence of the upper story could not possibly be discerned from any other part of the building, nor any way suspected except by a comparison of the height of the central room with that of the adjacent ones.

Madhav, anxious and trembling, sought die lock of this second door and, after two or three fruitless attempts in which the violent movement of the keys brought blood from his fingers, he succeeded, and threw open die plated door ringing and echoing. Tara entered with him, holding the light in her hand. The feeble glimmer it threw around, revealed to them an unexpected sight. Upon a small bedstead of varnished mahogany, splendidly ornamented with gauze and crape, lay a form apparently that of a female. Tara and Madhav ran to the bedstead with the light; and its dim and ghastly glare, as Tara held it over die bedstead, revealed to them the features—pale, emaciated, agonized, but still heavenly—the features of MATANGINI.

20

SOME WOMEN ARE
THE EQUALS OF SOME MEN

Tara and Madhav bore away the seemingly lifeless Matangini to an apartment which was secure from interruption. The exertions of Tara, materially aided by the wholesome fresh air to which Matangini had been for so many days a stranger, soon recalled the blood to her face, and long before the first streaks of day had brightened the eastern sky, Matangini was again a living being. Refreshments were provided for her, but she ate little. The little she did eat considerably revived her, and as Tara sat on the window eyeing the grey light in the east, Matangini softly and slowly unfolded to her the course of the painful events which had nearly consigned her to a living grave.

Briefly told, that dark story is this: When Mathur Ghose sent her home in Suki's mother's company, Matangini had no suspicion of the snare which had been laid for her by that wily monster. Suki's mother, who had been well-instructed in her part, asked her on the way if she had no apprehension in returning to her husband.

'To tell you the truth, Sukir *má*,' replied Matangini, 'I would not go, if earth held a place where I could remain.'

'Would you?' asked the wretch, 'I think I can serve you. I would conceal you in a place where nobody could find you out.'

'No,' said Matangini thoughtfully, 'I must not conceal myself. Evil tongues will be busy.'

'Then why not come to your sister's house?'

Matangini heaved a deep sigh. 'No! that is not to be thought of.'

The artful woman appeared to sympathize sincerely with her helpless situation, and at length suggested embarking for her father's house.

'How am I to find the means?' said Matangini sorrowfully.

'Oh! as for that, I dare say my elder mistress will find you a boat if she knew you wished it; and I can accompany and leave you there.'

Matangini wept, anticipating this act of kindness on Tara's part.

'Shall I go and tell her?'

'Yes,' said Matangini, joyfully.

'You then wait where I leave you till I come back. There no one will observe you. Come.'

Matangini went where the woman-fiend led. She led her to the little room above stairs in the godown *mahal*. The sombre and deserted appearance of the rooms shot a chill through her heart as she passed the approaches. She was surprised to find the deserted dark little room splendidly furnished. She turned to Suki's mother to explain the mystery. Lo! Suki's mother had vanished, bolting the door after her!

Matangini's intelligent mind now comprehended everything. Her resolution was formed at once with her usual promptitude.

In the evening, Mathur Ghose came and laid himself at her feet. The indignantly contemptuous repulse he met with, wounded and mortified him. He determined to gratify at once both revenge and lust.

'You shall be mine yet, life,' said Mathur, as with a demoniacal look he was departing for that evening.

'Never!' said Matangini, concentrating the energy of twenty *men* in her look, 'Never *yours*. Look here;' and she placed herself immediately in front of him 'look; I am a full-grown woman, and at least *your* equal in brute force. Will you call in allies?' Mathur Ghose stood bewildered at this wonderful challenge.

'Hunger shall be my ally. I lift not a finger against a woman,' said Mathur, recovering himself.

'Hunger shall be my ally,' said Matangini, in return.

Mathur had resolved to starve her to compel her compliance. Matangini had resolved to starve herself to be rid from his power.

Both kept their word. Mathur visited her daily, to watch the effect. Matangini was literally starving when Madhav rescued her.

Madhav departed before it was quite daylight. Matangini was too feeble to be immediately removed, and it was arranged between Madhav and Tara that Tara should keep her concealed till the ensuing night, when Karuna would come to fetch her.

After seeing Madhav safe out of the house, Tara returned to

Matangini, and observing playfully that it was now her turn to make her a captive, locked the door of the chamber to deceive appearances. She then returned to her husband's apartment, replaced the bunch of keys whence she had purloined them, and went to bed as if not a mouse had stirred during the night. Did she sleep? No! She had now learnt her husband's secret, and a terrible acquisition of knowledge it had proved to her noble heart. Perhaps of all the visitors in the scenes of that eventful night, none had suffered so deeply as the affectionate and confiding wife, appalled by the unexpected disclosures of the dark deeds of her husband.

Matangini spent the day in her safe but solitary chamber. Late in the evening Karuna came, as had been arranged, and at length, after so much suffering and wretchedness, Matangini had the pleasure of clasping Hemangini to her bosom.

'And you will never leave me again, sister, will you?' said Hem, after her joy at the meeting had subsided a little.

Matangini sighed. There were tears in her eyes.

'Why don't you answer?' asked Hemangini, a little impatiently.

'Alas! I fear we must part!'

'And for whom will you leave me?' said Hem, disappointed.

'I go to MY FATHER,' said Matangini.

21

THE LAST CHAPTER IN LIFE'S BOOK—AND IN THIS

The evening that followed was a tempestuous and gloomy one. The wind howled, the rain fell in torrents, and the thunder rattled loud and long. As Mathur Ghose sat alone, a sound like that of blowing at a conch shell fell on his ears, during intermissions in the violence of the storm. Twice he could distinctly hear it. His first thought was not to obey the well known signal of those whose unworthy association had just brought on him infamy and disgrace. But every time that the sound was heard it became louder and louder, and more and more urgent. At length he left his seat, and braving the storm, repaired to the spot which had been the scene of so many of his dark interviews. A form lurked beneath a tree, and he had no difficulty in recognizing it to be that of the robber chief.

'What brings you now here?' said he, pettishly, 'I have had enough of you. Rid me of your presence. My good name is lost, and your treachery the cause.'

'I do not deserve this reproach,' replied the robber, calmly; 'we did our best. He who takes us for his associates must abide by the consequences.'

The scoundrel was preaching philosophy to the great man! And, dear reader, was he very wrong?

'But our connection has ceased,' rejoined Mathur, angrily; 'you know it well enough. Why do you seek me at this stormy hour?'

'Because,' said the sardar, mournfully, 'because this is the only hour when I can dare come out now. The police are after us, as you know.'

'Then, why not rid Radhaganj of your presence at once?'

'You were not wont to speak thus to us, Baboo,' said the sardar, with a slight touch of his old manner, 'when these days had not come over us. Think as you may, I am come to convince you that we have a better memory than you suppose of those whom we serve, or those who serve us.'

'What do you mean?' asked Mathur.

'You do not see with me tonight, one who used to follow me as my shadow,' answered the sardar with a shade of melancholy.

'Yes—where is that man? Bhiku you call him, I believe?'

'In the hands of the police.'

Mathur was startled. 'Nothing worse?' asked he, tremblingly.

'Alas! yes!' replied the sardar in a desponding tone. 'He has confessed.'

'Confessed *what*?' asked Mathur with furious anxiety.

'Much,' said the sardar with the same despondency, 'much that may send *both you and me* across the black waters. *Me* they shall not catch. This hour is my last at Radhaganj. But you have done well by us, and it shall never be said we did ill by you. So I came to give you a warning.'

So saying the bandit vanished into the thicket without waiting for a reply.

Mathur Ghose turned back and regained the house. For a couple of hours he sat musing deeply. His was a strong mind, and speedily regained courage. The police was venal and corrupt; his wealth was vast; he would buy up the police. There was one hitch in the scheme. A shrewd and restlessly active Irishman sat in the district station as Magistrate, and it was his besetting sin to be meddling with everything. He was constantly shaking out ugly affairs of the police. But Mathur Ghose promised himself to see that Bhiku should recant before the meddlesome Irishman.

His meditations were interrupted by someone bounding into the room, dripping with rain, and bespattered with mud. It was one of his trustworthy agents employed in the Zila Courts.

'Fly, master, fly!' said the man, 'you have not a moment to lose.'

'How so?' asked Mathur, bewildered at this new warning.

'One Bhiku has this day at eleven o'clock confessed to the Magistrate to dacoities and other crimes committed, as he falsely said, at your instigation.'

'Confessed to the Magistrate?' repeated Mathur, almost mechanically, turning pale as death.

'Yes,' said the law agent, 'and I started immediately after the confession was worded. I saw the Saheb making preparations for starting, and I am afraid he will be at Radhaganj during the course of the night.'

'At Radhaganj during the course of the night?' again iterated Mathur, mechanically.

'Fly, Sir! immediately!' repeated the man.

'Yes; go,' said Mathur, mechanically again.

The man went away.

Next morning the busy Irishman came to Mathur Ghose's house, to arrest him personally, a whole posse of policemen following at his heels in a hundred varieties of dress, and an eager rabble pressing close upon them to have a peep at the sort of animal they call a Magistrate, and the pranks he liked to play. Arrived at the house, it was entered, and thoroughly ransacked for the owner, but he was not to be found. At length found he was. There in the godown *mahal*, in the very room which had formed the prison of Madhav and so many others of his victims, the master of the house was found—DEAD. He had hanged himself.

CONCLUSION

And now, good reader, I have brought my story to a close. Least, however, you fall to censuring me for leaving your curiosity unsatisfied, I will tell you what happened to the other persons who have figured in this tale.

The sardar successfully escaped—not so Rajmohan. He had been implicated deeply in Bhiku's confession, was apprehended, and under the hope of a pardon confessed likewise. They were however wise by half and made only partial confessions. The pardon was revoked, and both he and Bhiku transported.

Matangini could not live under Madhav's roof. This, of course, they both understood. So intimation was sent to her father and he came and took her home. Madhav increased the pension he allowed the old man, on her account. History does not say how her life terminated, but it is known that she died an early death.

Tara mourned in solitude the terrible end of a husband who had proved himself so little worthy of her love. She lived a long widowhood in repose, and, when she died, died mourned by many.

As to Madhav, Champak and the rest, some are dead, and the others will die. Throwing this flood of light on their past and future history, I bid you, good reader, FAREWELL.

DURGESHNANDINI
OR
THE CHIEFTAIN'S DAUGHTER

Part I

1

THE TEMPLE

One day, near the end of summer, in the year 998 of the Bengali era, a solitary horseman was journeying along the road which leads from Vishnupur to Jehanabad. Seeing that the sun was about to set, he began to gallop; for before him lay a long, lonesome, unshaded road, and if the evening should bring with it one of those thunder-storms so frequent at that season of the year, it would go hard with him in that shelterless place. By degrees the twilight sky was overspread with masses of dark clouds. As early as nightfall, such dense darkness enveloped the landscape that the guiding of the horse became extremely difficult; and the traveller could only with difficulty follow the path shown by the lightning flash. In a short time, the winds began to roar, accompanied by heavy rain. The horseman was now absolutely incapable of distinguishing his course. The reins were now slackened, and the animal went his own way. After going some distance in this manner, the charger stumbled at some hard substance. As the lightning played just then, the traveller caught a glimpse of some gigantic white object before him. Taking it to be a building, he jumped to the ground, and came to know that some stone stairs had occasioned the accident. Hence concluding shelter to be at hand, he let his horse loose, and in darkness cautiously began to ascend the flight of steps. By the help of the lightning he soon ascertained that the pile before him was a temple. He adroitly reached its little door, but found it shut. He felt it about with his hand and perceived that it was not fastened outside. 'In this temple, situated as it is in an uninhabited, solitary tract, who can have fastened the door within?'—the traveller asked himself with some surprise and curiosity. But the rain was beating pitilessly against his head, so that be the occupant whoever he might, the traveller fell to rapping at the door violently with his hand, again and again. But in vain. Irresistibly prompted to break it open by kicking, he refrained from going so far, lest thereby he should commit an act of graceless sacrilege. But notwithstanding this forbearance of his, the violence of his blows was such that the frail wooden thing was not able to bear it long—shortly it was deprived of its fastening pin. On the door being flung open, as the young man entered the temple, a faint shriek, issuing from it, entered his ear; and immediately a gust, rushing in, blew out the lamp which had been burning there. Who was in the temple and what the image of the god?—the newcomer could not at all determine. Finding himself thus placed, the dauntless young man only smiled, and first reverentially bowed down his head before the invisible image. He then arose and in darkness spoke, 'Who's there in the temple?' No answer; but the tinkling of ornaments was heard. Thinking it useless to waste words, the traveller then closed the door in order to keep out the wind and rain, and in place of the broken pin leaned against it. 'Whoever you may be, here,' again said he, 'listen. Here I sit at the door armed. Do not break my rest, or do it at your own peril, if you should happen to belong to the stronger sex. But if you be women, never fear; so long as sword and buckler are in the hands of a Rajput, not a hair of your head shall come to grief.'

'Who are you, sir?' was the question in a female voice.

The traveller answered in surprise, 'From the voice I gather this is asked by some fair one. What's the use, madam, of your knowing me?'

'O sir, we were so frightened!' answered the voice.

'Whoever I may be,' replied the young man, 'it is not our custom to make ourselves known by our own mouth. But rest content that so long as I am here, no danger shall befall the weaker sex.'

'I take heart at your words, sir,' said the woman. 'Till now we were almost dying of fright. My companion has yet not completely recovered from her swoon. In the evening we came to worship this *Siva*, called Saileswara. Afterwards when the storm broke out, our bearers and attendants left us and have gone, we know not where.'

'Be of good cheer, madam, I pray you,' said our young man. 'Rest here for the present. Tomorrow morning I will conduct you home.'

'The blessings of Saileswara upon you, sir!', returned the woman.

At midnight when the storm ceased, the young man said, 'Madam, please stay here alone for a while, summoning up courage. I'll just go and procure a lamp from the nearest village.'

At this the female interlocutor returned, 'Sir, you needn't go so far. The keeper of this temple, a menial, lives close by. The moonlight has now appeared, so that you will be able to see his hovel on going out. This man lives alone in this lonely region and has always by him articles for lighting a fire.'

Accordingly the young man went out and in the moonlight discovered the dwelling of the keeper. Coming to the door of his habitation, our traveller awakened him. The man, not opening the door at once from fear, began at first to peep out to ascertain who it was that had come. On close examination, no signs of a robber were recognisable in the traveller; moreover, it was not so easy for the former to overcome the temptation of gold held out by the latter. After some balancing, the keeper opened the door and lighted a lamp.

Having brought in the light, the traveller saw that an image of *Siva*, made of white marble, was established in the temple. Behind it were two women only. The more youthful of them, on seeing the light, sat down veiling herself, and looking down. But from the diamond-studded *Marwari*[1] that shone on her wrists and from her embroidered dress of exquisite workmanship, over which were displayed tastefully her jewelled ornaments, the traveller could clearly infer that she came of no mean family. From the comparatively inferior value of the second woman's dress, be concluded her to be the handmaid of the young lady, yet more well-to-do than the ordinary run of maidservants. Her age might be thirty-five. Naturally it appeared to the young man that he was speaking to the matron. He also remarked with surprise that the dress of neither was like that of Bengali women, both being attired after the fashion of the North-Western or Hindustani females.

After placing the lamp in its place, the young man stood facing the women. Then, as the rays of light fell full on his head, the ladies perceived that his age might be slightly over five and twenty. His body was of such a height as would not have looked beautiful in another, but owing to the young man's broad chest and the symmetrical largeness and fulness of every member, his tallness contributed singularly to his

---

[1] Bangles.

beauty. Over a complexion, like the hue of the tender grass brought forth by the rainy season, or rather like the more captivating colour of the fresh, spring leaves, shone amulets and other ornaments worn by the Rajputs. Over his loins hung his sheathed sword fastened to the girdle; in his long arm was a long spear; a turban, crested with a diamond, was on his head; from his ears hung pearl earrings; a jewelled necklace completed his dress. On viewing each other, both parties were eager for acquaintance, but neither could bring itself to stoop to the indecorum of making advances to the other.

2

ACQUAINTANCE

The young man was the first to betray his curiosity. Addressing the dame, 'I presume, madam,' said he, 'you belong to the *zenānā* of some respectable person. I should scruple to ask for your name and lineage, but you may not have the same objection that I have to make myself known. May I therefore take the liberty to enquire who you are?'

'No, sir,' replied the woman, 'that can not be. When do women first make themselves known?'

'What does precedence in acquaintance signify?' rejoined the young man.

'And how, I pray, is a woman to make herself known—she who is not allowed to bear her caste addition? How can she, whose virtue consists in living shut up from the world, disclose herself? When God forbade woman to utter her husbands name, didn't He thereby deprive her of the power of discovering herself?'

The young man returned no answer to these words; in fact, he was otherwise engaged. By degrees removing part of her veil, the youthful lady had been gazing at him steadfastly from behind her companion. In course of the conversation, the traveller's glance had also accidentally fallen in that direction and been fast riveted on her face. He thought it would never again fall to his lot to witness such a 'shower of beauty.' As soon as the young man's glance mingled with that of the damsel, she looked down. On the other side, the attendant, receiving no answer to her words, looked right into the traveller's face, and marked well which way he was looking. Knowing also that her fair companion was eying the young man ardently, she whispered into her ear.

'What's this, girl? Dost mean to marry in presence of the *Siva*?'

She who was thus spoken to, gave her attendant a pinch, saying, 'Beshrew thee!' Seeing how matters stood, the clever attendant reflected,

'I shrewdly fear the charms of this young man have begun to tell on my charge. Should she conceive a passion for him, even if worse consequences do not happen, her peace of mind, alas! would go for ever. Ah! that's to be averted. Aye, but how? Let me try artifice to rid ourselves of him.'

Having determined this, with the innate cleverness of a woman, she said, 'Sir, women's good name is so frail a thing that it can hardly bear the weight of the air, what shall I say of tonight's violent gale? Therefore, now that the storm is over, we shall with your permission see whether we can walk home.'

'If you needs must go home afoot at this hour of night,' replied the young man, 'I will convoy you. The sky has become clear, and I would by this time have set out for my quarters; but it is only because I have not the heart to leave a beauty like your companion without a guard, that I am still here.'

'Sir,' replied the woman, 'your kindness towards us has been very great—indeed so great that it alone prevents me from speaking out my mind fully to you lest you think us ungrateful. But, sir, what shall I tell you of woman's cursed luck? We are naturally looked on with suspicion. It would indeed be a very happy thing if you accompanied us, but pray consider when my master, who is the father of this girl, will ask her, 'Under whose safeguard have you come at this dead hour?' what shall she answer?'

The young man mused a little and then replied, 'Why, even thus, 'Under the safeguard of Jagat Singha, son of Maharaja Kinorh Man Singha?"'

Had the thunder burst there at that moment, the females could not have been struck with greater surprise. Immediately both stood up. The damsel slinked away behind the image; the clever-tongued dame wound the flowing border of her cloth round her neck and with clasped hands said, 'Pardon, noble Prince. We have unwittingly been guilty of a thousand transgressions.'

'Such grave transgressions are past all pardon,' replied the Prince laughing, 'but I'll forgive if you let me be acquainted with you; otherwise you cannot escape condign punishment.'

Soft words invariably breathe courage into a clever woman. 'Name it, sir—issue your fiat, we agree.'

'Nothing but this,' replied Jagat Singha, 'that I will conduct you home.'

The attendant was in a dilemma. For some very particular reason she was loath to make the damsel known to the officer of the Emperor of Delhi—that he should accompany them was far more objectionable, being, as it was, of grayer import. She hung down her head.

Just at this moment the treading of a good many horses at no great distance from the temple, was heard. Going out hurriedly, the Prince saw about a hundred horsemen passing by. He marked their uniform and recognised them to be his own Rajput soldiers. Some time ago the Prince had gone to Vishnupur on some military duty; and had been returning to his father's camp with a hundred horsemen. In the afternoon he had left his men and gone before; and afterwards following a path different from that taken by his soldiers, he had been overtaken alone by the storm and put to trouble. Now finding them again, in order to ascertain whether they had descried him, he exclaimed, 'Victory to the Emperor of Delhi!' Immediately a horseman approached. On seeing him, the Prince said, 'Dharam Singha, I stopped here on account of the storm.'

'After searching much for you, sir,' said Dharam Singha, humbly making obeisance, 'at length we have come here tracing the marks of your horse's hoofs. We have also brought up the horse, which we found near yonder banian tree.'

'Do you stay here with the steed,' said Jagat Singha, 'sending two men to fetch up a palankeen and bearers from a neighbouring village. Let the rest of the soldiers march on.'

Dharam Singha was rather taken by surprise at this order, but thinking it unnecessary to ask his master for any reason of his command, said, 'I will carry out your orders, sir.'

He then communicated to the soldiers the intention of the Prince. On coming to know it, someone smiled and enquired of his campanion, 'why things were ordered so wondrous strange that day.' 'And why shouldn't this be, Sir?' answered another. 'Remember, the Maharaja at the head of the Rajputs is surrounded by no less than five hundred queens.'

Meanwhile availing herself of the Prince's absence, the young lady withdrew the veil and said to her handmaid, 'Bimala, why are you so unwilling to make me known to the Prince?'

'I answer that to your father; but now, what's this noise again?'

'Methinks,' replied the maiden, 'some of his soldiers have come in search of the Prince. But why should you fear while he himself is with us.'

Before the return of the horsemen who had gone to bring up a palankeen, the bearers and guards who had left the ladies and taken shelter in an adjacent village, came back. Espying these, Jagat Singha re-entered the temple and said to the attendant, 'Some bearers accompanied by several armed men, are coming this way with a palankeen. Please come out and see whether they are your people.' Bimala looked out from the door, and recognised them to be their men. 'Then I mustn't stay here any longer,' said the Prince, 'my presence with you may be attended with evil. Farewell, then. I pray to Saileswara that you may reach home in safety. I only beg that you will not make known our meeting within a week. But O! do not forget me either. Rather keep this with you for remembrance. As for me, your memento is in my heart—even the fact that I could not learn who your lord's daughter is.' He thereupon took out a pearl neck-lace from his turban and placed it on Bimala's head. Bimala, after twining the precious gift around her hair, bowed to the Prince in great humility. 'Noble Prince,' said she, 'I beseech you not to blame me for withholding from you the information in which you have happened to take so much interest. Believe me, Sir, there is sufficient reason for this silence on my part. If however you are exceedingly curious, let me know where I may see you a fortnight hence.'

'In this very temple,' said Jagat Singha after reflecting a little. 'If you don't see me here, we shall never meet again.'

'God bless you, Sir!' said Bimala, humbly bowing. After looking once more on the youthful lady with burning ardour, the Prince leaped on his horse and was out of sight.

3

THE MOGAL AND THE PATHAN

I shall not, for the present, satisfy the curiosity of the gentle reader by following Jagat Singha from Saileshwara's temple, or by narrating the personal history of the charming damsel discovered in it. Jagat Singha was a Rajput. In order to explain why he had come to Bengal, and been journeying alone over a lonesome, open track, I shall briefly describe the political condition of Bengal at this time. This Chapter will therefore be historical, and an impatient reader may pass over it; but nothing like patience.

After Bakhtiyar Khiliji had planted the standard of the crescent in Bengal, the Pathans held undisputed sway over the country for several centuries. In 932, the celebrated Sultan Babar defeated the reigning Emperor Ibrahim Lodi, and ascended the throne of Delhi. But Bengal did not then pass under the sceptre of the Tamerlane dynasty.

Until the accession of that luminary of the Mogal dynasty—Akbar, Bengal remained under the sway of independent Pathan Sovereigns. In an evil hour, the foolhardy Daud Khan laid his hands on the person of the sleeping Lion. As the consequence of his rashness, he was defeated by Manaim Khan, one of Akbar's generals, and so lost his throne. In 982, Daud fled to Orissa with his followers, and Bengal passed into the hands of the Mogal Sovereigns. When the Pathans had established themselves in Orissa, it became an arduous task for the Mogals to dislodge them from their hold. In 986 of the Bengali era, Khan Jaha Khan, viceroy of the Emperor, worsted the Pathans a second time, and brought Orissa under his master's yoke. Afterwards, a disturbance broke out. The Jaigirdars and other landholders took umbrage at the introduction into Bengal of Akbar's new system of settlement for the collection of the imperial dues, and drew the sword in order to maintain their established rights. Taking advantage of this crisis, the Pathans of Orissa again raised their head, and investing one of their members, named Katlu Khan, with the insignia of royalty, again brought Orissa under their dominion; and with great demonstrations of power, opportunely took Midnapur and Vishunpur—two districts lying beyond the pale of Orissa.

Both the able viceroy, Khan Azim and afterwards, Shahabaz Khan failed to wrest the conquered province from the enemy. At length a Hindu warrior was placed in command for the accomplishment of this difficult task.

When bursting with new-born fanaticism and in all the pride of strength, the surges of the Musalman soldiery rushed from the Himalayan chains, Prithviraj and other Rajput heroes resisted the tide with matchless valour. But alas! India's downfall was in the counsel of the Eternal. Instead of combining their strength, the Rajput princes fell to quarreling with one another. By virtue of reiterated efforts, the Musalmans beat the Hindu powers one by one, and established the Empire of Delhi. But although they succeeded thus far, yet they could not at once render lifeless the Kshetriya-begotten Rajputs. Many Rajput Princes remained independent; and from this time down to the final disruption of the Moslem Empire, this warlike race repeatedly challenged the Javanas to the field and on many occasions put them to the rout. In course of time, however, many Rajput chiefs were compelled to pay tribute to the Emperor of Delhi; and in the decay of their prowess, to set aside their pristine dignity, in order to obtain the good graces of the Victor by alliances with the Imperial house and by other means. The Emperors, for their part, were anxious to lay under obligation their heroic antagonists, by extending to them their friendship and alliance. In course of time, the tributary Princes began to enter the imperial service. The high-minded Akbar was in every respect far wiser than his predecessors. It was his conviction that for the administration of this country, the children of the soil and not foreigners—are peculiarly fit, and further, that either in war or in civil administration, the Rajputs had no equals. Agreeably to this belief, he, as a rule, appointed the natives—more particularly the Rajputs, to important posts of Government.

At the time of our story, of those Rajputs who had gained eminent appointments, Maharaja Man Singha was one of the foremost. He was the brother-in-law of prince Selim himself, the son of Akbar. After Azim Khan and Shahabaz Khan had been foiled in their endeavours, Akbar sent this personage as Governor of Bengal and Behar.

In 997 Man Singha reached Patna and first suppressed the disturbances. Next year he marched towards Orissa. On arriving at Patna, he had appointed Syed Khan as his deputy in Bengal, himself intending to stay at Patna. Entrusted with this office, Syed Khan was residing at the city of Tanda, the then capital of Bengal. Now marching for Orissa, Man Singha summoned his subordinate, writing him to say that he must join him at Burdwan with his forces.

On reaching Burdwan, the Raja saw that Syed Khan had not come, but had simply sent a message. He reported that great delay was inevitable for him to levy troops—nay, that the rains would set in by the time that he could set out with his army; so that if the Raja would encamp till the wet season was over, he would join him with his men. Seeing no alternative, the Raja closed with this proposal, and encamped on the banks of the Darukeshwara river, in the village of Jehanabad, waiting for Syed Khan.

While at Jehanabad, the Raja received intelligence that Katlu Khan, emboldened by his inactivity, was plundering the country within a few miles of that village. Filled with apprehensions, the Raja thought it expedient to dispatch an officer to ascertain the actual state of affairs—where the enemy lay, what his aim, what he was doing, etc. His favorite son, Jagat Singha, had accompanied him in this expedition. Learning that the Prince was eager to be entrusted with this bold task, the Raja had dispatched him with a hundred horsemen, in the direction of the enemy. The Prince returned soon, after performing his work. It was when he was journeying back to the camp, that he has been introduced to the gentle reader.

4

THE YOUTHFUL GENERAL

When Jagat Singha returned to his father, Maharaja Man Singha learnt from the lips of his son that an army of about fifty thousand Pathans had encamped near the village of Dharpur, that they were plundering the neighbouring villages, and that having raised or captured forts, they were lying unmolested. Man Singha saw that a speedy check must be put on the excesses of the Pathans; but that this was a task of no small difficulty. With the view of deciding the appropriate course to be followed, he took counsel with the officers who had accompanied the expedition.

'Day after day,' said he, 'village after village, Pargana after Pargana are slipping off from the hands of the Emperor. Now, the Pathans must be chastised. But how to do this? The odds are against us—further, the enemy will fight from the shelter of forts; so that even if we could beat them, they could not be crushed or dislodged. But, mark, if on the contrary we are worsted, we shall be at once annihilated in this shelterless region of the enemy. Therefore, methinks, it would be a piece of hair-brained bravado to risk the lives of so many of the Emperor's troops, as also to blight once for all the prospect of conquering Orissa. To wait for Syed Khan, then, seems to be the best course; but then, in the meanwhile, some speedy means must be resorted to, for keeping the enemy in some check. What do you advise, Sirs?'

All the old officers returned with one voice that to wait for Syed Khan seemed the best course.

Raja Man Singha said, 'Instead of risking the whole army, my intention is to send a small force under some able officer.'

'Maharaj,' replied an old officer, 'where you are afraid to send the whole army, what will a detachment avail?'

'I don't mean to send it,' rejoined Man Singha, 'to face the enemy in the open field. A small force lying concealed will be able to keep in check small bands of Pathans who are harassing the villages.'

'Maharaj,' answered the Mogal, 'what officer will court certain destruction?'

Man Singha scowled. 'What?' said he, 'breathes there not one among so many Rajputs and Mogals who can look on death with scorn?'

Immediately a few Mogals and Rajputs started up, and expressed their readiness to go. Jagat Singha was present there. He was the youngest of all. From behind the others, he also said, 'With your permission, Sir, I am also willing to do the Emperor's business.'

'Ah! why shouldn't it be so?' said Man Singha with complacence. 'Now, I know the day is yet distant when the name of either Rajput or Mogal will be a thing of the past. So you are all ready to undertake this perilous task? Now, whom shall I select?'

'Maharaj,' replied a courtier laughing, ''tis fortunate that so many have come forward. Pray, Sir, make the most of this competition, and select him who agrees to take the fewest men.'

'Aye!' replied the Raja, 'this is sound advice.' He then asked the first that had volunteered, 'With what number are you willing to go?'

'With fifteen thousand, so please you.'

'Nay, that can't be. If fifteen thousand were detached, a sufficient number would not be left behind. What gallant is ready to take ten thousand?'

The officers were silent. At length Yasovantha Singha, a Rajput warrior and favorite of the Raja, solicited his permission to be placed in command. The Raja now began to eye them round with satisfaction. Prince Jagat Singha had been standing courting his glance, and as the Raja's gaze fell on him, he humbly said,

'Maharaj, under your favor, with the help of five thousand, I can engage to drive away Katlu Khan to the other side of the Subarnarekha.'

Man Singha was struck dumb; the officers began to whisper to one another. 'My son,' said he after a while, 'I know you are the pride of the Rajput race, but, child, you are rash.'

Jagat Singha supplicated with clasped hands,

'Sire, if instead of redeeming my word, I waste the Emperor's troops, let me meet with condign punishment.'

After thinking a while, the Raja said,

'God forbid that I should hinder the free exercise of your Rajput virtue. Look! here I entrust you with this business.'

Saying this, he embraced the Prince with much feeling and bade him farewell.

5

GARMANDARAN

The traces of the road along which Jagat Singha returned from Vishnupur to Jahanabad, still exist. At some distance to the south of it, is the village of Garmandaran. The women whom Jagat Singha met in the temple, went towards this village. Several ancient forts were situated in Garmandaran, which may probably have owed its name to that circumstance. The river Amodara flowed through it. At one place, it so much deviated from the right line, that two sides of a triangular piece of land were completely surrounded; on the third, rose a rock-cut fort. At the head of this piece of land, and just where the river first entered, rose a stupendous castle from the water, piercing Heaven. The pile was composed entirely of black stone. The strong current laved its two sides. The traveller still sees the massive ruins of this impregnable fortress;—only the lower part now remains, the building having been reduced to a heap of ruins by the destructive hand of Time. Over it, the tamarind, the *madhabi* and various other wild trees and shrubs have formed themselves into a wood, which affords shelter to the snake, the wolf and other ferocious beasts. Several other forts were situated on the other side of the river. These were inhabited by certain wealthy persons belonging to the same family. But our story has no connection with any other besides the first.

When Balin, the Emperor of Delhi, came to conquer Bengal, a soldier named Jayadhar Singha accompanied him. The night on which Balin obtained victory, the soldier performed prodigies of valour for the Imperial cause. In reward of his services, the Emperor gave him a *Jaigir* in the village of Garmandaran. The descendants of this Jaigirdar grew powerful, constructed forts at their own pleasure, and bade defiance to the ruler of Bengal. In 998 of the Bengali era, the castle which I have described in detail was inhabited by Virendra Singha, a descendant of Jayadhar Singha.

In his young days, Virendra was not on good terms with his father. He was of a haughty and impatient temperament, and seldom or never acted up to the wishes of his parent. Hence quarrel and altercation frequently ensued between the father and the son. The old landholder fixed his choice on the daughter of a neighbour, also a landholder and belonging to the same caste. The father of the girl had no son, so that by this alliance, Virendra could in all probability increase his fortunes. The bride too was beautiful. The match was therefore in every way highly acceptable in the eyes of the old man, and he accordingly made preparations for the coming ceremony. But instead of caring for all this, Virendra clandestinely married the daughter of a poor and forlorn widow who lived in the neighbourhood. When intelligence of this *mesalliance* reached the ears of the landholder, he drove out his son in a fit of rage. Driven out from his father's house, the young man set out for Delhi with the intention of entering the army. His spouse was then in the family way, and he could not take her with him; she remained in her mother's cottage.

Now, when his son had gone away, the old landholder began to lament over the separation, and became a prey to remorse. He assiduously tried every means to get news of his child—but in vain. Failing in his endeavours, he welcomed his daughter-in-law with open arms, and brought her from the house of her poor mother. In time, the wife of Virendra Singha, gave birth to a daughter, and died after a few days.

On arriving at Delhi, Virendra embraced the military profession and entered the Rajput army of the Emperor. In a short time, he rose to a high rank through his abilities. After having in several years acquired wealth and distinction, he received the tidings of his father's demise. Considering it further unnecessary to remain in a distant land, or to serve, he returned home. He brought many persons with him from Delhi—among whom were a maidservant and an ascetic. In the following story we shall have to do with these two only. The maidservant was called Bimala, the name of the ascetic was Abhiram Swami.

We have before called Bimala a maidservant, we shall also do so now. The report ran that she was the paid servant of Virendra. She managed the household affairs, and in particular tended Virendra's daughter—no other reason was visible for her stay in the castle. I am therefore obliged to call her a maidservant. But for all this, no signs were visible in her of the maidservant. She was respected by the inmates as a housewife; all of them rendered obedience to her. From her countenance, she appeared to have been surpassingly fair in her youth—a ray of that beauty still lingered, like the setting moon in the 'sweet hour of prime.' Gajapati Vidyadiggaja, a disciple of Abhiram Swami, was an inmate of the castle. Whatever his attainments in Rhetoric, he had an inordinate thirst to display his wit and to pass for a wag. 'The goodly maidservant,' he used to say, seeing Bimala, 'is like a pail of clarified butter: as love's fire is cooling more and more, her frame is getting more and more compact.' Here it should be remarked that from the day when he happened to make this display of his wit, Bimala nick-named him '*Rasikdas Swami*' (illustrious bond-slave of gallantry). Form and bearing apart, Bimala's civility and conversation were such as could by no means be expected from an ordinary maidservant. Many people said that for a long time she was an inmate of the Emperor's *Zenana*. Whether the report was true or false, Bimala alone could say; but she was never known to allude to the subject.

Was Bimala a widow? Who knows? She wore ornaments, did not fast like widows, and in other ways behaved like a woman in wifehood.

That she cherished Tilottama, the Chieftain's Daughter, with real affection, her conduct in the temple has clearly showed. Tilottama returned her love. The other follower of Virendra Singha, Abhiram Swami, did not always remain in the fortress. He often travelled, spending a month or two in Garmandaran, a month or two on the journey. The inmates and other people believed him to be Virendra Singha's spiritual guide—and very truly, to all appearance, considering the homage Virendra paid him. Nay, he did not transact any of his domestic affairs, without previously consulting Abhiram Swami—and the advice given by his spiritual guide was almost always successful. The fact was that Abhiram Swami was a man of experience and possessed an acute intellect. Moreover, by virtue of his austerities, he had learnt to control his passions in almost all worldly transactions: when required, he could master his passion and go through the business calmly. Under such circumstances, what wonder that his advice would be more effectual than the schemes of the impatient and haughty Virendra Singha?

Besides Bimala and Abhiram Swami, a maidservant, named Ashmani, had come with Virendra Singha.

6

ABHIRAM SWAMI'S COUNSEL

Tilottama and Bimala reached home in safety. Some three or four days after this, Virendra Singha was seated in his steward's Office on a *masnad*, when Abhiram Swami entered. Virendra Singha rose from his *masnad*, and Abhiram Swami sat down upon a seat of the *kusa* grass handed by Virendra, who then resumed his seat with the Swami's permission.

'Virendra,' said Abhiram Swami, 'today I have some very important talk with you.'

'I am at your service, Sir,' replied Virendra Singha.

'A great war is about to break out between the Mogals and the Pathans.'

'Yes, Sir; some serious event is likely to ensue.'

Abhiram. 'Likely. Now, what have you determined on for yourself?'

'This arm'—replied Virendra haughtily—'This arm will quell the enemy, should he come.'

'Virendra' said the ascetic still more mildly, 'this reply doubtless befits a warrior like you; but you must know that victory is not gained by feats of heroism only—it is gained by observing the principles regulating peace and war. You are yourself one of the first of heroes; but your force numbers not more than a thousand men. What warrior ever can with such a force beat an army a hundred times its number? Both the Mogals and the Pathans are vastly superior to you in point of number. How can you then hope to escape the hands of the one, unless you secure the assistance of the other? Pray, don't be angry at my words. Consider the matter calmly. Further, what's the use of being hostile to both. An enemy is an undoubted evil. Why then have two instead of one? In my opinion, therefore, you should choose between the parties.'

'Which party,' said Virendra after a long pause, 'would you have me join, Sir?'

"Victory aye attends the banner of Right,' says the adage. Side with that party which is in the right. Rebellion is no common sin; embrace the Sovereign's cause.'

'Who is the Sovereign, I pray?' asked Virendra after reflection. 'Are not both the Mogals and the Pathans contesting for empire?'

'He who takes tribute is the Sovereign,' said Abhiram Swami.

Virendra. 'Akbar Shah?'

Abhiram Swami. 'Of course.'

At this, Virendra's countenance showed signs of displeasure; by and bye his eyes reddened. Seeing these signs, Abhiram Swami said,

'Virendra, suppress your anger. I tell you to follow the Emperor of Delhi—not Man Singha.'

Virendra stretched out his right hand, and pointing to it with a finger of the left, said,

'By your blessings, Sire, this hand I will drown in Man Singha's gore.'

'Be calm,' said Abhiram Swami. 'Don't mar your interest through passion. By all means punish Man Singha for the old wrong. But why should you be unfriendly with Akbar Shah?'

'If I were to side with the Emperor,' said Virendra in a rage, 'what general shall I have to fight under—whom shall I have to aid—whom shall I have to respect? Man Singha? No Sire—Virendra Singha is incapable of so base an action so long as he lives.'

Abhiram Swami was silent in dejection.

'Then,' asked he after a while, 'Then you think it preferable to join the Pathans?'

'Is it necessary for me to choose between the parties ?' enquired Virendra.

Abhiram. 'Yes, it is.'

Virendra. 'Then I must join the Pathans.'

Abhiram Swami heaved a sigh, and was again silent; a tear stood in his eyes.

'Forgive my transgression, Sire,' said Virendra Singha, greatly surprised. 'I beseech you, let me know what offence I have been unknowingly guilty of.

Abhiram Swami wiped his eyes with his sheet, and said, 'Listen. For several days, I have been engaged in astrological calculations. You know your daughter is an object of greater affection to me than yourself. I naturally made various calculations concerning her.' Here Virendra looked blank; eagerly he asked, 'Pray, what have you found by your calculation, Sir?'

'Great harm to Tilottama from a Mogal officer.'

A cloud overspread Virendra's face.

'It is only when the Mogals are your enemy,' went on the Swami, 'that any danger may proceed from that source—not if you be friendly to them. It is for this reason that I was persuading you to side with the Mogals. It was not my intention to pain you by this disclosure; but human endeavours avail not—methinks, the decrees of fate must take effect—why else should you be so determined?'

Virendra Singha remained mute.

'Virendra,' said Abhiram Swami, 'the ambassador of Katlu Khan is at the gate. It is because I saw him that I have come to you. Owing to my prohibition, the guards have not so long allowed him to come before you. I have now said my say. You may now summon him and return fit answer.'

Virendra Singha raised his head with a sigh.

'Sire! so long as I did not see Tilottama,' said he, 'I did not so much as think of her as my daughter. Now, I have none in this world save her. I bow to your command—I will forget the past—I will follow Man Singha. Let the porter usher in the ambassador.'

In accordance with this order, the porter brought in the envoy. He handed a letter from Katlu Khan. Its purport was that Virendra Singha should send a force of a thousand horsemen and five thousand gold mohurs to Katlu Khan, otherwise he would send an army of twenty thousand men to Garmandaran.

Virendra read the note and said, 'Envoy, let your master send his army.'

The man bowed low and went away. Bimala had played the eavesdropper all through the conversation.

7

CARELESSNESS

Sitting at a window of a chamber belonging to that part of the castle by the base of which, the river Amodara flowed past, murmuring, Tilottama was listlessly gazing at an eddy of the stream. It was evening; and those clouds that had been painted in gold in the western sky by the mellow rays of the setting sun, were dancing under the ever-flowing water. The lofty buildings and the tall trees on the opposite bank were painted on the clear canvass of heaven. Within the castle the peacock, the Indian crane and various other birds were crying in sweet confusion—sometimes, a bird busy in quest of its nest at the approach of night, was so silently winging its airy way beneath the firmament. After gently waving the mango grove and touching the waters of the Amodara, the cool, grateful summer breeze was playing with the ringlets of Tilottama's hair, or with the cloth which fell so gracefully over her shoulders. Tilottama was a beauty, and how do I wish to hold up to the gaze of the gentle reader her matchless perfections! But O vain wish! Courteous reader, have you ever in your 'young days' seen, with a lover's eye, the fresh-budding loveliness of a calm, gentle, soft maiden, whose dear image has stamped itself indelibly on your memory and imagination—whose sylph-like form keeps aye gliding in and out as if in a dream—in your youth, manhood and old age; in your busy moments and in your repose; alike when you sleep and when you wake; yet which for all this, leaves not a tinge of impurity behind it—have you, gentle reader, seen such a maiden? If you have, then only you will be able to conceive what Tilottama was like. That form which illuminates our mental darkness, through the profusion of its radiant charms—that form which through the perfection of its arch playfulness plants its poisonous tooth into our heart, our heroine had not. Hers was that form which through its deliciously soft graces, instills the dew of gladness into the mind—that form which keeps so gently waving in the imagination like a shrub lightly stirred by the breath of the vernal evening breeze.

Tilottama was sixteen; her body had not yet therefore received the full development of grown women; nay, there was still visible a tinge of girlishness in her form and features. The well-arched forehead, not narrow, yet not too expansive either, was like a moonlit stream, expressive of perfect quiescence. The raven black ringlets fell on her eyebrows, cheeks, neck, shoulders and breast; while the dark hairs behind were gathered up by an elegant pearl chain. The superb arch of her eyebrows looked like the work of the painter; a shade thicker, and they would have been absolutely faultless. Reader, do you love playful eyes? If so, Tilottama must despair of victory over you; her eyes were gentle; they could not dart glances like the lightning flash. The two dear eyes were very expansive; exquisitely graceful and mildly gleaming. In colour, they resembled delicious blue which appears on the face of the heavens at the 'sweet hour of prime.' When the damsel gazed with those large clear eyes, not a shadow of guile lurked in them. She had not learnt to look obliquely—her look was all openness and sincerity—-an infallible index to the sincerity of her soul. But when any one happened to look at her in the face, she cast her eyes down. Tilottama's acquiline nose never knew the pain of bearing the burden of the nasal ring. The two sweet lips were rosy and swam in genial humors; they were small, a little curved, and their habitual expression was a gentle smile. Ah! if your eyes were but once blessed with a sight of a smile on those lips, then be you an ascetic or a sage, young or old, you could never forget it in this life—yet there was nothing in it except sincerity and girlishness.

Although well-made, Tilottama's limbs had not yet attained their full proportions; yet whether owing to her youth or to its natural make, not a tinge of corpulency was perceptible in her beautiful person. Yet all the members of her slender frame were well rounded and delicate—on the well-rounded wrist, the *Marwari* bracelet; on the well-rounded arm, the diamond-studded *tar*; on the well-rounded finger, the ring; on the well-rounded loins, the zone; over the well-rounded shoulders the golden chain; on the well-rounded neck the jewelled necklace—the make of all the parts was exquisitely beautiful.

What is Tilottama about, sitting alone at the window of her chamber? Is she surveying the splendour of the evening sky? Why then are her eyes fixed on the ground? Is she enjoying the fragrant breeze blowing from the banks of the river? Why then minute drops of perspiration stand on her forehead? The breeze can only touch one side of her face. Is she then watching at the cattle grazing in the fields? Not even that; for the 'lowing herd' are by this time 'winding' to their fold. Is she listening to the *kokila's* song? If so, why does she look so pensive? No. Tilottama is seeing nothing, hearing nothing;—she is chewing the food of sweet and bitter fancy.

At this girlish age, what contemplation can possibly have absorbed all her faculties? Has her bosom been warmed by the witching influence of the first breath of love? Perhaps.

A maidservant brought in a lamp. Leaving off thinking, Tilottama took up a book and sat down by the light. She knew to read, she had learnt Sanskrit from Abhiram Swami. What is she reading? Kadamvari. The book did not please her, and she put it down after reading a little. She then took up Vasavadatta by Subandhu. She read a while and then was plunged in abstraction; she read again, and was again lost in thought—*Vasavadatta* too failed to please. She next tried Gitagovinda. The book pleased for a time, but on coming to the following verse,

'मुखरमधीरं त्यज मञ्जीरं रिपुमिव केलिषु लोलं।'

> [Thy sounding bangles, wench, resign,
> Lest they the tell-tales play.
> Thy foes they are, sweet lady mine;
> For dal'ance restless they.]

she blushed from shame and threw it down. Then for a while, she sat still on the bed. At hand were a pen and inkstand. She now began absently to write this and that, 'क,' 'स,' 'म,' room, door, tree, man etc. By degrees, one entire side of the couch became filled with marks. When there was no further room left, she was awakened to a sense of what she was about. She smiled at her work, and began to read what she had written. What has she written? 'वासवदत्ता,' 'महाश्वेता,' 'क,'

'ই,' 'इ,' 'प,' a tree, a *Senjuti Siva*, 'गीतगोविन्द,' 'विमला,' shrubs, leaves, scrawls, a fort. Confusion! What more has she written!

'कुमार जगत सिंह'
(Prince Jagat Singha.)

Tilottama's face crimsoned with shame. Foolish girl! Who's there in the room that thou shouldst blush so. 'कुमार जगत सिंह.' Tilottama read the words once—twice—thrice, many times; she looked at the door and read, and looked and read—like a thief in the very act of stealing.

She had not courage enough to read it for a long while, lest any one should come in and catch her in the act. Hurriedly she fetched water, and washed off the writing; but could not depend upon the result. She then wiped the spot clean with her cloth; and then examined whether any writing was legible any longer. Not a mark was there, yet it seemed to her as if the writing was still to be seen; she again washed the place and once more wiped it—still, still it seemed as if there was writ,

'कुमार जगत सिंह'

8

BIMALA'S CONSULTATION

Bimala was standing in the cottage of Abhiram Swami, who was seated on the ground, upon his devotional seat. She was narrating in detail how they had met with Jagat Singha. 'Today,' said she, when she had done, 'is the fourteenth day; tomorrow the fortnight will complete.'

'Well, what have you determined on?' asked Abhiram Swami.

'It is to get sage advice' replied Bimala 'that I have sought you, Sir.'

'Good,' said the Swami. 'My advice is—think no more about the matter.'

Bimala remained silent, exceedingly dejected.

'Why do you look so sad? Eh?' asked Abhiram Swami.

'What, then, is to be done for Tilottama?' returned she.

'Why?' asked Abhiram Swami curiously. 'Have the germs of love sprung up in Tilottama's mind?'

'How much shall I disclose to you, Sire!' said she after a pause. 'I have been watching her motions daily and nightly these good fourteen days, and am perfectly satisfied that Tilottama has conceived a very deep feeling.'

'You, women,' replied the ascetic with a smile, 'as soon as you perceive signs of affection, outright conclude it to be deep. Bimala, don't be uneasy on the score of Tilottama's future happiness. It is because she's a girl that her mental balance has been disturbed at first sight. She'll no doubt soon forget Jagat Singha, should all talk on the subject be studiously refrained from.'

'Not so, Sire,' said Bimala, 'The signs seen in Tilottama are not what you take them for. Within this fortnight, a change has come over her nature. She no longer finds delight in talking with her youthful companions or with me; nay, she seldom or never talks nowadays. Her books are rotting under the couch; her flowers are withering for lack of water; her birds are pining for neglect—she doesn't eat—she dosn't sleep; she dosn't make her toilet; she, who was never given to thinking, is now wholly absorbed in thought every hour in the four and twenty. There's a palor in Tilottama's face.'

Abhiram Swami remained silent for a long while.

'I was under the impression,' he said, 'that deep affection can not spring up at first sight; but woman's nature, specially that of girls, is known to God only. But what are you to do? Virendra will never lend his consent to such a match.'

'For that very fear,' said Bimala, 'I haven't up to this time disclosed this matter; nor did I in the temple tell our name and lineage to Jagat Singha. But now that the noble Singha,' here Bimala's face underwent a slight change, 'now that the noble Singha has resolved to make friends with Man Singha, what's the harm in his accepting Jagat Singha for his son-in-law?'

Abhiram. 'Why will Man Singha consent to such a marriage?'

Bimala. 'If he doesn't, the Prince is free to act.'

Abhiram. 'And why, again, will Jagat Singha marry the daughter of Virendra Singha?'

Bimala. 'What side, I pray, is entirely free from caste blemishes? The ancestors of Jayadhar Singha belonged also to the Yadu dynasty.'

'Should a daughter of such a family marry the son of the Musalman's brother-in-law?'

Bimala fixed her look on the ascetic. 'And why not so?' said she. 'What family is too low for the Yadu dynasty?'

At these words, the eyes of the ascetic darted fire. 'Wretch!' exclaimed he in a stern voice. 'Wretch! thou hast not forgotten thy own wretched fate? Out of my sight!'

9

THE LUMINARY OF THE RACE

The movements of Jagat Singha after he had bidden farewell to his father, spread terror and dismay among the Pathan army. The Prince had promised to drive away the fifty thousand troops of Katlu Khan to the other side of the Subarnarekha, with the aid of only five thousand men. Although he was as yet indeed far from achieving such success, yet the news of the way in which he displayed his qualifications as a general within two weeks of his departure from Jahanabad, made Man Singha say, 'perhaps the pristine glory of the Rajput name will revive at the hands of my princely son'.

Jagat Singha knew perfectly well that to beat in open fight an army of fifty thousand men with a force of five thousand was out of the question—such a course could only end in certain defeat or death. Accordingly, far from trying to bring on an open engagement, he adopted a mode of warfare calculated to avert such a consummation. He always kept his small force strictly hidden in deep forests or in the hollows of the undulating grounds that exist in that country;—he selected such spots to pitch his tents on as lying behind elevations, could not be discovered even by one standing very near. Remaining in this manner, whenever he received intelligence of the presence of any small detachment of Pathans, he burst on it like a wave of the sea and made root and branch work of them. He employed many spies, who went about in various directions in the guises of fruiterers, fishmongers, beggars, religious mendicants, Brahmins, physicians, and they brought him news of the movements and intentions of the enemy. On receiving any intelligence, he rapidly yet cautiously, posted troops at such a place as would afford the greatest convenience for attacking the approaching soldiers without being foreseen. If the detachment happened to be too large, he made no attempt to attack it; because he knew that in his present position, a single defeat meant utter annihilation—that should he be defeated in a single encounter, all would be lost. In such a case, when he saw that the Pathans had gone out of sight, he kept cautiously following them, and then plundered them of their provisions, horses, cannon, etc. If, on the contrary, the party turned out to be small, he remained quiet in his ambush so long as they did not come up to the desired spot—then when the opportunity came, with loud cries, he fell on the foe, like a famishing tiger, and cut him to pieces. Under such circumstances, the men could not know the neighbourhood of the enemy, and as a matter of course were quite unprepared for fight. Accidentally falling into the jaws of the enemy, they lost their lives almost without a struggle.

In this manner, a great many soldiers were destroyed. The Pathans were profoundly agitated; and set about to bring on an open fight with the view of crushing Jagat Singha's men. But where they were nobody could tell—like the messengers of Death, they presented themselves once only before the Pathan soldiers at their last moments, and vanished as soon as they had accomplished their mortal work. Jagat Singha was a master of strategy; he did not always keep his five thousand together—here a thousand, there five hundred; at one place, two hundred, at another place, two hundred. As he received intimations of the presence of the enemy, he dispatched his men by detachments, each proportioned to the exegencies of the case. When a job was accomplished, he no longer kept his men at the scene of action. Where the Rajputs were and where they were not, the Pathans could not at all ascertain. Every day tidings of the destruction of troops came to the ear of Katlu Khan—every hour brought with it fresh news of disaster. Whatever the business, it became difficult for the Pathan soldiers to come out of the fort, in small numbers; their excesses at once ceased; the soldiers took refuge within the fort; and it became extremely difficult to procure provisions. On receiving news of the redress, the country, previously so much harassed, had met with at the hands of Jagat Singha, Man Singha wrote his son the following letter:—

'Luminary of the Race! I am convinced that the Imperial domains will be rid of the Pathans by you. To back your efforts, I send you ten thousand soldiers more.'

The Prince wrote in reply:—

'As you like it, Sire. If more troops come, so much the better; else, by your blessings, with the five thousand I shall redeem my Kshetriya-like word.'

Drunk with martial enthusiasm, the Prince went on achieving uninterrupted success.

Saileshwara! Had all recollection of the lovely damsel, the magic of whose sincere glance had vanquished this warrior in thy temple, vanished quite from his mind amidst the tumult and din of fight? If so, then Jagat Singha is verily composed of stone like thee.

Come, go we to Bimala; let's see whether Jagat Singha *is* a stone or a man; let alone the tumult of the fray—Bimala alone is sweet in all this.

10

PREPARATION AFTER CONSULTATION

In the evening of the day following that on which Abhiram Swami drove out Bimala, she was making her toilet in her chamber. A woman of five and thirty, and engaged in that sort of thing? And why not so? Does youth pass away with any particular age? Never. Youth only passes away with beauty and love: she that has no beauty, is old in the very flower of youth; she who has it, is blessed with a perpetual youth; she whose mind is unknown to love and joy, is never young; she who has experienced them, never old. To that day, Bimala's body seemed filled with genial humors, and her mind overflowed with love and the ideas and desires which love inspires. Moreover, advance of age serves but to mellow beauty—a remark the truth of which the reader will be all the readier to allow, if he happen to be a little advanced in age.

What man that saw the beauty of her cherry-ripe lips, crimsoned with the colour of the betel, could say that he did not look upon a youthful lady? Who, after seeing the quick side-glances of her expansive eyes, shaded with *kajjala*, could say that the woman was not younger than a damsel of twenty-five? What a lovely pair of eyes! So gracefully drawn out, so lustrous, so quick-glancing! The eyes of some women unmistakably show that they are ambitious, and that they are ever eager to tread 'the primrose path of dalliance.' Bimala's eyes were of this kind. I tell the reader that Bimala was youthful—nay, she may more justly be considered as enjoying a perpetual youth. Who that witnessed the melting softness of her skin, over which shone her *champaka*-like complexion, could honestly say that a girl of 'sweet sixteen' was mistress of a softer person than she? Who that saw the small, beautiful ringlet which, escaping from behind her ear, had fallen on her cheek in happy negligence, could affirm that a young female's hair had not fallen on a young female's cheek! Courteous reader, kindly do comply with our request; open your mind's eye, and lo! look where seated before her glass, Bimala is dressing her hair—look how taking before her yon thick lock in her left hand, she is applying the comb to it—look at the supressed smile with which she is contemplating her youthful charms in the glass. Ah! Listen to the faint, mellifluous strains which are flowing from her lips at intervals. Nay, should you feel inclined, you are at liberty to feast your eyes with a sight of the voluptuous grandeur of her well-formed bust; then candidly say whether they are Time-conquering or not. Having seen and heard all this, now say what youthful woman is more captivating to your fancy?

Having woven her hair, Bimala did not tie up the braid into a knot, but let it hang at length behind her back. She then wiped her face with a handkerchief soaked in fragrant waters; again stained her lips with a betel containing fragrant spices; and then donned a pearl-studded *kanchali*. All the parts of her body she decked with golden and jewelled ornaments; but on second thought, she put off some of them. She next wore the curiously embroidered clothes and the coral-studded slippers; and about her well-arranged hair wound the precious pearl chain given to her by the Prince.

When the dressing was over, Bimala went to Tilottama's chamber. On seeing her dress, Tilottama was surprised.

'What's the matter, Bimala?' she asked with a laugh. 'Why in this dress?'

'That's no concern of yours,' Bimala said.

Tilottama. 'In sober truth, say—where are you going?'

Bimala. 'And who, my dear, has told you that I'm going out at all?'

Tilottama was abashed. Perceiving her confusion, Bimala said, kindly smiling,

'I'm going far.'

Tilottama's countenance expanded with joy, like a full-blown lotus.

'Pray, where are you going?' she asked Bimala in a soft tone.

'Better guess.'

Tilottama fixed her eyes on her face.

'Listen, then,' said Bimala, and taking hold of Tilottama's hand, she drew her to the window.

'I'm going to the temple of Saileshwara; there to meet with a certain Prince.'

Tilottama's frame was convulsed with some powerful emotion; she made no reply.

Bimala went on,

'I had a talk with Abhiram Swami. In the opinion of the holy father, your marriage with Jagat Singha can never take place; your father will spurn such a proposal. Should this matter reach his ears, I will thank my stars, if I can escape disgrace and punishment.'

'Why go then?' With a downcast face, Tilottama faintly uttered these words;

'Why go then?'

Bimala. 'Why? Have I not promised the Prince that I will see him tonight, and acquaint him with our name and lineage? What he will do with the mere knowledge of us, I can't tell. But let me now make ourselves known to him, leaving him to do what he thinks best under the circumstances. If the Prince really loves you—'

Before she could finish, Tilottama gagged her mouth with her cloth.

'I am ashamed to hear your words,' said she. 'You may go wherever you like; but you shall not speak of me to any one or to me of any one.'

Bimala again laughed. 'Who then told you to plunge into this ocean in this girlish age?' said she.

'Off!' exclaimed Tilottama. 'I won't hear you any more.'

Bimala. 'Then I shan't go to the temple?'

Tilottama. 'Am I forbidding you to go any where? You may go wherever you will.'

'Then I must not go,' said Bimala laughing.

'Go,' said Tilottama, looking down.

Bimala again laughed. After a while she said, 'I go. Don't you sleep till my return.'

A smile was also visible on Tilottama's lips—it seemed to say, 'How can I?' Bimala understood this. When about to depart, placing one hand on Tilottama's shoulder, with the other, she took hold of her chin, and for sometime studied her face, sanctified by the presence of sincere love. She then kissed it with affection. When she was going away, Tilottama espied a tear standing on her eyes.

Now Ashmani came to the door of the chamber and said to Bimala, 'Master calls you.'

Tilottama, hearing this, came forward, and said in Bimala's ear, 'Change your dress before you go.'

'Never fear,' replied Bimala.

Bimala then went to Virendra Singha's bedchamber. Virendra was reposing; one maidservant was shampooing his legs; another was fanning him. Approaching the couch, Bimala said, 'What's your will, Sir?'

Virendra Singha raised his head, and asked in surprise,

'Bimala, are you going out on some errand?'

'Yes, Sir,' replied she, 'but pray, what's your will?'

Virendra. 'How's Tilottama doing? She was in a bad state of health. Has she come all right now?'

Bimala. 'Yes, Sir, she has.'

Virendra. 'Do you fan me for a small while; let Ashmani bring Tilottama here.' The woman who was fanning, went out.

Bimala directed Ashmani by a sign to wait outside. Virendra said to the other maidservant.

'Lachmani, go, prepare some betels and bring them here.'

The woman who was shampooing went away.

Virendra. 'Bimala, why are you with this dress on, today?'

Bimala. 'I have some business.'

Virendra. 'What is it. I must know it'

Bimala. 'Hear then, Sir.'

Saying this, she began to gaze at Virendra with eyes which resembled the field of Cupid.

'Hear then, Sir,' said she. 'I am an adultress; now I go to the appointment.'

And anon she darted off.

11

ASHMANI'S EMBASSY

All this while, Ashmani had been expecting Bimala outside, according to her sign. On coming out, Bimala said to her,

'Ashman, I have some very private word with you.'

'From your dress,' replied the maidservant, 'I gathered that something most important was going to take place today.'

'Today I go very far on some important errand,' said Bimala. 'I can't however go alone at night, nor can I safely take any other person. So, you shall have to accompany me.'

'Where are you going?'—enquired Ashmani.

'Ashmani,' said Bimala, 'you were not in the habit of enquiring so much in days of old.'

Ashmani was a little abashed.

'Then wait a bit,' replied she. 'I'll go and do some household duties, and then come back.'

'One word more,' said Bimala. 'Suppose that today you meet with someone of old days, will he be able to recognise you?'

'How's that?' asked Ashmani in surprise.

'Suppose' continued Bimala, 'that you meet with Prince Jagat Singha, eh?'

Ashmani remained silent for a long while, and then said in an agitated voice,

'Shall I live to see such a day!'

'You may,' said Bimala.

'The Prince will certainly recognise me.'

'Then you shall not go'—said Bimala. 'But then, whom shall I take? I can't go alone.'

'How do I long to see the Prince!' Said Ashmani.

'Suppress your desire as best you can'—returned Bimala. 'But what am I to do now?'

Bimala began to think. All of a sudden, Ashmani began to laugh in her sleeve.

'Ill betide thee!' said Bimala. 'Why are you laughing without rhyme or reason?'

'A thought has struck me,' answered Ashmani. 'What if my darling Diggaja goes with you?'

'Ah! well said,' replied Bimala joyfully. 'I'll take that gallant with me.'

'Gracious me! but I was jesting,' said Ashmani in surprise.

'No joke,' replied Bimala. 'I don't mistrust the numskull. Night and day are all one to the blind man. The Brahmin will understand nothing, and I have no misgivings about him. But then, he won't consent to go.'

'Leave that to me,' said Ashmani laughing. 'I'll bring him. Please wait a little at the gate.'

Thereupon, she directed her steps towards a cottage within the castle.

Gajapati Vidyadiggaja, the disciple of Abhiram Swami, has already been introduced to the gentle reader. He has also been enlightened as to why Bimala called him by the cognomen of *Rasik Das Swami* (illustrious bond-slave of gallantry). This personage was the occupant of the cottage. He was about nine feet in altitude—in breadth, scarcely so much as one foot. His legs, from the loins to the toe, measured about six feet. In breadth they resembled two slender sticks. His colour 'held divided empire' with ink; perhaps Agni had sat down to devour his legs, taking them for very sticks, but had found them so utterly devoid of sap, that he had left them in the shape of brands. Owing to his great height, the worthy tended to be double. Among all his members, the nose held the most prominent place—the general lack of flesh was more than made up there. His goodly crown was shaven like that of an *Uriya* palankeen bearer. The new-grown hairs were very short, and pierced like so many needles. 'The pomp and circumstance' of the *tilaka* on his forehead was something splendid.

He had not received the title of *Gajapati Vidyadiggaja* for nothing. His intellect was unusually acute. In his childhood, he had commenced upon Sanskrit grammar in a *chatuspati*. In not more than seven months and a half, he got by rote the rule 'सहर्णघ,' both text and exposition. What, through the kindness of the Bhattacharjya, and what, through the noise and bustle of the class, he read on for ten and five years, and finished the noun affair. Then before entering upon the other affair, 'Let me see what the affair is,' said the teacher to himself. He then asked his pupil, 'Say, child, what do you get, if the termination, अम् comes after the base, राम?' After much exercise of thought, the pupil said, 'रामाम्भ.' 'Child,' said the teacher, 'now you may go back to your home. Your education with me has been finished. There's no more learning in my stock to bestow on you.'

'I have only one word to say,' replied the pupil haughtily. 'My title?'

'My child,' said the teacher, 'you have acquired such uncommon learning, that some novel title must be conferred upon you. Accept then the title of *Vidyadiggaja*.'

Diggaja humbly bowed at his feet in perfect self-complacency, and went home.

'I have now mastered grammar,' thought he. 'Now I must study Law a little. I have heard that Abhiram Swami is a great scholar. Who is there under the sun save him to teach me? To him then I will go.'

With this determination, he became an inmate of the castle. Abhiram Swami taught a good many pupils, and was not the man to set his face against any one;—so that whether Diggaja learned anything or not, he did not deny him his teaching.

The holy Gajapati was not only a grammarian and a lawyer, but he had a touch also of the rhetorician and the wit; for instance, 'the pail of clarified butter.' His shafts were mainly directed against Ashmani; and there was a profound reason for this. 'The advent of such a one as I,' thought he 'is solely for dalliance. This is my fair Vrindaban; Ashmani is my Radhika.' Ashmani was also a votary of Mirth; and her Madan Mohan served but as a substitute for a baboon. Bimala, also upon the scent, occasionally came to make the baboon dance. 'Lo! this is my Chandravali', said Diggaja to himself. 'And why shouldn't this be, considering what a 'pail of clarified butter' I have discharged? 'Tis a mercy Bimala doesn't know it's a borrowed feather.'

Today great joy awaits Madhava's luck—today Vrikabhanu's daughter is hieing herself to the grove-embosomed cottage.

12

ASHMANI'S RENDEZVOUS

Of what pattern of beauty was Diggaja's charmer, Ashmani, the reader is no doubt curious to know; and I will satisfy his curiosity. But it would be highly impudent for so contemptible a person as I am to depart from the beaten path followed by authors when engaged in describing female loveliness. I will therefore begin with the beginning *i.e.* the invocation.

O word-presiding Goddess! O thou of the lotus seat! O thou with a countenance fine as the autumnal moon! Thou whose feet excel a group of chaste lotuses, and whose bosom overflows with the 'milk of kindness' for thy devotee, vouchsafe unto me the protection of those lily-like feet of thine, for I am going to describe the beauty of Ashmani. O thou who humblest the pride of beauteous damsels! O thou creator of cart-loads of confounded, big, elegant, compound words, do but once grant me shelter in a corner of thy feet; for I am about to describe a beauty. O thou giver of the milk and honey coveted by scholars, thou who scarcely favorest the illiterate! O thou saviour of the base! O thou mother of that perilous phenomenon—*cacoethes scribendi*! O thou who replenishest the lamp of learning at Bartala, do thou once vouchsafe to illumine

'—What in me is dark.'

Mother, I know that thou hast two several forms. Do not, I beseech thee, make my poor shoulders ache by riding them in that form in which thou didst bless Kalidasa—that form which breathed inspiration into the author of *Raghuvansa* and *Kumarsamvaba*, *Meghaduta* and *Sakuntala*—under whose inspiration Valmiki composed his *Ramayana*—Bhababhuti his *Malatimadhava* and Bharabi his *Kiratarjuniam*. But descend thou on my head in that form which inspired *Sri Harsha* in producing his *Naisadha*—which has enabled Bharata Chandra to fascinate all Bengal by his incomparable *Vidya*—which smiled on the birth of Dasarathi Ray, and which still illumines the depositories of Bartala; for I am going to describe the beauty of Ashmani.

Ashmani's flowing braid was like the snake. Owing to this, the pride of that animal was wounded. 'What is the use of again showing my cursed face to the world,' it said 'when I am vanquished by the braid of Ashmani? I will hide my shame under the ground.' Saying this, it entered its hole. Bramha perceived the danger, for now that the snake had disappeared, who was to bite people any more. Reflecting thus, he pulled it out by the tail. Seeing itself thus compelled to show its face again, it began to beat its head against the ground for grief, and the consequence was that its head got flattened. Ever since snakes have their present hood. The very Moon 'hid his diminished head' before Ashmani's face. Unable to rise for shame, that divinity went to Bramha for redress—who said, 'Never fear. Go, rise. Henceforth let woman's face be hid.' Thus came the veil into being. The two dear eyes were like the *Khanjana* bird—lest the bird should spread out its wings and fly away, the Creator wisely provided against that too possible contingency by creating the two lids, like the door of a cage. Her nose vied with that of Garura himself—that monarch of birds. Seeing it, the feathered monarch took fright and straightway flew to a tree. From that time, birds have lived in trees only. From another cause, the pomegranate left Bengal and fled to Patna; it was followed by the elephant, who fled to Burma with its proboscis. There only remained the Dhawalagiri. 'What may be my height?' it thought. 'Five miles at most, but these are at least six miles high.' Intensely brooding over this subject, its head grew heated; it thereupon fell to heaping ice on it. Ever since it has held ice on its head. Etcetera, etcetera.

Through the malice of Fortune, Ashmani was a widow.

On coming to Diggaja's cottage, she found the door shut; a lamp was burning within.

'What ho! holy man,' called she.

No one answered.

'What ho! Gosain, ho!'

Still no answer.

'Hang him! What is the hypocritical fellow about? Lord Rasik Das, ho!'

No reply still.

Ashmani peeped through a chink in the door, and saw that the Brahmin was engaged in taking his meal; and it was for this reason that he did not speak; for Brahmins do not eat if they happen to speak while eating their meal.

'*He* pretend to sanctity!' said Ashmani to herself. 'I shall see whether he eats after speaking.'

'I say, slave of a gallant!'

No reply.

'Ho! prince of gallants!'

Answer. 'Hum!'

'The Brahmin has answered with rice in his mouth. That's no speaking', thought Ashmani.

'Holla, mirror of gallantry!'

Answer. 'Hum!'

Ashmani. 'Speak first, man, and then eat.'

Answer. 'Hu-u-um!'

Ashmani. 'Is it come to this? You a Brahmin, and do this sort of thing! I will straight tell it to the holy Swami. Whom have you got in the room?'

The Brahmin eyed round with apprehension, but seeing nothing, began to eat again.

'What's this?' said Ashmani. 'Why do you eat again? Do you eat after speaking?'

Diggaja. 'Why? When have I spoken?'

Ashmani burst out into a laugh.

'Now you have!'

Diggaja. 'Right, right, right. No, then I shan't eat again.'

Ashmani. 'Certainly not. Why, get up then and open the door.'

Ashmani saw through the opening that the Brahmin was actually about to rise from his meal.

'No, no,' said she. 'You must finish the quantity of rice still left.'

Diggaja. 'No, that can't be. I have spoken.'

Ashmani. 'How's that? On my life, you must eat.'

Diggaja. 'Horrible! How can I, after speaking?'

Ashmani. 'I am going then—I had many confidential words for you, which you shan't hear. I am going.'

Diggaja. 'No, no, Ashman! don't you be so angry. I'll eat.'

The Brahmin began to eat again—as soon as he had taken two or three mouthfuls, Ashmani said,

'Well, you have done—rise and open the door.'

Diggaja. 'Let me but finish this handful.'

Ashmani. 'Your stomach will never cry 'hold'. Get up, or else I will divulge that you have eaten after speaking.'

Diggaja. 'Confound it! Here you are—I am getting up.'

The Brahmin sipped the *gandusha*, rose up and opened the door.

13

ASHMANI'S AMOUR

On the door being opened, as Ashmani entered the room, Diggaja conceived that since his dearly beloved was come, it behooved him to welcome her in a right gallant fashion. He accordingly waved his hand and exclaimed,

'ओं आयाहि वरदे देवि!'
[O blessing goddess hail!]

'This is a very fine piece of poetry' said Ashmani. 'Wherefrom have you procured it?'

Diggaja. 'Today I have composed it for you.'

Ashmani. 'Well have you been called the prince of gallants.'

Diggaja. 'रसिकः कौषिको वासः'.
[The gallant clad in silken vest.]

'My fair one, pray, sit you down; while I wash my hand.'

'Ill-starred wretch! you will wash your hand?' said Ashmani to herself. 'Beshrew me if I do not make you eat the rejected meal. How's that?' she said aloud. 'Why are you going to wash your hand? Eat, man.'

'What do you say? Haven't I risen from my meal? Shall I eat again?'

Ashmani. 'And why not? Is there not rice still left? Will you fast?'

'How can I help it?' replied Diggaja with regret. 'You were in such a hurry', and he eyed the rice eagerly.

'Then you must eat again,' said Ashmani.

Diggaja. 'O horrible! I have sipped the *gandusha*, I have risen from my meal, and shall I eat again?'

'Yes, you must. I shall see that.' Saying this, Ashmani grasped the Brahmin's arm, by main force dragged him to the dish, and made him sit down.

'O fie! O fie! What have you done! What have you done! Have you not touched me with my mouth still unwashed!'

Ashmani. 'And where's the harm, I pray? What is not allowable in love?'

The Brahmin was silent.

Ashmani. 'Eat, I pray you.'

Diggaja. 'I have sipped the *gandusha*, I have risen from my seat, moreover you have touched me—shall I eat again?'

Ashmani. 'You must—nay, you must eat after I eat of the dish.' Saying this, Ashmani took up a handful from the dish, and ate a mouthful.

The Brahmin was struck dumb.

Ashmani returned into the dish the quantity of rice that remained after filling her mouth, and said,

'Come, eat.'

The Brahmin was rendered speechless.

Ashmani. 'Fall to; listen', here Ashmani said something in Gajapati's ear.

The Brahmin cut a caper high in the air.

'Hey! then I must eat,' exclaimed Diggaja and began to gulp down the defiled rice like a very cow. The dish vanished in a twinkling. He then demanded,

'My fair one, now?'

Ashmani. 'Confound you! In unwashed mouth?'

'Yes, yes. I'm going to wash my mouth,' said he, and thereupon fell to washing his mouth in a blind hurry;—some parts of it were washed, while the others remained untouched by water. One bushel of rice remained deposited in the openings between his teeth.

'Where, my fair one, where is the nectar of your lips?'

Ashmani. 'Ill betide you! first wipe your mouth.'

Hurriedly the Brahmin wiped his hands and face with the forepart of his cloth.

'Now, my fair one?'

Ashmani. 'Come hither.'

Diggaja went to Ashmani and sat down by her.

Ashmani. 'Draw your mouth near to mine.'

Diggaja drew his mouth near to Ashmani's.

Ashmani. 'Open your mouth.'

Diggaja's obedience was implicit; he parted his lips a foot asunder. Ashmani took out a betel from her handkerchief, and began to chew it, Diggaja continuing with open mouth. When her mouth was entirely filled with saliva mixed with betel, she discharged the whole of its contents into Diggaja's mouth. The man was in sore straits; the beloved one had favored him with the betel juice; he had not therefore the heart to throw it out, for fear of being called ungallant, nor could he bring himself to swallow it, for how could he swallow a whole mouthful of saliva immediately after taking his meal? So it remained in his mouth, like the poison in the throat of *Nilakantha*.

Taking this opportunity, Ashmani took a toothpick and put it into one of Diggaja's capacious nostrils. On came the sneeze, and the next moment, his weak frame was deluged with the entire quantity of the nectarous fluid, which gushed out violently from his mouth.

Relieved from the dilemma, the Brahmin began to wash his body, reciting at the same time the following elegant line of verse:—

'दक्षिणे पश्चिमे वापि न कुर्याद्दन्तधावनं.'
[Facing the south ne'er clean thy teeth:
Facing the west do it neither.]

14

ABDUCTION OF DIGGAJA

On the other hand, Bimala grew impatient at Ashmani's delay, and thinking it inadvisable to wait any longer, went personally in search of Gajapati. On seeing her enter the cottage, Ashmani exclaimed,

'Welcome! welcome! Chandravali. O welcome!'

'Hey day!' said Diggaja. 'In what a lucky moment did I rise from my bed this morning! One alone is enough, and lo! there have arisen two! The *Shastra* hath it—

'एकश्चन्द्रस्तमोहन्ति नच मूर्खशतैरपि.'
[A single moon darkness defeats,
And not a thousand fools.]

'And have you heard that the prince of gallants has lost his caste?' said Ashmani.

'How so?' said the prince.

'Havn't yon eaten the rice defiled by me?' replied Ashmani.

'And what's the earthly harm in that, I pray?' returned he. 'It is my holy bread; you are my good mother *Bhagabati*.'

'Out open you!'

Here Bimala whispered into Ashmani's ear, 'Won't he go?'

Ashmani. 'I haven't yet spoken it to him.'

Bimala. 'I'll do it then.'

'Ho! gallant,' said she, addressing Diggaja, 'I have a word of very great importance with you.'

'What is it, eh?'

Bimala. 'Do you love us?'

Diggaja. 'What a question!'

Bimala. 'Both of us?'

Diggaja. 'Both, both.'

Bimala. 'Will you do as I say?'

Diggaja. 'Why should you doubt it?'
Bimala. 'Instantly?'
Diggaja. 'Yes, instantly.'
Bimala. 'At this moment?'
Diggaja. 'At this very moment.'
Bimala. 'Do you know why we two have come to you?'
Diggaja. 'No, I don't.'
'We'll elope with you,' said Ashmani.

The Brahmin was struck dumb, and for a time remained agape—Bimala suppressed her rising laughter with difficulty.

'Why are you silent?' asked Bimala.
'Nya-nya-nya-ta-ta-ta-ta,'—no articulation.
'Then you won't go?'
'Nya-nya-nya, ta-ta, let me first go and speak to the holy Swami.'
'What will you speak to him for? Is it an occasion for the celebration of your mother's funeral obsequies; that you will go to the holy man for instructions?'

Diggaja. 'No, then I needn't go; but pray, on what day are you going?'
Bimala. 'On what day! When but at this very moment? Don't you see me furnished with my ornaments?'
Diggaja. 'At this very moment?'
Bimala. 'And why not so? If you refuse, tell it—and we go in search of another. But know we leave our hearts with you.'

Gajapati could bear it no longer.
'Very well, I am ready.'
'Then take your sheet,' said Bimala.

Diggaja put on a *namabali*. Bimala was about to set out, and the Brahmin about to follow, when he said,

'My fair one?'
Bimala. 'What do you say?'
Diggaja. 'When are we returning?'
Bimala. 'Return! Am I not going away for good? We three will live like man and wives in another country.'

Diggaja's mouth filled with a laugh. He said,
'But shall I leave all these articles behind?'

Bimala. 'Doubtless you have no end of them!'
Diggaja. 'At any rate, the brazen utensils?'
Bimala. 'Never fear; I'll buy you all those.'

The Brahmin was rather sad; but what could he choose but consent, without running the certain risk of having his love to the women called in question. Making the best of a bad bargain, he said,

'*Khungiputi*?'

'The fellow sure has cartloads of them!' thought Bimala. 'Make haste,' said she.

Vidyadiggaja had two books in all, to wit—a Sanskrita Grammar, and a treatise on Hindu Law. Taking up the grammar, he said, 'What have I to do with this any more? I carry it on my fingers' ends.' He then took the other book in his *Khungi*, and uttering 'Durga-Sri-Hari,' sallied out with Bimala and Ashmani.

'Go on,' said Ashmani. 'I'll overtake you afterwards.'

Saying this, Ashmani entered the house. Bimala and Gajapati went out. They left the castle-gate, unperceived in the darkness. After having advanced a little, Diggaja said,

'How's this? Ashmani is not come?'

'Perhaps she couldn't come out,' answered Bimala. 'But are you not content with having me alone?'

The prince of gallants was mute. After a while, he sighed forth, 'O the utensils!'

15

DIGGAJA'S COURAGE

With hasty steps Bimala soon left the village of Garmandaran behind her. The night was pitch dark—she walked cautiously by the help of the starlight. On entering the field, she was rather alarmed; her companion was noiselessly following her, without wasting a single word. At such a moment, the human voice is cheering and welcome. Bimala therefore asked Gajapati,

'Gallant, what are you thinking about?'

'I say, the utensils,' said the gallant. Without returning any reply, Bimala laughed in her sleeve.

After a while Bimala again opened her lips.

'Diggaja, do you fear ghosts?' asked she.

'Ram! Ram! Ram!' exclaimed he. 'Take the name of Ram,' and drew a yard nearer to Bimala.

'This way is fearfully infested by ghosts,' said she, encouraged by her success. Diggaja came up and caught hold of the flowing end of Bimala's sheet.

'The other day,' continued Bimala 'we were returning after worshipping Saileshwara—when what should we see but a frightful shape under the banian tree at the roadside?'

From the pull at her dress, Bimala perceived that the Brahmin was shaking like an aspen leaf, and saw that if she went further, he would be deprived quite of his motion. She accordingly desisted, and said,

'Can you sing, gallant?'

'Yes, I can,' replied Diggaja. For breathes there a gallant to whom the 'concord of sweet sounds' is a sealed book?

'Pray, then sing a song.'

Diggaja began:—

> 'The hour was ill, I tell thee, sweet,
> My Shyam when I did see,
> Perch'd on a bough of Kadamba;
> 'Twas then all o'er with me.'

Hearing the preternatural sound, a cow which was reposing at the roadside and chewing the cud, fled for life.

The song however went on,

> 'My race that day I stain'd, my love,
> To follow Shyam alone—
> That crested buck holding the reed:
> I'm gone, my girl, I'm gone.
> He laughs and talks and laughs and talks;
> 'Milk-maid, my aunty dear,'
> Says he, 'thy pitcher, lass, ha! ha!
> In faith, I'll throw down here'.'

Diggaja could sing no longer; all of a sudden his ear was bewitched. Like the symphony breathed by 'harps angelical,'— nectarous, enchanting strains suddenly entered his ear; Bimala herself had begun to sing in the full compass of her voice.

The 'enchanting ravishment' begot of the seven notes flooded the still expanse of the nightly firmament. The sounds mounted the wings of the cool summer breeze and went away.

Diggaja listened with bated breath. When Bimala had finished, he said,

'Again.'

Bimala. 'What again?'

Diggaja. 'Pray, sing another dear song.'

Bimala. 'What shall I sing?'

Diggaja. 'Sing a Bengali air.'

'I will.' Saying this, Bimala began to sing again.

While thus engaged, she felt a strong pull at the border of her dress. She turned round and saw that Gajapati had well nigh come upon her heels, and held fast the flowing end of her sheet, as if his life had depended upon it.

'What is the matter?' asked Bimala in surprise. 'Is the ghost out again?'

The Brahmin could not speak, but pointed with his finger, 'There!'

Bimala looked at the direction in silence. Deep and hard breathing entered her ear, and she espied something near the road.

Summoning up courage, she drew nigh and discovered a handsome and well caparisoned horse lying on the ground, gasping for life.

Bimala resumed her journey; but the sight of the well-furnished steed filled her with apprehensions. For a long while she remained silent. After walking a mile, Gajapati again pulled at her.

'What?' asked Bimala.

Gajapati held up some object to her.

'This is a soldier's turban,' said she, and was again plunged in thought.

'The turban,' said she to herself, 'belonged to the same person that the steed belonged to? No, not so. The turban is a foot soldier's.'

Now the moon arose. Bimala was still more lost in thought. After a long while, Gajapati mustered courage and asked her, 'Fair one, why do you speak no more?'

'Do you see any marks on the road?'

Gajapati looked attentively at the way.

'Yes, I see the hoofmarks of many horses.'

Bimala. 'That's like a sensible man! Do you understand anything from it?'

Diggaja. 'No.'

Bimala. 'Yonder a dead horse, there a soldier's turban, here the hoof-marks of so many horses—can't you understand anything from all these? But to whom am I speaking!'

Diggaja. 'What's the matter, I pray?'

Bimala. 'Just now many soldiers have passed this way.'

'Let us then walk a little slow' said Gajapati with fear, 'to allow them time to get far ahead of us.'

'Numskull!' exclaimed Bimala, laughing. 'What do you speak of their getting ahead of us? Don't you see the direction to which the front of the hoof-marks points? These soldiers have gone to Garmandaran,' and Bimala was sad.

Presently the white grandeur of the temple of Saileshwara rose to the view. Bimala reflected that there was no necessity of the Brahmin's seeing the Prince—nay, it was rather calculated to produce evil; and she was thinking how to get rid of him, when Gajapati himself furnished the cue.

The Brahmin again drew near Bimala's back, and caught hold of her apparel.

'What again?' asked she.

'How far is it to that?'

Bimala. 'To what?'

Diggaja. 'To that banian tree?'

Bimala. 'Which banian tree, mean you?'

Diggaja. 'Where yon espied the other day?'

Bimala. 'Espied what?'

Diggaja. 'It must be nameless at night.'

Understanding how matters stood, Bimala availed herself of the opportunity, and uttered in a deep voice,

'Oh!'

'What's the matter, I beseech you?' enquired the Brahmin, with consternation.

Bimala with her finger pointed at the banian tree near Saileshwara's temple, and said in a hushed voice,

'Yonder's the banian tree.'

Diggaja did not move an inch more; in fact he was utterly incapable of proceeding any farther; and trembled like an aspen leaf.

'Come along,' said Bimala.

'I shan't go any farther,' replied the Brahmin, trembling.

'I too am affrighted,' said she.

The Brahmin now advanced a foot, ready to bolt.

Bimala looked at the tree and descried some white object beneath it. She knew that Saileshwara's bull used to lie there; but said to Gajapati,

'Take the name of your guardian god, Gajapati. What do you see under the tree?'

'Help! O! help! my God!' exclaimed Diggaja, and off he bolted. Blessed with long legs, in a trice he left a mile behind him.

Bimala knew the nature of Gajapati sufficiently well to infer that he would go straight to the castle gate—so that without any misgivings on that head, she proceeded in the direction of the temple.

Bimala had considered everything before she came out, except one: Had the Prince come?

The thought rendered her extremely uneasy. She saw that the Prince had given no certain assurance of his coming; but had only said, 'Here you will find me; if you don't, we shall never meet again.' In such a case, the probability of his not coming was very great.

If he had not come, then so much trouble had been taken in vain.

'Ah! why didn't I think of this before?' said she to herself. 'Why again did I drive away the Brahmin? How shall I return alone this night? Saileshwara, thy will be done!'

To ascend the temple, you had to pass underneath the banian tree. As Bimala was passing that way, she found that the bull was not there, nor was the white object which she had descried. She was rather surprised; for had the bull strayed, it must have been somewhere in the plain.

Bimala looked at the trunk of the tree, when it appeared to her as if she could see only part of the white dress of a man stationed on the other side. This increased her terror; with hurried steps she went towards the temple, ascended the steps by leaps, and vigorously rapped at the door.

It was shut.

'Who's there?'—was the question from within in a deep voice.

'Who's there?'—reverberated the empty vault.

Mustering courage with might and main, Bimala replied,

'A way-worn woman.'

The door opened.

A lamp was burning within; in front of her stood a tall man, with the sheathed sword in his hand.

Bimala saw and recognised,

Prince Jagat Singha.

16

IN PRESENCE OF SAILESHWARA

On entering the temple, Bimala sat down to rest a little. She then bowed down her head to Saileshwara and next bowed to the Prince. For some time, both remained silent, not knowing how to express their minds, each to the other. Both of them were confused. How to introduce the conversation!

Bimala, who was a consummate adept in the peace and war relative to such matters, said with a smile,

'Through the grace of Saileshwara, Prince, I have found you here; I was frightened to come across the plain at night—now I revive courage in seeing you, Sir.'

'All's well with you?' asked the Prince.

The object of Bimala was first to ascertain whether the Prince was really attached to Tilottama—and then to speak of other matters. She accordingly said,

'Yes, Sir, it is for the good of us that I have come to worship Saileshwara. Now I understand that the god is quite satisfied with your worship alone—and will not accept mine. I shall therefore return with your permission.'

Prince. 'Very well; but you shouldn't go alone; I must convey you home.'

Bimala saw that the Prince had not devoted all his time to the exercise of his arms.

'And why shouldn't I go alone, I pray?' asked she.

Prince. 'There are dangers in the way.'

Bimala. 'Then I will go to Maharaja Man Singha.'

'Why so?' enquired the Prince.

Bimala. 'Why? I have a suit to bring forward to him. The General he has appointed is unable to remove the fears of our way; he is incapable of destroying his enemies.'

'The General will reply,' said the Prince laughing, 'that the destruction of foes even the gods are not equal to—what is man? Witness, that enemy whom *Mahadeva* had reduced to ashes in the Grove of austerities—'tis only a fortnight since the same *Manmatha* has created strange disturbance in this his very temple. Such prowess!'

'At whom was the disturbance aimed, I pray?' asked Bimala, with a smile.

'At the General himself,' replied the Prince.

'Why,' said Bimala 'will the Maharaja believe in so impossible a thing?'

Prince. 'I have a witness.'

Bimala. 'And who is such a witness, Sir?'

Prince. 'You, good-natured—'

Bimala interposed by saying,

'Your humble servant is very ill-natured; call me Bimala, if you please.'

'Bimala is my witness.'

Bimala. 'No, Bimala will never give such evidence.'

Prince. 'Indeed, most probable. She that can in no more than a fortnight forget her promise—she can never prove a true witness!'

Bimala. 'Sir, kindly put me in mind of my promise.'

'To tell me the name and lineage of your companion.'

'Prince' said she, suddenly changing her tone of raillery for one of profound earnestness, 'Prince, I hesitate to satisfy your curiosity, lest it should not be for your peace of mind.'

The Prince mused for a while; he too renounced the light vein.

'Bimala,' said he, 'is the discovery of her name and lineage calculated to render me unhappy?'

'Yes, Sir,' replied Bimala.

'Come what will,' said the Prince, after reflecting sometime, 'do you satisfy my longing. Nothing can possibly be more harassing than the intolerable suspense which I am suffering. If what you apprehend turn out to be true, that even would be preferable to my present misery, for then I shall be able to console my mind with something. Bimale! I havn't come to you, prompted by mere curiosity—no, now I have no time to indulge in curiosity. Within this whole fortnight I have known no other bed than my steed's back. It is because my mind is exceedingly restless that I have sought you.'

It was to extort this confession that the previous endeavours of Bimala were made. With the view of extorting something more, she said,

'Prince, you are well versed in political morality. Pray, consider whether you should, in this time of war, suffer your mind to be absorbed in the contemplation of a lady hard to obtain? For the good of both, I conjure you to try to forget my companion. No doubt, you will succeed in the excitement of fight.'

'Ah! whom shall I forget?' replied the Prince, his nether lip showing a smile significant of his mental disquiet, 'whom shall I forget? The image of your companion has engraven itself deep on my mind at first sight; this heart can never get rid of it, without being reduced to ashes. People call me stonehearted; you know what is engraved on stone perishes with the stone itself. What do you speak of fight, Bimale? Ever since I saw your companion, in fight only I have been engaged. Whether in the field or in camp, I have never for a moment been able to forget that countenance. When the Pathan had raised his sword to cut off my head, my first thought was that if I then fell, I should never see her again—that our first sight was destined to be our last. Bimale, where shall I go to see your companion?'

What need of further confession. Bimala said,

'My companion you will find at Garmandaran—the lovely Tilottama, daughter of Virendra Singha.'

Jagat Singha felt as if an adder had stung him. He hung down his head and supported himself on his sword.

'Your words have, after all, proved true,' said he, with a sigh, after a long pause. 'Tilottama is not destined to be mine. I go to the field—there to drown all hopes of my future happiness in the enemy's blood.'

Bimala was touched by the Prince's grief. 'If true affection met with its reward in this world, noble Prince, you certainly deserved the hand of Tilottama. And why do you at once give way to despair, Sir? Today, Fortune is adverse, tomorrow, she may be friendly.'

Sweet is the voice of Hope; in the darkest day, she whispers soft into man's ear, 'The cloud and the storm will not endure for ever; why then are you cast down? Listen to my words.' Hope spoke through Bimala's mouth, 'Why are you cast down? Listen to my words.'

Jagat Singha listened to the voice of Hope. Who can know the Divine Will? Who can read beforehand the decrees of Fate? What is impossible under the sun? What impossibilities have not taken place in this world?

Yes, the Prince listened to Hope.

'Today my mind is exceedingly restless—I am incapacitated quite to judge the right course. What Fate has decreed must happen afterwards, for who can control Fate? Now I can only express my mind. Here, before the holy presence of Saileshwara, I vow never to accept the hand of any one save Tilottama's. I implore you to speak to your companion all that I have said. Pray, tell her that I long to see her once more only. I swear never to ask for this boon again.'

Bimala's countenance beamed with joy.

'How shall you, Sir, get the reply of my companion?'

'I cannot venture to trouble you again and again,' answered the Prince, 'but if you see me once again in this temple, I shall rest your debtor. Some time or other, you may expect a return from Jagat Singha.'

'Prince,' replied Bimala, 'I am your servant; but I greatly fear to come alone at night by this road. It is only because my promise had to be fulfilled, that I have come tonight. Now the country is infested by the enemy; I shall be exceedingly afraid to come again.'

'If you shouldn't think it wrong,' said the Prince, after reflecting a little, 'I can go along with you to Garmandaran. I'll wait at some fit place, where you will bring me her mind.'

'Come then, Sir,' replied Bimala delightfully.

They were about to sally out, when they heard the sounds of cautious steps outside the temple.

'Have you brought a companion with you?' demanded the Prince, with a little surprise.

'Oh no,' said Bimala.

'Whose steps can we have heard then? I am afraid somebody outside has overheard our conversation.'

He thereupon came out and went all round the temple, but found none.

17

VIRA PANCHAMI

After bowing down to Saileshwara, Jagat Singha and Bimala set out for Garmandaran, in an alarmed spirit. After proceeding in silence for some time, the Prince said,

'Bimala, I am curious about one thing. I don't know what you will say, when you hear it.'

'What is it, Sir?'

Prince. 'I am convinced you can never be a maidservant.'

'And why should you think so, pray,' asked Bimala with a smile.

Prince. 'There is some very particular reason why the daughter of Virendra Singha cannot be the daughter-in-law of the lord of Abnir. It is a very great secret. You could not possibly know it, if you were no better than a maidservant.'

'You have guessed right, Sir,' said Bimala with a sigh. 'I am not a maidservant, although behave like one, as my bad luck would have it; but why do I blame my luck? It has not been so bad either.'

The Prince perceived that the topic had awakened grief in the mind of Bimala. He accordingly dropped it.

'Prince,' went on Bimala, 'one day I will let you know who I am—but not now. But what noise is that? Is someone dogging us?'

The sound of human steps was now distinctly heard; it also appeared as if two men had been whispering to each other. They had then walked a mile.

'I begin to fear greatly,' said the Prince. 'I'll go and look out.'

Saying this, the Prince retraced his steps some way, and also looked aside, but saw no one. He returned and said to Bimala,

'I fear some body is following us. Let's talk cautiously.'

They went on, talking in an almost inaudible tone. Now they came up to the castle.

'How will you enter the castle now?' asked the Prince; 'the gate must be shut at this late hour.'

'Content you, Sir,' replied Bimala. 'I provided for that when I came out.'

'Is there any secret passage?' asked the Prince laughing.

'Where the thief is,' returned Bimala laughing, 'there's the breach.'

'Bimala,' said the Prince after a pause, 'I needn't go any farther. I'll wait in the mango wood by the castle. I beseech you, do you earnestly implore your companion in my name. I long to bless my eyes once more with a sight of her—be it after a fortnight; a month—or even a year.'

'Yonder mango grove is not solitary enough. Pray, Sir, come with me.'

Prince. 'How far?'

Bimala. 'Into the castle.'

The Prince mused a little, and then said, 'No, Bimala, I may not do this. I never will enter the castle without the permission of its lord.'

'What do you fear, Sir?' asked Bimala.

'Princes'—replied he haughtily—'Princes never fear to go any where. But, pray, consider whether it becomes the son of Abnir's lord to steal into the castle without the express knowledge of its master.'

'It is I,' said Bimala 'who am taking you in.'

'I beseech you,' returned the Prince, 'don't you think I am slighting you as a maidservant, if I enquire what right you have to welcome me into the castle.'

'You will not go' asked Bimala—'unless you know my right?'

'Never'—was the answer.

Bimala bent to the Prince's ear and said something.

'Proceed, madam, so please you,' said the Prince.

'I am a maidservant, Prince,' said Bimala, 'and should be commanded.'

'What you will,' said the Prince.

The way they were then following led to the gate of the castle; on its side was the mango wood, which was invisible from the main entrance. If you wanted to go where the Amodara flowed behind the castle, you must walk through this wood. Bimala now left the highway, and entered the wood, accompanied by the Prince.

After entering it, they heard the sound of the breaking of dry leaves, and of human steps.

'Again!' said Bimala.

'Once more stay a little,' said the Prince; 'I will look about.'

He drew his sword, and went in the direction of tho sound; but could see nothing. Underneath the mango wood, such dense thickets were formed by the exuberance of various wild shrubs and plants, and such a gloom was spread by the trees, that the Prince could nowhere see far before him. He thought it not impossible that the sounds had proceeded from some animals treading upon the dry leaves. Whatever it might be, thinking it expedient to dispel his doubts, he got up to the top of a tree, and began to survey round. After a long while, he espied the moonlit turbans of two men, whose persons were hid in the deep gloom formed by the boughs of some tall mango tree.

The Prince marked well and was perfectly satisfied as to the presence of the men. He also carefully marked the tree, so as to preclude the chance of his missing it on his return. Then softly coming down, he came up to Bimala, and related all that he had seen.

'If I had two spears now!' said he.

'What will you do with spears, pray?' asked Bimala.

Prince. 'Then I could ascertain who these men were. The signs bode no good. From the turbans, I think the rascally Pathans have been following us with some evil intent.'

Immediately the remembrance of the dying steed at the roadside, the turban, and the traces of horse's hoofs flashed upon Bimala's mind.

'Please stay here then,' said she; 'I'll bring you the spears presently.'

Saying this, she hastened to the base of the castle. A window of the room below that in which she had made her toilet in the evening, faced the mango wood. She got up to the window, and taking out a key from her garment, turned it in a lock which was attached to the doorcase. Then grasping a bar, she pushed the window in the direction of the wall. By the power of strange art, the window together with the doorcase and the bars entered an opening in the wall, and a passage stood ready open for the entrance of Bimala. After entering the room, she pulled out the doorcase, and the window was again placed in its former site. Bimala turned the key in another lock on the inner side, similar to the other one, and the window was fast established in its place, defying all attempts at opening it from the outside.

With hasty steps, Bimala went to the arsenal, where she said to the guard,

'Never tell any one of what I ask from you. Let me have two spears. You shall get them back.'

'What will you do with spears, mother, I pray?'

'Today I celebrate the *Vira Panchami* rite—which blesses the woman celebrating it with a heroic son. The ceremony requires the worship of weapons. I am desirous of getting a son. Don't tell it to any one.'

The guard understood as he was made to understand. All the servants in the castle paid her implicit obedience; and the man, without another word, went in and brought out two sharpened spears.

With her former speed, Bimala returned to the window, with the spears, opened the window as before, and hurried forth to Jagat Singha.

Whether through the excitement of hurry, or feeling secure in the thought that she should be by, and return immediately, Bimala did not lock the passage, when going out; and this afforded entrance to danger. An armed man stood behind a mango tree very close to the window. He perceived this error; but did not stir so long as Bimala was not out of sight. When she had disappeared, he left his sounding shoes, and by soft steps neared the entrance; and casting a glance within to see if any one was there, and seeing none, noiselessly glided in. He then entered the castle by the door of the room.

On the other side, the Prince took the spears from Bimala, and, as before, ascended the tree. He then looked at the other tree which he had marked; but now saw only one turban;—the second person had disappeared. Then holding one spear in his left hand, he took the other in the right, and aiming at the turban, sent the weapon after it, with all the mighty energy of his arm. Anon a powerful rustling of the leaves was heard, and then the heavy fall of some thing. The turban was no more there—the Prince concluded that his unerring aim had dislodged the person from his boughy station, and brought him low.

Jagat Singha speedily descended and came to the wounded person. He saw that an armed Musalman soldier was lying as if dead; the spear had penetrated beside one of his eyes.

The Prince looked attentively and found that life was quite extinct.

The spear had entered beside his eye, and went right through the brain. Taking out a note which was enclosed in his amulet, Jagat Singha came to the moonlight and read it. It ran:

> 'The followers of Katlu Khan shall obey the orders of the bearer, on sight of this note.
>
> Katlu Khan.'

Bimala had only heard the noise, but could not understand what it meant. The Prince came to her, and related all.

'Alas!' exclaimed she, 'beshrew me if I would ever have fetched you the spears, Prince, had I known this. I am a great sinner, and shall hardly be able to expiate the deadly sin I have been guilty of tonight, for a long time to come.'

'What room for regret,' replied the Prince, 'in destroying our enemies? Such an act is righteous.'

'Let warriors think so,' returned Bimala; 'we are women.'

'Prince,' said she after a pause, 'there's harm in further delay. Pray, come, let's enter the castle. I have left the door open.'

Hastily coming to the foot of the castle, Bimala entered in, followed by the Prince. While he was entering, his heart trembled and his feet shook. What could it bode to one a single hair of whose head would not be thrown off its accumstomed position in the face of innumerable odds—what did it bode to him while entering into this mansion of joy?

Bimala shut the door in the same way, and then led the Prince to her bedroom. 'I shall be back in a moment,' said she. 'If you please, for a while sit on this couch. If your mind is not otherwise engaged, pray, Sir, remember that the seat of the Deity was merely a banian leaf.'

She went out, and after a little while, opened the door of an adjoining chamber. 'Noble Prince,' said she from the room, 'will you please step in and hear a word?'

Again the Prince's heart trembled!—perhaps, it gave no uncertain sound! He rose up from the couch, and went to Bimala.

Anon she darted out like lightning; the Prince found himself in a perfumed chamber;—a silver lamp was burning. In a corner was a veiled woman—she was none other than Tilottama.

18

THE CLEVER PERSON AND HER FOIL

Bimala came back to her chamber and sat down on the couch. Her countenance betokened excess of joy at having fulfilled her desire. A lamp was burning there; before her stood the glass;—her dress looked as fresh as it did in the evening. For a moment, she looked at her image in the glass. The same happy entanglements of her braid, the same dark sheen of the *kajjala* on the underlid of her eyes, the same rosy betel stain on her nether lip, the same pendants ever and anon waving, touching her round cheeks. She was lying in a recumbent posture. Who that saw her manner then, could again pant for the love of a youthful woman? Bimala contemplated her own charms with a smile. Did it proceed from regret at having sent the peerless Jagat Singha to Tilottama, after having brought him with her own exertions? Oh no! Far from being pained at such a consummation, she was delighted by it beyond measure. She smiled at the thought that the erudite Diggaja did not consent to leave his home absolutely without reason!

Bimala was waiting for Jagat Singha, when suddenly the deep blast of a trumpet burst upon her ear from the adjoining mango wood. She started in alarm, for the trumpet used to sound only at the gate, and never at so late an hour. Anon the remembrance of all that she had seen and heard on her way to the temple and back flashed upon her mind. She immediately inferred that the sound was the harbinger of evil; and hurried to the window to look out; but could see nothing particular in the wood. Filled with apprehensions, she sallied out of the room. Next to it was the yard, beyond which was another suite of rooms containing a staircase for ascending to the roof. Bimala went to the roof and began to look around; but could see nothing on account of the deep darkness in the wood. With increased apprehension, she then came to the balustrade, and placing her breast upon it and bending down her face, surveyed the place to the very base of the castle; but with her former success. The shifting green foliage was bathed in the soft moonlight; at intervals, as the breeze swayed the leaves, they wore a glistening red. Beneath the wood reigned deep, palpable darkness; here and there the moonlight escaping through openings in the foliage glinted over certain spots. On the still breast of the Amodara was reflected the moon with the star-crested welkin. At a distance, on the other bank rose the heaven-kissing appearances of the stately buildings. Here and there the form of a sentinel was visible on their roofs. This was all that she could see. She was about to return in disappointment, when she felt as if someone had touched her back with a finger. She started and turned round—an armed individual unknown to her was standing before her. She was struck motionless as a statue.

'You mustn't cry,' said the armed person. 'Do so—and your tender frame I shall hurl down to the bottom of the castle.'

The man who thus suddenly stupified Bimala was dressed like a Pathan soldier. From the completeness of his costly dress, it might easily be inferred that the person held some important post. His age did not exceed thirty and he was eminently handsome. A diamond graced the turban on his lofty forehead. Were Bimala not then utterly confounded, she could perceive that the individual before her could almost challenge a comparison with Jagat Singha himself. His body was not so large, nor was he so broad-chested; but he had the same heroic and graceful mein, and boasted of a softer person. In his precious belt was a Damascus dagger in a sheath studded with corals. He held the naked sword in his hand, but had no other weapon.

'Don't cry; if you do so, I will instantly throw you down.'

The amazement of Bimala, gifted with presence of mind, lasted but for a moment. She understood the soldier's meaning when he spoke a second time. Just behind her was the verge of the roof; before her stood an armed soldier; soldiers, she knew, were no idle talkers, nor was the threat so hard of execution either. Revolving all this in her mind, the sensible woman said,

'Who are you?'

'Where's the need of your knowing me?' replied the soldier.

'Why have you come here into the castle?' asked she. 'Don't you know that thieves are led to the stake?'

Soldier. 'I am no thief, fair one.'

Bimala. 'How have you entered the castle?'

Soldier. 'Through your own kindness——when you left the window open, I came in; and have come up here in your wake.'

Bimala struck her forehead with her hand.

'Who are you?' again asked she.

'Why should I now hesitate to make myself known to you?' said he. 'I am a Pathan.'

Bimala. 'This is not enough—you are a Pathan by race; but who are you?'

Soldier. 'By God's grace, my name is Osman Khan.'

Bimala. 'I have never heard of any such person.'

Soldier. 'Osman Khan, the general of Katlu Khan.'

Bimala trembled. She burned with the desire of escaping any how and informing Virendra Singha of the tidings. But there was absolutely no way of her doing so, for before her stood the general obstructing her passage. Seeing no alternative, she thought that so long as she could keep him engaged in talk, so long she was free; afterwards, some sentinel on the roof might chance to come that way. Deciding this, she again set on to talk.

'Why have you entered the castle, Sir?'

'We sent a messenger to Virendra Singha,' answered Osman Khan, 'requesting him to side with us. In return, he has challenged us to enter the castle with our soldiers.'

'Because the master of the castle, I understand you to say'—said Bimala, 'has refused to ally himself with your people and has sided with the Mogals, therefore you have come to capture it. But I see you are alone.'

Osman. 'At present I am so.'

'Perhaps it is for this very reason,' asked Bimala 'that you are preventing my going.'

This was said with the vain hope of escaping from the hands of the Pathan, who, she thought, would feel piqued at the imputation of cowardice and prove his valour by making way for her.

'Fair one,' replied Osman with a smile, 'you have nothing to be afraid of, except your side glance. I have no very great fear even of that. But I have a suit to you.'

Bimala felt curious, and fastened her look on Osman Khan's face.

'Pray, kindly oblige me,' said Osman, 'by giving me the key which is tied up in the corner of your sheet. I should hesitate to insult you by laying my hands on your person.'

'That's very fine!' replied Bimala, gently laughing. 'Were you not but a moment before ready to crush my body by hurling me down?'

'Necessity has no law,' said the general. 'And if need be, I shall have to do it now.'

It required no long time for a clever woman like Bimala to understand that the key of the window was indispensably necessary to the soldier. But she did not know how to evade him. He that can take a thing by force, jests when he solicits for it. If the key was not voluntarily given, the general would master it by force. Any other person in her position would undoubtedly have handed the key, but the clever Bimala said,

'If I don't give you the key willingly, how will you take it, Sir?'

Whilst she was speaking, she took her sheet in her hand.

'If you don't,' replied Osman, his eyes fast fixed on the sheet, 'if you don't, I will enjoy the pleasure of touching your body.'

'Do it, Sir,' said she and sent the sheet in the direction of the wood. No sooner had she done so, than Osman, whose gaze had been rivetted to the sheet, stretched out his hand and caught hold of the flying cloth. Bimala was amazed at the vigilance of Osman.

Having secured the sheet, Osman Khan took hold of Bimala's arm with a firm grasp. Then holding the sheet between his teeth, he loosened the key and deposited it in his belt. His next action blanched the countenance of Bimala; he bound her hands fast to the balustrade with the sheet.

'What are you at?' enquired Bimala.

'It's an exigency of war,' replied Osman.

Bimala. 'You will soon reap the consequence of this foul deed!'

Osman was going away, leaving Bimala in that plight, when he returned, and saying, 'No trusting a woman's tongue,' gagged her mouth as well.

Osman then descended to the room below Bimala's. He there turned the key, as Bimala had previously done, and pushed the window into the wall. When a passage was made, Osman began to whistle softly. Immediately a bare-footed soldier came up from behind a tree and entered in. He was followed by another. In this manner, a large number of Pathan soldiers noiselessly crept into the castle. To the last man that came, Osman said,

'No more; do you all remain outside. When you hear my signal, attack the castle from the outside. Tell it to Taj Khan.'

The man returned. Taking the soldiers with him, Osman again noiselessly ascended to the roof. When passing by the place where Bimala was a captive, he said,

'This woman is very clever; not safe to trust her. Rahim Saikh! do you mount guard over her. Free her mouth; but should she attempt to fly or talk with anyone or talk aloud, don't scorn to kill a woman.'

'I will, Sir,' replied Rahim, and remained there.

From roof to roof, the Pathans went to the other side of the castle.

19

THE LOVER AND HIS LASS

When Bimala saw that the clever Osman was away, she revived courage, for now she could hope to regain her freedom by dint of her cleverness. She anon fell to thinking how to effect it.

After the sentinel had remained standing for sometime, Bimala began to converse with him. Sentinel or Pluto's messenger—who can ever willingly abstain from conversing with a fair woman? At first Bimala talked on various indifferent matters; gradually she introduced a variety of questions regarding the guard's name, country, home, employment, happiness and misery. The man was highly satisfied with the display of so much interest in him and his on the part of Bimala. Seeing the opportunity, she began to take out sharpened arrows from her quiver. On the one hand, her honied converse—on the other, the unerring discharge of the flowery arrows—these conspired to usher in the 'melting mood.' When Bimala perceived from the guard's manner that his ruin was not distant, she said in a soft, sweet tone,

'O! I am strangely afraid, Shaikhji. Will you kindly sit by me?'

The guard was in ecstacies—he came up and sat beside Bimala. After a little talk on other matters, Bimala saw that her medicine had begun to work, for ever since he had sat by her, the guard was casting his glances 'frequent and full' at her.

'Shaikhji, I see you are perspiring awfully; if you do but once release my hands, I can fan you a little—after that, you can bind me again.'

Not a drop of perspiration was visible on the guard's forehead; but Bimala must undoubtedly have seen it, why else should she say so? Further, to be fanned by such a hand! To whom is it given to enjoy such a luxury? Reflecting thus, the sentinel immediately loosened her hands.

Bimala fanned the guard a little with her sheet, and then without the least let or hinderance wore it over her body. The guard could not think of re-binding her, and there was indeed a particular reason for this. When instead of serving as a cord, the sheet graced Bimala's person, her charms began to burn the brighter—those charms at sight of which in the glass, Bimala had smiled in the morning, struck the guard dumb.

'Shaikhji,' said she, 'doesn't your wife love you?'

'Why should you think so?' asked the Shaikhji.

'Only if she did,' said Bimala, 'how could she in such a spring time (then the dog star was raging, about to usher in the wet season!) endure the absence of such a husband?'

A deep sigh was the answer!

The arrows were flying out incessantly from Bimala's quiver.

'Shaikhji, I feel shame to confess it, but were you my husband, I would never suffer you to go to war.'

The sentinel again sighed. Bimala went on,

'O that you were my husband!' and here she too fetched a little sigh, at the same time casting a side glance full of love. The sentinel was wrought up beyond bearing. By degrees, he drew nearer and nearer to Bimala, who imitated him. Their bodies now came into actual contact; the guard was all excitement!

Bimala placed her silken-soft hand in that of the sentinel; the man was ravished!

'I am ashamed to speak thus,' said Bimala, 'but if you go away victorious, will you remember me any more?'

Guard: 'Shall I ever forget you?'

Bimala: 'Shall I open to you my heart?'

Guard: 'Do so—Prithee speak out.'

Bimala: 'No, I shan't. What will you think when you come to hear it?'

Guard: 'No, no; speak out, I beseech you. Take me but your bondslave.'

Bimala: 'I am very anxious to fly with you, and stain the name of this cursed husband.'

Again the same side look darting love. The guard cut capers for very joy.

Guard: 'Eh? Will you do so?'

Diggaja, come and see there are other sensible people like you under the sun!

'I shall be really delighted to go,' said Bimala, 'if you kindly take me with you.'

'Shall I not take you? I shall ever rest your slave.'

'O how can I requite your boundless love! A trifle as it is, pray accept it.'

Thereupon she took the gold chain from off her neck, and placed it on that of the sentry. The man was at once carried up to the seventh heaven! Bimala went on,

'Our *shāstras* declare that when one person places her garland on another person's neck, this constitutes marriage.'

The guard's teeth stared as he laughed.

'Ha! then we have been married sure,' exclaimed he.

'To be sure,' said Bimala, and seemed plunged in thought.

'What are you thinking about, eh?' enquired the guard.

Bimala. 'No, I am not destined for happiness—meseems your people will never be able to take the castle.'

'Never doubt it; by this time the castle is almost ours.'

'Oh no'—said Bimala; 'there's a very particular secret about this matter.'

'What's it, pray?' enquired the sentry.

'I reveal it to you, if you can compass the capture of the castle.'

The sentinel prepared to listen with parted lips; Bimala feigned disinclination to speak out.

'What's the matter, eh?' impatiently asked the sentinel.

'You don't know,' said Bimala 'that Jagat Singha is lying close to the castle with ten thousand men. Knowing that you would come here secretly, he had laid an ambush before you came. Now he wont stir, but when victory shall make you repose in fancied security, he will come up and surround you.'

The sentry was struck dumb.

'How's that?' exclaimed he.

Bimala. 'These tidings are not unknown to any of the inmates, and I have also heard them.'

The guard was in raptures.

'My soul! this day you have made me. I'll go and tell it to the general. By bearing such important news, I shall earn a reward. Stay you here; I'll be back soon.'

There was not a shadow of doubt in his mind as to the fidelity of Bimala.

'But will you come back?' asked she.

Guard: 'Presently.'

Bimala: 'O forget me not.'

Guard: 'Never, never.'

Bimala: 'Nay, I conjure you by my life.'

'Why do you fear?' said the sentry and off he went.

No sooner was he out of sight than Bimala slipped away—thus verifying the saying of Osman, 'there's danger only in the eyes of Bimala.'

20

FROM ROOM TO ROOM

After regaining her freedom, Bimala conceived it to be her first duty to bring intelligence of the disaster to Virendra Singha; and with this view in breathless haste she directed her steps towards Virendra's bedchamber.

She had not gone halfway when the warcry of *allalla ho!* burst upon her ear.

'Is it the victorious shout of the Pathan soldiers?' exclaimed she distractedly. A loud uproar then breaking upon her ear convinced her that the inmates of the castle had risen up.

Flying to Virendra Singha's bedroom, Bimala witnessed the same noise and bustle there, the Pathans having broken open the door and entered the room. She peeped in and discovered Virendra with his waist fast bound, playing his sword like a maniac—his body deluged with blood. His exertions were presently rendered fruitless, for by a stroke of a long sword of a powerful Pathan, his weapon flew from his grasp and fell at a distance; Virendra Singha was taken prisoner.

Filled with despair at what she saw and heard, she left the place. Thinking that there was time yet to save Tilottama, she ran for the place. While on her way, she perceived it to be no easy task to go to Tilottama—the Pathan soldiers having overspread every creek and corner of the castle. There could be no room for doubt that the enemy had taken the castle.

Bimala saw that on her way to Tilottama's chamber, she should fall into the hands of Pathan soldiers. She immediately turned. Utterly distracted, she bethought herself how she could, in this time of imminent peril, bring Jagat Singha and Tilottama, tidings of the disaster. She was thinking of this, when she saw some soldiers coming that way after plundering another room. Exceedingly terrified, she hastily hid herself behind a chest. The men entered the room and began to plunder it. Bimala saw that there was no chance of her escaping their hands, for when they would come to the chest, she should certainly be discovered. Mustering courage, she remained there for a little while, and cautiously peeping over the edge of the chest, began to watch the proceedings of the soldiers. She was endowed with matchless courage—her courage rose with the prospect of danger. While they were each occupied in plundering, she emerged from her place of concealment, and with stealthy steps attempted to slip away. Bent on plunder, the men did not see her—she was on the point of leaving the door, when a soldier came up from behind, and caught hold of her hand. She turned and saw—Rahim Shaikh!

'Now, runaway,' exclaimed he, 'where shall you go now!'

Falling a second time into the grasp of Rahim, Bimala turned pale; but this lasted for a moment. Through the force of her powerful intellect, her face was again restored to cheerfulness.

'I must' thought she, 'secure my end through this very fellow! Hush!' said she, 'soft, come with me.'

Saying this, she took Rahim's hand, and dragged him out. The man followed nothing loth.

'O fie!' said Bimala, when they were alone, 'is this your deed? Where did you go, leaving me? There's not a place which I have not searched for you.' Again the same loving side glance! The ire of the magnanimous Shaikh was quenched.

'I searched for the general,' said he, 'to give him information of Jagat Singha. Failing to find him, I came back to the roof, but missed you. I have since been looking for you in every direction.'

'Seeing your delay,' said Bimala, 'I concluded you had forgotten me; and have accordingly come in search of you. But now what's the use of delaying any longer? Your people have captured the castle; and it is time we got ready for our flight.'

'Not tonight,' answered Rahim, 'tomorrow morning. How shall I go without telling it to the general? Next morning, I will take his leave and go.'

'Let us go then,' returned Bimala, 'and at once secure my ornaments and that sort of thing—or else some other soldiers may steal them.'

'Very well,' replied the soldier. The object of Bimala in taking

Rahim with her was simply to escape the hands of other soldiers; and a circumstance which happened soon after, bore testimony to the sagacity of her foresight. They had not gone far, when they came upon a second party of marauders. On seeing Bimala, they cried out, 'A wench! a wench! a wench!'

'Mind your several affairs, comrades,' said Rahim; 'don't look this way.'

The soldiers understood and desisted. 'Rahim,' said one, 'you are lucky, only if the general do not wrest the dear morsel from your mouth.'

Rahim and Bimala passed on. Bimala took Rahim to a room below her bedchamber.

'This is my nether chamber,' said she; 'collect whatever in it you choose. Above this is my bedchamber. I'll go and bring thence my ornaments and such gear.' Saying this, she threw him down a bunch of keys.

Finding the room loaded with articles, Rahim eagerly fell to unlocking the chests. Not a vestige of doubt now lingered in his mind as to Bimala's perfect honesty of purpose. On coming out, she fixed the fastening chain from the outside and locked the door. Rahim remained a prisoner in the room.

Bimala then ran upstairs. Tilottama's and her own apartment lay far removed in the interior of the castle, so that the plundering soldiery did not yet reach so far—nay, it might well be doubted whether Tilottama and Jagat Singha had yet heard the din and the clamour. Instead of at once entering the chamber, impelled by curiosity, Bimala began to view the manner of the lovers through a chink in the door. Who can override nature! Bimala could afford to be curious at such a terrible moment. She was rather surprised at what she saw.

Tilottama was seated on the couch; Jagat Singha stood by, holding the lily hands of the beauteous damsel. Jagat Singha was also wiping his eyes.

'This is perhaps the watery passage of Farewell,' thought Bimala. 'Whatever it may be, certain it is that these two have not yet dreamt the impending disaster. O! Love alone is mighty in this world! In this universal hubbub, he has rendered this couple stone deaf, although they possess the sense of hearing.'

21

THE RENCOUNTER

When Bimala entered and informed Jagat Singha of the impending calamity, he could not at first believe her. But the noise and din just then bursting upon their ears, at once dispelled his doubts.

'Pray, Sir, devise some instant means of escape, or we perish here!'

For a moment Jagat Singha was plunged in thought.

'What's Virendra Singha doing?' asked he.

'He's a captive in the hands of the enemy,' answered Bimala.

Tilottama uttered a faint shriek and sank down senseless on the couch.

Jagat Singha turned pale. 'Help, help! ho!' he exclaimed; 'look to Tilottama.'

Instantly Bimala took a vessel containing rosewater, and began to sprinkle it over Tilottama's mouth, neck and forehead; as well as to fan her with a troubled heart. The uproar drew nearer and nearer.

'There they come, Prince,' cried out Bimala. 'How shall we save ourselves?'

'God of Heaven!' exclaimed Jagat Singha, his eyes flashing fire. 'Is this thy will? Am I destined at such a moment of peril to remain cooped up here with women!'

This hurt the pride of the haughty Bimala.

'And what's the earthly need, Prince?' retorted she, her eyes filling with tears. 'If I can do no better I will at least die by the side of Tilottama.'

The Prince was touched. 'How can I go,' replied he, 'leaving Tilottama in this plight? I will also die for her sake.'

The fearful cry approached nearer every moment; the clang of arms also now became audible.

'Tilottama, Tilottama!' exclaimed Bimala, 'O! why are you senseless at such a moment! How shall I save you!'

Tilottama opened her eyes. 'Tilottama has revived,' said Bimala 'Prince! Prince! there's time yet to save her.'

'Nothing in heaven and earth,' said he, 'can avail us here. Could we yet leave the room, I could probably take you out of the castle. But, alas! Tilottama is helpless! Bimala, look! there they ascend the stairs. I will first lay down my life—but the regret is that I shan't be able to save you even at such a cost.'

In a twinkling Bimala took up Tilottama and said,

'Very well, Sir, I'll carry Tilottama.'

In an instant Bimala and Jagat Singha reached the door, when four Pathan soldiers swiftly ran up.

''Tis too late, Bimala,' said Jagat Singha. 'Fall back behind me.'

Seeing their prey before them, the men set up their warcry of *Allalla ho*, and leapt forward like devils. The arms around their loins rang as they descended. Their cry had scarcely died away when the sword of Jagat Singha was planted deep in the breast of one of them. The man expired, crying frightfully. Before the Prince could extricate his weapon, the spear-point of another Pathan ran towards his neck; but before it could alight, swift as lightning, with his left hand he arrested its course, and with one thrust of that same spear, prostrated his adversary. In a moment, the two remaining Pathans simultaneously aimed their blows at Jagat Singha's head; but without pausing to take breath, he lopped off the forearm of one, but could not parry the blow of the other—which without alighting on his head, inflicted a severe blow on his shoulder. On receiving the wound, the Prince grew doubly frantic, like a tiger smitten by the hunter's arrow; and scarcely had the Pathan attempted to strike again, when with both hands grasping his bloody weapon with his whole strength and spirit, the Prince leapt forward and by one blow severed the head of his enemy with the turban on. Meanwhile the man who had lost his arm, drew out a sharp dagger from his waist by the left hand, and aimed at the Prince's body. As the latter was descending from his leap, the poniard went deep into his spacious arm. Considering the wound as nothing more than the pricking of a needle, he administered such a tremendous kick to the man's waist as fairly flung him at a distance. The Prince hastened to cut off the Pathan's head, when with the terrible cry of *Allalla ho,* countless Pathans began to stream into the chamber. He now perceived that further fighting could only end in his certain destruction.

His body was dripping with blood, and he was being fast enfeebled by loss of blood.

Tilottama was still lying senseless in the lap of Bimala, who was weeping. Her clothes were drenched with the Prince's blood.

The chamber was now full of Pathans.

Supporting himself on his sword, the Prince took breath for a moment.

'Slave' exclaimed a soldier, 'surrender yourself. We will not take your life.'

This added fresh fuel to the expiring fire; the prince leapt forward like a flame and cutting off the man's head, placed it beneath his feet. Then flourishing his weapon in the air, he called out,

'Ye Javanas! See how a Rajput dies.'

His sword played like lightning. Perceiving that regular fighting was no longer possible, he determined to die after slaying as many of the enemy as possible. With this view, he dived into the thick of the hostile force, and with both hands holding his sword with an iron grasp, began to deal incessant blows, without in the least heeding his own safety. One—two—three—every blow either prostrated or mutilated a Pathan. Blows now began to pour in upon him like hail. His arms grew fainter and fainter from bleeding; his head became dizzy; his eyes grew dim; his ears could hear only an indistinct noise.

'None shall take the Prince's life—the tiger must be caged alive.'

The Prince could hear no more. Osman Khan had spoken these words.

The Prince's arms relaxed and hung loosely down; from his grasp, his sword fell down with a clang. He fell senseless over the body of a Pathan slain by him.

Some twenty Pathans rushed to rob the gem which crested the Prince's turban, but Osman Khan said in a voice of thunder,

'Don't touch the Prince, on peril of your lives.'

All desisted. Osman Khan and another soldier took up the Prince and laid him on the couch. It was a moment before that Jagat Singha indulged in the fond hope of one day sitting on that couch in company with Tilottama after their nuptials. That couch now became his bed of arrows (*Sarasayyâ*).

After setting down Jagat Singha, Osman enquired,

'Where are the women?'

Osman did not see Bimala and Tilottama. When the soldiers rushed into the room the second time, she read the future; and finding no other means, had hidden herself with Tilottama under the couch.

'Where are the women?' said Osman, not finding them. 'Search through the castle. The attendant woman is fearfully clever; and I shall be ill at ease should she escape. But have a care. Let no rudeness be shown to Virendra's daughter.'

Some of the soldiers went to the other parts of the castle: one or two began to look about the room. After searching in other directions, one of them took a lamp and looked under the couch. Discovering the object of his search, the man said,

'They are here, Sir.'

'Are they?' enquired Osman Khan eagerly.

Answer. 'Yes, Sir, they are.'

Osman's countenance brightened.

'Come out,' said he, 'no fear.'

Bimala first came out and then bringing out Tilottama, made her sit down. The latter was reviving, and could therefore sit up.

'Where are we?' she slowly asked Bimala.

'Never fear,' whispered Bimala into her ear, 'just veil yourself.

'May it please Your Excellency,' said the man who had discovered the women, 'I have discovered the women.'

'You are asking for a reward,' said Osman. 'What's your name?'

'My name is Karim Baksh,' replied the man. 'But no one knows me by that name. Formerly I was in the Mogal army, and people call me 'the Mogal officer,' by way of jest.'

Bimala shuddered. Abhiram Swami's astrological calculation came to her recollection.

'Well, I'll remember,' said Osman.

PART II

1

AESHA

When Jagat Singha opened his eyes, he found himself in a handsome chamber and lying upon a couch. He could not remember ever having been in the place before. The room was spacious and richly furnished. The marble-paved floor was covered with a soft carpet, over which were ranged rosewater pots and other articles of silver, gold, ivory and such things. Blue screens hung in front of the doors, and softened ere they admitted the day into the chamber. The place was perfumed with various odours.

All was still as death. A maidservant was noiselessly fanning the Prince with a fan sprinkled with fragrant waters; another stood at a little distance mute and motionless as a statue. Beside the Prince on the ivory-inlaid couch sat a woman engaged in applying some salve to his wounds. On the carpet below sat a well-dressed Pathan, chewing betel and reading a Persian work. But none was speaking or breaking the utter silence of the place.

The Prince looked round. He tried to turn but could not do so on account of severe pain all over his body.

'Be still, Sir. Don't move,' said the woman beside him in a soft, sweet tone.

'Where am I?' enquired the Prince faintly.

'Pray Sir, be quiet,' said she in the same musical tone. 'You are in a proper place, Sir. Don't be uneasy. Don't speak.'

'What's the time now?' asked the Prince still more faintly.

''Tis afternoon' replied she 'Be quiet, I beseech you. You won't come all right if you talk; and we must leave the place.'

'One word more,'—said he with an effort, 'who are you,?'

'Aesha,' replied the damsel.

The Prince fell to studying Aesha's countenance in silence. Had he seen her before? No.

Aesha might be twenty-two. She was beautiful to a degree; but it is not possible to depict that style of beauty in a word or two. Tilottama also was exceedingly beautiful; but Aesha's beauty was not of that type. The charms of the ever young Bimala also fascinated people; but neither could they claim fellowship with Aesha's transcendental graces. The loveliness of some damsels is like the blossoming of the vernal *Mallika*—fresh-blooming, closing for bashfulness, tender, serenely bright and deliciously fragrant. Tilottama was such an one. Some women are like the afternoon *Stala-padma*, odourless, about to close, wanting moisture, yet graceful, full-blown, splendid and ripe with honey. Such were the charms of Bimala. Aesha resembled the lotus expanding itself to the rosy touch of the morning sun—so beautifully blooming, so exquisitely fragrant, so overflowing with honey, so resplendent; neither closing nor lacking moisture, and 'clothed with transcendent brightness.' The rays of the sun are beaten off by the expanded leaves, yet its face ever beams with a smile. O reader, have you ever witnessed 'beauty's splendour'? You may at least have heard of such a thing. Many a fair one illumines all round with her beauty. The daughter-in-law of many a man illumines his home. In the land of *Vraja* and in the war of *Nisumbha*, the world was ablaze with dark lustre. But has the gentle reader now understood what I mean by 'beauty's splendour'? Bimala shined in beauty but her light was that of the *pradipa*, somewhat dim, wanting oil, though sufficient for domestic use; it can light you from room to room; with it you can cook your food, prepare your bed etc; but you must not touch it, on pain of being burnt. Tilottama too shined in beauty but her light was like the soft rays of the crescent moon—pure, balmy, cool, but ill fitted for daily use, not powerful and coming from afar. Aesha shined in beauty, and it was the full effulgence of the midday sun—flaming, darting myriads of rays and imprinting a laugh on whatever it fell.

What the lotus is to the garden is Aesha to this story; and I am therefore anxious to make the reader realize her form and face. Were I gifted with a cunning pencil—could I prepare that colour—not *champaka*-like, nor red, nor yet like the unblown white lotus, but a happy mixture of all three—could I truthfully paint that forehead of hers, so faultlessly round and deliciously expansive—the very field of Cupid—over which appeared the fine curves of her hair—could I prolong them as finely over her smooth and round forehead—could I turn them off in the same way over her ears—could I paint her black silken hair—could I in the same way part them above her forehead—could I dress them in the same neat and elegant fashion—could I weave her dangling braid—could I depict those dense eyebrows—could I show how they attempted to kiss each other and how by gentle degrees attaining bulk they visibly increased in breadth ere they had yet reached the middle, and then by as soft gradations ended in an exquisitely fine point near her hair—could I show all this—could I moreover paint those tender, nimble lids which looked like clouds flashing with lightning—could I transfer to the canvass the expanse of those eyes—the graceful curves of the upper and lower lids—that azure lustre so finely touched with red—those dark pupils—that aquiline nose with nostrils dilated with pride—those lips, the home of Nature's sweets—that alabaster neck over which fell her braid—those full blown cheeks which ever and anon attempted to kiss her pendants—those fully developed, delicate arms shining with gems—those fingers before which the gems on the rings grew pale—those hands which in hue might vie with the land lotus—the pomp and grandeur of her swelling bust, which shamed the brightness of the pearl chain which fell over it—the 'mighty magic' of her stature,

'O call it middle not tall!'

Could I do all this, yet I would not touch the pencil. Aesha's beauty was the only reality in this unreal world—she was the master work of nature's hand—her side glance was like the blue lotus waving in the evening breeze. Ah! how can I hope to paint her without the help of inspiration?

The Prince gazed at Aesha. Immediately the thought of Tilottama arose in his mind; and he felt the iron entering his soul. The blood coursed violently through his veins, and gushed out afresh from the deep wounds; he closed his eyes and sank in insensibility. The lovely lady on the couch immediately arose. The person who sat on the carpet reading, from time to time lifted his eyes from the book and saw Aesha lovingly—for a long while he gazed with insatiate eyes at her waving pendants, as she arose. Aesha softly approached to him and whispered into his ear,

'Osman, send for the physician, sharp'; for it was no other than the conqueror of the castle. On receiving this communication, he went out. Aesha took a vessel which stood upon a silver stool, and drenched the prince's forehead and face with some liquid.

Osman Khan soon came back with the physician, who after a variety of expedients succeeded in stopping the bleeding and handed to Aesha various medicines, giving directions in a low tone for their use.

'Pray, what do you think of him, Sir,' said she in the physician's ear.

'O the fever is awful!' replied he.

He saluted them and was going out, when Osman overtook him near the door and asked him in an undertone,

'What do you think of his recovery, Sir?'

'I am not hopeful, you know,' said he, 'but please call me again, when the fit returns.'

2

THE FLOWER-EMBOSOMED STONE

That night Aesha and Osman sat up by Jagat Singha till a late hour. Now he was becoming conscious and now he became insensible; the physician came and went many a time and oft.

Aesha was ceaseless in her attentions to the Prince. When it struck twelve a maid entered in and said that the Begum had sent for her.

'I go,' said she and rose up. Osman rose with her.

'You also up?'—asked she.

'It is late; let me convoy you.'

Aesha instructed the servants to be watchful, and then directed her steps to her mother's apartment.

'Do you mean to stay with the Begum tonight?' asked Osman on the way.

'No,' replied Aesha. 'I shall return to the Prince.'

'Aesha,' said Osman, 'your goodness nothing can equal. A sister does not more for her brother than you are doing for this mortal enemy of your father. You are actually rescuing him from the jaws of death.'

'Osman,' said Aesha, a gentle laugh illumining her countenance, 'Nature has made me a woman, and as such it is my first of duties to tend the sick. It would indeed be a great sin in me to neglect it, but I can claim no merit for doing my duty. But how does it touch you? That you are daily watching and striving hard for the recovery of one who is your mortal foe, who is your opponent in the field, ever bent on humbling your pride—of one reduced to this pass by your own hands—that you are doing all this for such a one can but redound to your credit.'

'You, Aesha,' said Osman, thrown a little out of countenance, 'look on the world as partaking of your own sweet nature. My motive, you must know, is not so virtuous as you think. Don't you perceive what gainers we shall be if Jagat Singha come all right? Should the

Prince now die, what do we gain by it? In the field, Man Singha is not inferior to his son; so that instead of one warrior we shall have another to cope with. But if we can keep Jagat Singha in durance when he recovers, we have Man Singha on the hip—he shall certainly be obliged to offer us favorable terms for the liberation of his beloved son—nay, Akbar too shall consider peace proposals seriously, to get back such an able officer. Further, if we can lay Jagat Singha under an obligation by treating him generously, he also will lend his influence to bring about the conclusion of a treaty favourable to us—and his endeavours may not go for nothing. At any rate, we cannot miss a good round sum as his ransom. His life then, you see, is more valuable to us than even a victory in open fight.'

No doubt these considerations weighed with Osman in determining his present conduct, but there was something more. It is the way with some men to give themselves out as hard-hearted, fearing to be convicted of the taint of the 'milk of human kindness,' and they do good with a perpetual sneer at kindness, as an effeminate quality. When pressed for explanation, they seek refuge in such expressions as, 'O, sir, content you, herein I serve my turn.' Aesha well knew Osman was one of this class.

'Osman,' said she laughing, 'would to Heaven, all were as selfish and far-sighted as you. Goodness could then very well be dispensed with.'

After an attempt at shuffling, Osman said in a softer tone,

'That I am selfish, I will show by another instance.'

Aesha fixed her eyes on Osman, like a cloud surcharged with lightning—Osman continued,

'I am living on Hope; how long shall I remain her borrower?'

Aesha looked grave; Osman now saw new beauties rising to the view. 'Speak to papa about it, pray,' said she. 'You know he can deny you nothing.'

Osman. 'I have not left untried that quarter.'

Aesha. 'And what does he say?'

Osman. 'He has pledged his word to the Begum that he will give you to the man of your own choice. But to this day, I have not known your mind.'

Again her sweet countenance gleamed through a smile.

'Pray, when have men,' said she, 'been able to read the thoughts of women?'

Osman—'What am I to understand by this?'

Aesha. 'That I do love you.' Osman's handsome face brightened with joy.

'As your future husband, eh?' enquired he.

'As my dearest brother.'

Osman's countenance fell.

'God! God! ever on that key!' ejaculated he. 'God of Heaven, in such a flowery frame hast thou closed in a heart of stone!'

After conveying Aesha to her mother's apartment, Osman returned to his quarters, with a heavy heart.

3

AREN'T YOU TILOTTAMA?

In the evening of the next day, Aesha, Osman and the physician were seated in silence in the room where Jagat Singha was lying. Aesha was seated on the couch, engaged in fanning the Prince and that sort of thing; the physician was momentarily feeling his pulse. The Prince was insensible. The physician had said, 'Most probably he dies when the fever remits. If he escape that, he will surely be cured.'

The remission was fast approaching; and it was for this reason that all were held in breathless suspense. The physician was incessantly feeling the Prince's pulse. 'Low,' 'lower still,' 'a little high,'—such were his frequent exclamations in a suppressed tone.

All of a sudden his face grew pale.

'The time is come' said he. Aesha and Osman listened motionless— the leech kept holding Jagat Singha's pulse.

'The state's bad' said he after a while, 'the pulse irregular.' Aesha's face grew pale. Suddenly Jagat Singha's face became white and showed an unnatural expression, his fists clenched fast, his eyes manifested a preternatural twinkling. Aesha understood that the *coup de grace* of the Destroyer was not distant. The physician who sat ready with his medicine, seeing the symptoms opened the patient's mouth and poured in the drug. The change was electric. By and bye, his face reassumed its natural expression and composed. The whiteness which spread over his body disappeared, the blood renewed its free circulation, his fists relaxed, and his eyes closed in composure. The physician felt his pulse, all attention.

'No fear any more' exclaimed he joyfully, after a long while, 'he will recover.'

'Has the fever gone off?' enquired Osman

'It has' answered the follower of Esculapius.

Both Aesha and Osman now looked cheerful. 'There is no more

danger' said the physician. 'I needn't wait any more. Let the patient take this medicine every now and then up to twelve o'clock.' He then went away. After a while, Osman too went to his house. Aesha sat as before on the couch beside the Prince, tending him.

A little before midnight, he opened his eyes. The first sight that struck him was Aesha's cheerful countenance. From his side glance, Aesha gathered that his mind was wandering, he looked like one who tried to recall some thing, but without success.

'Where am I?' asked he, after looking long at Aesha. This was the first time that he spoke after two days.

'In the fort of Katlu Khan,' replied Aesha.

The Prince again tried to recollect some thing.

'Why am I here?' said he after a long pause.

Aesha was at first silent.

'You are ill, Sir,' said she.

'No, no, I am a captive,' said the prince musing and shaking his head; his features now underwent a change.

Aesha made no reply; she found that the Prince's power of recollection was reviving.

'Who are you, I pray?'—again asked he after a pause.

'My name is Aesha.'

'Who is Aesha, beseech you?'

'The daughter of Katlu Khan.'

The Prince was again silent, lacking strength to talk for a long time together,

'For how many days am I here, pray?' asked he after a pause.

'These four days.'

'Is Garmandaran still in your possession?'

'It is, Sir.'

Jagat Singha again paused a little.

'What has become of Virendra Singha?' enquired he.

'He is a prisoner. Today his trial takes place.'

Paler grew the pale countenance of Jagat Singha.

'Pray, how fare the other inmates of the castle?'

'I don't know every thing,' answered Aesha anxiously.

The Prince muttered something to himself. A name escaped his lips; Aesha heard it:

'Tilottama.'

Aesha rose softly and went to bring the palatable medicine given by the physician.

The Prince fell to observing the matchless perfections of Aesha's person, as her pendants kept waving to and fro. She returned with the medicine. After drinking it, the Prince said,

'When lying insensible, I dreamt that a nymph of heaven sat at my head engaged in tending me. Isn't she you, Tilottama?'

'You may have dreamt of Tilottama, gentle Sir,' replied Aesha.

4

THE LADY OF THE VEIL

Two days after the capture of the fortress, about noon, Katlu Khan was holding his court in the fortress. On two sides stood his courtiers in array. On the tract of land in front, an immense crowd stood in silence. That day would take place the trial of Virendra Singha.

Several armed guards brought in Virendra. His face was overspread with crimson; but there was no trace of fear in it; his flaming eyes threw out scintillations of fire; his nostrils dilated and quivered; he bit his nether lip. When he was brought up, Katlu Khan said,

'Virendra Singha, this day I will try you for treason. Why did you assume a hostile attitude towards me?'

Virendra's face reddened. He suppressed his anger and said,

'Let me first know what I have done?'

'Be more respectful, Sir,' said a courtier.

'Why didn't you,' asked Katlu Khan, 'send me men and money?'

'You are a rebel,' replied the undaunted Virendra; 'one might well call you a robber. Wherefore should I give you money; wherefore supply you with troops?'

The spectators perceived that Virendra was preparing his own ruin.

Katlu Khan's frame shook with passion; but he had learnt to master his emotions with promptitude.

'Living in my domains,' said he somewhat calmly, 'why did you join the Mogul?'

'And where are your domains, may I enquire?' asked Virendra.

'Listen, miscreant,' exclaimed Katlu Khan in a rage, 'Listen, varlet, you shall meet your desserts. You could hope for your life; but you are mad. Your pride has undone you.'

'Katlu Khan,' said Virendra laughing scornfully, 'when I came before you, I never expected mercy at your hands; and what's the earthly need of a life saved through the mercy of an enemy like you? If you could rest satisfied with only taking my life, I would gladly lay it down, wishing you well. But you have stained me and mine; my life of life you have—'

He could no longer contain himself. His utterance was choked; his eyes filled with tears; the dauntless, haughty Virendra Singha hung down his head and wept like a child.

Katlu Khan was constitutionally hard; so much so that he delighted in the pain of a fellow-creature. Seeing the plight of his proud enemy, his face betokened joy.

'Virendra Singha,' said he, 'would you ask anything at my hands? Consider, Sir, your end is near.'

Tears had brought relief to the burning heart.

'Nothing save this,' answered Virendra calmly, 'order my execution soon.'

Katlu. 'It shall be so; anything more?'

Answer. 'Nothing in this life.'

Katlu. 'Would you not look your last upon your daughter?'

At this the spectators became silent for grief. Fire sparkled in Virendra's eyes.

'What!' cried he; 'will nothing less satisfy you than trampling under foot this crushed heart?' He then continued with less vehemence, 'Do so; I am powerless in this life. But in the next you shall answer for it before the tribunal of God.'

This touched the heart of Katlu Khan; for is there a sinner whose heart trembles not at the sound of that dread Name?

'No more' said he; 'executioner, do your office.'

Silence held that vast concourse of people in breathless suspense; so much so that the fall of a needle could have been heard.

The guards led Virendra to the place of execution. He had not yet reached it, when a Musalman whispered something into his ear. Virendra could not understand it. The individual then handed him a letter. Musing and absent, he opened it and saw that it was in Bimala's handwriting. He crumpled and threw it away from him, with signs of great displeasure. The bearer took it up and went away.

At this a spectator who was close by said to another in a low tone, 'Perhaps, Sir, 'tis a letter from his daughter.'

Hearing this, Virendra turned round and said,

'Who speaks of my daughter? I have no daughter.'

When the bearer of the note departed, he said to the guards, 'Await my return.'

'All right, Your Excellency,' replied they.

Osman himself was the bearer, and it was for this reason that the guards applied to him the epithet of 'Excellency.'

Taking the note, Osman went to the bottom of the wall of the inner apartment. There stood a veiled lady. Osman came to her, and after casting his eyes round, related to her all that had happened.

'I am giving you infinite trouble' said she; 'but you must remember it is you who have reduced us to this pass. You must thretfore do me this turn.'

Osman said nothing.

'If you refuse it,' continued she of the veil, in a voice trembling with emotion, 'I am helpless—but God will judge.'

'Mother,' said Osman, 'you don't know what a perilous task you are laying upon me. Katlu Khan will take my life, if he come to know it.'

'Katlu Khan?' returned the woman. 'Why are you deceiving me? Katlu Khan dares not touch a hair of your head.'

Osman. 'You do not know Katlu Khan. But come, I will take you to the execution ground.' When they came to the spot, Virendra, who was conversing with a Brahmin disguised as a beggar, did not mark her. The woman looked from within her veil and recognised the Brahmin to be Abhiram Swami.

'Sire,' said Virendra, 'here then I make my last obeisance to you. What more shall I say? Whom have I in this world on whose behalf I should offer up my prayers to Heaven? For whom shall I pray?'

Abhiram Swami pointed with his finger to the veiled lady behind. Virendra turned round; anon she threw back her veil and cast herself at the chained feet of Virendra.

'Bimala!' cried he in a choked voice.

'Husband! My life! My all!' she exclaimed in a frenzy, 'this day I will proclaim it to the four winds. None shall prevent me. Husband! Life of life! Where are you going—where are you going, leaving us?'

The floodgate was opened in Virendra's eyes.

'Bimala! Beloved,' exclaimed he, lifting her by his arm, 'O! why should you make me weep at such a moment! my enemies will think me afraid to die.'

Bimala was mute.

'Bimala!' he went on; 'Farewell!—Do you follow me straight way.'

'No; after a little delay.' Here she proceeded in an inaudible tone. 'First I will avenge my wrong.'

Virendra's countenance brightened up like an expiring flame.

'By your own hands?' enquired he.

'By this very hand'—said she, painting her right hand with a finger of the left. 'Here I cast away gold from my arms. What further the need of it?' She thereupon flung away her bracelets and other ornaments at a distance and proceeded, 'No more shall these arms of mine bear any ornaments—but sharp steel must now supply their place.'

'You will certainly succeed,' said Virendra joyfully. 'May Heaven help you.'

'I can't wait any longer,' cried the executioner.

'Well then, you may go now,'—said Virendra.

'Not so,' replied Bimala. 'I will with my own eyes witness the fell stroke that makes me a widow. I will drown all scruples in your blood.'

Bimala's voice was awfully calm.

'Be it so,' said Virendra. He then made a sign to the executioner. Bimala saw the raised axe flash in the sun; for a moment her eyes closed of themselves; when they opened again, the severed head of Virendra Singha was rolling before her in the bloody dust.

Bimala stood like a statue; not a hair of her head waving in the wind; not a tear standing in her eye. Without shrinking, she fixed her gaze steadily upon the severed head.

5

THE WIDOW

Where is Tilottama? Ah! where the fatherless, forlorn girl? Where is Bimala? Whence had Bimala come to the place of execution? Where did she go after that grim proceeding?

Why did not Virendra Singha seek an interview with his beloved daughter in his last moments? Why did his wrath kindle at the simple mention of her name? Why had he exclaimed, 'I have no daughter!' Why had he flung away Bimala's letter without even perusing it? Ah! why? Bring but your recollection of Virendra's rebuke of Katlu Khan and see what a terrible thing had taken place.

'You have stained me and mine.' had roared out the chained lion.

Do you ask where Tilottama and Bimala are? Search the seraglio of Katlu Khan and you will find them.

'Tis the way of the world! Such is the inexorable turning of Fortune's wheel! Youth, beauty, sincerity, purity—all, all are crushed out by its relentless pressure.

Katlu Khan had made a rule that whenever any beautiful woman should be taken captive in the capture of any village or fort, she should be sent for his pleasure. The day after the capture of Garmandaran, he went to the place and was engaged in disposing of the prisoners, in placing a garrison there and that sort of thing. On seeing Bimala and Tilottama among his captives, he forthwith sent them to enrich his harem. He was afterwards engrossed with other matters. He had heard that the Rajput army on hearing of the captivity of their leader, lay close, meditating an attack. He was therefore engaged in providing means for expelling them in case of an attack, and could not consequently find time to enjoy the company of his new slaves.

Bimala and Tilottama were kept in separate chambers. Reader, no use of casting a look where the tender, youthful, fatherless girl is rolling in the dust, her person covered with dust. What is the good of doing that? Who will now cast a glance at Tilottama? When decked in bud and blossom, the fresh shrub waves a welcome to the Spring, who does not court it for its fragrance? And in a summer storm, when down it goes with the tree round which it has entwined its embraces, who goes to it, leaving the uprooted trees? The woodman takes away the wood only, the shrub he tramples under foot.

Come, reader, let's go elsewhere. Let's look in where with the flowing end of her cloth over her eyes sits the dusty, grave, mourning widow, instead of the active, clever, gay and sportive Bimala.

Is this Bimala?

Bimala! where is that dressing of your hair? Why is your head so full of dust? Where is your curiously embroidered sheet? Where is your *kanchali* sparkling with gems? What's this? Why is your cloth so dirty? Why with this short cloth on, pray? Where have gone those ornaments—those pendants that ever and anon longed to kiss your cheeks? Why are your eyes swollen? Ah! where that side glance? Wherefore is this wound in your forehead? Who has drawn the blood there?

All this has but one answer: Bimala is a widow now. She was waiting for Osman.

Osman was a person of whom the Pathans might justly be proud. He had entered war as a profession and accordingly did not hesitate to do anything which promised to bring martial success. But when the exigencies of war were at an end, he never allowed the least unnecessary outrage to be committed on the vanquished. Had not Katlu Khan himself reduced Bimala and Tilottama to that pass, they would never have been captives through Osman's hands. It was through his kindness that Bimala succeeded in seeing her husband before his death. When afterwards Osman came to learn that she was the wife of Virendra Singha, his kind heart at once melted. He was the nephew of Katlu Khan; and had leave to go everywhere in the inner apartments. This has already been seen. But the threshold of Katlu's seraglio none could cross—not even his own sons—not even Osman. But he was the right hand of Katlu. It was owing to his strength of arms that Katlu Khan had advanced so far as the shores of the Amodara. Consequently the inmates obeyed Osman even as they did Katlu himself; and it was for this that none hindered Bimala from seeing her husband that morning before his execution.

Two days after this, she gave her remaining ornaments to the maidservant appointed to serve her. 'What's your will, Madam,' asked the woman.

'Pray, do you go to Osman, as you did yesterday,' said Bimala. 'Tell him that I beg him to see me once more. This is my last request; I will not ask for a like favor again.'

The maidservant did so. Osman said, 'There's danger to both of us in my going there. Tell her to see me in my lodgings.'

'How can I go?' asked Bimala.

'He has said he would provide for that,' returned the menial.

At nightfall one of Aesha's maidservants came in and after talking something with the eunuchs, who guarded the interior, took Bimala to Osman.

'What more do you require of me, pray?' asked Osman.

'A trifle,' said Bimala. 'Is the Rajput Prince, Jagat Singha, alive?'

Os: 'Yes, he is.'

Bi: 'Is he a captive?'

Os: 'He is a captive but not in prison now. He is bedridden because of his wounds.'

'Every one connected with these wretched women is destined to fare ill!' exclaimed she. 'The hand of God is in all this. Should he recover, pray, do you, Sir, give him this letter. At present let it remain with you. This is my request.'

Osman returned the note and said, 'Excuse me; I may not do this. In whatever case the Prince may be, he is to be considered a captive now. It is improper to take any letter to such a person without first reading its contents; moreover this is against the orders of my master.'

'Believe me, Sir,' replied Bimala 'it contains nothing which you can take exception to; you may without scruple convey it. And talk you of your master, Sir? You are your own master.'

'In other things,' said Osman, 'I can act against the wishes of my uncle; but not in this. I perfectly believe you when you say the letter is quite harmless, so far as we are concerned—but I can not break the rule for its sake. I am powerless to serve you in this matter.'

'Well then, you may read it,' said Bimala sadly.

Osman took the letter and began to read it.

6

BIMALA'S LETTER

'Prince,

I promised that one day I would unfold to you the history of my life. The time has now come for my doing so.

I hoped to narrate my personal history, when Tilottama should have ascended the throne of Abnir. That hope, alas! has been dashed to the ground. In a few days you will probably hear there is no Tilottama on earth—no Bimala. Our days are numbered.

It is for this reason that I am now writing you this note. I am a great sinner—I have committed many sins in my time. When I shall be no more, people will speak ill of me; what a load of uncharitable things they will heap on my memory! Who then will wipe out the stigma from my name? Who is such a friend?

There *is* a friend; but he will soon renounce the world and be engaged in austerities. My object will not be gained through Abhiram Swami. Prince, for one day at least, I ventured to indulge in the hope of being reckoned among your kindred. Pray, do you, for one day, act like a relative. But to whom am I saying this? The fortunes of these wretched women are like flames; they have touched the friend who was near us. Be that as it may, do you, Sir, remember this petition of your humble servant. When people will say that Bimala was a harlot, that Bimala was a mistress in the guise of maidservant, pray, do you say that Bimala was low-born, Bimala was wretched, that solicited by strong sensual promptings, she committed a thousand wrongs, but Bimala was no harlot. He who is now in heaven, as my good luck would have it, married me in the proper form. My lord did not for a single day suspect me of infidelity.

This was not known so long; who will believe it now? Why, again, being a wife, did I behave like a maidservant? Listen.

A certain Brahmin, named Sasi Sekhara Bhattacharya, lived in a village adjacent to Garmandaran. Sasi Sekhara was the son of a wealthy Brahmin. In his youth, he received a finished education; but his education could not remove the fault of his character. Although God had lavished upon him every virtue, yet He had implanted in him a certain strong passion: that passion is always strong in youth.

A woman then lived in Garmandaran, who pined for her absent husband, a follower of Jayadhara Singha. She was uncommonly beautiful. Her husband was a soldier in the army of the Emperor, and was long away from home. The woman fell in love with Sasi Shekhara; in a short time, she conceived.

Fire and sin cannot be hid long; the misdeed of Sasi Shekhara reached the ears of his father. With the view of removing the stain cast by his son on the race of another, the father of Sasi Sekhara wrote to the husband of the woman and hastily called him home. He reprimanded his backsliding son severely. Thus disgraced by his parent, Sasi Sekhara left his country.

He went to Benares. There, hearing of the fame of a *dandi*, who was extraordinarily learned, he began to receive lessons from him. Possessed of an acute intellect, he became proficient in the *darsanas*, and attained the highest excellence in astrology. The tutor taught him with the greatest delight.

Sasi Sekhara had put up at the house of a *Sudra* woman. She had a blooming daughter. From veneration for a Brahmin the young lady arranged things for his cooking, etc. It is the duty of the child to throw the veil over the shame of the parent. What more shall I say? The *Sudra* girl gave birth to this wretch of a woman.

On coming to know this, the teacher said to his pupil, 'My boy, I don't teach wrongdoers. Don't show your face in Benares any more.'

Sasi Sekhara left Benares for shame.

My grandfather turned my mother out of his house, as a fallen woman.

My poor mother came with me to a cottage; she maintained herself and me by bodily labor. None cared for the poor thing; neither could any news be got of father. Several years after, in winter, a wealthy Pathan was going to Delhi from Bengal. He was going through Benares. Arriving at the city late at night, he could not get lodgings. His wife and his babe were with him. Coming to our cottage, he begged permission to spend the night there. 'None of the Hindus' said he, 'consent to give me shelter. Where shall we go now with this infant? He cannot bear cold. I have not many persons with me, and there will be room enough for us in the cottage here. I will reward you handsomely.' The Pathan was hastening to Delhi on some urgent business; he had only one servant with him. My mother was poor as well as kindhearted; either from love of gold or from compassion for the infant, she allowed the Pathan a place in our cottage. He lay in a part lighted up by a lamp, with his wife and son. In the other, we lay. The populace of Benares were then full of apprehensions for boy-kidnappers. I was then six years old; I can't tell all that happened; I relate what I have learnt from mother.

The lamp was burning at midnight. A thief entered in through a breach, which he made in the wall, and was stealing away the boy of the Pathan. I had then awaked from sleep and saw it. I set up a loud cry, which awakened all.

The wife of the Pathan not finding her child beside her, at once shrieked. The thief was then going out with the boy. The Pathan rushed on the man, drew him by the hair and snatched the boy from him. As the culprit implored hard for mercy, the Pathan let him go after cutting off one of his ears.'

Coming up to this point, Osman became plunged in thought. He then said to Bimala,

'Had you no other name before?'

'Yes, I had,' replied Bimala. 'That is a Musalman name, and father has therefore changed it.'

'What's that name? Maharu?'

'How could you know it, Sir?' asked Bimala in surprise.

'I am that very boy,' replied Osman.

Bimala was surprised; Osman again began to read.

'Next morning, when the Pathan was about to depart, he said to mother, 'Now I have no means to repay the obligation your daughter has laid me under; but let me know your wish. I am going to Delhi, wherefrom I will send you whatever you require. If you want money, I will send it.'

Mother said, 'I don't want money; I pass my days easily enough by bodily labor. But if you have any influence with the Emperor—'

'Yes, I have,' interposed the Pathan. 'I shall be able to serve you at court.'

Mother said, 'Then, will you kindly try to get news of this girl's father and send it me?'

The Pathan promised to do so. He offered gold to mother, which she declined. According to his promise, the Pathan employed some of the imperial officers to get news of my father; but to no purpose. Fourteen years after this, the men got tidings of my father, and information of it was communicated to mother. He was at Delhi; he had changed his name of Sasi Sekhara Bhattacharya for Abhiram Swami. When this intelligence reached us, mother departed this life. If heaven can be the portion of a woman who marries without 'sanctimonious and holy rites,' then mother sure has ascended heaven.

When I received tidings of my father, Benares could no more please me, now that mother was no more. There was none on earth to me save father, and when he was at Delhi, why should I be at Benares? Thinking thus, I set out alone for him. At first he was dissatisfied at seeing me; but as I wept bitterly, he allowed me to be engaged in tending him. He changed my former name of Maharu for Bimala. I employed myself in serving father with the greatest assiduity; my attentions were constant and ceaseless. All this was not prompted by any selfishness to secure his love, I really felt an inward delight in serving him. I knew that I had none save him, I thought I had no other happiness on earth save serving my father. Whether it was owing to my respectful attentions or to any other law of human nature, he began to feel an affection for me. Affection is like the flowing river: the more it flows, the more it attains strength. When my dear lord was about to suffer on the execution ground, then I knew how deeper beyond 'plummet's sounding' was that love.'

7

BIMALA'S LETTER (CONCLUDED)

'I have already told yon, Prince, that a certain poor woman living in Garmandaran conceived by my father. Her fate singularly resembled my mother's. She also gave birth to a daughter; and on becoming a widow soon after, began, like my mother, to maintain herself and child by bodily labor. It is not necessarily the case that the product should resemble its source; the tender flowering plant is found in the bosom of mountains; the dark mine produces the burning gem. An 'earth-treading star' rose at the cottage of the poor woman. The daughter of the widow came to be recognised as a paragon in Garmandaran. Time performs wonders; Time blotted out the stain of the widow; many forgot that her daughter owed her birth to an unchaste sheet. Some did not know—few or none of the inmates of the castle knew it. What more shall I say? That beauty became the mother of Tilottama.

When Tilottama was yet in her mother's womb, took place the principal event in my life—growing out of this marriage. One day, about that time, father brought in his son-in-law to the cottage. He gave him out as his disciple; I got the true information from my espoused saint.

As soon as my eyes fell on him, my heart ceased to be mine. He came every day to father, and stayed long—he talked of various things; he told stories. My rapt ear took in the honied strains—mentally I sold myself off to him—body and soul; he too did not scorn me. In brief, we came to read each other's thoughts. I spoke with him; his whispering accents still sound in my ears like the music of the spheres.

Although I sold my heart cheap, still the wretched fate of mother was ever present to my mind; I declined to sell the jewel in my dower—virginity. But this in no way cooled his fervour. Father too had come to understand how matters stood. One day I overheard the following conversation between him and my lord.

'I shan't be able to remain anywhere, leaving Bimala,' said father. 'But if she become your wedded wife, then I will live with you. But if your intention be otherwise—'

'Sire!' interposed my lord, somewhat angrily, 'how shall I marry a Sudra woman?'

'And how could you marry the illegitimate girl?' said father sarcastically.

'I did not know that she was such, when I married her,' replied my lord, rather regretfully. 'But how can I marry a Sudri, having full knowledge of the fact? Moreover, your elder daughter, although natural, was not a Sudri.'

'You refuse to marry, then' said my father. 'Well, your visits are objectionable—you need not come to the cottage. I will see you at your place.'

From that day, he discontinued his visits for a time. Daily I remained eagerly expecting his coming, but in vain. At length, (perhaps being unable to remain still) he again resumed his visits. During his separation, I had known what a thing a lover is. Therefore, during his latter visits, I determined not to be so bashful as before. Father perceived this. One day, he called me and said, 'You see I have adopted the ascetic life; it is not possible for me to be always with you. I will go on travel. Where will you go when I leave you?'

I fell to weeping, apprehensive of my separation from father. 'I will go with you' said I. Anon the thought of my lord occurred to my thoughts; and I said, 'Or I will remain alone as before at Benares.'

'No Bimala,' replied father, 'I have a better plan. I shall provide a good protection for you, when I go. You shall be an attendant of Man Singha's new queen.'

'O! do not leave me, Sir,' cried I.

'No, no,' replied he. 'At present I am not going any where. Do you now go to Man Singha's palace. I will be here for the present, and see you every day. I shall do the needful after satisfying myself as to your reception there.'

Prince, I became an inmate of your house. By this mœnuvre father removed me from the sight of his son-in-law.

Prince, I was an inmate of your father's palace for a long time.

But you don't know it. Then you were a mere boy of ten years old, and lived with your mother at the palace at Abnir. It was then that I became engaged in tending your new stepmother, at Delhi. Countless women hung round the neck of Maharaja Man Singha, like flowers in a garland. Do you know all your stepmothers? Will you be able to remember Urmila—the daughter of the chief of Jodhpore? How shall I tell you of Urmila's kindness to me? She did not consider me as a maidservant and attendant—she looked upon me as an affectionate sister. Under her fostering care, I received a good education; it was through her kindness that I learnt embroidery; it was to please her that I learnt music and dancing. She herself taught me letters. That I am able to send you these lines is owing to the kindness of Urmila.

I reaped still better good fortune at the kind hands of Urmila—she introduced me as favourably to the Maharaja as she loved me. I had attained some proficiency in music and dancing, and the Maharaja took delight in seeing and listening to my performance. Whatever may be the reason, he looked upon me as one belonging to his family. He revered my father, who came often to see me.

I was perfectly happy with the Princess; my only cause of sorrow was that he for whom I was prepared to give up everything, save my honor, could no longer be seen by me. Had he (on his part) forgotten me? No, Prince, do you remember the maid, Ashmani? It may be. I became intimate with Ashmani. I despatched her to bring news of husband. She brought me news of him. What shall I say how much he said in reply! I wrote to him *per* Ashmani. He replied. Thus passed day after day. Even while separated, we conversed with each other.

Three years passed away in this manner. When we did not forget each other after such a long seperation, we understood that our love was not shallow like moss but deep-rooted like the lotus. I don't know why but at last my lord lost all patience. One day he marred every thing. I was lying at night in my chamber alone, when waking suddenly, I saw a man at my head, in the glimmering light.

These words sweetly entered my ear—'My love, don't fear. I am your own.'

What could I reply? Meeting after three years! I forgot everything. I caught hold of his neck and wept.

When my speech returned, I asked him, 'How have you come into the inner apartment?'

'Ask Ashmani' said he. 'I entered the palace with her as a water-carrier. Since then I have been hid.'

'What then now?' asked I.

'What?' replied he. 'What you will.'

I thought what I should do; what way to adopt.

My mind led me to the side which had been espoused by my feelings. I was thinking thus when suddenly the door of my room opened, and stood in my front—Maharaja Man Singha.

What need of details? My lord was made a prisoner. The Maharaja expressed his intention of punishing him by law. Perhaps you can guess what it was with me. Crying I fell down at the feet of Urmila; I frankly confessed my indiscretion; I took the burden of every offence on my shoulders. On meeting father, I fell at his feet also. The Maharaja used to respect him, he reverenced him as his spiritual guide; of course (thought I) he would comply with his request. I exhorted, 'Consider the fate of your elder daughter.' I think father had concerted with the Maharaja; he turned a deaf ear to my entreaties, and angrily said, 'Wretch! you have at once bidden adieu to shame?'

With the view of saving me, Urmila interceded strongly with the Maharaja. He replied,

'I can forgive the thief, if he consent to marry Bimala.'

I becalmed myself, when I understood the intention of the Maharaja. My lord got wroth at the proposal and said,

'I shall ever remain a captive, I shall lay down my life, but I shall never marry a *sudra* girl. How can you, being a Hindu, make such a request?'

'When I could' replied the Maharaja 'give my sister in marriage to the Prince, Selim, what wonder that I shall request you to marry the daughter of a Brahmin?'

But my lord did not consent. He said 'Maharaja, what is done, is done. Do you kindly release me. I shall never name Bimala more.'

'What then is done by you to expiate your guilt?' replied the Maharaja. 'You will leave Bimala, and others will spurn her as a fallen woman!'

Still he held out. At length when the sufferings of durance 'vile' were no longer bearable, he half consented, and said, 'If Bimala consent to live as a maidservant, if she never in her life put me in mind of this marriage, if she never give herself out for my wedded wife, I can marry a *Sudri*—else not.'

With the greatest alacrity, I consented to do all this. I did not set a pin's fee on wealth and name, I was only mad for my lord. Both my father and the Maharaja consented; I came to my husband's roof in the guise of a maidservant.

My husband had married me under compulsion. Who ever cherishes his wife with love, having married under such circumstances? I became the eyesore of my husband after our marriage, and his former love at once vanished. He constantly took me to task, remembering the indignity he suffered from Man Singha. His scolding I accounted as love. In this way passed some time, but what's the use of mentioning all that? I have done with narrating my personal history; no more. In time I regained the affections of my husband; but he still maintained a feeling of bitter animosity against Abnir's lord. It was the will of Fate, else why would all this take place? But I have done. It is not only to fulfil my promise that I have written you. Many think that I lived at the house of the chief of Garmandaran, relinquishing my honor. When I am no more, you will wipe out that stain from my reputation. This has actuated me to write you.

In this letter I have only narrated what concerned myself; I have not once mentioned her for whom you are anxious. Think that her name has vanished from the face of the earth. Pray, forget that such a one as Tilottama ever breathed on earth.'

Having read the letter through, Osman said, 'Mother, you have saved my life. I will requite you.'

'Alas! what can you do for me now?' said Bimala with a sigh. 'What can you do for me? Still one thing—.'

'I will do that.' said Osman. Bimala's eyes sparkled; she said, 'Osman, what do you say? Why do you decieve this burnt heart?'

Osman took out a ring from his finger and said,

'Take this ring. Nothing can be done in a day or two. Katlu Khan's birthday is about to come; there will be joy and revelry that day. The guards will be engrossed in pleasure. I will deliver you that night. Do you come to the gate of the inner apartment at midnight; there if any one shows you another ring like this, come out with him. I hope you will escape without obstruction. But all depends upon His will.'

'God bless you,' exclaimed Bimala. 'What more shall I say?'

Her utterance was choked; she could say no more.

She was about to depart after offering him her benediction, when he said,

'I will warn you of one thing. Come alone. If you take another with you, your object will fail; nay, it may bring on danger.'

Bimala understood that Osman was prohibiting her to take Tilottama. She thought within herself, 'Well, if we can't come both, Tilottama alone will come.' She then took leave of Osman.

8

THE RECOVERY

Time flies. Do whatever you will, Time will fly and not remain still. Whatever condition you may be in, Time will fly and not stop its career. Wayfarer! are you being roughly handled by the storm and rain? Are the clouds roaring loud and deep over your head? Are the winds blowing wildly? Are you dripping in rain? Is your helpless body being mercilessly pelted by hailstones? Don't you find a shelter for your head? A little patience, friend; this day will go away and not stand still. Wait a bit, this ugly day will pass away, 'there's a gude time coming'; the sun will rise again. Wait for the morrow.

Whose days do not go away? Whose days stand still to perpetuate his misery? Brother! why then weep? Whose days sit down to perpetuate his happiness? Why then swagger?

Whose days do not go? Tilottama is rolling in the dust, yet the days are going away.

Revenge has made Bimala's bosom its home, and with its tooth has spread venom into every fibre of it. A moment of suffering from its sting is insupportable, how many moments go to make up a day! Still have her days not gone away?

The victorious Katlu Khan is lying in the lap of luxury. His days are passing happily, but still they are passing away and are not stationery.

Jagat Singha is lying on a sickbed. Who does not know what a lazy foot Time has with sick people? But still the days have gone away.

Yes, the days *have* gone away. By degrees, Jagat Singha began to recover. Having escaped the jaws of death, the Prince rallied daily. First his bodily uneasiness disappeared, then his appetite returned, next his strength returned, and with it brought anxiety.

His first thought was—'Where is Tilottama?' The more he rallied, the more he asked all that came in his way concerning Tilottama, in a disconsolate temper of mind; but none returned any satisfactory answer. Aesha did not know—Osman did not say—the servants and maids either did not know or did not say, having been forbidden. It was a bed of thorns with the Prince.

His second thought referred to his future. 'What is to come?' Who could return a ready answer to this question? The Prince saw that he was a captive. Through the kindness of Osman and Aesha, he was living in a well furnished and perfumed chamber instead of in a prison; he was tended by servants and maids; he had everything ready before asking; Aesha was tending him with more than a sister's care. Still a person mounted guard at the door; he felt like a bird in a golden cage, fed with sweet drinks. When should he get free? Where was the likelihood of his getting free at all? Where were his troops then? How did they fare, deprived of their officer?

His next thought respected Aesha. 'How has this fascinating and bewitching creature—how has this image of benevolence and goodness descended upon this clay world of ours!'

Jagat Singha saw that Aesha knew no rest—no fatigue—no neglect. She was ceaseless in her attentions. So long as the Prince's illness continued, he daily saw her coming in the morning, like the 'sun new risen', with a graceful pace, holding a nose-gay in her hand; daily he saw her remaining in the room even till the usual hour of bathing and breakfast had gone by; daily he saw her returning soon, after performing those necessary actions, to be engaged in tending him so long as the Begum did not send her maid (with the exception of short interruptions from urgent business).

What man has not lain on a sickbed? But if ever it has fallen to the lot of any to have been tended by a radiant girl at his head, and to have been fanned by her lily hands—he alone can say that disease is not altogether unpleasant.

Reader! wish you to form a lively image of Jagat Singha's situation? Well then, lie down (in imagination) on his sickbed, your entire body suffering from severe pain. Fancy yourself a captive among foes; next fancy a richly furnished, deliciously cool and perfumed chamber. Fix your gaze at the door; suddenly your countenance shows expressions of joy; yonder comes the person who under this hostile roof looks on you as a brother; the person is moreover a woman—a youthful woman—a very full-blown lotus. Lying at length, you are looking at her steadily. Look what a grace is seated on that form—just tending to be tall, with all the members perfectly symmetrical—a very goddess with her divine perfections—a very queen by virtue of Nature's sanctifying chrism. Look, how graceful is her step. Have you heard of the elephant's gait? What is that? You talk of the motion of the swan? Mark the girl's step. The sounding instrument keeps measure in music; your heart keeps time to the music of her steps. See the bouquet in her hand. Do you see the flowers have lost their hue before the superior brightness of her hands? Do you see that the golden chain has grown dim before the brightness of her throat? Ah! what's this? Why have your eyes forgotten to twinkle? Do you see the graceful manner of her neck? Do you see how happily the dark ringlets have fallen over her alabaster neck? Do you see how sweetly her pendants are waving? Have you marked the gentle inclination of her head? That is owing only to her slight tallness. Why are you looking so steadfastly? What will Aesha think of you?

So long as the illness of Jagat Singha required her services, Aesha was every day ceaselessly engaged in tending him. As the Prince grew better and better, the visits of Aesha became rarer and rarer; and when he was perfectly cured, she seldom came to him, only visiting him once or twice at long intervals, and when she came, she almost always came attended by Osman. As in winter the sun imperceptibly glides away from the body of a shivering person, as it gets late, even so did Aesha disappear from Jagat Singha as he recovered.

One evening the Prince stood at the window, looking beyond the fort. Men intent on business or pleasure were streaming to their respective destinations. Sadly the Prince fell to comparing his lot with theirs. At one place some people had formed themselves into a ring round some person or thing. The Prince's glance fell that way. He gathered that the men were engaged in some amusement; and that they were attentively listening to something. What the person or the object in the middle was like, the Prince could not see. He felt rather curious. After sometime, several of the audience went away; and his curiosity was satisfied. He saw a man was treating the people to some reading from a few leaves, which resembled a *puti*. The person of the reciter rather awakened his curiosity. He might pass either for a man, or for a middle-sized palm tree 'scathed by heaven's fire,' and shorn of its leaves. He was as tall and as broad; but the palm is never loaded with so huge a proboscis of a nose. His manner was of a piece with his shape. The Prince fell to studying most heedfully the various gesticulations of the hand, the head and the proboscis with which the reciter accompanied his reading. Now Osman entered.

When they had saluted each other, Osman asked,

'Pray, Sir, what are you looking at so intently at the window?'

'Something like a piece of wood,' replied the Prince. 'You can see it, Sir, if you like.'

'Hav'nt you seen him before, Prince?' asked Osman after seeing the man.

'No,' replied the Prince.

'He is one of your Brahmins, Sir,' said Osman. 'His conversation is quite elegant. I saw him at Garmandaran.'

The Prince grew anxious. He was at Garmandaran? Couldn't he then tell anything of Tilottama?

'What's his name, Sir,?' asked he in agitation.

Osman thought for a while, and said, 'His name is rather hard to tell; it can't be so easily recalled to mind, *Ganapat?* No, *Ganapati?*— *Gajapat?* No, *Gajapati?* What more?»

'*Gajapati?*—It's not a Bengali name; yet I see the man is a native of this country.'

'Right! He is a Bengali; a Bhattacharjya. He has got some title. *Elem—elem*—what next?'

'O no, Sir, Bengali titles never take in the word *elem*. The Bengali for *elem* is *vidya*. He might be a *Vidyabhusan* or a *Vidyabagish*.'

'Yes, yes, *vidya* and something more. Say—what do they call an elephant in Bengali?»

'*Hasti.*'

'What more?'

'*Kari, danti, varana, naga, gaja*—'

'Ah! here it is; his name is Gajapati Vidyadiggaja.'

'Viddyadiggaja! A rare title as I live! Nothing could match the title except the name. I feel curious to talk with the man.'

Osman Khan had heard a wee bit of Gajapati's conversation; and saw no harm to any talk the Prince might hold with him.

'No harm,' replied he.

They thereupon went into the next room and had Gajapati called in by a servant.

9

DIGGAJA'S TIDINGS

When Gajapati Vidyadiggaja was ushered in by the servant, the Prince asked, 'Are you a Brahmin, Sir?'

Diggaja replied with a wave of the hand,

'यावत् मेरौ स्थिता देवा यावत् गङ्गा महीतले,
असारे खलु संसारे, सारं श्वशुर मन्दिरं।'

[So long as the gods choose to inhabit the Himalaya, so long as the Ganges waters this sublunary sphere, in this unreal world, verily the only reality is the father-in-law's house.]

Jagat Singha suppressed his rising laughter and bowed down his head. Gajapati uttered the benediction, 'May *Khoda Khan* bless the noble Babu!'

'I am not a *Musalman*, Sir,' said the Prince. 'I am a Hindu.'

'The rogue!' thought Diggaja. 'He is certainly a Yavan; he is only trying to humbug me. He has some motive for this, else why should he call me in? Noble Khan Babu,' said he sadly in alarm, 'I know you, Sir, I live upon your bread; do not ill treat me, I pray you; I am your bond-slave, Sir.'

Jagat Singha perceived the hitch.

'You are a Brahmin, Sir,' said he, 'and I am a Rajput. This language to me is therefore not befitting. Your name is Gajapati Vidyadiggaja?'

'Ha! look there!' thought Diggaja. 'The fellow wants my name! God knows what a scrape he will bring me into! Have mercy upon me, noble Shaik,' exclaimed he with joined hands. 'Have mercy, I am a poor man, Sir. On my knees I beseech you.'

From the Brahmin's extremity of fright, Jagat Singha saw it was impossible to make him answer his purpose by any direct means. Accordingly with the view of diverting his attention, he said,

'What *puti* have you got in your hand?»

'A work on *Manikpir*, so please you, Sir.'

'You a Brahmin and carry a work on *Manikpir*?'

'Hem! hem! I was a Brahmin once, but not now.'

The Prince was at once astonished and vexed.

'What say you? Didn't you live at Garmandaran?'

'Death and damnation O!' thought Diggaja. 'He has even discovered that I lived at Virendra Singha's castle! He will deal with me even as they have done with Virendra Singha.' Here the Brahmin burst into tears.

'Have mercy, noble Khan!' cried out Diggaja, rubbing his hands with might and main. 'Do not belabour me, I beseech you; I am your slave.'

'Are you in your senses?'

'Yes, your honor! I am your slave, Sir; I am your own, Sir!'

'No fear, man,' said Jagat Singha, with the view of calming the Brahmin. 'Pray, entertain us with a reading from your book.'

The Brahmin fell to reading the *puti* in a sing-song way, his eyes still bedewed with tears. His tone was as much a borrower from crying as from sing-song. So sings a little boy who has just been pulled by the ear by the opera master.

After he had read for sometime, the Prince asked,

'Being a Brahmin, why were you reading a book on Manikpir?'

'I am a convert now,' answered the Brahmin, stopping his sing song.

'How's that?' asked the Prince.

'When the Musalman Babus entered the fort,' said Gajapati 'they said to me, 'Come, Brahmin, we'll spoil your caste'; and thereupon they dragged me away, and forced me to eat the fowl *palo*.'

'What is *palo*?'

'The *atapa* rice boiled in clarified butter.'

The Prince understood what was meant.

'Go on'—said he.

'Then they made me read *Kalmi*,' said Diggaja.

'*Kalma*; well then?'

'Then they said, 'You have become a Musalman.' Since then I am a Musalman.'

'What of the other inmates?' here enquired the Prince.

'All the other Brahmins have fared like me.'

The Prince fixed his eyes on Osman. Understanding his silent rebuke, Osman said,

'And where's the harm in it, Prince? We consider Mahommedanism as the only true faith; and consider it no sin but a virtue to spread it by any means.'

'Noble Vidyadiggaja—' said the Prince without replying to Osman.

'Now, Shaikh Diggaja, if you please.'

'Very well; noble Shaikh, know you anything of any other inmates of the castle?'

Osman grew anxious, understanding the motive of the Prince.

'Besides, Abhiram Swami has escaped,' said Diggaja.

The Prince saw that he must (if he should learn anything) speak directly.

'What has become of Virendra Singha?' asked he.

'The Nabab has beheaded him,' replied the Brahmin.

The Prince's face reddened.

'What does he say?' he asked Osman. 'Is the Brahmin telling a fib?'

'After trying him,' replied Osman seriously, 'the Nabab has executed him as a rebel.'

The Prince's eyes flashed fire.

'May I take the liberty, Sir, to ask one thing more?' he asked Osman. 'Was it done with your consent?'

'No; it was against my advice,' replied Osman.

The Prince paused for a long while. Taking the opportunity, Osman said to Diggaja,

'You may go now.'

Diggaja rose and was about to go away, when the Prince prevented him by catching hold of his hand.

'One word more,' said he. 'Where is Bimala?'

The Brahmin heaved a sigh; he also cried a little.

'Bimala is now the concubine of the Nabab,' said he.

The Prince cast at Osman a glance like the lightning. 'Is this also true?' asked he.

'What have you to do here any more?' said Osman to the person, without replying to the Prince. 'Go away.'

The Prince grasped his hand firmly; so that the Brahmin could not choose but stay.

'Wait a moment longer,' said he. 'One word more and I have done.' Here his red eyes began to flash with living flame. 'One word more; Tilottama?'

'Tilottama,' replied the Brahmin, 'also is now the Nabab's concubine. They are living in peace in the midst of every comfort.'

The Prince violently pushed away the Brahmin's hand; the man luckily escaped going head over heels.

Osman was ashamed; he said in a soft tone,

'I am an officer merely.'

'You are the Devil's officer,' replied the Prince.

10

SWEET IMAGE, AWAY!

It is needless to say that Jagat Singha could not sleep a wink that night. His bed was full of scorpions; his heart burnt in anguish and pain. That Tilottama whose death would before have rendered his existence insupportable—that the same Tilottama still lived—this was the only thing which he regretted.

How so? That Titottama still lived! That tender flower, that angelical sweetness, that soft splendour, that frame which rises before Jagat Singha'a vision whichever way he turns his gaze, shall the jaws of the grave close over such a frame! This earth—this spacious earth, shall it not contain a vestige of that frame? O heavy thought! O insupportable hour! Jagat Singha's eyes drop tears as fast as the Arabian trees their medicinal gum—

Anon the thought of the hellish Katlu Khan's pleasure chamber flashes upon his imagination; he sees that tender frame on the lap of the villain, *and* again his heart barns like a volcano,

That Tilottama whose image has been enshrined in his heart of hearts—that Tilottama is now an inmate of the Pathan's—aye—that very Tilottama is now the concubine of Katlu Khan!

Can a Rajput pay his devotions to such an image any more? Is a Rajput worthy of his race who hesitates with his own hands to tear that image from his mind for ever?

That image has rooted itself deep in the mind of Jagat Singha; and to uproot it is to rend the heart itself. Ah! how shall he banish that lovely image for ever? Is it possible? So long as 'memory holds a seat in his distracted globe,' so long as flesh and blood remain, so long will that image lord it over his heart and soul.

Not to speak of his mental quiet, these distracted thoughts were fast depriving the Prince of his reason; his memory began to fail. When the night was about to go away, the Prince still sat up supporting his head upon his hands; his brain was reeling; he had lost all power of thinking.

His body ached for having sat long in the same posture; his violent mental agitation had spread fever heat all over his body. He came up to the window.

The cool summer breeze touched his forehead. There was darkness all round; a thin cloud had spread itself in the sky; the stars were not visible; only here and there a mildly gleaming star peeped out from behind a fleeting cloud. The trees at a distance had blended themselves into one another's being in the dark, and stood under the sky like a wall of darkness; the trees close by were glittering with crowns of glow-worms, which shone like so many diamonds. In a tank in front, the image of the trees and the sky appeared indistinct in darkness.

The night breeze which had stolen its coolness from the clouds, somewhat allayed the bodily heat of Jagat Singha. He remained at the window and stood placing his hand over his head. He had become exhausted through prolonged mental agitation, and from want of sleep. The contact of the grateful breeze made him desist a little from thinking, and somewhat diverted his thoughts. The dagger which had hitherto been piercing his heart was being replaced by the less poignant dagger of despair. The pain is in forsaking hope; when despair has once established itself in the mind, the pain is not so much; it is the blow which is attended with very great pain—not so the wound, which though lasting, is not so painful. Jagat Singha was now suffering the lesser pain of despair. He looked at the dark, starless appearance of the heavens, and then with tearful eyes looked at the dark starless appearance of his own heart. The past now gently began to start into life at the touch of remembrance; childhood, youth with its delights, all came before his view; he was lost in his reflections; by and bye he became still more absorbed; by and bye his body began to cool down; he was fast growing insensible from fatigue. He felt sleepy, as he kept hold of the window. In his sleep the Prince dreamed a dream. It was of a very painful and agitating nature. He frowned in sleep; his face showed expressions of agony; his lips quivered; perspiration stood out on his forehead; his fists clenched fast.

He awaked with a start; he began to pace the room hurriedly; it is difficult to say how long he suffered in this way.

When the walls of the room were laughing in the morning sun, Jagat Singha was sleeping, stretched at length on the ground, without a bed, without a pillow.

Osman came and awakened him. When he rose, Osman saluted and handed him a letter. The Prince took it, and without saying anything, fixed his gaze on Osman. The latter understood that the Prince's mind was wandering. Thinking the time, therefore, as unsuitable for any talk on business, he said,

'Prince, I don't feel curious to know the reason of your lowly bed—not I. I had promised the writer of this note to deliver it to you. The reason which made me so long withhold it from you, exists no longer, you have learnt it all, Sir. I leave the letter with you; read it at your leisure. I'll call again in the evening. If you should wish to send a reply, I will have it conveyed to the writer.'

Saying this, Osman left the letter with the Prince, and went away.

On being restored to his senses when left alone, he began to read Bimala's letter. After having read it from beginning to end, he prepared a fire and cast the note into it. He kept his gaze fixed at it, so long as it burnt; when it was completely consumed, he said to himself,

'I have succeeded in destroying the remembrancer, by committing it to the flames; memory too is burning in anguish, but why is it not reduced to ashes?'

He then finished his daily morning duties. After finishing his devotions, he reverentially bowed down his head to his guardian deity, and then clasping his hands and looking upwards, said,

'Father! forsake not Thy servant. I will act as becomes a Kshatriya; I only ask Thy blessing. I will banish from my mind the concubine of the casteless wretch; should the effort cost me my life, I shall have Thee in the next world. I have done what man can do, I will do what man can. O! Searcher of hearts! look thou into the very recesses of my soul and see whether I any more long for Tilottama, any more wish to see her. Only fell remembrance is torturing me incessantly. I have resigned the desire, shall I never be able to get rid of the memory? Father! have mercy upon me! or cruel remembrance will undo me quite.'

The image is banished.

Tilottama! what are you dreaming of, girl, lying on the ground? The sole star at which you had been gazing amidst dismal gloom, will no more impart its light to you; the plank to which you had clung for life in this violent tempest, has slipped from your hold; the raft on which you had embarked your fortunes for crossing the ocean, has gone to the bottom!

11

CHANGING THE ROOM

According to his word, Osman came in the evening and said,
'Do you wish to send a reply, Prince?'
The Prince had written a reply, which he now handed to Osman. Osman took it.
'Please excuse me, Sir,' said he; 'but we make it a point never to allow one inmate of the fort to send any note to another, unless we first satisfy ourselves as to its contents.'
'It is needless to say it,' replied the Prince rather sadly. 'You can read the letter, Sir, and then send it, if yon like.'
Osman opened and read the letter. It contained simply the following lines:

> 'Ill-fated woman! I will not forget your request. But if you really loved your husband, you must follow him, and thereby wipe out the stain that has attached itself to your name.
>
> Jagat Singha.'

'Prince!' said Osman after reading the note, 'you are very cruel.'
'Certainly not more than the Pathan, Sir,' replied the Prince drily.
Osman's countenance reddened; he said rather harshly,
'The Pathans may not have behaved with you so very shabily, after all, Sir.'
The Prince was at once angry and ashamed.
'No, Sir' said he; 'I speak not of myself. You have treated me very kindly, sure, and although you have taken me captive, you have given me my life; you have effected the recovery from serious illness of one who had been destroying your forces. He who should be loaded with chains, and confined in a dungeon, lives in a perfumed chamber, through your kindness. What more can you do, Sir? But what I say

is this; you are laying me under embarassing obligations; I do not see the end which all this comfort points to. If I am a prisoner, send me to gaol, Sir; release from this net of kindness; but if I am not a prisoner, what's the use of keeping me in this golden cage, pray?'

'Prince,' replied Osman with composure, 'why are you so impatient for evil? Evil requires no courting—it comes of itself.'

'The Rajputs,' replied the Prince haughtily, 'consider it no evil to exchange this flowery bed of yours for one of stone.'

'It would not matter much' said Osman 'if Misfortune had no greater terrors than the stone-bed.'

The Prince eyed Osman keenly and said,

'When I have failed to chastise Katlu Khan, to me the executioner's axe is no evil.'

'Take care, Sir,' said Osman. 'The Pathans are no babblers.'

'General!' said the Prince with a scornful laugh, 'if you have come to cow me, you will not succeed.'

'No, Sir,' replied Osman; 'we know each other too well to waste words. I have come to you on some particular business.'

'Let me hear it, Sir,'—said the Prince, rather surprised.

'The proposal which I make—is made under the express orders of Katlu Khan. Please to bear this in mind.'

Prince. 'Very well.'

Os. 'The strife between the Rajputs and the Pathans is injuring both parties.'

Prince. 'Our object is to make root and branch work of the Pathans.'

'True' replied Osman; 'but Sir, consider the chance of destroying us without at the same time undergoing destruction yourselves. You, for one, can testify whether the captors of Garmandaran are so utterly weak.'

A slight smile appeared on the lips of Jagat Singha.

'I grant them skill.'

'Whatever it be,' Osman went on; 'it's not my object to praise self. It will never be easy for the Pathans to live in Orissa, if they are at daggers-drawn with the Emperor. But, depend upon it, Sir, he will never succeed in subjecting them. Don't tax me with national vanity; you are well conversant with political matters. Consider what a long way off Orissa is from Delhi. Suppose that the Emperor succeeds in bringing the Pathans under his yoke through the arms of Man Singha; how long will his banners float in Orissa? As soon as he turns his back, all the possessions of the Emperor in Orissa will slip from his grasp. Did not Akbar conquer the country before? But how long did it pay him tribute? And if he succeed in taking it again, it can but end in a like result. He may once more send his forces, and once more conquer the province; but again will the Pathans be free. The Pathans are not Bengalis, mind; they never have bowed down the knee to any one, they never will, so long as a single Pathan breathes. That is certain. Where then is the necessity of deluging the earth with the blood of Rajputs and Pathans?'

'And what would you propose, Sir?' asked Jagat Singha.

'*I* propose nothing' said Osman; 'but my master proposes peace.'

Jagat: 'And what kind of peace?'

Os: 'Let both of us concede a little. The Nabab Katlu Khan is ready to relinquish what be has possessed himself of in Bengal; let Akbar waive his claims to Orissa, and, withdrawing his troops, desist from any future warfare. He is not a whit the loser by this bargain; the Pathans indeed might, to a certain extent, be considered as losers. We are parting with that which we have made ourselves masters of by our own exertions, Akbar is only parting with what he could not make his own.'

'Good and well' replied the Prince. 'But why do you speak this to me? The man to make peace and war is Maharaja Man Singha; you should send an envoy to him.'

'We did so, good Prince,' returned Osman. 'Unfortunately for us some body had reported to him that the Pathans have taken your Highness' life. Through grief and anger at this report, the Maharaj would listen to no proposal of peace. He did not believe in the assurances of our envoy. But if you, Sir, personally propose the terms to him, he may consent.'

The Prince fixed his look on Osman and said,

'Be plain, Sir, I beseech you. When the Maharaja may believe it at sight of my handwriting, why do you wish me to go personally?'

Os: 'The thing is this. The Maharaja is not very well informed of our strength; you will be able to enlighten him on that point; and we hope a good deal from your kind intercession. A letter cannot do as much. One of the first results of the peace will be your Highness' release; the Nabab has accordingly thought that you would try to bring about this treaty.'

Prince: 'I do not refuse to go to my father.'

Os: 'I am glad of it, Sir; but I must provide one thing. If you don't succeed in concluding the peace we offer, will you kindly pledge us your word to come back into the fort.'

Prince: 'And how can you be sure that I shall return if I promise?'

'Yes, Sir, I am sure' replied Osman with a smile. 'That a Rajput is true to his word is a well-known fact.'

'Very well, Sir,' said the Prince complacently; 'I engage to come back alone into the fort, soon after seeing my father.'

Os: 'Kindly promise one thing more and you oblige us completely. Promise that you will bring forward the terms offered by us, when you see the Maharaja.'

'Worthy general' replied the Prince, 'excuse me, Sir, I cannot promise this. The Emperor has appointed us to subjugate the Pathans; and to subjugate them is our only duty; he has not appointed us to conclude peace, and peace we shall never conclude. Nor will I ever propose such a thing.'

Osman's face showed expressions both of satisfaction and regret.

'Prince,' said he, 'you have replied like a Rajput, but consider there is no other way of your getting free.'

Prince: 'And what's my freedom to the Emperor, pray? The Rajput race has many a Prince like me.'

'Prince,' said Osman with sorrowful earnestness; 'take my advice, Sir; resign your present purpose.'

Prince: 'And why so,?'

Os: 'To be plain, it is only in the hope of inducing you to bring about his end that the great Nabab has, up to this time, shown you such consideration. If you set your face against his object, he will be very severe upon you, Sir.'

Prince: 'On that key again? Did I not a moment before ask you to take me to prison?'

Os: 'Young Prince! it would be lucky indeed for you if that only satisfied the Nabab.'

The Prince frowned.

'If it doesn't, I will increase Virendra Singha's bloody torrent.' His eyes flashed fire.

'I go then'—replied Osman. 'I have done my duty. You will learn Katlu Khan's intention by some messenger.'

A messenger came after a while. He was dressed like a soldier; he was of a rank above that of the foot-soldier. Ho had with him four armed foot-soldiers.

'What's your message?'—asked the Prince.

'You will have to change your quarters, Sir,' said the man.

'I am ready, Sir, proceed,' said the Prince and followed him.

12

THE SINGULAR ORNAMENT

A great festivity was come—the celebration of Katlu Khan's anniversary. Dancing and drinking, mirth and frolic, feasting and alms-giving filled the day. The night was even more jovial. It was just past sunset. The fort was ablaze with light. Every creek and corner was filled with officers, soldiers, courtiers, servants, beggars, drunkards, actors, actresses, dancers, dancing girls, musicians, jugglers, fruiterers, vendors of perfumes, betel sellers, vendors of various kinds of food, of various products of art, etc., etc. Wherever you went, you came upon illumination, music, fragrant waters, betels, flowers, jugglery and prostitutes. It was partly the same with the inner apartments. The Nabab's seraglio was comparatively calm, but comparatively more gay. Every chamber was mildly lighted with fragrant silver and crystal lamps; there were fragrant flowers on the flower stands, over the pillars, and on the beds, the cushions and the persons of the inmates. The air was sick with the smell of the rose. No end of maids, clad in gold brocade, or in blue, yellow, black, or pale red *chin* cloth, were passing and repassing, their golden ornaments glittering in the light. Their fair mistresses sat each in her chamber, and all care and attention were engaged in making their toilette. That day, the Nabab would make merry with every one in his pleasure-house; there would be music and dancing; every one would that night obtain her desire. Some fair one (intending to secure a situation for her brother) was lustily applying the comb to her hair; another with the view of increasing the number of her maids had brought her curled locks down to her very breast; a third intended to secure some property in the shape of dower on behalf of her new-born son, and in order to make her neck blush, had rubbed it until blood had actually began to flow. Another woman envying a set of ornaments the Nabab had recently given to a favored mistress, was painting the underlids of her eyes with *kajjala* through their whole lengths. A maidservant in donning the cloth on the person of her gentle mistress, unwarily pressed her *peshwaj* with her feet; and the gentle fair one administered her a goodly slap on her cheek. By the inexorable virtue of age, the hairs of some dame had grown rather thin, and a quantity came out with the comb which the maid had been applying to them. Seeing this, her mistress began to cry, the tears streaming down her cheeks.

Like the land lotus in the grove, like the peacock among birds, a certain fair one, after having finished her toilette, was roving from room to room. One could go anywhere that night. Nature had made the woman the receptacle of her sweets; Katlu Khan had given her every member its appropriate ornament; yet her face did not show any marks of pride either for her beauty or for her ornaments. She knew no mirth, no laugh. Her face was grave—calm—her eyes showed the fire burning within.

After roving here and there, Bimala entered a handsome chamber. She fastened the door. On this festive occasion, a solitary lamp only cast its pale beams around. On the further side stood a couch on which lay someone covered from head to foot with a blanket. Bimala came up to the side of the person and said faintly,

'I am come.'

The person on the bed started and withdrew the cover from off her face.

Having recognised Bimala, she put away the blanket and sat up; but spoke nothing.

'Tilottama,' said Bimala again, 'I am come.'

Still Tilottama kept silent; she steadily gazed on Bimala's face.

She was then no longer the bashful girl she had been. Alas! if you saw her then by the pale light, you would think her ten years older than she actually was. Her body was lean and emaciated; her countenance was pale; she wore a short, unclean cloth; her hair was covered with dust; there was not a single ornament on her person, only the traces of her former ornaments remained.

'I told that I would come' again Bimala said, 'and have done so. Why don't you speak?'

'What I had to say' replied Tilottama, 'I have said. What more shall I say?'

Bimala perceived from Tilottama's voice that she was weeping. Bimala laid her hand on Tilottama's head, and raised her face; it was bedewed with tears; Bimala felt the flowing end of Tilottama's cloth, and found it thoroughly wet. She then touched the pillow on which the latter had reposed her head, and also found it wet.

'How long can you stand this constant weeping?' said Bimala.

'And wherefore should I stand it?' said Tilottama eagerly. 'The only regret is that I have stood it so long.'

Bimala became silent and began to weep.

'But what's to be done for tonight?' asked Bimala with a deep sigh, after a pause.

Tilottama eyed Bimala's ornaments with displeasure.

'What's the need of thinking of that?' said she.

'My child,' replied Bimala; 'don't you slight me. You don't yet know Katlu Khan well. Partly for want of leisure, and partly to allow our grief to subside, the villain has spared us so long. I have ere this told you, today ends our freedom. I don't know what danger will befall us, should he miss us at the dancing saloon.'

'What more danger can possibly befall us?'—said Tilottama.

'Tilottama,' said Bimala rather calmly, 'why do you at once despair? Still we have life—still we have innocence. So long as we have life—so long we will keep our innocence intact.'

'Why then, mother?' Tilottama then said, 'Fling off those ornaments; they are an eyesore to see.'

'Child'—said Bimala with a smile, 'don't chide me without seeing *all* my ornaments.»

Saying this, she drew out from her waist a sharp dagger, which she had hidden in her dress. It flashed like lightning on meeting the glare.

'Where have you procured it? Eh?' asked Tilottama, starting and looking blank.

'Havn't you seen,' said Bimala, 'a new maidservant who came yesterday into the inner apartment?'

Til. 'Yes, I have,—it is Ashmani.'

'I have brought it in through Ashmani, from Abhiram Swami.'

Tilottama was surprised; her heart trembled.

After a while, Bimala asked, 'Will you not change this dress tonight?'
'No,' replied Tilottama.
'Neither will you go to the dancing and music?'
Til. 'No.'
Bi. 'Still you will not be let alone.'
Tilottama began to weep.
'Be calm and listen,' said Bimala. 'I have found means for your escape.'

Tilottama eagerly looked at Bimala's face. The latter handed to her the ring given by Osman.

'Keep it with you,' said she; 'don't go to the merry-making. It will not end before midnight. I shall up to that time be able to keep the Pathan engaged. He knows that I am your stepmother; and I will make him restrain his desire to see you till the dance and music is over, under the pretext that you can't come in my presence. At midnight, go to the gate of the inner apartment; there a person will show you another ring like this; go with him without hesitation. He will take you wherever you should like to go. Tell him to take you to Abhiram Swami's cottage.'

Tilottama was astonished. Either from amazement or from excess of joy, she could not speak for a while.

'What's this?' said she. 'Who has given you this ring?'

'That's a long story to tell,'—said Bimala. 'I will tell it to you at leisure. Now do without hesitation as I have told you.'

'And what of yourself?' asked Tilottama. 'How will you go out?'

'Don't be uneasy on that account,' said Bimala. 'I will by some other means go out and meet you tomorrow morning.'

She thus silenced Tilottama. The latter could not understand that she closed her own way in providing deliverance for Tilottama.

For many a day, Tilottama's face had not expressed joy. She now looked quite cheerful at this joyful intelligence.

This filled Bimala with delight.

'Then I go now,' said she with tearful eyes and a choked utterance.

'I see,' said Tilottama hesitatingly, 'you know every thing that has taken place within the fort. Will you tell me (before you go) how and where our friends and acquaintances are?'

Bimala saw that even in this imminent danger the remembrance of Jagat Singha was lively in Tilottama's mind. Bimala had received Jagat Singha's cruel note, in which he did not mention the very name of Tilottama. To tell this to her would but add to the misery of a heart already bending beneath the weight of its sorrow. Therefore without alluding to that subject, Bimala said,

'Jagat Singha is in the fort. He is in good health.'

Tilottama remained silent.

Bimala kissed her and went out, wiping her eyes.

13

PRESENTING THE RING

When Bimala had gone out, seated alone in her chamber, Tilottama began to indulge in melancholy as well as cheerful reflections. That a way was now opened for her speedy deliverance from the clutches of the fiend, almost engrossed her thoughts—the thought that Bimala loved her more than life, that she owed her expected deliverance to Bimala, came repeatedly before her mind and increased her delight. Then she thought, 'And where shall I direct my steps when I go out? Alas! where is my father's roof now.' Anon the tears trickled down her cheeks. When other anxieties had been stifled, another troubled her mind: 'The Prince then is safe. But where is he? How is he? Is he too a captive?' The thought brought tears to her eyes. 'Lack-a-day! the Prince is a captive for me. Shall I be able to requite him by laying down my life at his feet? Ah! what shall I do for him?' Again thought she, 'Is he in prison? What is the prison like? Can none go there? What can he be thinking now, sitting in his prison? Is he remembering such a one as Tilottama? Oh yes! Am I not the cause of his present distress? I don't know what lots of names he is calling me.' Again thought she, 'And how so? Why should I think so? Does he know how to call any one names? No, no, that can't be. But the fear is, he may have forgotten me; or banished me from his thoughts for being an inmate of the Yavan.' 'No, no,' she went on, 'why will he do so? I am a mere captive in the fortress even as he is. Why then will he despise me? If he do so, in spite of this, I will take hold of his feet and explain it to him. Will he not be satisfied? By all means, he will. If he will not, I will die before him. Formerly they used to go through the fiery ordeal; it is not so now in this *Kali* age. Never mind, what if I throw myself before him in the fire?' 'Ah! when shall I see him?' she continued; 'how shall he get free? What purpose is served by my deliverance? Wherefrom has my stepmother procured this ring? Could this serve to deliver him? What if I send this ring to him? Who will come to take me out? Cannot any means be found through him? But how shall I ask him about it? Shall I not be able to see the Prince once more?' She again thought, 'Ah! how shall I ask for an interview with him? How open my lips to him, in his presence? By what words shall I relieve this wretched heart?'

Tilottama thought incessantly.

A maidservant entered. Tilottama asked her,

'What o'clock is it?'

''Tis struck twelve,' was the answer.

Tilottama waited for the disappearance of the menial. When she had gone out after doing what she came for, Tilottama took the ring and issued from the room. She then became subject to apprehensions; her feet trembled; her heart quaked; her face grew blank; she advanced one pace and receded another. By degrees, summoning courage, she reached so far as the gate of the inner apartment. The inmates, the eunuchs, the negro-slaves,—all were knee deep in merriment; nobody saw her; and if any did, he did not care to notice her. But it seemed to Tilottama as if she was marked by every one. She however got courage to proceed to the gate. There the guards who had been making merry over 'potations pottle-deep,' were either asleep, or awake but insensible, or half insensible: no body marked her. One person only was standing at the gate; he too was dressed like a guard. On seeing Tilottama, he said,

'Have you got a ring, madam?'

In a flurry, Tilottama presented the ring given by Bimala. The man carefully examined it and showed her another on his finger.

'Come with me, madam, no fear,' said he.

Tilottama followed him in agitation. The guards in the other parts of the fort were as lax as those who guarded the inner apartment. More particularly, as the gates were thrown open that night to all, no one said anything to the pair. The guard crossed many a threshold, many a room, many a yard, and at last reached the main gate of the fortress. He then said,

'Where would you go?'

Tilottama could not bring to mind the instruction of Bimala; she first remembered Jagat Singha. She burned to say, 'take me to the Prince;' but shame, her former enemy, prevented her, and the words stuck in her throat. The guard again asked, 'Where shall I take you?'

Tilottama could say nothing, she was almost out of herself; her heart trembled she knew not why; her eyes failed to see; her ears to hear; she knew not what escaped her lips; a faint sound like *Jagat Singha* entered the guard's ear.

'Jagat Singha is in prison now,' said he; 'no one can go there; but I have been ordered to take you wherever you should like to go. Come along, madam.'

The guard re-entered the fort. Unconscious of what she was about or where she was going, she turned and followed her guide, like a puppet in pulling wires. The man found that the guards of the prison were not lax like those belonging to the other parts of the fort; here the men were watching in their posts.

'Where is the Prince?' asked the guide.

The man addressed pointed with his finger.

'Is the prisoner awake or asleep?' asked the guide to the guard of the prison. The man went up to the gate and returned.

'I have received the answer of the prisoner,' said he. 'He is awake.'

'Please open the door to me,' said the bearer of the ring; 'this lady will go in to see the prisoner.'

'How is that?' said the guard in surprise. 'Don't you know there is no such order?'

The guide showed him the ring of Osman. The man bowed low, and opened the door.

The Prince was lying upon a common four-footed bed. On hearing the sound preceding from the door, he looked at it curiously. Tilottama neared the door but could approach no further. Her feet could not do their office; she took hold of the door, and stood there.

'What's this?' asked the bearer of the ring, seeing Tilottama pause. 'Why do you stop here?'

Still Tilottama could not go.

'If you don't wish to enter in' said the man, 'please return then; this is not the time to linger here.'

Tilottama prepared to return; but she could not go that way either.

What could she do? The guard was impatient. While vacillating thus, Tilottama unconsciously advanced a foot, and was in the room.

No sooner she saw the Prince, than she was again deprived of farther motion. She held by the wall and paused near the door, hanging down her head.

The Prince could not at first recognise Tilottama. He was surprised to see a woman. Seeing her pause near the wall, without approaching him, he was still more surprised. He rose from his bed and approached the door; he saw, and—he recognised.

For a moment their eyes met; anon Tilottama's were cast to the ground; her body slightly inclined forwards as if seeking the feet of the Prince.

He drew back a little, and anon Tilottama stood like one spellbound and motionless as a statue; her bosom which but an instant before had bloomed like a lotus, became suddenly withered.

'Virendra Singha's daughter?' said the Prince.

Tilottama felt as if a dagger had entered her vitals. 'Virendra Singha's daughter?' Is that the present address?

Has Jagat Singha forgotten the very name of Tilottama? Both remained silent for a while.

'Why here?' asked the Prince.

'Why here?' What a question! Tilottama's head became dizzy—on all sides, the room, the bed, the lamp, the walls, all began to turn round; she supported herself by leaning her head against the wall.

For a long while, the Prince stood for reply; but who would reply? Seeing no chance of it, he said,

'You are suffering much. Return, and forget the past.'

All doubts were now dispelled from Tilottama's mind; she fell down upon the ground, like a leaf torn from its parent tree.

14

THE TRANCE

Jagat Singha bent down and saw that Tilottama was quite senseless. He began to fan her with his cloth. Still not seeing any signs of sensibility, he called the guard.

Tilottama's guide came in.

'This woman has suddenly gone off in a trance,' said Jagat Singha. 'Who has come with her? Tell her to look to her.'

'I alone have come,' answered the guide.

'You!' exclaimed the Prince in surprise.

'None else,' replied the guard.

'What's to be done then? Tell it to a maidservant of the fortress.'

The man was going away, when the Prince called him back and said, 'Look here! The matter shall take air, if you speak to any body about it; and who will leave the merry-making to help the woman?'

'That's too true,' returned the guard. 'And why will the guards allow any one to enter the prison? I don't dare bring any other into it.'

'What shall I do then?' said the Prince. 'There is only one means. Do you hastily convey the news to the Princess, through a maidservant.'

The guard hurried out to attend to the Prince's instructions. The Prince tended Tilottama so far as the circumstances of the case permitted. What were his thoughts then? Who can say? Did a tear stand in his eyes? Who can say?

The Prince was greatly embarrassed with Tilottama alone in the prison. If the tidings did not reach Aesha; if, again, she could not devise any means, what should it come to?

By degrees, Tilottama began to revive. Immediately the Prince saw through the open door two women (one of them veiled) approach with the guard. Seeing from a distance the stately form, the rhythmical gait and the graceful neck of the veiled beauty, the Prince perceived that Aesha herself was coming with her maid—and as if she had been bringing Hope with her. When Aesha and her maid came up to the door with the guard, the sentry asked the bearer of the ring,

'Shall I also permit these?'

'That's your option—I can't say,' said the guide.

'Well,' said the man, and prohibited the women to enter. Aesha removed her veil and said,

'Sentry, allow me to enter. If you incur any censure for it, lay it all to my account.'

Seeing Aesha, the guard was surprised. He bowed and said with joined hands,

'Your Highness, pardon your humble servant. To you no place is forbidden.'

Aesha entered the prison. She was not smiling then, but her features having a habitual expression of smile, it seemed as if she had been smiling. What a grace then sat on the dark brow of the dungeon; it was no longer a prison.

Aesha saluted the Prince and said,

'Prince! what's the matter?'

What was the Prince to reply? He simply pointed with his finger to the prostrate Tilottama.

'Who is she?' asked Aesha, after seeing Tilottama.

'The daughter of Virendra Singha,' answered the Prince, reluctantly.

Aesha took up Tilottama in her lap. Any other female in her situation would have hesitated—would have calculated, but Aesha at once took Tilottama in her lap.

Whatever Aesha did, looked beautiful; she could do every thing gracefully. When she took Tilottama in her lap, both Jagat Singha and the attendant thought, 'how beautiful!'

Aesha had brought vessels of rosewater, sherbet, etc. through her maid. She now fell to reviving Tilottama with these. The attendant began to fan her. Tilottama who had been regaining her consciousness already, now completely revived by the attentions of Aesha, and sat up.

She looked round, and remembered what had occurred. She was immediately going to rush out of the room; but her frame having been exhausted through the physical as well as the mental agitation of that night, she could not go; her head became dizzy on remembering what had taken place; and down she sat.

'Sister,' said Aesha, taking hold of her hand, 'why are you uneasy? You are now very weak; come now to my room to rally. Afterwards I will send you wherever you should like to go.'

Tilottama made no reply.

Aesha had learnt all from the guide. Suspecting apprehension in Tilottama, she said,

'Why do you mistrust me? I am indeed the daughter of your enemy; but you should not therefore think me unworthy of your confidence. You needn't fear any discovery from me. Before the night is out, I will send yon with an attendant whereever you should like to go. No one shall know anything.'

This was said so sweetly that Tilottama could not entertain any doubts as to Aesha's sincerity. Further, she was now incapable of walking; nor could she remain with Jagat Singha. Consequently she consented.

'You won't be able to walk,' said Aesha; 'do you go supporting yourself on the maid.'

Tilottama supported herself on the shoulder of the attendant, and began to walk slowly. Aesha too was going to take leave of the Prince, when he fixed his gaze on her, as if he had had something to say. Aesha understood it and said to the attendant,

'Do you take the lady to my bedchamber; and then come back to take me.'

The woman proceeded with Tilottama.

'Farewell, for ever!' thought Jagat Singha within himself, with a profound sigh. So long as Tilottama was visible, he fixed his gaze on her.

'Farewell, for ever!' also thought Tilottama. So long as Jagat Singha could be seen, she did not turn; when she turned, the Prince was no longer visible.

15

THE DECLARATION

When Tilottama and the maidservant left the room, Aesha came forward and sat down on the bed. There being no other seat, Jagat Singha stood by.

Aesha pulled out a rose from her braid, and, beginning to tear the leaves, said,

'Prince, you look as if you had something to speak to me. If I can be of the least service to you, Sir, pray, do not scruple to speak out your mind. I shall be really delighted to serve you.'

'Princess,' said he 'nothing avails me now. No, Your Highness, it was not for that reason that I longed for an interview with you. What I would say is this. Judging from what I have been reduced to, I cannot indulge the fond hope of seeing you again; perhaps here we see our last of each other. Ah! how shall words express how deeply I stand indebted to you! As for ever requiting it, I dare not hope to do it, considering my ill luck. But if ever I again possess the power to do you a good turn—if ever better days dawn on me, do not, I pray you, scruple to express your mind to me. As a sister unreservedly expresses her wishes to her brother, do you, Madam, do likewise.'

Jagat Singha's tone was so very disconsolate—so very despairing, that Aesha was touched.

'Don't give way to despair, Sir,' said she; 'the evils of today are removed by the morrow.'

'I am not given up to despair,' answered Jagat Singha. 'But what have I again to hope for in this life? To resign this existence, not to maintain it, is my sole wish now. But I am unwilling to quit it in prison.'

The pathetic tone of the Prince went direct to the heart of Aesha—she was moreover surprised at this display of feeling. The Princess was now put aside—distance and reserve now vanished—like an affectionate woman, with a woman's tender concern, she took hold of the Prince's hand.

'Jagat'—exclaimed she, looking up into Jagat Singha's face, and then stopped for a moment. She had addressed the Prince, 'Jagat.'

'Jagat,' resumed she, 'O why is this anguish in your heart! Do not look on me as one foreign to you. If you permit me I'd ask—Is Virendra Singha's daughter—'

'I cry you mercy,' interposed he; 'that dream has vanished.'

Both remained silent for a long while, their hands continuing joined as before. Aesha bent down her face over them.

All of a sudden the Prince started, for a warm teardrop had fallen on his hand.

Lowering his head, the Prince examined the lovely countenance of Aesha, and saw tears streaming plentifully down her cheeks.

'Gracious Heaven!' exclaimed he, in surprise; 'what is this, Aesha? Why are you weeping?'

Without returning any answer, she gently pulled Jagat Singha's hand, and made him sit down beside her on the couch.

When he had sat, she again took his hand and said,

'Prince! I did not dream that I should have to bid you farewell in this manner. I can suffer a great deal—but I can never suffer the thought of leaving you in prison, under this extreme anguish. Come out with me, I beseech you—I will give you a horse from our stables; escape to your father's camp this very night.'

Had his guardian angel appeared before him personally, to confer blessings on him, the Prince could not have been struck with greater surprise. He was speechless from very astonishment.

'Jagat Singha! Prince! come, O come,' again importuned she.

'Aesha,' said he, after a pause, 'you will set me free?'

'Yes, instantly'—replied Aesha.

Prince. 'Without your father's knowledge?'

Aesha. 'No fear; I will break the matter to him when you shall have been beyond his reach.'

'But how will the guards allow me to go out?'

'This talisman will induce them.'

She thereupon tore her jewelled necklace, and held it before the Prince.

'When the matter will come to light' said he, 'you shall come to grief at the hands of your father.'

'No great matter.'

'No, Aesha, I never will go.'

Aesha looked blank.

'Ah, why so?' asked she sadly.

Prince. 'I owe you already nothing less than my life—and I shall never do an action which shall make you miserable.'

'Then must you persist in refusing?' asked she in a choked voice.

'Pray, go out alone,' said he.

Aesha was again silent—tears gushed out afresh from her eyes, defying her utmost efforts at restraining them.

'Aesha!' exclaimed the Prince in amazement—'Aesha, why do you weep, maiden.'

Aesha was silent.

'Aesha,' the Prince went on, 'if you can well express to me the cause of your silent weeping, do so I beseech you. I shall lay down my life to remove it. That I have chosen to remain in prison cannot have brought tears to the eyes of Aesha. Have not thousands of prisoners rotten in your father's goal?'

Without returning any answer, Aesha wiped her eyes.

'Prince,' said she after a pause, 'I shall weep no more.'

The Prince was rather sorry for not receiving any reply. Both hung down their heads in silence.

The shadow of a third person now fell on the prison wall, unmarked by those in the room. He came up and stood by them. After standing still like a statue for a while, he said in a voice faltering with passion,

'Princess! this is capital!'

Both raised their heads and saw—Osman.

Osman had learnt the particulars from his follower, the bearer of the ring; and had come in search of Aesha. On seeing Osman, the Prince became greatly apprehensive for the sake of Aesha, who might come by disgrace or reproof at the hands of Osman or of Katlu Khan himself; and that this was more than probable, the angry tone in which Osman had made the taunt, rendered clearly manifest. Aesha understood the import of the remark as soon as it was made. For a moment only her fair features grew crimson; but there was no other sign of impatience.

'And what is capital, Osman, I pray'—asked she calmly.

'It is capital,' said he in the same tone of raillery, 'it is capital for a Princess to be at night in the company of a prisoner. Aye; it is capital for her also to enter the prison in perfect contempt of rule.'

This was more than Aesha's spotless innocence could bear. She rivetted her eyes on Osman's face, and in such haughty accents as Osman never remembered to have heard before, said,

'It is my will to enter the prison alone at this dead hour of night—it is my will to talk with the prisoner. You are not the man to sit in judgment on the correctness or otherwise of my conduct.'

Osman was amazed; he was still more angry.

'You shall see that tomorrow morning before the Nabab,' said he.

'When father will ask'—replied she in the same manner, 'I shall answer him; you needn't be uneasy on that score.'

'And what if I asked?' said he in the same railing tone.

Aesha started to her feet, and for a while fixed her gaze on Osman. Her expansive eyes became more expansive, her lily-like countenance became still more blooming, her head with the raven-black locks slightly inclined to one side, her bosom heaved with rising emotion, like moss swayed by the waves. In clear, ringing tones, she said,

'If *you* ask, Osman, I can tell you that the prisoner before us is—the lord of my bosom.'

Had the thunder burst there at that moment, neither the Rajput nor the Pathan could have been startled more highly. The Prince felt as if someone had illumined his mental darkness;—he now understood the meaning and import of Aesha's silent weeping. Osman had ere this surmised as much, and had therefore rebuked Aesha in such a way; but that she should declare her love in his very presence, had not entered his head. Osman was silent.

'Listen, Osman,' continued she, 'this prisoner is the lord of my bosom. While a particle of life continues to warm this frame, none else can hope to find a place there. If it so happen that tomorrow the ground of execution be drenched with his blood—' here she shuddered, 'still, still, you will find me enshrining his dear image in my heart of hearts and worshipping it for ever and a day. If this moment is destined to be the last of our seeing each other, if he be released tomorrow, and being encircled by hundreds of wives, cry shame upon the name of Aesha and turn it into a bye-word—still, still shall I remain his for ever, panting for his love. What, think you, I was speaking to him here secretly? I was telling him, I would win the guards over by soft words or by reward. I would furnish him with a horse from our stables—and importuned him to escape at once to his father's camp. The prisoner himself declined to go away, or by this time you would not have found the least trace of him.'

She wiped away her tears, and paused a little, and then resumed in an altered voice.

'But Osman, I have pained you. Forgive me, I beseech you. We cherish each other with affection; and my conduct looks rank unkindness. But you suspected my innocence. Whatever her other faults, impurity has no share in Aesha. Whatever Aesha does, she can avow it before the world. Now I have declared it to you—if necessary tomorrow I will declare it to my father.' Then turning to Jagat Singha, she said,

'Prince! do you also forgive me. Had not Osman touched me to the quick, the grief that knawed my vitals, would never have come to your ears—nay, to any human ears.'

The Prince stood speechless, his heart burning in anguish. Osman also was silent. Aesha resumed,

'Osman! I say again, if I have offended you, do you forgive me. I shall ever remain your affectionate sister. Do not, O do not, lessen your affection for me. As my bad luck would have it, I have plunged into this ocean; do not add to my woe by depriving me of your brotherly love.'

Saying this, the fair damsel rushed out, without waiting for the return of her maid. Osman remained speechless for a while like one that had lost his senses, and then returned to his apartment.

16

YOUR SLAVE'S AT YOUR FEET, LORD

There was dancing that night in the harem of Katlu Khan. He did not, like the Mogal Emperors, celebrate his anniversary in festive mirth and gaity in the midst of his courtiers—his nature was intensely selfish, and ever craved for the lusts of the flesh. That night he was surrounded by his sweethearts, and was engaged in mirth and fun with them. There was no other dancing girl—no other spectator. No one could go there except the eunuchs. Some were dancing, some were singing and some keeping measure; the rest sat round Katlu Khan and listened.

Nothing that could please the sense was lacking there. You entered the chamber, and a grateful coolness spread itself over your body, on account of the odour of fragrant waters, which kept continually sprinkling. The splendour of ever so many silver, ivory a crystal vessels dazzled your sight. No end of flowers—here in garlands—there in heaps—and there again in *bouquets*—they graced the hair of the fair ones,—they gleamed mildly over their neck. Some carried the flowery fan—some were decked in flowers—some were throwitng *bouquets* at others, the odour of the flowers—the odour of the perfumes—the odour of the lamps—the odour of the fragrant bosoms of the lovely damsels themselves—the air was sick with odour. The splendour of the lamps, the splendour of the flowers, the splendour of the ornaments, and finally the splendour of the side-glances darted incessantly from the eyes of the women. The music of the *vina* and other instruments swelled the air, accompanied by the sweeter, clearer strains of the females; at intervals the tinklings proceeding from the feet of a dancing-girl took the soul with 'enchanting ravishment'.

Look there! reader, how yonder female dances; so dances the lotus-embosomed swan when the waves are up. She is looked on by a circle of lovely, cheerful faces. Look where sits she of the blue attire—her cloth glittering in stars of gold—what a pair of expansive eyes! how deliciously blue like the sky!—what lightning flash in her side glance! Look at the other fair one, who bears a diamond-star on that spot of her forehead where her hair begins to part. Do you see what a sweet forehead she has? Serene, expansive, clear—has such a creature been meant by Heaven for the harem? Look at that lovely brown girl decked in flowers. Do you see how well her floral dress sets off her person? Flowers were meant for the fair. Do you see yonder girl with cherry-ripe lips, which are at present slightly compressed. Mark how her bright complexion comes out from behind her glossy, blue vesture—so looks the moon at its full in the cloudless heavens. Do you see that fair one there with the swan-like neck. She is talking and laughing. Look how her pendants are waving. Who are you, my fair one, with such a fine head of hair? Why have you let your ringlets down to your breast? Do you show how the snake twines itself round the lotus-bud?

And who are you, my fair one, who seated beside Katlu Khan, are pouring out the 'rubied nectar' into the golden glass? Who are you at whose 'bright, consummate' charms Katlu Khan is incessantly casting eager glances? Who are you that are firing his bosom with your infallible side-looks? I know that glance—you are Bimala. Why are you pouring out so much liquor? Go on—go on—more—you have, sure, got the dagger within your dress? Of course. How can you then laugh in such a manner? Ah! it is no common laugh. Katlu Khan is looking at you in the in the face. What's that? Side glance! What's that? What again? See if you have not maddened the flushed Musalman! Perhaps, it is by means of your wiles that you have at once made yourself the sole mistress of his heart. And how could it be otherwise? Such a laugh! Such a carriage! Such a sweet, playful talk! Such a side glance! Again the cup! Have a care, Katlu Khan! And what can Katlu Khan do? With what a glance Bimala is offering the glass! Ha! what's that sound? Who is singing? Does it proceed from human or from angelic lungs? Bimala is singing with the singers. What a voice! what strains! how fine the measure! Katlu Khan, what's this? Who has captivated your mind? What are you gazing at? She is smilingly casting her side-look at every cadence; she is piercing your heart with more than a dagger's sharpness. Do you see that? The glance alone is bewitching and it is accompanied by music! And do you see how her head waves gently with every glance? Do you see how her pendants are waving? Ha! Pour the liquor again, pour, for God's sake. What's this? What's this? Bimala has risen up and begun to dance. How beautiful! What a manner! The glass! What a person! What a frame! Katlu Khan, my lord! Have patience! Patience I say! You are in a flame! Ah! Katlu's body is burning! The cup! Ah! The cup! Ha! What again? Again the laugh! again the glance! Wine! Wine! What is is, eh? *Kanchali?*

What's that, my lord? What's that?

The circle of women rose up with a chorus of laughter, and fled.

Suddenly the lamp went out; Katlu Khan cried 'Where are you, my charmer?'

Laying one hand on Katlu's shoulder, Bimala said, 'Your slave's at your feet, lord.' Her other hand held the dagger.

Katlu Khan drew Bimala to his breast, and embraced her deeply. The next moment he shrieked out frightfully, cast her away at a distance, and sank in the bed. Bimala had sent her sharp dagger to the hilt into Katlu's breast.

'Vile murdress! damned wretch!' exclaimed he; his throat gurgled he spoke.

'No murdress, no wretch, but the widowed wife of Virendra Singha!' said Bimala, and off she went.

Katlu was fast losing his speech; still he kept up crying with all his might. Bimala too ran and cried. On reaching another room she heard some people talking. She flew like wind. She found some guards and eunuchs in the next room. Hearing the cry and seeing her flurry, they asked,

'What's the matter?'

'Death and ruin,' exclaimed the inventive Bimala, 'make haste, Sirs; some robbers have entered the chamber; perhaps they have murdered the Nabab.'

The men ran off in hot haste towards the room; Bimala ran to the gate of the inner apartment. There she found the guard in a profound sleep through inebriation, and crossed the gate without hindrance. It was the same throughout. She ran uninterruptedly. On coming to the outer gate, she found the guard awake. One of them, on seeing Bimala, said,

'Who is there? Where are you going?'

There was now a tremendous uproar within the inner apartment; all were running in that direction.

'What are you doing here, sitting idle?' said Bimala; 'don't you hear the noise?'

'What is it about?' enquired the guard.

'Confusion!' exclaimed Bimala, 'the Nabab has been attacked.'

Off ran the guards, leaving the gate; Bimala slipped out without obstruction.

When she had gone some way from the gate, she found a man standing under a tree. Bimala immediately recognised him as Abhiram Swami.

When she came up, Abhiramswami said,

'I was extremely anxious. What's the noise for?'

'I have avenged my wrong!' replied Bimala. 'We shouldn't tarry here; let us hasten to the cottage. I will let you know all afterwards. Tilottama is there already?'

'She is going with Ashmani,' said Abhiramswami. 'We shall overtake her soon.'

They walked away hastily. On reaching the cottage soon, they found that through Aesha's kindness, Tilottama had just come with Ashmani. She saluted the feet of Abhiram Swami with a low reverence, and began to weep. After solacing her, he said,

'By the grace of God, you have come out of the clutches of the sinful wretch. No tarrying here a moment more. Should the Musalmans trace us out, they will avenge their murdered lord by taking our lives. Let us quit this place this very night.'

All agreed to this proposal.

17

THE LAST MOMENTS

Immediately after the flight of Bimala, an official of Katlu Khan hastily entered the prison of Jagat Singha and said,

'Prince! The Nabab is dying, and wants to see you.'

'How's that?' exclaimed the Prince, astonished.

'Some enemies entered the inner apartment' said the man, 'and have fled after striking the Nabab. He is still alive, but has not long to live. Pray, Sir, make haste or it will be too late.'

'And why does he wish to see me at such a moment?' asked the Prince.

'I don't know that' said he, 'I am a mere messenger.'

The Prince went to the interior with the person. There he saw that the light was really flickering, about to sink into eternal night. Round the dying man thronged Osman, Aesha, his youthful sons, the partner of his fortunes, his mistresses, servants, courtiers, etc. The air was filled with wailing and lamentation; loudly wept almost every one of that crowd; the infants wept without understanding what the matter was; all were crying aloud save one. It was Aesha. Tears were trickling down her cheeks plentifully. She sat silent, holding in her lap the head of her father.

Jagat Singha saw that her manner was awfully calm, like a flame unfanned by the lightest breath of air.

As the Prince entered, a courtier named Khwaja took hold of his hand, and brought him to the side of Katlu Khan.

Addressing him as if he had been a deaf person, the courtier said, 'The Prince Jagat Singha is come.'

'Your enemy, I die,' said he faintly; 'resign all anger and enmity.'

'Very well,' said Jagat Singha, understanding him; 'I do so now.'

'A request—promise,' said Katlu Khan, in the same tone.

'What shall I promise?' asked Jagat Singha.

'Your hand,' said Katlu Khan.

Understanding his intention, Osman took Jagat Singha's hand and placed Katlu Khan's in it.

A fire spread over Jagat Singha's body, but he did not prevent the action.

Katlu Khan went on,

'Lads all—war—O I die of thirst!'

Aesha poured the sherbet into his mouth.

"'Tis no use—fighting—peace.'

Katlu Khan stopped. Jagat Singha made no reply. The former remained fixing his gaze on the Prince's face, expectant of a reply. Not receiving any, he said with an effort,

'Refuse?'

'If the Pathans acknowledge the supremacy of the Emperor,' the Prince said, 'I can promise to try for peace.'

'Orissa'—said Katlu Khan in a half articulate voice.

'If my endeavours do not fail,' returned the Prince, understanding him, 'your sons will not be deprived of Orissa.'

The features of Katlu Khan, which had been before writhing in the agonies of death, brightened up with joy. He said,

'You—free—God—good.'

Jagat Singha was going away, when Aesha bent down her head, and said something to her father. Katlu Khan first looked at Khwaja Isa, and then at the departing Prince. Khwaja Isa said to the Prince,

'Perhaps the Nabab has something more to say.'

The Prince returned.

'Your ear,' said Katlu Khan.

The Prince understood. He drew closer to the dying person, and brought his ear near to the lips of Katlu Khan.

'Vira,'—said he still more indistinctly.

He paused a little, and then went on,

'Virendra Singha—O! I thirst!'

Aesha again poured the drink into his mouth.

'Virendra Singha's daughter'—

The Prince felt as if an adder had stung him; he started and slightly drew himself up. Katlu Khan went on,

'The orphan—I am a sinner—O thirsty!'

Aesha repeatedly poured the drink into his mouth. But now articulation became difficult. He breathed hard and said,

'I burn!—I burn!—chaste—you'll see that.'

'What?' asked the Prince.

His voice entered like a thunder peal into Katlu Khan's ear. He continued,

'Never saw—so chaste—didn't see—didn't touch—you—how thirsty!—O I die, I die, dear Aesha.'

No more articulation. He had exerted beyond his power. His exhausted head fell down dead on her lap. Aesha's name was the last word which Katlu Khan articulated, as the flickering spirit went out into the darkness of death, and life and the world passed away from him.

18

HOSTILITY

After regaining his freedom, Jagat Singha went to his father's camp; and, as promised, brought about the conclusion of a treaty between the Moguls and the Pathans. The latter acknowledged the supremacy of the Emperor, and were allowed to retain the possession of Orissa. For the details of the treaty, the reader is referred to the pages of the historian; and we shall not enter into them. Some days after the conclusion of peace, both parties remained where they were. With the view of cementing the new-made alliance, the chief minister, Khawja Isa, and general Osman visited the camp of Man Singha, with the youthful sons of Katlu Khan. They won his good graces by the present of fifty elephants and various precious articles. The Raja received them with many marks of respect, and dismissed them loaded with honors.

It took some days to break up the encampment At length, on the eve of the departure of the Rajput army for Patna, Jagat Singha and suit went one afternoon to the Pathan fort, to take leave of Osman and other acquaintances. Ever since their meeting in the prison, Osman had shown a coldness towards the Prince. He now dismissed him with a few merely formal words.

In a sad temper of mind, Jagat Singha then went to Khawja Isa, and next to Aesha. He sent her word through a guard of the inner apartments, saying, 'Tell her, I have not had the good fortune of seeing her, since the demise of the Nabab. I am about to depart for Patna, and the chances of my again seeing her are few. I am therefore anxious to bid her farewell before I go.'

The eunuch returned after a while, and said,

'The Princess directs me to say that she is unable to see you, Sir; and begs you will excuse her for it.'

With increased mortification, the Prince set out for his quarters. On coming to the gate of the fortress, he found Osman, waiting for him.

The Prince again saluted him; and was about to leave the place, when Osman followed him.

'General,' said the Prince, 'if I can be of any service to you, pray, let me know it. I shall be very glad to do your bidding.'

'I have some very particular word with you,' said Osman 'which must not be told in the presence of so many people. Kindly tell them to advance, and follow me.'

Without the least hesitation, the Prince directed his retinue to go forward, and rode with Osman. The latter called for and mounted his horse. After proceeding some distance, Osman entered a deep *sal* forest, in the heart of which stood a dilapidated building. Probably in former days, some rebel had taken refuge in the bosom of this forest. Fastening his horse to a *sal* tree, Osman entered the ruin, followed by the Prince. It was a deserted mansion. In the middle there was a spacious yard. On one side of it there was a new-made open grave, but no corpse; on the other, a funeral pyre, but no dead body.

'What are these for?' enquired the Prince, entering the yard.

'These have been prepared by my directions,' replied Osman. 'Should I fall this day, pray, bury me in yonder grave; nobody will know it;—should you die, I will have your last rites performed by Brahmins; no one will know it.'

'What do your words moan, Sir?' enquired the Prince in surprise.

'I am a Pathan' replied Osman, 'when our heart burns, we do not judge between right and wrong. This world cannot contain two rivals longing for Aesha's love; one of us must die here today.'

The Prince now understood all, and became sad.

'What then is your intention, Sir?' demanded he.

'You are armed,' replied Osman; 'fight with me. If you can, clear your way by slaying me, or else lay down your own life and make way for me.'

With these words Osman attacked the Prince with his sword, without even allowing him time to reply. Tho Prince was compelled to draw his sword hastily, and defend himself. Osman made repeated attempts on the life of the Prince, but the latter did not attempt to strike his antagonist, he only maintained the defensive. Both were masters of their weapons, and the fight continued for a long time, without resulting in the defeat of one or the other. But the blows of the Pathan made sorry work of the Prince's body, which was drenched with blood; Osman on the contrary was untouched, as the Prince had not aimed at him a single blow. Finding himself gradually enfeebled by loss of blood, and knowing death to be certain in such an unequal encounter, the Prince cried out imploringly,

'Desist, Osman, desist, I say—I acknowledge myself vanquished.'

'Ha! I did not know before,' replied Osman with a laugh, 'that a Rajput officer feared to die. Fight on—I will slay you—I will never forgive; whilst you live, Aesha will never be mine.'

'I am not for Aesha,' said the Prince.

'No, you are not, but Aesha is for you,' said Osman flourishing his sword, 'fight on—no forgiving.'

The Prince flung away his sword at a distance, and said,

'I will never fight. You have served me in my misfortune; and I will not fight with you.'

Transported by rage, Osman dealt a kick at the Prince's chest.

'Thus!' exclaimed he, 'thus do I fight with a warrior who fears to fight.'

The Prince's patience became exhausted. Hastily recovering his rejected weapon, he leaped forward, like a lion bitten by a jackal, and attacked the Pathan. The latter was ill fitted to bear the force of that tremendous onslaught; and he measured his length on the ground, borne down by the stalwart body of the Prince. The Prince got up upon the breast of his enemy, and wresting his sword from his hand and holding his own over his throat, said,

'How now? Has your craving for fight been satisfied.'

'Not while I live,' returned Osman.

'Your life I can end this moment,' said the Prince.

'Do so—or else your mortal enemy will live,' said Osman.

'Let him,' replied the Prince; 'the Rajput scorns to fear it. I would have killed you; but you spared my life, and so do I.'

He then bound together the hands and feet of Osman, and one by one deprived him of all his weapons.

'Now betake yourself to your home in peace,' said he, after releasing him. 'Being a *Yavan*, you durst kick the person of a Rajput Prince, and it is only for this guilt of yours that I have reduced you to this plight; otherwise the Rajputs are never so ungrateful as to lay their hands on the persons of their benefactors.'

Without making any reply, Osman mounted his horse, and galloped in the direction of the fortress.

The Prince let down his sheet in a well close by, and washed his body with the water. He then unfastened the reins of his steed and mounted it, when he perceived a letter fastened to the reins by twigs and shrubs. On releasing it, he found that it was tied by a quantity of human hair. The superscription ran thus:

'Pray, Sir, do not open this letter for two days—if you do so, the object intended by it will be defeated.'

The Prince reflected a little, and decided in favor of the writer. He kept the note enclosed in his amulet, and giving a lash to his horse, rode for the camp.

The day after his arrival there, the Prince received another letter through a messenger. It was from Aesha; but of this in the next chapter.

19

AESHA'S LETTER

Aesha sat down to write a letter. Her countenance was serious and grave. She was going to write to Jagat Singha. She took a piece of paper and began. She first wrote, 'Dearer than life!' She immediately struck out the expression, and wrote, 'Prince!' In doing so, tears streamed down her cheeks, and dripped upon the paper. Aesha tore it, and took up a fresh piece of paper. She had not written many lines, when it also shared the fate of its predecessor. Aesha destroyed it also; and at the third time finished a letter unsullied by a tear. She then began to read what she had written. While doing so, her sight was obstructed by tears. With difficulty she folded the letter, and delivered it to a messenger. The man went in the direction of the Rajput camp. Aesha then lay down alone on the couch, and wept.

Jagat Singha opened the letter, and read as follows:

'Prince,

'That I did not see you was not owing to any fear I felt in regard to my endurance. Pray, do not charge Aesha with want of endurance; the thought will give me pain. Osman, you know, has kindled a fire in his bosom; and I did not see you, lest I should thereby give him pain. That you should feel pain at my refusal, I could not think. As for my own pain, my happiness and misery I have resigned to the hands of God. If I had had to give you farewell personally, I would have borne that pain easily; that I could not see you, I have borne like a woman of stone.

'Why then do I write this letter? I have a request. If you have heard that I love you more than a sister, pray, forget it. I had determined not to express it in this life, but God has willed otherwise. But now forget it.

'I am not for your love. What I had to give, I have given to you. I do not ask for any return. My affection is so deep-rooted, that I am happy even without your love. But I must have done with this business.

'I saw you unhappy. If ever you see better days, inform Aesha of it; but should you not like to do so, do not do it. If your heart ever feel pain, will you remember Aesha?

'People may blame me for writing you now, or in future. I am innocent; and you should not much care wkat they may say. Whenever you like, write to me.

'You are going away; you leave this place for the present. These Pathans are not quiet folks; so that the odds are for your having to come to this country again. But you will never see me more. I have decided so, after much reflection. Much confidence should not be placed in a woman's heart, which it is naturally difficult to curb.

'I intend to see you once more only. If you marry in this country, give me notice of it. I will be personally present at your marriage. I have kept some petty ornaments for the fair one that is to be your wife. If I find time, I will deck her person with them, with my own hands.

'Another request. When you receive intelligence of Aesha's death, pray, come here once. Accept, for my sake, what you will find in a chest inscribed with your name. Through the kindness of an affectionate father, although a daughter, I have inherited an amount of wealth which in a poor country might pass for much. Should it not be unacceptable to the race of Abnir, pray, take possession of it.

'The deed of gift you will find in the same chest.

'What more shall I write? I wish to write a great deal more; but 'tis no use. May God make you happy; but never feel unhappy at the thought of Aesha.'

After reading the letter, Jagat Singha began to weep; and for a long while paced up and down the camp, holding Aesha's letter in his hand. Then he hastily took up a piece of paper, and dashing off the following lines, delivered the note to the messenger.

'Aesha! you are the glory of the fair sex. Perhaps it is the Will of God to render the world miserable. I am unable to reply to any of your remarks; your letter has overpowered me. Know this much only that I shall ever cherish you as my dearest sister.'

The messenger took the note, and returned to Aesha.

20

THE FLICKERING LAMP

Ever since Tilottama took leave of Aesha and went away with Ashmani, no body could tell where she was. No news could be had of Tilottama, Bimala, Ashmani, or Abhiram Swami. When peace was concluded, feeling commiseration on Virendra Singha, for his sad end and the deplorable circumstances that had befallen his family, both parties agreed to search out Virendra's wife and daughter, and establish them in Garmandaran. Accordingly, Osman, Kwaja Isa, Mansingha and others, searched for them diligently; but beyond the fact of Tilottama's coming out from Aesha with Ashmani, none could learn anything. At length disappointed in his exertions, Mansingha placed a trustworthy follower of his, in Garmandaran, instructing him to 'search for the wife and daughter of the deceased *jaigirdar*; and should he succeed in finding them out, to establish them in the castle, and go to him. He would reward the official, and give him a *jaigir*.'

Having disposed of this matter, Mansingha prepared to go to Patna.

Whether the dying words of Katlu Khan had produced any change in Jagat Singha's mind, could not be known. True it is that he spared neither men nor money, to find the women out; but whether his efforts owed their origin to a mere remembrance of the past, to the same motives that influenced Mansingha and others, or to a revival of his former love, could not be known. Whatever the cause, his endeavours proved vain.

Mansingha's army began to break up the encampment. Next day they would march. The time for reading the note that had been attached to the reins of Jagat Sinhga's steed, came the day before the march. Eagerly opening it, the Prince read the following lines;

'If you righteously fear sin, if you fear a Brahmin's curse, please come here alone as soon as you read the contents. Thus much,

A Brahmin.'

The Prince was taken with surprise. Once he thought, 'This may be the artifice of an enemy. Should I go?' Next he remarked that the letter was written in pure *Devanagari* characters; and concluded it to be most likely as coming from a Brahmin. In a Rajput breast, the fear of a Brahmin's curse outweighs every other fear. The Prince accordingly decided on going. He directed his followers not to 'wait for him, should he not join them before they marched. No matter if they went before: he could meet them at Burdwan or at Rajmahal.' Having given these directions, he proceeded alone towards the *sal* forest. On reaching the gate of the ruined habitation, he (as before) fastened his charger to a *sal* tree. He looked around him, but found none. He then entered the ruin. There was the same grave on one side, and the funeral pyre on the other. A Brahmin sat upon the wood of the pyre. He had hung down his head, and was weeping.

'Is it you, Sir,' asked the Prince, 'that have desired me to come here?'

The Brahmin raised his face; the Prince saw it was Abhiram Swami.

Wonder, curiosity and joy struggled in the Prince's bosom for mastery. He humbly saluted the Brahmin, and eagerly said,

'What shall I say to you, Sir, as to how much I have tried to see you? Pray, Sir, why here?'

Abhiram Swami wiped his eyes, and said,

'For the present, I am living here.'

The Prince had scarcely heard the Swami out, when he began to pile question upon question.

'Why have you wished to see me? Why, again, do you weep, Sir?'

'The reason why I have called you is also the reason of these tears. Tilottama is on her deathbed.'

Slowly—gently—softly, sat down the warrior upon the ground. Then,

Remembrance waked with all her busy brain, Swell'd in his bosom, and turned the past to pain.'

The first sight at the temple—the vow in presence of Saileshwara—the true love tears at their first meeting with each other, in the chamber,—the incidents of that black night—the face of Tilottama in her swoon—her suffering in the den of the Yavan—his own heartless behavior in the prison—and finally her imminent death in this exile;

the memory of all, all these at once dashed against the Prince's mind with the fury of a storm; the former fire blazed out with a tenfold fury, and spread itself into his vitals.

He sat mute for a long while; Abhiram Swami went on,

'The day on which Bimala avenged her widowhood by slaying the Yavan, I fled with my daughter and grandchild; and roved from place to place secretly, for fear of the Musalmans. Tilottama's illness dates from that day. The cause of it you well know.'

The iron entered Jagat Singha's soul.

'Ever since I have kept her in various places, and treated her in various ways. Having studied the *Nidana*, from my youth upwards, I have treated many a disease; I know many an unknown medicine. But what can the doctor do for a patient suffering from a sorrow that has struck its roots deep into the heart? Seeing this place very solitary, we have been living in a retired part of this mansion, for a week or so. Providentially finding you here, I fastened the letter to the reins of your horse. I had always intended to bring you once more to Tilottama, to soothe her last moments, if I failed at last to cure her. It is for this that T wrote to you. Then I had not given up every hope of her recovery; I understood that if she did not get better in two days, she would die; it is for this reason that I advised you to read the note after two days. Now the worst is come. No farther hope remains of her life. Ah! the lamp is flickering.'

He again wept. Jagat Singha was also weeping.

'You must not present yourself to Tilottama all of a sudden,' continued the Swami; 'lest her frail system should not be able to bear the excess of joy. I have ere this given her to understand that I had told you to come here, and that your coming was likely. I'll now go and inform her of your arrival; you may see her after.'

Saying this, the ascetic directed his steps towards the inner apartment of the ruined building. Returning after a few moments, he said to the Prince,

'Come.'

The Prince proceeded to the inner apartment with the ascetic. He saw that a room was entire. In it was an old, time-worn couch; on it lay the lean, yet still beauteous form of Tilottama. Still was she surrounded by the mildly gleaming lustre of her former beauty. There she lay in her loveliness, like the 'fairest of stars, that crowns the smiling morn with his bright circlet,' about to disappear from our blessed sight. Beside her, sat a widow, who was gently passing and repassing her hand over her body. She had no ornaments on her person; she was a dirty, forlorn widow. The Prince could not at first recognise her; and how could he? She that had been perpetually young, was now an old woman.

When the Prince came in and stood beside Tilottama's bed, her eyes were closed. Abhiram Swami called her, saying,

'Tilottama, Prince Jagat Singha is come.'

She opened her eyes, and gazed at the Prince; her look was soft and tender; there was not a shadow of rebuke in it. As soon as she saw the Prince, she cast her eyes down. By and bye, tears began to trickle down her cheeks, in a continuous stream. The Prince could not contain any longer; all bashfulness and reserve vanished; he threw himself down at the feet of Tilottama, and bedewed her flowery frame with his silent tears.

21

THE CONSEQUENCE THE DREAM BELIES

The fatherless, forlorn girl is on her sickbed, Jagat Singha is at her side. The day passes away, and the night. Again the day comes, and again passes away, and again comes the night. The glory of the Rajput race sits by the bedside of Tilottama, and is engaged in tending her; he is incessantly assisting the bereaved, silent widow. Whether the suffering girl look on his face, and whether her countenance, (resembling the tender lotus weighed down by 'the dews of Heaven refined,') again sweeten with her former laugh, to ascertain this, Jagat Singha sits fastening his look on her face.

Where's the encampment? Where's the army? They broke up their encampment and are now in Patna. Where are Jagat Singha's own followers? They are expecting their master's return on the shores of the Darukeshwara river. Where's the master? He is reviving with the 'eye-offending brine,' the tender floweret that had been dried up to the point of death by the fierce, cruel rays of the midday sun.

The floweret did revive. Love is the only magician in this world; in curing love-sickness, your only physician is Love himself. Who else can cure it?

As a lamp gradually brightens up by a fresh supply of oil, as by degrees the creeper shrivelled by the summer sun, again puts forth bud and blossom by the fresh showers of autumn, Tilottama began to recover in the company of Jagat Singha.

She attained strength to sit up on the couch. During the intervals when Bimala was out of sight, she opened her heart to the Prince and related many an incident. She told him manythings; she confessed to many faults on the score of unjust surmises; she told of many unjust hopes which had arisen and died in her mind; she related many a fair dream which she had dreamt, waking or in sleep. One day she narrated the following dream, which she had dreamt, while lying insensible on her sickbed.

She saw herself and Jagat Singha sporting with flowers, on a hill clad in the freshness of spring. She gathered flowers and laid them in heaps: she made two garlands, one of which she wore herself; the other she placed around Jagat Singha's neck. Happening to come in contact with the Prince's sword, his wreath was torn. 'No more will I lay any garland on your neck,' said Tilottama; 'I will bind your feet with chains.' Thereupon she made chains of flowors. She went to bind Jagat Singha's feet with the floral gyves, when he drew off a little; Tilottama hastened to catch him; he removed further: Tilottama ran after him; Jagat Singha began to descend the hill rapidly. In the way ran a slender rill. Jagat Singha crossed it by a leap; Tilottama being a woman could not cross it in that way. Hoping to cross it at the spot where the brook was the narrowest, she ran down the mountain beside it. Far from growing narrower, the waters grew broader as she advanced; by and bye it became almost a rivulet; and then a large river; Jagat Singha could no longer be seen. The banks were high, and frightfully uneven; walking was no longer possible. Further, parts of the bank near Tilottama gave way and fell into the water with thundering noises. Below whirled furiously a whirlpool, fearful to look at. Tilottama tried to fly from the place, by re-ascending the hill; but the way was impracticable. Tilottama began to cry aloud. All of a sudden, the horrible shape of Katlu Khan came out from the grave and barred her way. Anon the garland of flowers was turned into a heavy chain of iron; the floral shackles escaped her hand, and all of a sudden became iron shackles round her feet; suddenly her body came to a stand-still, when Katlu Khan grasped her by the neck; and whirling her body, throw it into the torrent.

'Prince!' said Tilottama, when she had done, her eyes glistening with tears, 'Prince! this is no idle dream. Perhaps the flowery chains which I strung for you, have really proved iron chains round my feet—the garland of flowers which I placed round your neck, you have cut off with your sword.'

The Prince laughed; and taking out his sword from his side, and laying it at Tilottama's feet, said,

'Tilottama! here I resign my weapon to you. Pray, do you favor me with the garland once more, and I will with these hands, break the sword in twain.'

Seeing Tilottama silent, the Prince said,

'Tilottama! I am not jesting.'

Tilottama hung down her head in bashfulness.

Seated in another room, Abhiram Swami was that evening reading a manuscript book in the light of the *pradipa*. The Prince came to him, and said in all humility,

'Sir, I have a request. Tilottama is now in a position to bear the fatigue of a journey. Why then should she undergo the privation of remaining in this deserted house? If tomorrow do not happen to be an in-auspicious day, take her to Garmandaran, Sir, I beseech you. And if you have no objection, do you make me the happiest of men, by giving your granddaughter in marriage to a member of the house of Abnir.'

Leaving his book, Abhiram Swami started up and warmly embraced the Prince, utterly unconscious that he was, while so engaged, treading the sacred volume under his foot.

When the Prince came to Abhiram Swami, guessing something, Bimala and Ashmani had softly followed in his wake; and from the outside had learnt all. On coming out, the Prince found that Bimala had suddenly changed her former manner. She was incessantly laughing, and tearing Ashmani's hair, and dealing her blows right and left. Taking no heed of the beating, Ashmani was learning to dance from Bimala. The Prince stole away quietly.

22

THE CONCLUSION

The flower blooms. Abhiram Swami went to Garmandaran; and with great pomp and *eclat* celebrated the nuptials of his granddaughter and Jagat Singha.

Jagat Singha had invited his friends and acquaintances from Jahanabad to his wedding. The friends and relatives of Tilottama's father also came and made merry on the auspicious occasion.

Jagat Singha had given notice to Aesha as desired. She came with her youthful brother and some of the inmates.

Although she was a Musulmani, yet such was the regard and affection which both Tilottama and Jagat Singha bore to her, that she was welcomed into the inner apartment of the castle, with her maids. The reader may think that, weighed upon with a load of grief, Aesha could not enter into the general joy and gaity of the occasion. But it was not so. Blessed with a cheerful heart, she delighted all, like 'a bright consummate flower,' waving in the crystal brook and gleaming in the autumnal moonlight; her laugh spread lustre before her path.

The small hours had begun when the marriage ended. Aesha then prepared to return with her attendants. Laughing, she took leave of Bimala. The latter, who knew nothing of Aesha's heart, said with a laugh,

'Dear Princess, now it will be our turn to be invited on the auspicious occasion of your wedding.'

Leaving Bimala, Aesha came to Tilottama, and took her to a soliary chamber.

'Sister,' said she, taking Tilottama's hand, 'I go now. May you enioy happiness and length of days. This only is my heartfelt prayer.'

'And pray,' said Tilottama, 'after how long shall I see you again?'

'Alas! How can I' replied Aesha, 'entertain the hope of ever seeing you again?'

Tilottama became sad. Both remained silent.

'Whether we meet or not,' said Aesha after a pause, 'but will you forget Aesha?'

'Would the Prince,' replied Tilottama, laughing, 'ever forgive me if I forget Aesha?'

'I am not pleased with these words of yours,' said Aesha seriously. 'You must never mention me to the Prince; promise this.'

Aesha understood that the circumstance that her future happiness had been utterly blighted for Jagat Singha, smote him severely; and the least mention of her to him would awaken his grief.

Tilottama promised to do so. Aesha went on,

'But don't forget me either. Pray, do not reject the things which I give you for memory.'

She thereupon called her maid, and gave her orders. The woman brought in an ivory box, containing jewels. Aesha sent her away, and began with her own hands to deck Tilottama.

Although the daughter of a wealthy landholder, Tilottama was struck with the rare workmaship of the various ornaments, as also with the brilliant lustre of their gems. With her own load of ornaments which had been given to her by her father, Aesha had caused these rare jewels to be prepared for Tilottama. The latter spoke in admiration of the jewels.

'Sister,' said Aesha, 'do not admire these. What tinsel are they in comparison with the gem with which you have adorned your bosom this day!' Here she strove hard to check her tears. Tilottama knew nothing.

When the adorning was over, Aesha took hold of both hands of Tilottama, and fixed her eyes on Tilottama's face. 'Me thinks'—thought she, 'my love will never be otherwise than happy with the possession of this open, lovely countenance. When Heaven has willed it so, my only prayer to Him is, may the Prince be ever happy with this girl!'

'Tilottama!' said she, 'fare-well. Your husband may be engaged; no use of losing any more time in taking his leave. May God grant you long life. Wear these jewels. And my—your best jewel wear on your heart.'

Her utterance became almost choked in saying 'your best jewel.' Tilottama saw that Aesha's eyelids were trembling with the weight of tears.

Tilottama melted in sympathy, and said,

'Why are you weeping? Eh?'

Anon the flood gates were opened.

Without staying there a moment more, Aesha hastily left the chamber and got into the litter.

When she reached home, it was still night. She changed her dress, and stood at the window of her room, through which the cool air was blowing in. The sky more deliciously blue than the dress she had just changed, was studded with myriads of twinkling stars; the trees in the dark sent a murmur as their leaves were swayed by the breeze. On the top of the castle, the owl was shrieking low and deep. Below the rampart in front, on the other side, and the wall of the castle down Aesha's chamber, lay the moat filled with water, holding silently and still the image of the sky.

Sitting at the window, Aesha reflected long. She took out a ring from her finger. The gem which graced it was the home of poison. Once she thought,

'I can at once quench my thirst for good, by sucking this gem.' Again she thought,

'And is it for this that God has sent me into the world? If I am not equal to this trial, why was I born a woman? And what would Jagat Singha say, on hearing it?' She thereupon put on the ring. On some thought or other, she again took it out.

'It is beyond the power of a woman to resist this temptation; I'll cast it away.'

Saying this, she threw the ring into the waters of the moat.

KAPALKUNDALA

Part 1

1

AT THE ESTUARY OF THE GANGES

Nearly two hundred and fifty years have passed away since the grey hours of one Magh morning saw a passenger boat making her way up the river on her voyage back from the Saugor Islands. It was usual at that time for such boats to sail in strong parties on account of the scare of the Portuguese and other pirates. But these passengers had no companion boats. The reason was that a thick fog had overspread the horizon towards the latter part of the night. The crew, having lost their bearings, drifted a far long way from the little flotilla. Now there was no knowing which direction she was making for. Most of the people on board were asleep. Only an old man and a youth lay awake, the former conversing with the latter. The former for a moment broke off and addressed one of the crew: 'Boatman, what distance can you cover this day?'

'I can hardly say,' replied the boatman after a short indecision.

The interrogator took offence and began railing at the boatman. 'What is in the hands of Providence, Sir,' chipped in the youth, 'can't be foretold by the wise, far less by a simpleton. You must not bother over that.'

'Not bother!' echoed back the other furiously. 'What do you mean? The fellows forcibly cut away paddy from some twenty odd bighas of my land and what my children would live upon the whole year?'

This news he received from the fresh arrivals not before he had come out to the Saugor Islands. 'So I observed already,' rejoined the youngman, 'when you have none other guardian left home, it was wrong of you to venture out.'

'Not venture!' snapped the old man as sharply as before. 'Three quarters of my life have been spent and only the fourth is left. Now or never to work for one's next life.'

'If I have read the scriptures aright,' added the youth, 'the merits of pilgrimages accruing to after-life are equally within the reach of those who stay at home.'

'Why did you stir out then?' returned the old man. 'So I told you at the very outset', replied the other, 'I had a great mind to have a look at the sea. So I came.' Then he exulted half to himself, 'Ah! what a sight! This is never to be forgotten in ages of the soul's migrations.'

> 'From afar, as on a wheel of iron, slender
> All blue with tamarisks and palms extended,
> Outshines the briny oceans' margin yonder,
> Like streak of rust mark with the wheel-rim blended.'

The elderly man's ear was not following the poetry but he was listening raptly to the conversation passing among the crew.

'Eh, brother, our folly is looking the bigger,' spoke one of the crew to the other, 'Are we out on the open sea now, or in what corner of the globe the boat has got to, can't understand.' The speakers voice had the ring of a great fright. The old man scented some danger ahead and nervously enquired, 'Boatman, is anything the matter?' The man addressed to did not answer. But the young blood waited not for the reply. He came out into the bare open and saw the day was dawning. The heavy pall of a thick mist lay over everything. The stars, the moon, the sky, the coast-line were all blotted out. He understood that the crew had lost all directions. They were not certain which way they were steering the boat. They feared they would perish in the boundless open sea.

A screen hung out in front as cold protector and the passengers were quite in the dark about all this. But the young man knew the plight and explained to the old man the whole thing in detail. Then arose a great uproar aboard. Of the female passengers some awoke at the sound of the conversation and no sooner had their ears caught the remark than they set up a loud wail. 'Row shoreward, row shoreward, row shoreward,' vociferated the elderly man.

The youth smiled softly and put in, 'where is the shore? If we could but know this, how would the danger arise?'

Now louder grew the hub-bub. The youth quieted them down

somehow and said, 'Have no fear. The day has broken and the sun rises within two odd hours. The boat can never sink by that period. Now stop rowing and let her go adrift. Next when the sun breaks through, we would lay our heads together'.

The crew approved of this bit of advice and acted accordingly.

All boathands sat stockstill. The passengers ate their hearts out in an agony of suspense. The wind blew a gentle sigh. The shake of the boat was scarcely felt on account of the smooth glassy sea. However, they felt sure that their last hour had struck. Silently did men say their prayers and loudly did women raise a babel of cries uttered in vocal contortions of different keys. One of them had given a watery grave to her babe in the deep water of the Bay—she had dropped her child but could not rescue it—she of all others did not weep.

While in this nervous mood of expectancy, they guessed it to be nine o'clock. At that time the crew all on a sudden shouted out at the top of their lungs the names of the five Pirs of water and kicked up a row. All on board burst in one voice, 'What, what is up?' All the boathands cried out in a chorus, 'The sun has appeared. Land ahoy.' Every body crawled out into the open space and began to observe the locality and the surroundings. They saw the sun had come out and the mist rolled away like a curtain before the sun revealing all sides in their naked clearness. The sun shone pretty above the horizon line. The water on which the boat floated was not the sea but the estuary of a river though the same expanse was scarcely observable any where else. One side of the river was within easy reach—it was twenty-five yards more or less from where the boat lay. But the coast-line was hardly visible on the opposite side. Every other way besides, shimmered the wild waste of water in the glare of the brilliant sun and sweeping off immeasurably melted into the misty sky-line. The adjacent water had a turbid appearance as is usually noticeable in river water though the same looked blue at a distance. They felt certain that they had drifted down into the deep blue sea. But by some stroke of good luck they were pretty near the land. So they screwed up some courage. They calculated the direction from the sun's position. The fringe of the frontal ground was easily concluded to be the western seaboard. At a close range from where the boat floated was the mouth of another river pouring its gurgling flow of gold into the channel. Innumerable water birds of diverse description were playing joyously on the broad patch of sand that lay on the southern side of the estuary. This stream now takes the name of the Rasulpur river.

2

ON THE COAST

The first impulses of elation being over, the crew proposed that as there was still time for the tide to come, the passengers in the meantime might cook and dine on the sands before them and with the rising tide might start on the way home. The men fell in with the suggestion. Then the boatmen having secured the boat along the bank, the men landed. They had had their dips in the water before they attended to their morning ceremonies.

After bath before starting kitchenwork another difficulty presented itself in the shape of the absence of any fuel on board. Every one was loth to fetch firewood from the high bank on account of tigerscare. At last the dread of sheer starvation staring them in the face, the old man proposed to the previously mentioned youth, 'Nabokumar, my boy, so many people would die, if you can not cast about for any means.'

Nabokumar reflected a few seconds and replied, 'All right, I shall go. Let a man bear me company with a woodcutting knife and an axe.'

No body, however, responded to the call.

With the words, 'The affair would be squared up at the mealtime', Nabokumar girded up his loins and axe in hand, set out in search of fuel.

When Nabokumar ascended the higher ridges of the river slope, his wandering eye could not see any vestige of human habitation within the whole stretch of ground. It was but a weald, though the wood consisted neither of stately trees nor dense brushwood. Only at intervals, shrubs grew up in circular forms and covered the ground. As Nabokumar could not find there any firewood proper to fell, he wandered on to the remoter reaches of the upland in quest of any suited to his purpose. At last he found out a fellable tree and provided himself with the necessary fuel. The transport of the load seemed another uphill task. Nabokumar was not born of a poor parentage. So he was not inured to such hard jobs. Besides, he had not considered the question in all its bearings before he started on his mission. Now the carrying of the wood proved a sharp work. However Nabokumar was not a man to shirk a task to which he had set his hand because of its arduous nature. Therefore, he trudged along with the bundle over a certain distance and when he grew tired, he rested at stages and again proceeded. He plodded his way back in this way.

This delayed Nabokumars' return. On the other hand his companions felt nervous as there had been none of the noticeable signs of his return. They feared Nabokumar had been killed by a tiger. The allowable time-limit being over, they came to that positive conclusion. Still no body ventured to go up the bank and advance a few paces in search of Nabokumar.

The passengers were indulging in such idle thoughts when the terrible moan of rushing tide was audible in the water. The crew fully knew it to be the on rush of the coming tide. Besides, they knew that with the flood tide, the heaving water dashed against the coastline with such a fury that any boat happening to lie on the coastal water was sure to be smashed to smithereens. So with great bustle they unfastened the mooring and made for the midstream. No sooner was the boat untied than the river-fringe was flooded over. The passengers could scarcely find time to spring on to the boat's side when the rice and grain deposited on the margin were clean washed-away. To add to their misfortunes, the crew were not skilled boatmen. They could not steady the boat. So the boat was pitched into the Rasulpur river channel with the violence of the current. One of the passengers cried, 'Nabokumar is left behind.' One of the crow replied, 'Alas! Is your Nabokumar alive? He is safe in the stomach of a jackal.'

So the boat was being rushed up the Rasulpur river by the rapid current. But as it would be an arduous task to get the boat downstream afterwards, the crew were trying their level best to emerge from the river. Even in that cold month of Magh sweat started out and trickled down their brows. Though they forced their way back from the river channel with such exertion, yet no sooner did the boat come out than she was caught up by the more violent stream outside. The boat shot up due north like an arrow and the crew could not bring themselves to control her. The boat never returned.

By the time the current slackened down so as to let the boat being tackled, the passengers were carried over a long distance past the mouth of the Rasulpur river. Now the question whether they would retrace their course furnished food for discussion. We ought to say here that Nabokumars' fellow passengers were all his neighbours but none his kinsmen. They concluded that they would have to await another low-tide to come back. Then night would fall when further navigation would be impossible and they would have to wait for another hightide. This meant starvation for each and all throughout the period. Thus two days' privations would bring them within an ace of death. The more so, when the crew remained obdurate and would obey no orders. They asserted that Nabokumar had been killed by a tiger. This was possible. If so, then what would all their worries avail?

Concluding thus, the people thought it judicious to get back homeward without Nabokumar. Nabokumar was thus left to his fate in the howling seaside wilderness.

If at this, any body sets his face against bestirring himself in search of firewood to save others from starvation, he deserves the world's ridicule. Let those people whose nature it is to send out their benefactors into exile ply their 'dirty work' an the while; but men who run about to collect firewood for others must do the same, over and again, whatsoevertimes they are banished from their hearthstone. Because you are bad makes for no reason why I should not be good.

3

IN SOLITUDE

Not far off from the place where Nabokumar was cast away, now stand two straggling villages under the names of Daulatpur and Dariapur. But at that period of which we are speaking, there could scarcely be visible any signs of human habitation. It was all woodland. The part of this countryside was not so as other parts of Bengal which are usually flat. An unbroken range of sand dunes traversed the whole stretch of ground lying between the mouth of the Rasulpur river and the Subarnarekha. If the series of the sand elevations would have been a little bigger in height, these might have claimed the appellation of a chain of sandhills. Now people call these the Baliari. The white cliffs of the Baliari or sandhills appear unusually bright under the hot meridian sun. No tall trees grow on those heights. Shrubs and undergrowths abound at the feet of these sand mounds though the arid desolate belt and summit generally emit a white glow. Of the plants overgrowing the downward slope, there is plenty of waterside shrubs comprising bushes and flowering creepers.

At such an unpleasant spot was Nabokumar abandoned by his companions. The first thing that struck his eye, on return to the riverside with the load of wood, was the absence of the boat at the water edge. Though a sudden great fear immediately sent a shiver into his heart, it looked next to impossible that he could be ever forsaken there by his fellow-travellers. An impression gained upon him that due to the swamping of the down by the hightide they might have taken the boat to some secure place and so they would find him out in no time. Fed by this hope, he sat down and lay in wait for some time. But neither the boat came nor did the men put in their appearance. Nobokamar's little mary craved for food and drink. Unable to wait any longer, he wandered over the river fringe hunting for the boat. But the boat could not be found any where. So the retraced his steps and came back to the starting ground. Though till then he could not see the boat he laboured under the delusion that the boat might have been carried away by the tide stream and so they would be late in getting back against current. Even when the tide ebbed he thought the boat could not return owing to violence of the stream against which she could hardly make any headway. Now she might come back as the tide was out. But now the ebb tide settled into a slacker stream, the day declined and the sun went down. The boat would have returned by this time if she had been put back on the reverse course.

Then he concluded either the boat was wrecked by the violence of the tidal water or he was left to his fate in this lonely place by his fellow-passengers.

Nobokumar saw no village there—the place without shelter, without men, without food, without drink. The river water tasted bitter brine and his heart was being rent under the agony of hunger and thirst. He found not the shelter that could save him from the biting cold nor had he sufficient clothing on. He had the gloomy prospect of lying down for the night on the icy-cold-wind-swept river bank under the canopy of the unkind sky, unsheltered and unprotected. During night there was the chance of his meeting tigers and bears. In any case death was certain.

Owing to the restlessness of mind Nabokumar could not sit still on one spot for a considerable time. He left the foreshore, clambered up and wandered aimlessly. Gradually the colour faded out from the sky and darkness fell. The stars came out in the frosty sky overhead as silently as they used to do in his native clime. Now this wooded countryside was hushed in darkness—the sky, the field, the sea were all bathed in a stillness punctuated with the dull continuous roar of the sea and the occasional howling of wild beasts rising above all this. Still in that darkness did Nabokumar tramp around these sand-dunes under the bleak sky. Up hill and down dale, now at the foot of the sandhills and then on their crests did he ramble about ceaselessly. At every step of this aimless ramble had he the chance of an attack from the wild beasts. But he had the same fear even when he placed himself on one spot. Nabokumar grew footsore and fatigued with such wandering. He had been fasting all day and so he became all the more weary. He sat down at a certain place supporting his back against a sand mound and remembered his cosy bed at home. When a man broods in an exhausted condition of his mind and body, sleep sometimes steals a march and closes his drooping eyelids. Thus Nabokumar blooded and glided into a vague sort of forgetfulness. Perhaps, had this not been the order of things, then men in all ages could ill-stand the stress and strain of domestic troubles.

4

ON THE TOP OF A SAND-HILL

It was deep into night when Nabokumar awoke. He wondered that till then he was not killed by a tiger. He gave all sides his searching glances, to be sure whether a tiger was stalking him or not. Suddenly he espied before him the glimmer of a light at a long distance. To guard against delusion, he strained his eyes after it. The orb of light grew by degrees in magnitude and brightness and he concluded it to be a fire light. No sooner did Nabokumar conclude this, than his hope of life revived. No such light was possible without man because it was not the season of forest-fire. Nobokumar started to his feet. He ran towards the direction of the light. Once he thought 'Is the glow of light a will-o'-the-wisp?—It might be so. But what life is saved if anybody lacks courage to confront the danger?' Prey to such thoughts, he moved forward with a brave heart aiming at the light. Trees, creepers and sandheaps obstructed him at every step. He trampled under feet plants and trailers, crossed over sand dunes and walked onward. When he drew near the light, he saw a fire burning at the pretty altitude of a small sand elevation and the picture of a man sitting on the top silhouetted against the skyline in the glow. Resolved to approach the man seated on the hill crest, Nabokumar pressed on with unslackened pace. At last he began to ascend the sand hill. Then he felt a bit nervous. However, he went on through the work with unshaken limbs. On nearing the man squatted there, his flesh creeped at what his eyes met with. He was indecisive whether to advance or withdraw.

The man seated on the height was absorbed in meditation with closed eyes. So he could not observe Nabokumar at first. Nabokumar saw the man on the verge of fifty. He could not perceive whether the man had any cloth on or not. He had a tiger skin wrapped round his loins that reached to his knee and a string of Rudrakha round his neck. His big broad face was overgrown with shaggy hair and surmounted with a crown of matted locks.

A fire glowed before him—the same that acted the lodestar to Nabokumar to guide his steps there. An offensive smell stinked into his nostrils and he made out the reason when he happened to glance at the mans' seat. The man of matted locks sat on a headless corpse in a state of disintegration. He grew all the more alarmed when he detected a skull lying before him with some crimson liquid in the hollow. Around him were strewn about here and there bones whitened in the sand. Even the string of Rudrakha suspended round his neck had small bones fastened between them at intervals. Nabokumar was rooted to the spot spell-bound. He could not decide whether to move before or behind. He had heard of Kapaliks and he knew the man to be a Kapalik.

When Nabokumar arrived, the Kapalik was so much engrossed either with worship or contemplation that he paid no attention to Nabokumar. After a long time he enquired in Sanskrit, 'Who are you?'

'A Brahmin,' replied Nabokumar.

'Wait,' rejoined Kapalik and then slipped into his work which preoccupied him. Nabokumar stood on his legs all the while.

Thus half the watch of the night passed away. At last, the Kapalik left his seat and said to Nabokumar in Sanskrit as before, 'Follow me.'

It might be safely said that, at a time other than this, Nabokumar could hardly persuade himself to follow the Kapalik. But he was more dead than alive with hunger and thirst. So he said, 'I am under your Emimence' orders. But I am overcome with hunger and thirst. So kindly tell me where to get my food and drink.'

'You are sent by Bhairobi,' returned the Kapalik. 'Follow me and you will be satisfied.'

Nabokumar went behind the Kapalik. The two together walked a weary long distance. But none spoke on the way. At last they reached a hut overtopped with leaf-thatched cover. Kapaiik was the first to go inside and then invited Nabokumar within. He struck a light in a way mysterious to Nabokumar and enkindled a piece of wood. With the aid of light Nabokumar saw the cottage entirely built of Keya leaves. Within it were a few pieces of tiger hides, a pitcher of water and some fruits and vegetables.

After lighting fire, the Kapalik said, 'You may help yourself to the fruits and vegetables. Drink the water from the pitcher in cup which you must make of tree leaf and sleep, if you so mind, on the tiger skin. Stay secure and have no fear from tiger. You shall meet me later on. Never leave this cottage until I see you again.'

With these words, the Kapalik went away. Nabokumar having for his repast the few fruits and vegetables, and for his drink, the brackish water, was mightily pleased. He made his bed on the tiger skin and after the day's troubles and worries fell into a sleep.

5

ON THE SEA—SIDE

As soon as Nabokumar left his bed the next morning, he, as a matter of course, worried himself over going home; the more so, as the presence of the Kapalik boded evil. But, for the nonce, how was he to get out of this trackless forest? How would he strike out the right path that would take him home? The Kapalik was sure to know the way. Would he not, if asked, give him the direction? However, the Kapalik, so far he marked him, never showed in his manners anything wrong. Then why was he on earth to be afraid of him? On the other hand, the Kapalik warned him against leaving the cottage till the next meeting and that, if he now ran counter to his wishes, it might upset him. Nabokumar had heard that Kapaliks were capable of impossible feats. Then it was wrong of him to show any insubordination. After much anxious consideration, Nabokumar made up his mind, for the present, to remain within the cottage bounds.

But by degrees, the day wore on. Still there was no sign of the Kapalik's return. Previous day's fast added to the privation all this time sharpened his hunger. The little store of fruits and vegetables had been eaten up overnight and now the hunger threatened to kill him in the event of his not leaving the hut-precincts in quest of fresh fruits and vegetables. Before the day faded away, hunger drove Nabokumar outdoor to seek out fruits, if he could find any.

Nabokumar wandered in and out between these neighbouring sand-dunes in search of fruit. He tried the fruits of one or two trees growing on the sands and found the fruit of only one tree had the delicious taste of almond. With these he satisfied his hunger.

The aforesaid sandhills were of small width and so Nabokumar surmounted these obstacles by a short detour. Then he entered a dense sandless forest. Those who, ever, for a short time have travelled an unknown wooded terrain know that the sense is confused almost immediately amidst the pathless forest tract. The same happened to Nabokumar. After walking forward a little distance, he failed to pick out the way that led him there from the hermitage. The deep roll of rushing water met his ear and he learnt it to be the roar of the sea. Soon after, which looked too sudden for him, he emerged from the forest belt and saw the vision of the spreading sea before him. His heart thrilled with wild delights at the sight of the ever-stretching circle of deep blue water. He advanced and rested on the sandy beach. The foaming, blue, ever-spreading sea sprawled out before him. So far his eye could strike stretched away, both ways, the foam line of the sea surf cast up by the breaking splashing waves. The snowy foam streaks were left deposited on the golden-yellow sands like a mass of milk white flower garlands worked into fantastic shapes and figures. The waves breaking in foam at thousand places amidst the blue circle of water served meet decorations for the love locks of the wood-tressed earth. If ever, there be the possibility of a fierce gale through whose violence the myriads of stars are displaced from their sockets and tossed up in the blue dome of the sky then it might conjure up the image of that breaking dashing sea. At this time, a portion of the saphire water shone like liquid gold in the mellow tints of the setting sun. At a far-off end a European merchant man with her bulging white sails looked like a monster bird skipping over the surface of the water.

Nobokumar had no idea of the measure of time he spent in observing the beauty of the sea. Afterwards 'grey hooded' evening came and at once settled over the dark blue water. Then Nobokumar awoke to his sense and the idea was brought home to his mind of finding out the cottage. He drew a deep sigh and rose to his feet. No reason could be ascribed why he drew that sigh. But who could say there might not arise some happy thoughts in his mind of his joys in the days before? As he stood up he wheeled round moving his back upon the sea. No sooner did he jerk his head than behold! A beautiful silhouette—the delightful phantom of a radiant female form standing on the sandy fringe of the booming sea greeted his eyes in the waning light of the faded evening. The rich mass of her dishevelled hair fell in disordered profusion across her back and floating in clustering waves reached down below her waist-line. From amidst the dark silken tresses shone out an exquisite face that looked the beautiful painting framed in a fine setting. The face though partly hid under the thick heavy curls appeared like the envious gleams that lace the severing clouds. The glance of her big bright eyes was very quiet, very soft, very deep, though full of brilliance, shining like the streaks of moonlight playing across the glassy sea. The luxuriant tresses enveloped her neck and shoulders. Though the shoulders were fully concealed, the transparent colour of her arms, however, gleamed through the dense locks. The feminine figure was wholly denuded of any of the artificialities. The subtle charm pervading the beautiful figure can not be described in words. The happy graceful effects were heightened by the bold contrast of the rich complexion, which shone like the faint glow of a half moon, to the raven black of the dark hair, and, any attempt at conveying an adequate impression of the liquid graces, would fall far short of the reality if not actually perceived on the thundering sea coast in the purple haze of grey twilight. Nabokumar stood rootbound at the sudden appearance of such a joyful vision in the midst of wilderness. His speech lost its articulation and he looked agape quivering with admiration. The maiden also stood standstill fixing the winkless steadfast gaze of her big wide eyes on Nabokumar's face. The difference between the two lay in the fact that Nabokumar had the startled look of a man lost in wonder while the damsel's stare showed no such evidence though it had the troubled air of anxiety in it.

Subsequently on this lonely sea coast both kept on looking into each other's face. After a long time, the sweet tremulous voice of the damsel was heard softly enquiring, 'Traveller, have you lost your way?'—and at that musical voice all the magic wizardry was touched.

The flute of her treble voice swept a touch on a chord in Nobokumar's heart. At times, the wonderful gear of the heartstrings goes out of tune in such a way that with all our efforts no music can be struck out of them, though the defect can be remedied at the fine touch of a single word or the soft voice of a woman. Then everything becomes full of harmony and life an unending flow of music. The voice sent a drift into Nabokumar's ear in such sweet strains.

The melody rose in symphony and thrilled a music into Nabokumar's ear—'Traveller, have you lost your way?' The meaning failed him and he found no word of reply. The melody struck the air awhirl thrilling in wild ecstacy, floated through the evening sea breeze that rustled in tree-leaves and died away in faint thin cadence until lost into the tumult of the sea.

The sea-girt earth was enchanting—the woman enrapturing—the voice thrilling—and the tune ran its whole gamut on heart's vibrating strings.

The maiden receiving no reply said, 'Follow.' With these words, she moved forward with such light gait as could scarcely be visible. Like a fleecy cloud sent adrift by a gentle sigh of the spring, she advanced with slow, easy and unperceived steps with Nabokumar following behind mechanically like a doll working on spring hinges. At one stage, the path wound round a copse and when Nobokumar was opposite to the thicket that intercepted his view, the fair guide gave him a slip and was lost sight of. Nabokumar hardly cleared the brushwood, when the cottage sprang to his eye.

6

IN THE KAPALIK'S COMPANY

On entering the hut Nabokumar closed the door and sat down with the head on his hand. He did not lift his head for a long time.

'Is she a goddess?—or a woman in flesh and blood?—or a phantom of the Kapalik's creation?' were the thoughts uppermost in his mind as he sat immobile. He was at his wit's end.

Nabokumar was far too much occupied with his own thoughts to see any other object. A log of wood was burning in the cottage since before his return. Afterwards, when far into night, it occurred to him that till then he had not performed his evening ceremonies, he struck up a truce with his cogitation in order to find out water. It was only then that the oddity forced itself upon his mind. Besides fire, there were rice and many other sundry things for the preparation of a meal. Nabokumar was not astonished at the sight of these as he believed them to be also the work of the Kapalik and at such a place as this it did not set him moping over it. Having finished the evening ceremonies, Nabokumar cooked the little rice in an earthen pot he found in the hut and had his repast.

As soon as he left his skinbed the next morning, he struck for the sea coast. The previous day's outing helped him in feeling his way before him with less difficulty. He performed his morning ceremonies there and stayed in a mood of expectancy. Whom did he expect? We are not sure how far the thought gained its ascendancy in Nabokumar's mind that the previously seen apparition would visit the place again but anyhow he could not leave the ground. However, nobody came even when the day was far spent. Then Nabokumar fell into strollmg through the grounds. The search proved but fruitless.

He could not detect any trace of human footsteps. He came back again and sat himself down on the same spot. The sun went down and the shadows of evening were falling fast. Nabokumar, crestfallen, retraced his way to the habitation. On his return from the sea-side in the evening, he found the Kapalik silently squatted on the cottage floor. He first of all enquired about his health but the Kapalik made no rejoinder.

'Why was I denied your grace,' visit all this time?' asked Nabokumar.
'I was engaged in my worship,' replied the Kapalik.

Nabokumar made the proposal of return to his homelands. 'Neither do I know the way nor have I the means,' added he, 'but I counted on you as the line of action may be settled as soon as I see your worship again.'

'Follow me,' simply said the Kapalik. With this word, the hermit got up on his legs. Nabokumar, also, expecting that some feasible means of his return home might be devised, followed him.

The glow did not depart from the western sky, when Nabokumar was following the Kapalik who led the way. He, suddenly, felt the touch of some soft hand on his back and turning round stopped short at what he saw. It was the same wood nymph with the glorious crown of rich silken tresses that clustered around her back—as speechless and immoveable as before.

From whence could the figure unexpectedly glide out behind him? Nabokumar saw the girl had a fingertip placed across her lips. He understood that the damsel warned him against the danger of speech. Was there any necessity for caution? He stood there agape wondering all the while. The Kapalik could not observe any of the enactments of this silent drama. So he moved onward. When they were out of the Kapalik's hearing, the maiden spoke something in an undertone. The words audible to Nabokumar were, 'Whither are you going? Desist—get back—flee.'

Scarcely had the words issued from her lips when the fair speaker slipped away without waiting to hear the reply. Nabokumar stood there for sometime as one obsessed of a ghost. He yearned to follow in her wake. But he failed to strike the line of her escape. He thought within himself, 'Whose fantasy is this?—or is it the creation of my own mind?—what I heard is certainly frightful. But what the deuce do I care to be afraid of? Kapaliks can work miracles. Then shall I fly?—or why shall I fly?—when I lived the other day I must also live this day. The Kapalik is but a man, so I am too.'

Nabokumar was meditating thus when he observed the Kapalik getting back as he could not see Nabakumar behind. 'What makes you tarry?' asked the Kapalik. The Kapalik having reiterated the question, Nabokumar without a word followed him. After walking a little distance Nabokumar's eyes rested on a cottage encircled with a mud-wall. The tenement struggled betweeh the debatable styles of a cottage and a small house. But with this we have no concern. Yonder over across the back-ground gleamed the rolling sanddowns. The Kapalik was leading Nabokumar to the sands along the edge of this hut. At this moment the previously seen damsel ran past Nabokumar with the quickness of an arrow. When alongside with him, she whispered into his ears. 'Escape yet. Don't you know Tantrick's rituals lose their merits if not supplemented by human flesh?'

Sweat started out on Nabokumar's forehead. As ill-luck would have it, the maiden's admonition entered the Kapalik's ear. 'Kapalkundala,' broke forth the Kapalik.

The voice fell upon Nabokumar's ear with the detonation of a thunder. But Kapalkundala did not answer.

The Kapalik conducted Nabokumar grasping him by his hand. The manslayer's touch sent Nabokumar's blood coursing through his veins with a thousand-fold pulsation and his lost courage revived. 'Leave off my hand,' said Nabokumar. The Kapalik made no reply. 'Where do you lead me to?' asked Nabokumar again. 'To the place of worship,' answered the Kapalik.

'Why?' added Nabokumar.

'For immolation,' joined the Kapalik. With a violent tug did Nabokumar pull out his hand. The force, with which Nabokumar jerked his hand, might have run an ordinary man down to the earth instead of allowing him to retain the hold on his hand. But not a part of the Kapalik's body bent and Nabokumar's hand was left in his grip as in a vice. The impact rebounded upon Nabokumar's system and sent a rattle through his bones. Nabokumar saw that strength would not avail but trick might serve the purpose. He allowed himself to be dragged along with the conclusion, 'Well, let me watch the flow of events.'

When Nabokumar was led on to the central ground on the sands, he saw a log of wood crackling there as on the previous night. On all sides were arranged things adapted to the requirements of the Tantrick rites of worship including a human skull filled in with Ashab or wine. Only a human corpse was Wanting. He guessed his body would furnish the corpse.

A small stack of dry stout plants and creepers was piled up there from before-hand. The Kapalik began to bind Nabokumar tightly with these. Nabokumar exerted every ounce of his whole strength but his strength did not stand him in good stead. Nabokumar gained the belief that even at such an advanced age, the Kapalik could muster the strength of a mad elephant. Finding Nabokumar use violence, the Kapalik said 'Fool, why do you pull your weight? The mass of your mortal flesh shall furnish the sacrifice for the Bhairobi worship. What a better luck than this can a man of your run expect?'

After fastly securing Nabokumar, the Kapalik laid him down on the sands and set himself to attend to the preparatory rites of worship. In the meantime Nabokumar tried to burst the bonds. But the dry creepers proved too strong and the knots too firm and he saw death before him. He resigned his soul to the sacred feet of his cherished god. The visions of his native land and his blessed home and the images of his long-lost parents passed before his mind in quick succession and a drop or two of scalding tears trickled down to the earth to be soaked into the parched sea-sands. Having finished the preliminary rites, the Kapalik left his seat to get his execution axe. But he could not find the axe where it was kept. What a surprise! The Kapalik wondered a bit. He was cocksure that he brought the axe in the afternoon, put it at the right place and did not remove it anywhere else. Then what became of the axe? He conducted a hurried search here and there. But the axe could not be traced. Then facing the hut, he called out to Kapalkundala but despite repeated calls no answer came. Then the Kapalik's eyes inflamed and his eyebrows contracted. He hastened to the cottage side. At the interval, Nabokumar made another attempt at burstmg the binding creepers but that effort, too, shared its former fate.

At that time, hushed footfalls were heared pattering on the sands—not the heavy footsteps of the Kapalik. Nabokumar looked up the direction and saw the same enchantress Kapalkundala with the axe flourishing in her hand.

'Silence,' enjoined Kapalkundala. 'Speak not—the axe is with me—I secreted it'.

With these words Kapalkundala deftly set her hand to cutting open the creepers that made up Nabokumar's bondage. In a brace of seconds, she freed him and exhorted, 'Escape—follow me—I shall act the guide'. Scarcely the words died on her lips when she vaulted forward and sped away like a bolt directing the way. Nabokumar, at a jump raced after her.

7

IN QUEST

On the other hand, the Kapalik, after having had some hunting for the axe within the cottage bounds, found neither the axe nor Kapalkundala. So he hastened back to the sands in a suspicious mood of mind. On his return he could not see Nabokumar there. At this, his astonishment grew intense. Soon after, his wandering eyes lighted on the broken bonds of creepers. Then the conviction was borne in upon him and he started out in search of Nabokumar. But it was impossible to make out in such a wilderness either the path or the direction the runaways had taken. The visibility being low owing to darkness, he could not spot either of them. He moved about for sometime aiming at the sound of voice. But the voice was not audible everytime. So with the object of a close survey of the outlying grounds he mounted the crest of a sand hill of a higher elevation. The Kapalik climbed the height from one side. He did not know that the base of the sand mound on the opposite side was worn out and loose with rivulets of water running down in the rains. No sooner had the Kapalik got on the summit than the crown of the sand hill in its tumble down condition gave way under the heavy weight of his body and came down with a terrific crash. The falling debris dragged down the Kapalik along with it like a wild buffalo torn from its crest.

8

IN SHELTER

Under the wing of the inky darkness of the moonless night, both ran into cover of the wood at their top-most speed. The wood path was unknown to Nabokumar and he had no other choice left him than to follow the lead of that fair guide of sixteen summers. This, too, was writ on my brow by that unknown scribe thought he within himself. The reflection betrayed Nabokumar's ignorance that the Bengalee is always the slave and never the master of circumstances. If he even knew this, he would never have felt either sick or sorry for it. On they travelled, they gradually slackened their paces. The gloom enveloped everything under its deep fold. Only at places the chalky crests of sand dunes seldom loomed sentinel-like under the star-lit night. At odd intervals, in the tiny glow of the fireflies, the tall trees of the forest stood out in their ghostly outlines against the dark blue sky.

Nabokumar in company of Kapalkundala arrived at a lonely recess in the wood. The turret of a temple was descried in the foreground through the forest gloom. Near the temple was, also, visible a house with a brick wall around it. Advancing, Kapalkundala knocked at the door in the wall and after short sharp raps came out a man's voice from inside, 'I presume you are Kapalkundala'. 'Open the door please,' chimed in Kapalkundala.

The speaker came down and unfastened the door. The man who threw open the door looked either the caretaker or the owner of the edifice raised to the Goddess inside, and appeared to have been on the wrong side of fifty. Kapalkundla with both hands drew the thin-haired head of the man near her lips and explained in a whispering word or two the plight of the stranger. The proprietor or the Adhicary of the shrine placing the head on his hand revolved the question in his mind for a long time.

'It is a serious affair,' observed the man at length. 'The saintly man can work miracles. However, through the grace of the Mother Goddess no misfortunes can befall you. Where is the man?'

'Come in,' trilled out Kapalkundala to Nabokumar. Thus invited, Nabokumar, who kept himself well under cover, slipped into the house.

'Hide your head for the night here,' said the Adhicary to him. 'Before the day breaks tomorrow I shall put you on the Midnapore highway.'

The Adhicary in course of conversation gathered that Nabokumar till then had not had a morsel of food. So he bustled himself arranging for Nabokumar's repast. But Nabokumar showed his disinclination to have had any food at all and simply prayed for the resting place. The Adhicary made Nabokumar's bed in his own kitchen room. After Nabokumar had laid himself down to rest, Kapalkundala was making herself ready to get back to the sea shore.

The Adhicary eyeing her affectionately said, 'Don't go. Rest a while. I have a request.'

'What you mean?'

'Since these eyes saw you, I have begun to call you mother and I can swear by the feet of the Goddess that I love you more than my own mother. Won't you keep my request?'

'Certainly, I will.'

'My only request is that you must not get back there any more.'

'Why?'

'If you go, you are undone.'

'That I know too.'

'Then what makes you question again.'

'Where am I to go, if not there?'

'Go forth into otherland in company of this stranger.'

Kapalkundala remained silent.

'What gives you furiously to think over it, mother?' asked the Adhicary.

'When your disciple came, you urged the immorality of my accompanying, as a young maid, another young man. But why do you tell me to do so again?'

'Then your life was not in jeopardy. Besides, the opportunity, which was lacking men, might prove golden now. Come, let us have the sanction of our Mother.'

Saying this, the Adhicary holding a lighted lamp in his hand issued forth and went over to the temple porch and opened the door. Kapalkundala, also, went behind him. Inside the temple was established the frightful Goddess Kali of the height and measure of a human figure. Both bent low before her in deep reverence. The Adhicary, after going through the holy preliminaries and reciting incantations in invocation of the deity, took a trident leaf from the flower stand and placing it at the feet of the Goddess looked intently on it. Shortly after, the Adhicary remarked to Kapalkundala, 'Look, mother, the Goddess has accepted the offering as the trident leaf has not dropped down. The idea with which the offering has been made is sure to materialise favourably. Go forth with this foreigner with a light heart. But I know the manners and conduct of the worldly people. If you literally prove a dead weight round his neck, then a blush might rise to the cheeck of this stranger to have a young girl by him in society. Besides, the world might treat you contemptuously. You say this man is a Brahmin and I see, too, he has a sacred thread around his neck. If this man takes you home after marriage then it is happy and good. Otherwise I can never advise you to bear him company.'

Kapalkundala slowly drawled out the word, 'M-a-r-r-i-a-g-e.'

'I heard the word "Marriage" from your lips,' went on she, 'but have never understood the honest meaning of the expression. What's to be done?'

The Adhicary gave a silent and slight laugh and said, 'To woman wedlock is but a stepping stone to the soul's flight to holihead and for this she is called the better-half of man. Even, the Mother of the Universe is Shiva's married wife.'

The temple-keeper thought he explained everything and Kapalkundala thought he understood everything.

'Let it be as you say,' added Kapalkundala. 'But my heart is loth to let him severely alone as he brought me up by hand for so long a time.'

'You don't know why he reared you.'

After this, the Adhicary or temple keeper made a feeble attempt at making a half-hearted exposition to Kapalkundala as to the relation of woman to the Tantrick rites of worship. Though Kapalkundala could not take in all this, still a chill gripped her heart.

'Let me be led to the marriage altar then,' stammered out she.

Afterwards, both went out of the temple. The temple keeper, making Kapalkundala wait in a room, approached Nabokumar's bed and sat at the head of the bedstead.

'Sir,' enquired he, 'are you asleep?'

Nabokumar was not in a mood to fall into a sleep. He lay brooding over his own condition.

'No, Sir,' answered he.

'Sir, I have turned in here,' resumed the Adhicary, 'to gather your particulars. May I ask if you are a Brahmin?'

'Oh! yes, I am.'

'Of what sect?'

'Of Rahri sect.'

'I, too, belong to the Rahri order of Brahmins. So, please, never take me for a Brahmin that came of the Uriya stock. By family pedigree, I am a first rate Kulin though, for the present, I have taken refuge under the foot-stool of the Mother Goddess. Your name please'

'Nabokumar Sharma.'

'Native village?'

'Saptagram.'

'Of what branch of Kulins?'

'Bandoghati.'

'How many times did you marry?'

'For the first time.'

Nabokumar did not lay bare his whole heart. In fact, he had no wife at all. He married Padmabati, the daughter, of Ram Govinda Ghosal. After marriage Padmabati stayed at her father's place for a short time and at times visited her father-in-law's house. Her father had been on a holy pilgrimage to Puri with the whole family when she was barely thirteen. At this time, the Pathans who were expelled from Bengal by Akbar found an asylum in Orissa. Akbar had quite a tough job to quell them. The Moghuls and Pathans had been on their war-path when Ram Govinda Ghosal was getting back from Orissa.

On the way he fell into the hands of the Pathans, who, at that time, were in the habit of trampling down the codes of war etiquette and so used violence to innocent passers to squeeze out money. Ram Govinda was of choleric temper so he abused the Pathans. The up-shot was that he with the whole family was thrown into prison. At last he and the family changed faith and were released on their apostacy. Though Ram Govinda and the family returned home unhurt, they were treated as outcasts by the relation and society. Nabokumar's father was living and he discarded his daughter-in-law as well as her father who had cast away the faith. Nabokumar did not any more set his eyes on his wife. Renounced by the relation and society, Ram Govinda could not hold his head high in his native village for long. What with these grounds and what with his high ambition to secure some fat billet through royal favour did Ram Govinda move to Rajmahal with his family and settled there. Having turned renegades, he and the family adopted Mussulmun names. Since they repaired to Rajmahal, Nabokumar had no means of knowing the whereabouts of either the wife or the father and so far he received no news about them. Nabokumar was reluctant any more to take to second wife. For this, we are entitled to say that Nabokumar had no wife at all. Adhicary was not aware of all this. He concluded that there might be no harm for a Kulin's son to be a polygamist.

'I came to tell you one thing,' he spoke aloud. 'This girl who saved your life has sacrificed her own life for other's good. The saintly man under whose protection she lives is a horrid being. If she goes back she needs must share the same fate as you were almost doing. May I ask whether you can suggest any way out of this?'

Nabokumar sat up on the bedstead.

'I, too, feared that,' said he. 'You know everything so you can suggest the means. If my self-immolation can repay anything, I am ready to sacrifice myself. I have so made up my mind as to return to the manslayer and surrender myself to him. In that case her life may be spared.'

The Adhicary laughed silently.

'You are insane,' said he, 'What would this result in? The flame of your life would be put out though it would not extinguish the wrath of the personage. It admits but of one solution.'

'What is it?'

'It means her flight with you. But that, too, is a risky adventure. If you tarry in my place any longer, you are sure to be apprehended in a day or two. That saintly man frequents this holy shrine. So it portends misfortunes to Kapalkundala.'

'What risk is there,' returned Nabokumar quick with eagerness, 'in her escape with me?'

'You don't know this girl's parents and lineage—whose wife she is and of what character? Would you take her as your companion? Granting you take her as your companion in life, would you shelter her under your paternal roof? Besides, if you refuse her any asylum where would this orphan go?'

Nabokumar reflected for sometime and joined, 'I shall not let the grass grow under my feet to be of any service to my saviour. She shall find a place in the inner ring of my family.'

'Well and good. But when the people would come and ask whose wife she is what answer would you give?'

Nabokumar mused again and added, 'You must tell me that and I will say to each and every one accordingly.'

'Good. But how is it possible for a young man and a young maid to go together alone on a fortnight's journey? what will men say to all this? How would you explain it to your friends and relatives? Besides, when I have called this girl my mother, does it behove me to pack her off to a far-off country in company of stranger?'

The prince of matchmakers was not ill-adept in matchmaking.

'Be pleased then to come with us,' urged Nabokumar.

'Indeed! Then who would offer Pujah to the Goddess Bhowani?'

Nabokumar was at a quandary and replied, 'Can't you point then to any solution to this riddle?'

'There may be one and only one solution that waits upon your generosity.'

'What might it be? In what do I not acquiesce in? Please tell me the way out.'

'Listen. She is the daughter of a Brahmin father. In her infancy, she was carried away by the wicked pirates but was abandoned on the sea coast due to shipwreck. You will have the details from her later on. Chance had given her over to the Kapalik who nursed and tended her so that his ritualism might attain its fruition. He could, by this time, have encompassed his own end but affection forged a fetter that held him with a hand of iron. Marry her and take her home so that none will have their say. I shall conduct the marriage according to scriptural rites.'

Nabokumar rose on his legs and paced up and down with quick steps silently.

'Take your bed now,' resumed the Adhicary after a brief interval. 'I shall wake you up early tomorrow morning. If you like, you may go alone. I shall place you on the Midnapore highway.'

With these words, the Adhicary took leave. While retiring, he thought within, 'Is it that I have forgotten the ways of marriage negotiations in Western Bangal?'

9

IN THE HOLY SHRINE

The Adhicary hastened back to Nabokumar at daybreak and found that he did never take his bed for the night.

'What is advisable now?' asked he.

'From this day forward,' said Nabokumar, 'she shall be made and remain my lawful wife. If the act needs the renunciation of the world I am ready to do so for her sake. Who will give her hand away in marriage?'

The face of the man of the first-rate matchmaking abilities beamed up with joy.

'After so long, O Mother of the Creation, perhaps, my hapless daughter's star has risen,' thought the Adhicary within himself.

'I shall bestow her upon you in the marriage ceremony,' said he aloud. Then the Adhicary re-entered his bedroom. An old piece of cloth wrapped some ancient worm-eaten palm leaves. Within it was preserved an astrological record of the stellar movements and positions. He drew up a chart, made minute calculations and then came out and said, 'Though the day is not auspicious enough for nuptials, yet there can be no harm in disposing of her hand in marriage. I shall hand her to you in the twilight moments and you shall have only to keep fasting the whole day. Do the sacred family rites at home. I have a place where I can hide you for a day only. If he happens to look in here in the course of daylight hours, he shall have no scent of you. After the marriage is over, you can, with your wife, leave the place next morning.'

Nabokumar agreed to the proposal. Shastric observances were followed as far as practicable in the circumstances. On the border line between light and darkness did Nabokumar lead to the marriage altar the ascetic girl, nursed by the Kapalik. So far no news reached them of the Kapalik. The following morning, the trio prepared for the journey. It had been settled that the Adhicary would accompany them as far as the Midnapore high road. Against departure, Kapalkundala went to make her last obeisance to the Goddess Kali. After she had devotedly bowed down her head, she took a trident leaf, whole and unbroken, from the flower basket and placing it at the feet of the idol, intently gazed down at it. The leaf dropped down. Kapalkundala was intensely religious. She was horror-struck to see the trident leaf slip away from the feet of the holy figure and so informed the Adhicary who was aggrieved to hear of it.

'Now there is no help for it,' said he. 'You have been united in holy bonds so you must follow your husband to the funeral pyre if it is so needed. Go forth silently.'

All of them moved noiselessly forward. The morning waxed hot when they arrived at the Midnapore high road. Here the Adhicary bade farewell to the party whereupon Kapalkundala burst into a rain of tears. The only friend, she had in this wide world over, was taking his final leave. The Adhicary also felt a mist rising over his eyes. He brushed the tears from Kapalkundala's eyes and whispered into her ears, 'Mother, you know, through the grace of the Mother of the Universe, your son stands in no need of wealth. Both the high and low of the Hijli country-side bow their knees to the Goddess and send in their offerings. Give your husband what I have tied to your cloth-end and tell him to hire a palanquin for you and ever and always remember your son.'

The Adhicary retired from the scene with streaming eyes. Kapalkundala, as well, went her way with her sight bedimmed with tears.

PART II

1

ON THE HIGHWAY

On his arrival at Midnapore, Nabokumar engaged a maidservant, an escort and palanquin bearers for Kapalkundala through Adhicary's money and sent her away on the road before him in the palanquin. He, himself, tramped along on account of the scantiness of his purse. He felt much fatigued on account of the worries of the day before, and so the palanquin bearers outdistanced him a long way after midday meal. Gradually the evening drew near. The wintry sky was littered over with light grey clouds that threatened rain. By degrees, the evening wore away into night that was settling down upon the earth with the mantle of darkness closing in upon everything. A thin rain began to fall in drib drabs. Nabokumar bustled forward to join Kapalkundala. He had the firm conviction that he would meet with her at the first roadside inn but so far no inn fell upon his eyes. The night was deepening. Nabokumar threw in an extra energy into his gait. Suddenly his feet came upon something hard and uneven. The thing crashed into splinters under the weight of his body and a dry crackle leapt to his ears. He stopped short and then moved onward again. Again the same crack met his ears. He picked up the trampled-down things and found them appearing like pieces of broken bedstead. Even when the sky is cloudy it never gets dark enough for material things not to be seen lying in front in the open. A large object lay on the ground in front of him and he felt it to be the broken part of palanquin boards. Scarcely had he perceived this than a suspicion crossed his mind that Kapalkundala might be in danger. He hastened towards the direction of the travelling palanquin when his feet touched some objects of a different category. It was like the soft touch of a human body. He sat down and moved his hand across the surface of the object. The impression gained confirmed his suspicion. The touch felt cold and icy and brought along with it the perception of some liquid flow. He felt for the pulse but could not find any as life had been extinct. He surveyed the thing in the darkness with increased attention and thought he heard some breathing sound. If the breath is left then why the pulse does not beat? Is it a sickman? He put his hand near the nose but perceived no respiration. Then where did the sound come from? Might be some living humanity happens to be here. Thinking thus he enquired at the top of his voice. 'Is there any living man here?'

Softly a murmuring answer came, 'yes.'

'Who are you?' asked Nabokumar.

'Who are you?' echoed back the reply.

The voice seemed to be the voice of a woman. Quick with eagerness Nabokumar querried, 'Are you Kapalkundala?'

'I don't know who is Kapalkundala,' replied the woman. 'I am a traveller and have been robbed of my Kundalas (ear pendants), for the present, by the highway robbers.'

Nabokumar was somewhat flattered with the joke in the form of a pun and asked, 'What is the matter with you?'

'The robbers smashed my palanquin,' said the answering voice, 'and killed a bearer as the rest stampeded. The rascals carried away all the ornaments I had on my person and tied me to the palanquin.'

Nabokumar saw through the haze of darkness that actually a woman remained there bound up with the palanquin. He undid the fastenings with quick fingers and interrogated, 'Can you rise?'

'One stroke fell upon me,' said the woman. 'So I feel a burning pain in my leg. But, I think, with a little help I can rise on my legs.'

Nabokumar stretched a helping hand. The woman got up with the assistance.

'Can you walk?' enquired he.

'Have you seen any other traveller coming behind you?' brusquely asked the woman without answering the question.

'No,' replied Nabokumar.

'How far is the inn?' questioned the woman again.

'I am not sure how far it is,' said he. 'But more possible than not it is close by.'

'What good is there in sitting on alone on such a wild heath in darkness?' added the woman. 'It is better, certainly, to follow you into the inn. I think I can walk over the distance if I get any support.'

'It is foolish to fight shy in the hour of danger,' joined he. 'Please lean on my shoulder and move along.'

The woman did not play the fool. She walked forward with Nabokumar's assistance. As a matter of fact, the inn stood at an easy distance. In those days, the robbers feared not to ply their dirty trade at a close radius from the inn. Before it was long, Nabokumar arrived at the estaminet followed by the woman. He found Kapalkundala placed at the same inn where her people appointed a room for her. He engaged the adjoining room for his companion and lodged her in it. At his bidding, the landlady brought in a lamp. When the flood of light fell upon the person of his fair companion, he was startled to find her an uncommon beauty. Like the full-coursed river overflowing its bank in the rains, the profuse full-blown graces of her exquisitely modelled youthful figure threw in an indescribable charm and created an atmosphere of loveliness around her.

2

AT THE INN

If this woman happened to have been reproachlessly beautiful then I might venture the remark, 'Gentleman reader, she is as much beautiful as your sweetheart, and, fair reader, she is just your shadow reflected in your looking glass.' This would have been penportraying to its finish. Unfortunately she was not a faultless beauty. So I have to resist the temptation. The reason in saying that she was not a perfect beauty is, first, she was a trifle taller than the average medium figure; secondly, her upper and lower lips slightly curled up inwards; and, thirdly, she had not a complexion of cream-and-rose. Though comparatively of a taller height, her body was full of a buxom bosom and her limbs showed perfect fulness and rotundity. As in the rains the cringing creeper sways majestically with its green gorgeous foliage, so her form displayed all the infinite graces on account of the lusty fulness of life. As a matter of course, her figure, though, to some degree, a shade taller in size, looked all the more resplendent because of its full-blooded roundness. Amongst the class of beauties of the really milk-and-rose style, some wears the hue of the liquid silver of the full moon and some the colour of the russet-tinted dawn. She had none of the complexions of the above two categories, so we can never say she had actually any brilliancy of skin though in magic effects her charms played no less a potency. She was a little darker. But that never suggests the blackness, of which Shyama's mother or Shyama, the goodlooking, is the type. The transparency of her skin had as much sparkle as the glow of the dissolved gold. If the white splendour of the full moon or the first flush of the saffron-coloured dawn be taken the criteria of the skin of the dainty eves, then the refreshing yellow-and-green of the new shafts of mango blossoms shooting up in the divinest of seasons may be made the comparing standard of this damsel's complexion. If amongst readers there might be many who are chivalrous enough to press the claims of the olive-complexioned beauties to the forefront, and, also, as chance would have it, there might be anyone whose smitten soul has been left to the care of a dark-skinned witch, then the latter in any case can never be called colour blind. If any body is offended at this, let him paint before his mind's eye the dark silky locks kissing the bright forehead like the deep rows of black bees lining the new-blown mango blossoms—let him imagine the pair of arched eyebrows under a shapely forehead, as beautiful as a three quarter silvery moon, overblown by ringlets—let him idealise the smooth velvety cheeks of the rich mellowed hues of golden mangos—let him portray a couple of small thin red lips like two streaks of scarlet, and, it is then, that he might have the impression of this fair stranger as the queen of beauty. Her eyes, though not wide, were full of brilliance and fringed with bowed lashes. The glance was steady but keen and searching. When the eyes are fixed upon you, you, at once, feel that this woman is probing the bottom of your heart. By degrees, the glaring intensity is apt to melt and the looks soften and become mellifluously affectionate. Sometimes, again, they bespeak certain languor and lassitude, born of voluptuous abandonment, appearing the soft dreamy bed of the blind baby-god with bow and arrows. At times, the eye-balls expand and dilate hot with desires full of amorous coyness. Again, they shoot up, at intervals, some sinister side-long glances resembling vivid flashes amidst dark clouds.

The face was lit up with two fine expressions—first, the forcefulness of an all-mastering intelligence,—secondly, an over-weening conceit. So, when she chanced to stand up imperiously and bend her swan-neck, she looked the right royal type of the feminist. She passed her seven-and-twenty summers—she the torrential river of the rich, ripe, golden autumn that has but set in. Her charms flowed and sparkled full to the brim, ready to break over the contents. The ripening fulness of those graces was more soul-enrapturing than the colour, the eye and all else besides. In her youthful sleekness, the whole frame coloured and quivered with a virility like the autumnal river sheening and shimmering under the gentlest sigh of a wind and the graceful rippling spread out the charms in all their shifting colours and contours.

Nabokumar with eager eyes was gazing upon this glorious form with all the changing shades of beauties. The fair creature caught sight of Nabakumar's hard stare and watchful speculating eyes. 'What do you look into intently?' asked she, 'My beauty?'

Nabokumar was gentle-born. He felt awkward and hung down his head in shame.

Seeing him silent, she archly remarked, 'Have you not ever seen a woman?—Or you think me an extraordinary beauty?'

Naturally, this might have amounted to a reproach. But the radiant smile that accompanied the words, took off the biting sting. So it savoured more of a jest than anything else. Nabokumar saw her tongue had sharp edges. Then why should he not reply her sharp remark?

'I have seen many a woman,' answered he, 'but never such a beautiful one.'

The woman boastfully asked, 'Not a single one?'

The soft sweet charms of Kapalkundala floated before Nabokumar's mind, and, he, too, proudly returned, 'Not a single one! No—I can never say that.'

'So far so good,' rejoined the woman. 'Is she your wife?'

'Why? What above all things sends you on the thought of a wife?'

'The Bengalee always regards his wife as an unsurpassed beauty.'

'I am a true-born Bengalee. But you, too, speak the Bengali dialect. To what country else do you belong then?'

The damsel glanced at her own style of dress and said, 'As ill luck would have it, this hapless self is not a Bengalee woman but an upcountry Mussalmani.'

Nabokumar eyed her up and down and saw the dress exactly suited the up-country fashion, though she was speaking the Bengali as much chastely as a born Bengalee.

After a short spell the young woman resumed, 'Sir, you have gathered all the information about me by parry of words. Now be pleased to let me know your own particulars. May I enquire the place where that incomparable beauty rules the household?'

'Saptagram is my native land' replied Nabokumar.

The foreigner added no answer. Suddenly she bent her head and plied her fingers brightening up the lamp-light.

Shortly after, without raising her head, she softly broke in, 'The servant's name is Moti. May I have the pleasure of knowing your name?'

'Nabokumar Sharma,' said Nabokumar.

The light was blown out by a deep sigh and a hush fell in the room.

3

MEETING WITH THE BEAUTIFUL WOMAN

Nabokumar ordered the inn-keeper for another light. He had heard a deep sigh before another light was brought in. A few minutes later, a Mussulman in servant's livery made his appearance. At his sight, the foreigner burst out 'Eh! What made you delay so much? Where are others gone?'

'The palanquin bearers were all drunk,' meekly joined the servant, 'and as I had to collect them together, I lagged behind. Afterwards, the broken palanquin and your disappearance frightened us out of our wits. Some men are left on the spot and others conducting the search in different directions. I turned in in this quarter on a scent.'

'Conduct them before me,' rang out the silver voice of Moti.

The servant made a deep bow and retired. The fair stranger remained seated for sometime, resting the head on her hand. Nabokumar asked leave to withdraw and then Moti shook herself as if coming out of a reverie. Without relinquishing her previous pose, she asked, 'Where are you going to put up for the night?'

'The room next to this.'

'I saw a palanquin there. Have you any companion with you?'

'My wife is with me.'

It gave another opportunity of showing Moti's vein of humour.

'Is she the non pareil beauty,' asked Moti.

'When you see, you will guess it,' replied Nabokumar.

'May these eyes see her?'

(In thoughtful air) 'What harm is there?'

'Then be pleased to show me this favour. My curiosity to see this peerless beauty has been piqued to the extreme. I shall carry the tale to Agra—but it is not befitting the time—goodbye for the present. I shall send you information afterwards.'

Nabokumar left the place. Soon after, a troop of retainers with a retinue of servants and servantmaids, with kits, and bags and baggages appeared on the scene. A palanquin, too, accompanied them with a chambermaid inside it.

Later on, the news reached Nabokumar. 'The mistress has remembered you.' Nabokumar reappeared before Moti. He saw a new departure this time. Moti changed and made a fresh toilet. She put on her embroidered garments splashed with gold and pearls and garnished her unadorned figure with ornaments. The enamel works of diamonds, rubies and other precious stones on the gold ornaments worn on every available inch of space on the body—the sidelocks, the braided knot, the brow, the temple, the ears, the neck, the bosom. the arms and the shoulders—glinted in ten thousand glittering points and dazzled the eyes of Nabokumar. Like the countless stars bespangling the sky, the innumerable gems setting off the exquisite charms and contours of the splendid figure heightened the effects which blended in a harmonising whole were thrown off into boldest relief.

'Sir, let me be conducted and introduced to your wife,' said Moti to Nabokumar.

'There is no use wearing jewelleries like that,' joined Nabokumar. 'Of ornaments my wife has none at all.'

'But what does it matter if I deck my person to display my jewellery? Women possessing jewelleries can not help making a show of them. Let us go now.'

Nabokumar showed her the way. The woman who had ridden the palanquin also accompanied them. Her name was Peshman. Kapalkundala was seated alone on the wet ground of the shop-room. The faint glimmer of a lamp light made the darkness visible only. Her rich mass of untied hair fell in a heap and darkened her back. At the first sight, the feeble ray of a faint smile glistened in the eyes and flickered on the lips of Moti. To get a closer view, did Moti hold aloft the light and bring it near Kapalkundala's face and then the flicker of the smile fled away. Moti's expressions hardened up in a rigid setting and she gazed on throbbing with admiration, holding her bated breath in aesthetic enjoyment. None spoke—Moti charmed and spellbound and Kapalkundala touched with surprise. Afterwards Moti began to pull off the ornaments from her own person. She denuded her body of all the jewelleries and proceeded to place these one by one on Kapalkundala's person. Kapalkundala did not speak a word all this time.

'What you mean by all this?' exclaimed Nabokumar in wonder. But Moti made no rejoinder.

After finishing the work on hand, Moti said, 'You told me a perfect truth. Such a flower never blooms in a king's garden. The regret is I can not show this blooming beauty in the capital. These jewelleries are befitting such a framework. So I set these on her. You, too, I hope, will bedeck her person, at times, with these and remember this sharp-tongued stranger.'

Nabokumar was amazed and said, 'How is it? These jewelleries are worth a king's ransom. How can I accept these?'

'Through Providence's kindness, I have more of these and I shall never have the occasion to miss them. If I feel any happines in embellishing her what on earth might be the reason of your objecting?'

With this, Moti left the place in company of her dressing maid. When they had reached some removed ground Peshman asked Moti 'Dear Lady, who is he?'

'My dearest,' answered the Mussalmani mistress.

4

IN THE PALANQUIN

Now let us have the story of the ornaments. Moti made a present of an ivory box inlaid with silver for the preservation of ornaments. The robbers carried off only a small booty—they laid their violent hands on the articles she had near her person but nothing more than these. Nabokumar left one or two ornaments on Kapalkundala's body and put away the rest in the jewel box. Moti left for Burdwan the next morning and Nabokumar with Kapalkundala went forth towards Saptagram. Placing Kapalkundala in the palanquin, Nabokumar put the jewel box with her. The bearers, as a matter of course, trotted off at a fast pace and left Nabokumar a long way behind. Kapalkundala opened the palanquin doors and looked about enjoying the landscape. A beggar espied her and followed the palanquin droning piteously for alms.

'I have nothing with me,' said Kapalkundala. 'So what can I give you?'

The beggar pointed to one or two ornaments Kapalkundala had on and said, 'How strange, mother! Pearls and diamonds gleam and glitter on your person and you have nothing to give away?'

'Are you satisfied if you get these?' asked Kapalkundala.

The beggar was stupefied. He pitched his aspiration a point higher and in a trice added, 'Of course I do.'

Without a second thought, Kapalkundala gave away the jewel-box with all the jewelleries into the beggar's hands. She even tore off a few ornaments she had on her and made a gift of these. The beggar stared for a moment, with those droll expressions peculiar to the class. The servants and servantmaids did not have a scent of all this. The beggar's bewildered expression was, however, of a moment's duration. Immediately he gave his furtive glances all the country round and at a bound ran off with the ornaments.

'What made the beggar dash away for his dear life?' thought Kapalkundala.

5

IN HIS NATIVE LAND

Nabokumar returned home with Kapalkundala. He had no father though he had his widowed mother and two sisters. The first sister was also a widow and we shall have no occasion to introduce our gentle reader to her. The second one was Shyamasundari. She had her husband alive though she looked a widow to all intents and purposes as she had been married to a high class Kulin. She alone will make her appearance in our midst once or twice. We are not sure how far Nabokumar's relations would have been satisfied if he chanced to marry an ascetic girl and carried her home in a changed set of circumstances. After all, Nabokumar encountered no difficulty in this respect as every body despaired of his return.

On return home, his erstwhile companions bruited it far and wide that Nabokumar was killed by a tiger. The gentle reader may think that these people who bore the hallmark of veracity invented the story according to their own beliefs and opinions. If this be his honest opinion, then he does a grave injustice to the fantastic inventiveness of these wise acres. Of the returned pilgrims, many made solemn affirmations that they saw with their own eyes Nabokumar run into the jaw of the tiger. At times, long-winded frothy debates were held as to the size of the tiger. Some asseverated that the tiger measured twelve feet but others negatived the idea and solemnly affirmed that the beast measured close upon one-and-twenty feet. Our previous acquaintance, the old pilgrim, said, 'It seems I have had a clean shave. The tiger took its first spring towards me but I showed him a clean pair of heels. Anyhow, Nabokumar was not such a daring spirit so he could not make off.'

When all these versions reached the ears of Nabokumar's mother and relations they set up such a howl as raged with unabated fury for days end on. Nabokumar's mother was stricken down with grief at the news of the bereavement of her only son. Just at this psychological moment the son made his way back home with his newly married wife. Now there was none in the whole countryside who dared raise issues on the topics of his bride's caste and origin! Every body was overjoyed to see him come back. Nabokumar's mother gave the bride a hearty reception and after the performance of the requisite after marriage ceremonies carried her home shoulder high. His joy passed all bounds on seeing Kapalkundala warmly received within his home circle. Even when he won Kapalkundala's hand he betrayed not the least sign of joy or affection fearing a cold shoulder might be given the party at home which might serve the damper. Still the thoughts of Kapalkundala filled his whole mental horizon. This was the only consideration weighing with Nabokumar that explained his shyness to close in with the offer of the proferred hand of Kapalkundala—that precluded his utterance of a single endearing term for a single time to Kapalkundala even when he got back home after marriage and, lastly, that prevented the smallest wave to ruffle the calm surface of his rising sea of love and affection. But the fear that haunted him all this time was now gone for ever. As a rushing stream gathering its volume before an obstacle in its path crashes down with redoubled fury when that impediment is dislodged so the growing enthusiastic love of Nabokumar surged and broke over all restraints. These pregnant feelings of affection though not often expressed in words could be read in Nabokumar's glistening ardent gaze upon Kapalkundala every time she chanced to cross his line of vision—in his constant visits to Kapalkundala on the pretext of urgency on the most trivial grounds—in his hovering around Kapalkundala without any occasion for it—in his attempts at driving at the topic of Kapalkundala in the midst of conversation without any necessity for it—in his ceaseless efforts to encompass Kapalkundala with all the comforts and well being of home life—and, in fine, in his halting gait of walk due to the distraction of his mind. Even his tone of life underwent some change. An air of seriousness settled in place of buoyant sportiveness—vivacity supplanted languor and Nabokumar's face brightened up at all times with joy. The heart being the mainspring of love, it blossomed into greater and nobler things. His love grew for all others—his tolerance extended to the undesirables—his heart overflowed with the milk of human kindness towards all mankind—the earth appeared the creation for piety and goodness and everything looked joyful and radiant. Such is love. It gives its colouring to everything. It sweetens harshness—turns iniquity into virtue—gives a halo to unholiness and ushers light into darkness. But what about Kapalkundala? In what mood is she now? Well, reader, let us go and have a look at her.

6

IN DOMESTIC SECLUSION

Everybody is aware that Saptagram was a city of considerable importance in her past days. Once she formed the trysting ground of maritime traders of every clime from Java to Rome. But her old splendours were much on the wane between the Bengali 10th and 11th centuries. Its main reason was that the river that washed the edge of the city was shrunk up in its channel so that sailing crafts of larger draughts could not push up well within her harbour. So she lost much of her commercial importance. A city of commercial greatness loses everything with the loss of her commercial glory. Such was the case with Saptagram.

Hooghly, in the 11th century, was leaping into existence and fame as her rival with all her nascent glories. The Portuguese established their business houses there which drew the wealth and opulence of Saptagram. But till then Saptagram was not shorn of all the vestiges of her fallen greatness. She still formed the headquarters of Fouzdars and other important Government officials though a large area of the city lost much of her attractiveness and, being uninhabited, gradually wore the aspect of a village.

Nabokumar's house was situated in an out-of-the-way nook on the periphery of Saptagram. The streets in her much ruined state were sequestered and overgrown with shrubs and trailers. In the background of Nabokumar's dwelling place lay a thick forest. A small stream ran across a mile's distance in the fore-ground that meandering its course around a small field entered the wood. The house was brick-built though on an all-round consideration it did not rise much above the commonplace. Although double-storied, it was not enormously high and so could not have any pretension to a mansion. Its specimen height can, now-a-days, be seen in the basement in many instances.

Two young women stood on the house top and were viewing the

country round below. The house was framed in a beautiful setting. It was evening and the landscape was really beautiful and fascinating. Close by, lay the dense woodland with the innumerable feathered choristers singing their piping chorus inside with the rivulet flowing at a distance, looking a thin silver ribbon. Yonder across the grounds unrolled the panoroma of landscape and town where gleamed ten thousand edifices of the vast city the windows and casements of which were thronged with citizens eager to have an airing in the soft breeze of the fresh spring. Far away on the otherside, were the shadows of the evening thickening over the broad water of the Bhagirathi crowded with sailing smacks.

Of the young women on the terrace, the complexion of one had the gleam of the moonshine. Her figure was half concealed amidst her loose dark tresses. The other dark-skinned and of clear cut features was neither just in nor well out of her gushing sixteen. She was thin and small. Her small ringlets were blown over the upper half of her tiny face like the petals of a full-blown lotus encircling the cup in the centre. Her eyes were large and of a mild white as of the fish. Her tiny fingers were enmeshed in her companion's flowing mass of curling hair. Our presumption is at par that the reader has recognised the girl with the tint of the silver moonbeam to be our Kapalkundala. We may let him understand, besides, that the dark-complexioned one is her sister-in-law, Shyamasunari.

Shyamasundari was addressing her brother's wife at times as 'Bow' (brother's wife), sometimes endearingly as sister and at other times as Mrino. The name Kapalkundala was a bit horrible so womenfolk called her Mrinmoyee. We, too, shall hence forward call her by this name though not too often. Shyamasundari was reciting verses from a nursery poem:

> They say the lotus queen that veils her
>   face when falls the night
> Makes buds to ope and bees to flee as her
>   dear lord's in sight.
> With leaves spread out to the tree the
>   woodland creeper flies,

> So the river stream when comes the
> > flood to the ocean hies.
> O, what a shame the bashless lily blooms
> > when the moon doth shine,
> And the newly wedded bride, her wedlock
> > o'er, does for her husband pine.

Shyamasundari. 'Would you lead an ascetic's single life all your days?'

'Why? what asceticism do I practise?' replied Mrinmoyee.

Shyamasundari with both hands lifting Mrinmoyee's rich curling locks exclaimed, 'Would you never gather this heap of hair in a knot?'

Mrinmoyee with a soft smile gently extricated her hair from Shyama's clutches.

'Well and good,' continued Shyamasundari. 'Do but fulfil my wishes. Once attire yourself after the style of our household women. How long, Oh God, would you play the ascetic?'

'I had ever been an ascetic girl before I fell in with this son of a Brahmin.'

'Now you must forego that.'

'Why forego?'

'Why? Would you see? I will break your asceticism. Do you know what a philosopher's stone is?'

'No.'

'The philosopher's stone turns the rusty bars of iron into gold.'

'What of that?'

'Women have, too, their philosopher's stone.'

'What is it?'

'Man. The forest-maid with his touch blossoms into a full blown housewife. You have touched that stone.'

Then she hummed in the following air in a tuneful voice:

> I shall bind thy ample locks of hair
> And give thee shining robe to wear;
> Your braid shall shine with flowers fresh,
> A tiara shall thy temple grace;
> There shall be a girdle for thy waist,
> For ears, a pair of pendants best;

Nut, leaf and betel spices sweet,
Sandal and ingredients meet,
Delicious shall thy cup overflow;
Thy ruddy lips shall ruddier glow.
There shall, a boy, as bright as gold
And fair, as doll, thy arms enfold;
And, I am sure, such a sight as this
Will fill your heart with joy and bliss.

'Well, now I understand. Granted, I have touched the philosopher's stone and in contact with it have turned into gold; granted, I have braided the hair and stuck up flower in the braided knot; granted, I have dangled the waistband on the loin and hung up earrings in the ear; granted, I have used plenty of sandal, kumkum, chooa, betel and betel nut and am delivered even of the precious sweet boy babe; granted, it gave a fillip to my pleasures. After all, do these make up happiness?'

'Answer if the flower has any joy in its bloom.'

'Men are delighted to see it. But what does it matter to the flower?'

Shyama's looks fell and dark shadows flitted across her face. Like the petals of a lotus blown by the morning wind, her big blue eyes stared hard and twinkled.

'What has it to do with flower?' echoed she, 'That I can never say. I never grew up into a flower that blossomed. But if ever I could be a rose-bud like you, then perhaps I would have a taste of the thrill of delights in the blossom.'

Seeing her silent, Shyama continued, 'Well and good. But if it does not follow, then let me hear your idea of happiness.'

Mrinmoyee bethought herself a while and said, 'I can not explain it. Perhaps I would have been happy if I could but wander through the seaside wilderness.'

Shyamasundari was no little disconcerted to hear this. That their care and good treatment bestowed no benefits upon Mrinmoyee stung her and ruffled her temper.

'Is there any means of return?' asked she.

'No. Not any.'

'Then what you propose?'

Adhicary used to say, 'We do as we are ordained to do.'

Shyamasundari hid her face with her cloth and shook with laughter.

'As you please, your most Noble Eminence,' added she. 'What is the conclusion?'

Mrinmoyee heaved a heavy sigh and rejoined. 'Let God's will be done. Come what may.'

'What? What else in store? There are brighter and happier days for you. Why you drew that sigh?'

'Hear me,' proceeded Mrinmoyee. 'Just before we left the place on the day I started forth with my husband I went to place the trident leaf at Bhowani's feet as I used to undertake no work until I had done the same. The trident leaf used to stick up if the work in hand was sure to prosper and it shook and fell if the work was to end in a fiasco. I had my misgivings with regard to my adventure into a foreign land in company of a foreigner and so visited the Goddess to read the auguries. Mother Goddess let fall the trident leaf and so I am afraid what the future may bring forth.'

Mrinmoyee ended. A shudder crept into Shyama and she gave a start.

PART III

1

IN THE LONG PAST

When Nabokumar left the inn with Kapalkundala, Moti also bowled off towards Burdwan along a different route. Let us have a resume of her early career so long she is on the highway. Moti had an erratic career and her character though stained with dark vices was as well adorned with great virtues. A review of such a character may not bore the reader.

The time, her father embraced Musalman faith, her Hindu name was converted into Luthfunnisha. She never assumed the name Moti in any part of her life. But she might have had recourse to the name when she happened to travel incognito in foreign lands. Her father came to Dacca and took service under Government. The place was, however, too full of his countrymen. It ill-becomes almost every gentleman to live and move in a community wherefrom he has been blackballed. As a matter of course, when he won some feathers in his cap of success under the subadar he provided himself with credentials from many Omrahs who were his friends and made for Agra. Merits were sure to have been unearthed by Akbar and so his merits were rewarded. Luthfunnisha's father in a surprisingly short time gathered more leaves to his laurel and was reckoned as one of the most powerful Omrahs of the realm. On the other hand, Luthfunnisha was fast coming of age. On her advent into Agra, she received her lessons in Persian, Sanskrit, dance, music, wit and what not and became accomplished in all these. She was in no time looked upon as the first and foremost amongst the first-rate beauties as well as the 'blue stockings' of the capital. As ill luck would have it, her education was ill-grounded in religion and was not of a piece with her proficiency in other branches of knowledge. When Luthfunnisha blossomed into her glorious womanhood she showed signs of an unbridled temper. She had no control over her passions far less any inclination for it. She set her mind upon any work without arguing its pros and cons and did what pleased her. She did right when her heart took fancy for it and did wrong when it pleased her passing whim. So Luthfunnisha imbibed all the vices as the fruit of her unlicensed youthful follies. Her first husband was alive so none of the Omrahs consented to marry her. Marriage, too, had not its much attractiveness for her. She thought she found no earthly necessity in clipping short the wings of the dallying amorous bee sipping from flower to flower. The first whisperings culminated in a deep-mouthed public scandal. Her father was annoyed and she was expelled from her father's residence. The heir apparent, Selim, was one of those upon whom her favours were bestowed in secret. Selim, however, could not make Luthfunnisha an inmate of his harem lest his actions cast a blot on the family escutcheon of an Omrah and he, himself, incurred the flaming wrath of his imperial father. Now the moment proved opportune. Selim's chief Begum was the sister of Mansinha, the Rajput chief. The prince gave Luthfunnisha the situation of the first maid-of-honour to the Begum. Luthfunnisha publicly showed, herself, as the maid to the Begum, while in secret was in liaison with the heir apparent.

It can be easily imagined that a woman of the intellectual stamp of Luthfunnisha could shortly win the heart of the prince. She gained such an unrivalled ascendency over Selim's mind as made her cocksure that she bade fair to be Selim's prospective chief Begum at the right nioinent. Not only was Luthfunnisha cocksure about it but all the palace household thought it a possibility. Luthfunnisha bore her charmed existence under the spell of such golden dreams when one day she received a rude awakening. Meherunnisha, the daughter of Khowja Ayesh (Aktimud-daulah), Akbar's High Treasurer, held the first rank amongst Moslem beauties. The Chancellor of Exchequer one day invited Selim and other shining lights to a dinner at his residence. That day Selim saw Meherunnisha for the first time. At the first sight he lost his heart and confided his smitten soul to her care. What followed then is known to every reader of the Indian History. The High Treasurer's daughter was, before this, affianced to a powerful Omrah named Sher Afgan. Selim blinded by passion approached his father to have the engagement cancelled.

The result was that he met with a stern rebuff from his impartial father. But his ardour received a temporary set-back only. Being disarmed for sometime he did not give up the game. Though Meherunnisha was married off to Sher Afgan, Luthfunnisha, however, looked through Selim's soul as if in a mirror and she knew it for certain that the fate of one thousand-fold stout-hearted Sher Afgan was sealed for ever. With the death of Akbar his life would be violently cut short and Meherunnisha would perforce be made the Begum wife of Selim. Luthfunnisha gave up the idea of the throne as a thing not worth a moment's purchase. The days of Akbar, the glory of the Moghul race of emperors, were drawing to a close. The glaring sun that shed its effulgence over the sweep of the country from the Brahmaputra to Turkistan was on its decline. Luthfunnisha at this time planned a bold coup to assert her personality.

The Begum of Selim was the sister of Mansinha, the Rajput chief and Khasru was her son. One day Luthfunnisha was conversing with her on the topic of Akbar's illness and was congratulating her on her being a Badsha's wife.

'Life's highest ambition may be attained,' retorted the mother of Khasru, 'in the exalted position of a Badshah's wife but the mother of a Badsha is the highest of all.' At this the fertile mind of astute Luthfunnisha formed a daring scheme.

'Why not let it be so?' replied she, 'This, too, is under your thumb.'

'What is it?' asked the Begum.

'Have the kindness to bestow the throne on Khasru,' archly added the sly schemer.

The Begum made no reply. No further issue was raised on the same topic on the same day but none forgot about it. That the son should sit on the throne instead of the father was not after the liking of the Begum but Selim's affection towards Meherunnisha was as much gall and wormwood to Luthfunnisha as to the Begum herself. Why she, the sister of Mansinha would brook the bondage of an upstart Turkoman's daughter? Luthfunnisha had also a deep motive to be an instigator to the scheme. The same question cropped up on a different day and the two came to a decision. It could never be canvassed an impossibility to place Khasru on Akbar's throne to the exclusion of

Selim. Luthfunnisha impressed this fact on the Begum's mind.

'The Moghul empire has been won by the Rajput sword,' exhorted she, 'and Mansinha, the maternal uncle of Khasru, is the noblest of the Rajput race. Also Khan Ajim, Khasru's father-in-law, is the Prime Minister and head of the Moslems. If the two pull together on his behalf, who would not follow the suit? 'On whose support else can the prince count to seize the throne? It rests on you to make Mansinha pull his whole weight into the boat and it remains with me to bring over Khan Ajim and other Mahomedan Omrahs to our side. With your benediction I am sure to succeed but the dread is lest Khasru on his accession to the throne drives this miscreant out of the Palace.'

The Begum divined the lady-in-waiting's motive. A happy genial smile relaxed her expressions and she said, 'Any Omrah of Agra in whose household you choose to be a mistress shall accept your hand in marriage. Your husband shall be created a Manshabdar and shall command 5000 horse.'

Luthfunnisha was mightily pleased. This also was her heart's choice. If she was to be an obscure harem woman in the palace what joy was there for the flirting flapper who won't come flapping any more. If she was to buy this at the cost of shackling her liberty, then what happiness could there be in her serfdom to Meherunnisha, her friend since the time they were lasses. Rather is it a thing of greater honour to be the supreme ruler of a minister's household. So this did not hold out sufficient bait to lure Luthfunnisha into the marrying business. Besides, her ruling idea was to avenge the wrong she suffered at the hands of Selim, the more so as he overlooked her claims upon his affection and hankered so much after Meherunnisha. Khan Ajim and other Omrahs of Agra and Delhi were under great obligation to Luthfannisha. So it did not appear strange that Khan Ajim would bestir himself in the interest of his son-in-law. He and the rest of the party agreed to the proposal.

'Suppose the scheme fizzles out through any inopportuneness,' said Khan Ajim to Meherunnisha, 'then it might not offer us any chance of escape. Therefore it is meet that we should have at least some loop-holes of retreat.'

'What is your advice?' asked Luthfunnisha.

'There is no shelter other than Orissa,' said Khan Ajim, 'where the Moghal grip is not so tight. The army of Orissa should be brought under our palm anyhow. As your brother is a Manshabdar in Orissa, I shall proclaim it tomorrow that he has been wounded in a battle there. Start positively next day ostensibly to visit him and return quickly after fulfilling the mission so far you think it feasible.' Luthfunnisha consented to this proposal. The reader saw her when she was journeying back from her visit to Orissa.

2

AT THE PARTING OF WAYS

The day Moti or Luthfannisha as she was called bade farewell to Nabokumar, she started out on her journey towards Burdwan. She could not reach her destination the same day. So she stopped at a wayside inn. Towards the evening when she sat tete-a-tete with her Peshman or chambermaid she suddenly asked, 'Peshman, how did you see my husband?'

Peshman was a little taken aback at the abrupt question and replied 'What to see other than a plain man?'

'If he is not a handsome person?' interrogated Moti again.

Peshman developed a great aversion for Nabokumar. She had an eye on the ornaments Moti gave away to Nabokumar and was anxiously looking forward to the day when she would get the same on her mere asking for them. That hope was blighted now. So she came to hate both Kapalkundala and her husband. Accordingly on her mistress questioning her on the subject she retorted, 'Gainly or ungainly is all the same for a poor Brahmin.'

Moti took in the significance of the maid's observation and hilariously said, 'If the poor Brahmin blossoms into an Omrah whether he would not look all the more handsome?'

'What a new idea!'

'Why? Don't you remember the Begum's promise that my husband shall be created an Omrah when Khasru becomes the Badsha?'

'Know it I do, of course. But what earthly reason is there that your former husband shall be made an Omrah?'

'Besides, what other husband have I got?'

'I mean the prospective new husband.'

Moti jestfully added, 'It is a wicked thing for a chaste woman like me to be in possession of two husbands!—who goes there?'

Peshman happened to recognise the man, whom Moti challenged, to be a creature of Khan Ajim of Agra. Both looked flurried. Peshman called in the man who came forward, saluted Luthfunnisha and handed in a letter to her. Moreover, he said, 'I was carrying the letter to Orissa because of its urgency.'

The reading of the missive gave a death-blow to Moti's high hopes and cherished aspirations of life. The letter ran as follows:—

'Our energies are of no avail. Even on death-bed Akbar Shah defeated our ends by his art and sagacity. His soul has passed away into eternity. Under his orders Prince Selim has assumed the title of Jehangir Shah. You need not worry yourself about Khasru. Come back posthaste with a view to baffle any design of hostility towards you on the occasion.'

The way Akbar Shah broke up the conspiracy is described in history. So it is out of place to give an account here.

When the messenger was sent away with a reward, Moti read out the letter to Peshman.

'Good Heavens! Any means now?' exclaimed Peshman.

'Every thing has gone by board now.'

Peshman. (Thoughtfully) 'But what a harm can there be? You shall be as you had been. The inmate of a Badsha's harem is far more powerful than the sovereign queen of any other land.'

(With a slight laugh) 'That can never be a possibility any longer. I can not live any more in the Palace as Meherunnisha shall be married to Jehangir in a short time. I know Meherunnisha from her nursery days and once she is an inmate of the harem, Jehangir shall be a Badshah in name. It will be an open secret to her that I once stood between her and the throne. Then what will be my condition?'

Peshman was about to burst into tears.

'Alas! what should be done then?' cried out she.

'There is one hope yet—how is Meherunnisha inclined towards Jehangir?' said Moti, 'As for her singleness of purpose, if she has actually set her heart upon her husband and has no affection for Jehangir, then Jehangir despite slaying one hundred Sher Afgans must fail to secure Meherunnisha. But if Meherunnisha takes a fancy to Jehangir, then everything is given up for lost.'

'How are you to understand Meherunnisha's heart?' enquired Peshman.

'Is any feat impossible with Moti?' joined Moti with a smile. 'My friendship with Meherunnisha is as old as our childhood. I shall proceed to Burdwan tomorrow and stay with her for two days.'

'Supposing Meherunnisha does not love the Badshah, what happens then?'

'I heard my father say, "Things should be done as judged on the spot by the test of circumstances."'

Both remained silent for sometime. A thin smile curled the lips of Moti.

'What makes you laugh,' interrogated Peshman.

'Some new impulses are coming,' answered Moti.

'What new impulses?'

Moti did not speak that to Peshman. We, too, shall not speak that to the reader. This should be told later on.

3

IN HER RIVAL'S HOUSE

Sher Afgan, at this time, was working under the Subadar of Bengal as the chief functionary of Burdwan and was living in that far-off station. On reaching Burdwan, Moti went straight to Sher Afgan's quarters. Sher Afgan with the whole family warmly received her and made her lodge with them. Moti was much known to them since the time Sher Afgan and his wife resided in Agra. A jolly good friendship existed between her and Meherunnisha.

Eventually both played each other's rival in their game of high stakes for the throne of Delhi and the empire. Now when united together, Meherunnisha thought within herself, 'Who is destined to wield the first power in India? Providence knows, Selim knows and if anybody else knows it is this Luthfunnisha. Let me see if she gives me to understand a bit of her mind.' Moti, too, had a mind to gauge Meherunnisha's feelings.

Meherunnisha at that time won a celebrity as the first in beauty and talent in India. As a matter of fact, a woman of her calibre is such a rarity in this world. It is an admitted fact with every historian that she stands out pre-eminent in the historical group of celebrated beauties. Scarcely any even among contemporary men could hold his own with or excel her in either artistry or knowledge whatsoever. Meherunnisha was unsurpassed in dance and music and had the added charms of her skill in painting and verse-writing. Her wit had a greater fascination than her beauty. Moti, too, was no lesser an ability. These two witches set their wits today to know each other's minds. Meherunnisha was at her easel with paint and brush in her private appartments with Moti chewing betel, looking over Meherunnisha's shoulder and poring over the drawing.

'How do you judge the drawing?' asked Meherunnisha.

'It is what your painting always looks like,' replied Moti. 'It is a regret that no one is as much finished an artist as you are.'

'Even if it be the fact, what causes the regret?'

'If any one else could have your painting skill then the likeness of your face might have been preserved.'

'The entombing earth shall preserve the impress of my face.' Meherunnisha made this remark in a somewhat serious air.

'Sister, what makes you awfully of a bad humour today?'

'Where is the lack of humour? But how can I forget even the thought of your leaving me tomorrow morning? Why should I not have the added pleasure of your few day's extended stay?'

'Who lacks the taste for pleasure! If it be in my power, why do I leave you? But I am other's subordinate how can I stay further?'

'You have only the ashes of your former affection left for me. Otherwise you could have remained anyhow. When you have come, why can't you lengthen the stay?'

'I have had my say. My brother is a Manshabdar in the Moghul Army. He was severely wounded in an engagement with the Pathans in Orissa and his life was in jeopardy. I had heard the unwelcome news and with the Begum's permission came out on a visit to him. I delayed much in Orissa and it ill-behoves me to delay any longer. I did not see you for long so I came and spent a few days with you.'

'What is the approximate date you gave the Begum in your timetable to reach back?'

Moti understood it to be the tanut flung out by Meherunnisha. She was no match for Meherunnisha in tilting polished and pointed home thrusts. However, she did not blanch at the banter and stood her ground well.

'Is it possible to fix an exact date in a three month's return journey?' replied Moti 'I am already belated and any more delay may cause displeasure.'

'Whose displeasure you risk? Prince's or his chief Begum's!' added Meherunnisha with her world-bewitching smile.

'Why do you shame this shameless woman,' rejoined Moti with a little confusion. 'I may incur the displeasure of both.'

'But may I ask the reason why you don't publicly assume the role of the Begum? I heard that Prince Selim shall marry you and make you his beloved Begum. When does it come off?'

'I am always at other's command. Why am I to forego the little liberty I have? As a maid to the Begum I came out to Orissa but as the Begum of Selim I could never visit Orissa.'

'What urgency can there be for the prospective Begum of the Delhi Emperor to come out to Orissa?'

'I can never boast that I am in the running for the chief Begumship of the Delhi Emperor. None but Meherunnisha alone is worthy enough to be the deserving consort to the Delhi Lord in this wide land of Hindustan.'

Meherunnisha hung down her head.

'Sister, I can never persuade myself that you made the remark either to offened me or to probe my heart,' added she after a brief respite. 'But I beg of you, when you speak, never to lose sight of the fact that I am the married wife of Sher Afgan—nay, the whole-heartedly ever faithful bondslave to Sher Afgan.'

Brazen Moti took the reproof with a good grace as it rather gave her the opportunity.

'I know it for certain that you are a devoted wife,' urged Moti, 'and on that score I ventured to broach the subject before you under some pretext. My object is simply to let you know that Selim has not forgotten the glamour of your charms as yet. Beware.'

'Now the whole thing has cleared up. But what do I care?'

'Fear of widowhood,' put in Moti after a little hesitation.

With these words did Moti look hard and steady in the face of Meherunnisha but failed to detect any trace bespeaking either joy or terror.

Meherunnisha took up the cue and joined in a high tone of bold hauteur, 'Fear of widowhood! Sher Afgan is not too weak to defend himself. The more so as in the empire of Akbar the son even can not murder an innocent man with impunity.'

'Of course! But the recent despatches from Agra advise that Akbar Shah died and Selim has ascended the throne. Who now shall curb the Delhi Lord?'

Meherunnisha heard not a syllable more. Her whole frame shook and quivered. She again dropped down her head and a flood of tears streamed down from her eyes.

'What makes you weep?' enquired Moti.

Meherunnisha gave a sigh and vented her feelings, 'Selim is installed on the throne of Delhi but where am I?'

It served Moti's purpose. 'Have you not wiped off the Prince's image as yet from your heart?' added she.

Meherunnisha felt a lump coming to her throat and she groaned, 'Whom shall I forget? I can forget my ownself rather than forget the Prince. But look here, sister, you have been all at once let into the secret of my heart and you must swear on oath that you shall not breathe a syllable of it into other's ears.'

'Good. Your wishes shall be respected,' said Moti. 'But when Selim will hear that I came to Burdwan and enquire what you said about him what answer shall I make?'

Meherunnisha mused a little and then replied as an afterthought, 'Tell this that Meherunnisha shall worship him in her heart of hearts and, if needed, shall sacrifice herself in his interest. But she can never dishonour herself and shall always stand up for her rights and dignity. So long her husband is alive she will never show her face to the Lord of Delhi. Besides, if her husband is killed by the Emperor's own hand then there can never be the chance any more of her union with her husband's murderer on this side of the grave.'

After this peroration, Meherunnisha rose on her legs and left the place. Moti was electrified at this revelation. But it was she who scored the success. Moti caught Meherunnisha tripping though the latter could not have an inkling of the hopes and aspirations that surged in the mind of the former. She who by her own resourcefulness afterwards won the overlordship over the Lord of Delhi now admitted the defeat. The reason is Meherunnisha bubbled with love and affection while Moti was a self-seeking adventuress. Moti knew perfectly well the strange composition of human heart. Her conclusion on the premises supplied by Meherunnisha proved too true afterwards. She gained by the conviction that Meherunnisha bore no tinsel affection for Jehangir. So despite her bold front and fierce talk, her frigidity was sure to thaw one day when the time struck. The Emperor, if needs he, would perforce gain his objective.

Moti's hopes and disires were all blasted at this decision. But did this make her cross-grained all the more? Far from this. Rather she felt some jubilation. Whence this unnatural pleasurable feeling came Moti failed to realise first. She started out and moved along the road to Agra. Few days were spent on the journey and in these few days she understood the mood of her mind. She dimly awakened to the glimmerings of her first consciousness that she was beginning to recover her soul.

4

IN THE PALACE

Moti reached Agra. We have no more necessity of calling her Moti as the new impulse completely chastened her soul.

She was given an audience with Jehangir who as usual warmly received and questioned her on her brother's health and the comforts of her journey. What Luthfunnisha had told Meherunnisha came out true. At the name Burdwan in the midst of other topics Jehangir enquired what Meherunnisha said about him during her two day's stay with her. Luthfunnisha with an open mind gave him a true story of Meherunnisha's affection for him. Then the Emperor dropped into a sort of blissful forgetfulness and a blank pause ensued. One or two large drops of tears rolled down from his big eyes.

'Your Majesty,' broke in Luthfunnisha, 'the slave has carried you the happy tidings. Why no orders have issued till now for her reward?'

The Badshah smiled and joined, 'Dearest, your ambition is boundless.'

'Your Majesty, why this charge is laid at this slave's door?'

'The Delhi Emperor has placed his body and soul at your feet and still you press for further reward!'

'Women have many desires,' added Luthfunnisha laughingly.

'What more desire you have?'

'Let the royal orders be forthcoming first that the slave's prayer shall be granted.'

'Provided the royal duty is not hampered.'

'The Delhi Lord's work can never suffer on the score of a single poor soul.'

'Then I agree. Now let me hear the proposition.'

'I have a mind to marry.'

Jehangir burst into a salvo of laughter.

'This is a novel sort of desire,' said he. 'Has the negotiation ended in a compact anywhere?'

'Yes. Only the royal assent is wanting. No contract is valid without the royal warrant.'

'What is the use of my permission? Whom you mean to help afloat in the ocean of bliss?'

'Because the slave has served her Emperor she can never be held unchaste. The slave craves permission to marry her own husband.'

'Indeed! What would be the fate of this old slave then?'

'He shall be left to the care of Meherunnisha, the prospective mistress of Delhi.'

'Who is this Delhi mistress Meherunnisha?'

'She who is in the running.'

Jehangir thought that Luthfunnisha must have been boldly confident that Meherunnisha was the Empress elect of Delhi. As she had quite a way to go with the chance of being jockeyed out of the objects of her ambition she wished in disgust to retire from her harem life. This feeling sorely pressed down upon Jehangir's heart and he remained silent.

'Does your Majesty veto this proposal?'

'I can not withold my assent. But where is the necessity of marrying a husband?'

'Ill-starred as I am, the husband of my first marriage sought a divorce from me. Now he shall dare not forsake His Majesty's slavegirl.'

The Badshah had a jocund laugh which shortly stiffened down into a rigid expression.

'My darling, you are given a "carte blanche",' joined he. 'If you have the inclination, then follow the bend of it. But why are you to leave me for good? Do the sun and moon not shine in the same firmament? Do the twin buds never flower on the same stalk?'

Luthfunnisha focussed the full glare of her large wide eyes on the Badshah and rejoined, 'The tiny flowers may bloom but the twin lilies can never blossom on the same stem! Why am I to remain a prickly thorn at the base of your jewelled throne?'

Luthfunnisha retired into her own apartments. She did not explain to Jehangir the cause that furnished the motive power. Jehangir was satisfied with the surface view of the question as he never cared to look a little lower down than the surface. Luthfunnisha had the heart of an adamant. The fascinating graces of the royal debonair Selim failed to entrap her mind. Marble-hearted as she was, a worm now began eating into that unimpressionable heart.

5

IN HER OWN APARTMENTS

On entering her apartments, Luthfunnisha called out to Peshman who helped in undressing her. She got out of her immensely rich gold-braided garment wrought with pearls, diamonds and rubies and said to Peshman, 'Take this dress.'

Peshman wondered not a little. The dress was recently made to order at an enormous cost.

'Why this dress to me?' asked Peshman, 'What is today's report?'

'It is reassuring news, indeed!'

'This is but too evident. Are you relieved of Meherunnisha incubus?'

'Yes, now I have no more anxiety in that quarter.'

Peshman made an exhibition of great delight and said, 'Then I count a maid to the Begum.'

'If you want to be the Begum's maid then I shall speak to Meherunnisha about that.'

'Why? You say that Meherunnisha is out of the running for the Badsha's Begumship.'

'I never spoke that sort of stuff. What I said is I have no more anxiety on that head.'

'Why no more anxiety?' snarled Peshman crossly, 'Everything is thrown overboard if you fail to be the Delhi mistress.'

'I must cut off all connections with Agra.'

'Why? Alack! I am too much a goose to grasp the situation. Let me have a full significance of today's happy tidings.'

'The joyful news is that I leave Agra for good.'

'Where do you go then?'

'I shall move down and settle in Bengal. If I can, I shall marry a gentleman.'

'What a huge joke! I simply shudder at the idea.'

'I don't jest. But I am, in all earnest, quitting Agra and have said an revoir to the Badshah.'

'What an evil idea has possessed you?'

'Not an evil idea, to be sure! I sauntered through the prime of my life in Agra but what is the result? The thirst for pleasure grew into a passion with me since my childhood. To slake the thirst I left Bengal and came up here. What treasures did I not sacrifice to purchase the trash? What dark and shady tricks did I stick at? What ends I strove for were not encompassed? I had a surfeit of all these—wealth, power, glory, fame. But what did these lead to? Sitting, this day here, I can make a mental reckoning of every day as it passed out but I can make bold to say that I neither felt happy for a single day nor enjoyed unalloyed happiness for a single moment. The thirst was never quenched rather it grew and quickened. I can add to my hordes that are reckoned in millions and amass greater fortunes for the mere striving for it. But what for? If the true happiness lay in these, I could have been happy even for a day in all this long weary period! The yearning for pleasure is like a thin mountain stream. The clear slender rivulet at first issues out from the secret spring, lies hidden in its own bowels and no body knows about it. It bubbles and gurgles and no body hears it. On it courses down, the volume increases and the muddier it grows. This does not exhaust the whole story. Sometimes, again, the wind blows, lashes angry waves, and, sharks, crocodiles and other sea monsters make their home therein. Farther the size grows, the water becomes all the more muddy and it tastes brine. Myriads of desolate dreary islets spring into existence in the river channel, the movement becomes sluggish and then the body of the river with all the mud and dirt loses itself into the wide deep ocean where who can say?'

'This too passes my wit. What makes the reason that all this palls upon your senses?'

'This puzzle why I have grown up blase has been solved at last. The pleasure I experienced though for a single night on my way back from Orissa, by far and away, out-measures the giddy round of pleasures, I tasted at a three year's stretch, under the shadow of the palace. This is the key to the problem.'

'What is the explanation?'

'I looked so long like the Hindu idol. The get-up is of gold and jewel though the interior is hewn out of the hard stone. For the sake of my sense-pleasures I sported with fire though I touched not the flame. Now let me see if I can seek out a full-blooded vein in the heart of the granite.'

'This, too, is all an unintelligible jargon to me.'

'Have I ever loved any one in Agra?

(In an undertone) 'None?'

'Then what am I if not a stone?'

'If you now be pleased to bestow your heart on any one why don't you do so?'

'This, too, is in my mind. That is why I am bent upon quitting Agra.'

'What necessity is there of doing things like that? Is there none to woo in Agra that you will go down into the land of savages? Why not set your heart on the man who now loves you? What a greater lord is there on the earth than the Delhi Emperor in grace, in wealth, in power and all else besides?'

'Why does water run down the lower incline despite the sun and moon's gravitation?'

'Why?'

'It is the scroll of fate!'

Luthfunnisha did not open out her whole mind. The fire entered into the marble soul and was dissolving it into fluid.

6

DOWN AT THE FEET

When the seed is sown in the soil, it germinates of itself. As the sprout shoots up, no body cares to know and see it. But once the seed is strewn, it sends its roots into the ground and bursts into a shaft of sprout which forces its way upward independent of the human agency. Today the plant's growth is but of a few inches and no body cares to look upon it. It grows up by degrees. Gradually the shooting sprout increases and it measures half a cubit, one cubit and so on up through all scales of progressive increase. Still if it lacks any body's interest then no body casts his eyes upon it. The days roll into month and months lapse into year when it attracts men's eyes. There can no more be the talk of inattention any longer. By degrees the tree grows and its shadow destroys other trees, or, it might be, it favours the growth of weeds and tares.

Luthfunnisha's love had a similar developement. One day, all on a sudden, did she come across the man after her fancy when she had hardly the consciousness of the first birth of the tender sentiment. But the sprout burst into a rank life at that very instant. Afterwards she had no other occasion of meeting him. But in his absence, she had occasional peeps into his face from her minds' eye and enjoyed a sensuous pleasure in indulging the reminiscences which were dyed deep on her heart's tablet. The seed burst into a green sprout. The nebulous affection took colour and form. The nature of thought is to move along worn-out grooves which are the lines of least resistance until the work by its frequency develops into a habit. Luthfunnisha had always this beautiful penumbra before her mind's eye. She developed strong desires for an interview and the flow of kindred passions and inclinations grew violent pari passu. The bigger thought of the Delhi throne grew small before it. The throne appeared to have been surrounded by flames set alight by Cupid's arrows. The ideas of throne, capital and the empire were knocked on the head and she hastened down to have a look at the object of her hearts' desire. For this Luthfunnisha did not feel sick at heart at Mehernunisha's words and thoughts at which her high ambition and splendid enthusiasm went up into thin air. For this, on her return to Agra, she gave not an ounce of thought to safeguard her interests and for this she took her farewell leave of the Badshah.

Luthfunnisha reached Saptagram. She fixed her habitation in a mansion inside the town at the farthest corner from the street. All at once, the phenomenon of a splendid house thronged with troops of servants and lackeys in their brilliant uniforms of braided gold and silver burst upon the view and arrested the attention of the passersby. Every appartment had costly furniture in it. Perfumes, perfumed waters and flower vases with flowers on them scented the atmosphere. Furniture inlaid with gold, silver and ivory and other valuable odds and ends displayed the splendour and samptuousness. In such a gilded chamber amidst a blaze of colour and decoration sat Luthfunnisha with a dejected look with Nabokumar on a separate seat. In Saptagram Nabokumar had utmost one or two interviews with Luthfunnisha. How far was Luthfunnisha successful in her objective is given out in today's conversation.

'Then let me say goodbye,' said Nabokumar after a brief silence. 'Don't remember me any more.'

'Please do not go now,' joined Luthfunnisha. 'Would you, if you don't mind, wait a little longer as I have not said everything I have a mind to?'

Nabokumar waited for sometime more but Luthfunnisha did not speak a word.

'Have you anything to say?' added Nabokumar shortly after. Lutfunnisha gave no reply. She was weeping silently. On seeing her weep Nabokumar rose to his feet whereupon Luthfunnisha caught hold of the hem of his cloth. He was somewhat annoyed at this and exclaimed, 'Ah! What do you mean?'

'What do you want?' demanded Luthfunnisha. 'Have you nothing to desire in this world? I shall give you wealth, honour, love, wit, mirth and jollity and everything else that make up happiness on this earth without wishing a return for the same. What I wish is simply to be a servantmaid to you. I don't long for the glorious position of a wife but the mere situation of a housemaid.'

'I am a poor Brahmin and shall always remain a poor Brahmin,' protested Nabokumar with vehemence. 'I shall never stand the ugly name of a Javan woman's favourite by accepting the gift of your proferred wealth and property.'

A Javan woman's secret lover! Nabokumar did not know yet that the woman was his married wife. Luthfunnisha sank down crestfallen when Nabokumar extricated the cloth end from her grasp.

Luthfunnisha again clutched the hem of his cloth and said, 'Well, let that pass. If it so ordained, I shall tear out my heart-strings and fling them into fire. I don't crave anything more than that you would fain pass this way at odd intervals, look up as towards a house-maid, and my eyes shall be feasted on the sight.'

'You are a Javan woman—a second man's wife and a guilt shall be fastened upon me by such an intimacy with you. This is the last of such meetings between you and me.'

A brief silence ensued. A tempest was raging in Lutfunnisha's heart. She sat motionless like a statue carved in marble. She let go the cloth end of Nabokumar and said, 'Walk out.'

Nabokumar walked forward and had advanced three or four steps when, all on a sudden, Luthfunnisha like a tree blown off by a tornado threw herself at Nabokumars' feet. She clasped the feet with both her hands and piteously cried out, 'Stone-hearted, I renounced the throne of Agra for your sake. You must not leave me.'

'Go back to Agra again and give up the hope on me,' said Nabokumar emphatically.

'Not in this life.'

Luthfunnisha stood up straight like a bolt and haughtily said, 'I will never abandon your hope in this life.' Drawing up to her full height, she slightly bent her swan neck and fixing the big steadfast eyes on Nabokumar's face threw herself in the right royal style. That fire of inflexible hauteur that grew less under the soft mellowed warmth of her heart's flame again flared up—that invincible iron will that daunted not at the attempt at grasping the sceptre of the Empire of Hindustan—that indomitable energy again quickened up the feeble framework of her love-smitten soul. The nerves swelled out on her forehead and drew out a fine tracery. The bright eyes shone like the glassy sea lighted up by a brilliant sun. The nostrils dilated and throbbed. As the goose sporting along the current straightens up its neck and throws out its head threatening men and things blocking its way—as the down-trodden serpent stands erect spreading out its hood—so this furious Javan woman proudly stood up towering her head in an imperious air.

'Not in this life—you shall be made mine,' exclaimed she in her rich ringing voice.

Nabokumar was terror-stricken at gazing upon this angry serpent-like form. The glory of Luthfunnisha's charm that spread out now had never before been eyed by Nabokumar. That beauty had the fatal fascination of the deadly lightening flash. It struck a chill into his heart. Nabokumar was about to walk out when the vision of a similar picture of haughty pose darted across his mind. Nabokumar, one day, being offended at the conduct of Padmabati, his first wife, tried to force out her ejection from the bedchamber. The twelve year girl similarly wheeled round facing him with a bold look of defiance, similarly her eyes burnt, similarly her nostrils expanded and vibrated and similarly her head leaned back in a fine throw. That figure was a past memory. It now flashed in upon his mind and the parity at once struck him. Nabokumar had the shadow of a suspicion and he in a hesitatingly soft voice enquired, 'Who are you?'

The eye-balls of the Javan woman expanded to a greater extent and she replied 'I am Padmabati.'

Without waiting for the answer, Luthfunnisha hurried away from the scene. Nabokumar, too, being a bit frightened, wended his way home, his brain busy with thoughts.

7

ON THE OUTSKIRT OF THE CITY

Luthfunnisha entered another chamber and closed the door. For full two days she cloistered herself inside the room. In these two days she determined the course she would follow. She arrived at a conclusion and set her mind upon it. The sun went low. Luthfunnisha began preparing her toilet with Peshman's help. It was a strange toilet as it had no evidence of a female make-up. She looked up the dress in the mirror and asked, 'How now, Peshman? Do you recognise me?'

'Impossible.'

'Let me start then. See neither man nor maid follows me.'

Peshman timorously added, 'If you pardon your slave, then she may ask one thing.'

'What?'

'What is your object?'

'Final separation between Kapalkundala and her husband for the present. He shall be made mine afterwards.'

'Would your ladyship just think over the project in its every possible light? The dense jungle—the approaching night—and your lonely position?'

But, without a word whatsoever, Luthfunnisha tripped forth silently. She directed her steps towards the lonely wooded outskirt of Saptagram wherein Nabokumar lived. Night had come ere she reached the place. The reader may have some recollection of the thicket which lay at a short distance from Nabokumar's dwelling place. When she gained the skirt of the forest-belt, she sat herself down beneath a tree. She sat on there for a considerable length of time, meditating the adventure She was embarking upon. Chance, however, brought her some fortuitous help.

Luthfunnisha could hear from her seat under the tree a dull continuous murmur that was maintained in its uniform key and seemed to issue from human throat. She started to her feet, looked about and saw shafts of light that cut the darkness of the wood. Luthfunnisha could outmatch a man in boldness so she guided her legs towards the place where the light burnt. First she reconnoitered the ground from behind the tree and observed that the light that shone was but the flame of the sacrificial fire and the voice she heard was the sound of incantation. She distinguished a sound in the midst of chants which she deciphered to be a name. At the mention of the name Luthfunnisha approached the man who was feeding the sacrificial fire and seated herself in proximity to him.

Let her be seated there for the present. But as the reader has not heard of Kapalkundala for a long time, we must needs enquire her 'goings on.'

Part IV

1

IN BEDCHAMBER

It took Luthfunnisha almost a year to complete her return journey to Agra and thence to move down to Saptagram where Kapalkundala lived over a year as Nabokumar's wife. The same evening, when Luthfunnisha was out on her excursion amidst the wood, Kapalkundala sat in her bedroom in an abstracted mood of mind. She was not the self-same Kapalkundala whom the reader saw on the sea beach, unadorned, with her loose curls flowing down her waist. The prophecy of Shyamasundari has materialised and the hermit girl with the touch of the philosopher's stone has bloomed into a full-fledged housewife.

Now the mass of her raven-dark hair that once hung out in heavy serpent-like coils, sweeping down her waistline, has been gathered up and twisted in a massive knot that perched high on the back of her head. The braiding of locks even was worked up into an elaborate artwork and the fine skilled designs and figures displayed in the pleating spoke highly of Shyamasundari's finished style of hairdressing. Every detail was faithfully attended to. Even the chaplet of flowers that encircled, like a coronet, the base of her braided coil, was not lost sight of. The unbraided locks of loose hair maintained not a uniform level of height on the crown of her head because of their crispness. So these ringlets showed themselves in small dark waves on the surface. The face is no longer half-concealed amidst her thick folds of hair. Rather it shone out bright and radiant. Only at places, the loosened stray locks caked on to parts bedewed with moisture. The skin displayed the same colour—the silver grey of a half moon. Now gold ear-rings suspended from her ears and a gold necklace hung round her neck. The brightness of the gold rather than paling before the lustre of the skin gained in effect like the night flowers adding to the charms of the sweet earth bathed in a flood of the weird mellow light of a quarter moon. The figure was draped in a piece of white cloth which appeared a milky cloud sailing in the silvery sky flooded with the splendours of a glorious moon. The skin showed the same gleam of moonshine though it looked to have acquired a darker tinge than before like a speck of black cloud gathering in some distant corner of the far off horizon. Kapalkundala was not seated alone, having Shyamasundari by her side. We shall narrate a portion of the conversation passing between them to our reader.

'How long will the brother-in-law stay here?' enquired Kapalkundala.

'He leaves tomorrow evening,' replied Shyamasundari. 'Alas! If I could but root up the medicinal plant tonight, I would have scored a success over him in taming him into submission. But what indignities did I not suffer because of my last night's escapade! So how can I go out this night also?'

'Does it not yield the same effect, if pulled out, at daytime?'

'How can it be of the same virtue if uprooted during daylight hours? It must be taken out just at midnight, in loose hair, if it is to have any efficacy at all. Well, sister, that cherished hope of my heart shall never have its realisation.'

'Right. I have myself seen the plant at daytime, today, and have, besides, seen the jungle it grows in. You must needs make no stirring tonight. I alone would bring you the plant.'

'Our mind is not a clean slate, so we must take stock of our experience. What has happened one day may not happen over again. You must not go out at night time anymore.'

'You have no reason to have any anxiety on that score. You might have heard that night walk grew up into a habit with me since my childhood and you must bear in mind that, if it had not been the case, I would never have come into your midst, and these eyes could not have shone upon you.'

'It is due to no fear that I say that. Does it behove a house-hold maid or wife to wander in wood and forest at night time? When we received that sharp rebuke despite our combined moves the other day, think, what it would come to, if you venture out alone at night?'

'What harm is there? Do you imagine I would count a lost character for my mere night outing?'

'I never think that way. But bad people may badly speak of you.'

'Let them say as they like. The taint shall never touch me.'

'We can't pass things to drift that way, as any ill-talk about you, will cut us to the quick.'

'Let not yourselves be so touchy.'

'I can stand even that much. But why should you make my brother unhappy?'

Kapalkundala cast a significant glance of her big bright eyes towards Shyamasundari and said, 'If it destroys his peace of mind, then there is no help for it. If I could but know that wedlock is a serfdom, I would never have suffered myself to be led to the marriage altar then!'

What followed then grew distasteful to Shyamasundari. So she left the place and went about her own work. Kapalkundala, as well, busied herself in doing the daily round of her household duties. Having finished her day's-work, she left the house in quest of the drug. The first watch of the night passed away. It was moonlight then. Nabokumar was seated in a room in the front wing of his house, so he could clearly see, through the window bars, Kapalkundala steal away from it. No sooner he saw this than he went out and, going forward at quick step, grasped her by her arm. Mrinmoyee turned back and questioned, 'What is the matter?'

'Where are you going?' asked Nabokumar. He had not the slightest ring of reproof in his voice.

'Shyamasundari wants to charm her husband,' replied Kapalkundala 'so I am going to search the drug.'

'Good,' added Nabokumar in his former silky voice. 'You had already been out overnight. What is the use of going over again tonight?'

'I could not find it out last night. So I would essay my second try this time.'

'Very well,' said Nabokumar in his blandest tone 'You might as well conduct the search at daytime.' His voice was full of pathos.

'The day-light finding won't give the desired effect,' rejoined Kapalkundala.

'What necessity is there for your drug-searching? Just tell me the name of the plant and I shall bring you the thing.'

'I know the plant but do not know the name. Besides, if you root it up, it won't serve the purpose. It is for women to pull it out in loose hair. So you should not put a spoke into other's wheel.' Kapalkundala had a tone of displeasure in her words.

Nabokumar made no further objection and added 'Move on. I shall accompany you.'

Kapalkundala with a touch of swagger replied 'Come and see with your own eyes if I hold not the plighted troth.'

Nabokumar could not speak a word more. With a sigh he dropped down Kapalkundala's hand and got back home. Kapalkundala alone went on her way and entered the wood.

2

IN THE WOOD

A little mention has been made before of the wooded character of this side of Saptagram. A thick forest lay at a short distance from the village. Kapalkundala wended along a narrow sylvan alley to hunt out the drug. The night was sweet and cool and an unearthly stillness hung in the air. In the vernal nightsky was the cold shining moon cleaving her way silently athwart the fleecy clouds. The forest trees and creepers were shimmering noiselessly in the cold moonlight on the earth below. Smoothly did tree leaves reflect the moonbeam and softly did milk-white flowers put forth their blossoms inside the shrubs and foliage. The whole countryside was bathed in a gracious peace. The atmospheric closeness was hardly punctuated with the occasional wing-flutter of birds disturbed in their night-roosts—with the crackle of a dead leaf falling down on the earth—with the whish of the serpent kind crawling amidst dry leaves lying about underneath—and with the faint barking of some night dogs at a far-off distance. It was not that no wind was blowing—it was the soft, refreshing, rippling breath of the spring. It was as much soft and silent as shook the top-leaves of trees, tossed the green verdure and foliage bowing down to the earth, and drifted the broken vapoury clouds scudding along the deep blue nightsky. The soft touch of that gentle sigh of wind was only awakening in one's mind the reminiscences of the past happiness experienced with such an association.

The remembrance of Kapalkundala slowly and gradually flew back to her jolly good old days and was reviving the past with all its realism. She remembered the surf-touched cool sea breeze that playfully shook her dishevelled hair on the sand dunes of the Bahari. She gazed into the unrelenting blue of the sky and recollection brought back to her mind the cameo-cut impressions of the boundless stretch of the sea resembling the vast deep azure of the sky overhead. With a heart heavy with such reflections did Kapalkundala walk onward.

In her distracted mood of mind she never gave a thought either to the object of her mind or the scene of her action. The track she was following proved gradually impassable. The forest grew denser and the moonbeam was almost entirely intercepted by the thickly interlaced branches and leaves making an archway above until by degrees the narrow pathway was blotted out from her eyes. Through the uncertainty of the forest path, Kapalkundala awoke from her deep reverie and the real conception of the truth was burnt into her soul. She cast up her eyes on all sides and saw a light burning in the distant reaches of that thicket. Luthfunnisha, too, had similarly observed this glow of light before. Kapalkundala, as a result of her past habits, was always bold and on the tip toe of curiosity on such occasions. So she slowly headed towards the glimmering light. No body could be found there where the fire was glowing. But at a few yard's distance stood a dilapidated house which was invisible from a distance on account of the forest shadows.

The house, though brick-built, was very mean and ordinary, and consisted of one room only. The sound of hushed human voices was heard issuing from it. Kapalkundala with cat-like paces approached the outer wall and, no sooner she gained it, than it appeared two men were conversing in whisper. At first she could not make out any meaning from the indistinct words but, afterwards, her repeated efforts set an edge on her hearing and she read the following conversation.

'Death is my objective,' said one voice. 'But in case, you don't agree, I can't bring myself to help you. I also don't want any assistance from you in the fulfilment of my design.'

'I, too, never count a wellwisher,' replied the other voice. 'But I wish her rather to be sacked and packed off, for good, to some distant place than to be myself an abettor in her murder. On the other hand, I shall oppose the act.'

'Thou art foolish and insensate,' joined the first voice, 'so I must impart some wisdom to you. Now give me your undivided attention as I shall unfold some deep-hidden secret. Meanwhile, go out and have a searching glance, all around, as I seem to hear human respiration.'

As a matter of fact, Kapalkundala stood almost in touch with the house wall, posing her fine head intently to catch the faint sound inside and breathed deep and hard like a tiny pair of bellows out of white-hot eagerness and terror.

At the companion's behest, one of the plotters came out and at once perceived Kapalkundala who also distinctly saw the person's contour and lineaments in the clear moonlight in the glade. Hardly could she make out whether her spirit lifted or fell at the sight. She found the stranger in Brahmin-garb—in dhoti—and the exterior well-covered under a muslin. The Brahmin looked of tender age with the down of youth hardly visible on the upper lip. The face was exceedingly beautiful—as beautiful as that of a woman—but unlike women it was full of glowing spirit and pride. The hair, quite unusual with men showed no sign of a razor's touch and being unclipped, as with women, crowded upon the muslin and bespread the back, the shoulder, the arm and, least of all, the bosom. The forehead was broad and high, though a bit swollen with a solitary vein showing out in the middle—the eyes full of brilliance as of lightning flashes—and a long drawn sword in the hand. But amidst all this colouring, gleamed a spectre of frightfulness, as if, a black gaunt shadow of a dark, sinister design lent its pigment to the lustrous gold of the skin. The glance, keen as a knife blade, cut into Kapalkundala's heart. Both stared on at each other's face for sometime. Kapalkundala was the first to flutter her eyelids and, with the first flutter, the stranger asked, 'Who are you?'

If a year ago, the same question would have been put to Kapalkundala in the forest of Hijli, then her response would have been quick and pertinent. But she now partook of the character of a gentle-born housewife. So she could not make any immediate rejoinder.

The Brahmin-looking person seeing Kapalkundala demur added in a grave tone, 'Kapalkundala, what has brought you to this deep part of the forest in this dead of night?'

She was in wild stupefaction to hear her name on the lips of an unknown night-walker and looked a bit scared. So no instantaneous reply issued from her lips.

'Have you heard the conversation passing between us?' querried the Brahmin-attired person again.

All on a sudden did Kapalkundaia regain her lost speech.

'I, too, am asking you the same question,' said she without answering the querry. 'What a dark plot were you two hatching at this depth of night in this depth of forest?'

The man with the Brahmin's appearance remained mute and silent, for a short while, his mind lost in thoughts. Suddenly, a new scheme seemed to evolve itself in his mind congenial to his purpose. He advanced and grasped Kapalkundala's arm and under his firm grip led off her to a place, a little removed from the dilapidated house. But Kapalkundala, indignantly, tore herself away from his clutch when the Brahmin-guised man brought his mouth near Kapalkundala's ear and spoke in a soft undertone 'Have no fear. I am not a man.'

Kapalkundala was all the more startled at this. She partly believed the words though the words could not carry their full weight with her. She followed the person in Brahmin's habit and when the two reached a spot from where the house was lost to sight, the latter whispered into the former's ear, 'Do you want to hear what a yarn we were spinning? It concerned you only.'

This whetted Kapalkundala's eagerness and she said, 'Yes.'

'Wait here till I return,' joined the other.

Then the sham Brahmin retraced his steps towards the ruined house while Kapalkundala was left seated there alone. But what she saw and heard excited some fear within her. While seated alone. in the dark deep forest, her anxiety waxed intensified. Because, who could divine the motive why the false man left her seated there alone? Might be, she was kept there waiting to give the masqueraded Brahmin the facility for the execution of his dark sinister design! On the other hand the disguised Brahmin was overdue to re-enter his appearance. So Kapalkundala could hot wait any longer. She rose to her feet and quickened her steps to get back home.

At that time black rolling clouds gathered in the horizon. The lowering sky took on a leaden hue that drew its drab lines across everything. The insufficient light that struggled into the wood through the interstices of luxuriant foliage grew smaller and it could scarcely direct Kapalkundala on to the track. So she could not tarry a moment longer. She went her way back in hurried steps in order to issue out of the forest. While on the retreat, she thought she heard a second man's footfalls behind. But on looking back, her eyes could not peer through the thick cloak of gathering gloom. She believed the Brahmin-garbed person to have been dogging her steps. So she left the forest belt and re-entered the previously spoken woodpath. The place was less dark here and so a man happening to be in the line of vision was sure to be discerned. But so far nothing was visible. Accordingly she acclerated her speed. But again the shadowing footsteps distinctly struck her ear. The sky was thickly overcast and the dark grey thunder clouds looked all the more threatening. Kapalkundala threw in an extra ounce of energy into her gait. Before the gleam of the house-top sticking across the ground met her eyes, the storm burst with the savage snarl of a tornado and rain began in torrents. Kapalkundala dashed forward. She guessed from the footsteps behind that the other man also ran. The thunderstorm had pursued its mad career over her head, before she reached the doorstep. Thunder clapped and the air vibrated with the crash of terrific electric discharges. The sky opened sheets of flame that played in zigzag way and the rain continued its pourings. Saving her skin anyhow, Kapalkundala regained her homestead. She bounded across the yard and lightly jumped on to the house terrace. The door of the room stood ajar, so she burst inside. No sooner she wheeled her back, facing the inner yard, to close the door, than it appeared she saw a big burly man standing at the centre of the quadrangle. At this moment, the lightning flashed once for all and under the solitary gleam of that light she recognised the man. The man was no other than the former Kapalik who dwelt upon the lonely sea shore.

3

IN DREAM

Slowly and silently Kapalkundala closed the door—slowly and silently she crept into the bedroom—and slowly and noiselessly she laid herself down on the bedstead. Man's mind is like a boundless ocean. What man is there who can count the tumbling, rollicking waves that are whipped into fury by the storm and wind raging across its breast? Who could reckon, then, the endless waves that tossed and swelled on the storm-swept ocean-like mind of Kapalkundala?

Nabokumar did not come into the inner appartments that night through heart-sickness. So Kapalkundala lay alone in her bedroom though sleep did never visit her eyes. She seemed to see around her, in the midst of darkness, that terrible face, surmounted by a crown of matted locks tossed up by the high wind and drenched in the rain that dribbled from it. Her mind retrospected the past events, chapter by chapter, as they happened, and dangled before her vision, the slovenly treatment she accorded to the Kapalik on the eve of her departure—the fiendish acts he used to perpetrate in the sea-side wilderness—his Bhairobi worship—and Nabokumar's bondage—and she gave an involuntary start. Her thoughts flew backward again across space and time and recalled the same night's incidents—Shyama's feverishness for the drug—Nabokumar's warning—Kapalkundala's admonition—the weird moon-light beauty in the shaded glade—the gathering gloom under the forest trees—the chance companion in the forest purview—and the strange commingling of a shapely form with the leering spectre of horridness in him.

When the first glitter of the radiant dawn emblazoned the eastern sky, did Kapalkundala fall into a light sleep and in that short light sleep she saw dreams. It appeared she was out in a pleasure boat on a joy row across the bosom of the previously seen ocean. The boat was gaily dressed with bunting, and pennons of gold and yellow flew from the peak, bow and port. The oarsmen rowed merrily with flower garlands festooned round their necks and sang jolly tunes of the amorous ditties of Radha Shyam. The sun was raining down liquid gold from the western sky and under the sunny shower of that golden cascade the sea smiled and gaily rippled by. Clouds scudded along the sky steeped and refreshed in the riotous profusion of the sparkling light and colour. In the midst of such simpering mirth and rollicking jollity, the sun suddenly went out and night came up. Dark blue clouds mantled the sky and everything was kicked up into confusion. The crew turned the head of the boat though they knew not which way to steer her as the compass lost its bearings. They stopped singing and tore through the flower garlands. Flags of yellow and gold were rent through and the flagstaff crashed overboard. Wind rose, mountain-high waves leapt into fury, and out of this tumult of elements, a bulky man of matted locks came forward and, seizing one side of Kapalkundala's boat, was about to hurl her into the mid-ocean. At this psychological moment, the same person of graceful mien tinged with a grim humour depicted on every line of the face and dressed. in a Brahmin's guise appeared on the scene and held fast the boat.

'Whether I shall rescue or drown you?' asked he.

'Drown me,' issued from the lips of Kapalkundala.

The seeming Brahmin gave a shove to the boat and the boat got her voice and spoke, 'I can't carry this load any further. Let me go deep down into the bowels of the earth.'

With these words, the boat flung away Kapalkundala into water and went down into the pit far into the earth below.

Dripping in perspiration, Kapalkundala startled out of her dream and rubbed her eyes. It was dawn and the window stood wide open. Puffs of balmy, soft spring breeze came stealing into the room through the window bars. Wild birds of the wood were singing their joyous carols amidst tree branches rocked by the wind. Sundry lovely wood trailers laden with sweet-scented flowers traced a natural trellies-work around the window casement and were gently gesticulating before it. Kapalkundala, through her tender womanly nature was engaged in arranging the blossoms in a bunch and patting the blooms in places when lo! a missive came out from their midst. Kapalkundala was brought up under Adhicary's tutelage and so she learned to read. She read the contents as follows:-

'Please see the last night's Brahmin boy, after evening, tonight. You shall hear important things which you want to.'

One in Brahmin's disguise.

4

AT THE TRYST

The same day until sundown, was Kapalkundala taken up, in thinking out the reasonableness of her meeting with the masqueraded Brahmin. She never paused over the profaneness of the thought for a faithful wife to visit, at night time, a strange man which goes, always, without a social warrant. The basic idea of her mind was that so long there is the purity of purpose such an action can never be judged impious. The social claim of intercourse exclusively between men or women is as much a legitimate natural right as between men and women specially when the Brahmin-dressed youth is of uncertain description. So her qualms were set at rest. But whether such a meeting would produce beneficial or baneful results gave an uncertain outlook to the whole affair that made her indecisive. First, the Brahmin-like boy's conversation, then the Kapalik's appearance and, lastly, the dream—all these conjoined to confirm her suspicion that she might have some smack of the danger that cast its shadows before. The flutter of a suspicion as to the existence of a connecting link between the advent of the Kapalik and some sort of evil-doing looked to have some substratum of truth. The young boy of a seeming Brahmin appeared to be the Kapalik's associate and the adventure of an interview might have all the risk of ensnaring her into a trap deeply laid in the plot. Did not the disguised Brahmin clearly tell her, the other day, that the conspiracy was set on foot against her alone? Besides, it can be suggestive of the beginning of the end. The man with whom the Brahmin-looking boy was in secret conversation appeared to have been the Kapalik. This is the sure indication that they were plotting either somebody's murder transportation. Whose it might be? When she was the subject of all these secret plottings and machinations, then her death or transportation was certainly being contemplated. Come what may! Then the dream!—but what is the significance of it? In vision she saw the Brahmin-guised boy rush forward to save her in the supreme moment of crisis and the dream now looks to have all the appearance of a reality.

'Drown me' said she in dream to the masqueraded Brahmin. Is she to re-iterate the same in actuality? Oh, no! the votary-loving Bhowani graciously sent instructions for her preservation and the Brahmin-garbed youth volunteered to her rescue. Now, in case of refusing the help, she is sure to be drowned. Therefore Kapalkundala made it a point to see the young man. It is under doubt whether a sane man would have similarly concluded. But we have nothing to do with sane conclusions. Kapalkundala had no wisdom of a wise woman and so she had not a wise woman's counsel all to herself. She came by her conclusion like a young woman eager after the curious—like a girl bewitched by a finely moulded form with a dark sinister air hanging about him—like a Sannyasi-trained girl used to rove gaily amidst wild landscapes at night—like a holy woman actuated under deep reverential feelings towards Bhowani—and like an insect on the eve of its headlong plunge into the shooting flame of a burning fire. Kapalkundala finished her household work and set out towards the forest after nightfall. She had stirred the lamp flame before she went out and the lamp burnt all the brighter. Scarcely she left the room when the light went out. She had forgot one thing before she started on her parlous errand. What could be the place the imposter of a Brahmin fixed as the meeting ground in the letter? So she came back and searched the place high and low where she put the letter. But, alas! no letter could be found there. It occured to her that in order to keep it on her person she had tucked it up in her pleated hair. Accordingly, she ran her finger nails in and around her braided knot. When her finger tips did not come across it, she unloosened her hair. However, the letter remained untraced as before. Then she rummaged every part of the house but still it could not be found. At last, when she lost every trace of it, she thought she might see him where they had met before. Due to the lack of spare moments, she could not arrange the mass of her hair. Thus, she went forth, as with her unmarried days before, her figure within her rich glorious hair that hung down, all around, in wavy curls about her.

5

ON THE DOORSTEP

When towards evening, Kapalkundala was engaged in doing her round of household duties, the letter, loosening from its hold in the braided hair, fell on to the ground. Anyhow she was unaware of the incident. But Nabokumar saw the letter slipping down to the floor from her hair which set him wondering: When Kapalkundala was called away by some other work, he picked up the missive and read over it. The reading suggested the same conclusion 'You will hear of things you, yesterday, wanted to.' What is it? Is it a love affair? Is the Brahmin-looking person, the secret lover of Mrinmoyee? The story pointed to a single moral to the man who never knew overnight's occurrence.

As when a devoted wife in practising the Suttee, or, for some other reasons, mounts her funeral pyre and sets fire to it with her own hands, then, first, the rolling volume of smoke makes a curtain all around, puts out the sight and blots out everything. Then, by degrees, the fire-logs begin to burn and crackle, the sharp tongues of flame begin to loll out from underneath and lick the body at places, and, afterwards, when the fire bursts with a terrific roar into a huge ring of flame, it envelopes the quick body and all else besides. Lastly, the leaping flames soar heavenward, enliven the horizon and reduce all and sundries to ashes.

Nabokumar had a similar taste of sensation when he finished the letter. First, he could not clearly define it, but, next moment, dark suspicion which always flutters like an owl in twilight, crossed his mind, and, finally. the dim outlines took shape and form of the burning truth which left a stinging smart behind. Men's minds are so moulded that they are unable to bear extremes of pleasure and pain. First, the dense smoke and fume sorrounded Nabokumar, then, the fire set his soul alight and, lastly, the flame burnt out his heart-string. He had already marked Kapalkundala's rebelliousness in many respects. Besides, inspite of all his warnings, she always went out alone of her own free will and choice and deported irresponsibly with each and everybody. Moreover, she never cared to mind his words and would rather move about, unattended, in his nightly wanderings amidst forest and wilderness. Other people might have their suspicions, but, Nabokumar, apprehending, that once the green-eyed jealousy is aroused, its torment will be as much a hellish fire as the never-quenching stinging bite of a scorpion, never harboured any distrust about the good conduct of Kapalkundala for a single day. He would never have entertained such a feeling even this day. But these were no mere doubts any longer that crystalised in unchallenged hard facts. He sat mute and alone for sometime and wept hot tears of sorrow. The free vent of tears brought him some relief and, then, he settled his line of action. He determined in his mind that he would throw up no hints to Kapalkundala, but would, rather, follow her, when in the evening, she would go out into the forest, see with his own eyes her sinful enactments and then, at last, violently cut short his own miserable existence. He would kill his ownself rather than communicating anything to Kapalkundala. What other alternative was left open to him? He was unable to muster sufficient strength to bear the fardels of humanity any longer.

Having thus made up his mind, he fixed his eyes upon the back exit of the house on the lookout for Kapalkundala's outing. Kapalkundala, as usual, went out and after she had traversed some distance, Nabokumar also left the house and followed her. But she was seen retracing her steps again to have a look at the previously spoken lost letter whereupon Nabokumar gave her a slip. Afterwards, when Kapalkundala walked out of the house for the last time and crossed over some ground forward, did Nabokumar issue out of the back door to do his shadowing work. Just at this moment, the outline of a big bulky man was thrown up against the doorway darkening the threshold. What that man might be and what business had he to let fall his shadow across the doorstep, Nabokumar had no mind to enquire, least of all, he scarcely bestowed even a look upon him. All he bustled about was to follow Kapalkundala with his eyes. So he gave the big man a big push in his breast in order to clear his way though the big push could scarcely shove him an inch.

'What are you? Get you gone. Make room for me,' burst from

Nabokumar's lips.

'Who am I?' exclaimed the stranger, 'Don't you know me?'

The deep bass voice had the resonance of the sea. Nabokumar looked up and saw him, his former acquaintance, the Kapalik, with a crown of matted locks trailing down on all sides. Nabokumar was startled but not frightened.

A ray of hope darted across Nabokumar's face and he, immediately, asked, 'Is Kapalkundala going out to see you?'

'Oh! No,' answered the Kapalik.

The last ray of hope had departed before it gleamed and dark shadows flitted across Nabokumar's face.

'Don't cross my path anymore,' uttered Nabokumar.

'I will let you pass,' said the Kapalik, 'but you must hear me, first, what I shall speak to you.'

'Words I have none with you,' cried out Nabokumar. 'Do you hover after me to take my life again? Slay me this time and I shall not any more thwart you. Now, wait here till I come back. Why did I not give up my mortal flesh to appease gods? As I have sowed so I reap now. She who preserved the sacred flame of my life is extinguishing it now. Kapalik, you must not distrust me any longer. No sooner I got back than I will surrender my body to you.'

'I have looked in here,' said the Kapalik, 'not for your annihilation as this is never the will of Bhowani. I have called at this quarter to settle some old accounts which must needs have your approval. Lead me into the house, first, and listen what I say to you.

'Not now,' joined Nabokumar. 'I shall lend you my ears afterwards. Wait here for the present and let me come back after despatch of some urgent work.'

'My son, I know everything. You are going to follow that miscreant. I know perfectly well where she will go. I will take you with me there and show you over the place. Now hear what I say and take no fright on any account.'

'I have no longer any fear from you. Come along.'

Then, Nabokumar took the Kapalik inside his house and gave him a small mat to sit upon. Having seated, himself near him, he said, 'Just begin.'

6

IN CONVERSATION

Having taken his seat, the Kapalik showed Nabokumar his two hands which were broken.

The reader may remember that the same night when Nabokumar fled from the sea shore in company of Kapalkundala, the Kapalik, in hunting down the couple, fell from the crest of a sand hill. In course of his fall to the earth, he tried to save his body by clutching the ground with his two hands. Thus he saved his body but could not save his arms which were fractured. He narrated the whole story to Nabokumar in detail and then said, 'I feel not much difficulty in going through my daily necessary work though I possess no strength in them. They are of no service to me, even, in collecting dry sticks of wood.'

Afterwards, he said, 'At the moment, I fell to the earth, I could not feel that my hands were fractured though the body was uninjured, as I swooned away at the time. First I lay in a perfect comatose state which was later on broken by half-conscious states. I have no clear recollection how long I lay in this condition but at its rough guess it might be estimated at two nights and one day. It was in the morning that I came to. Exactly before this, I had a dream. 'As if Bhowani'—and at this stage a shudder passed through his framework—'as if Bhowani appeared in flesh and form before me and browbeat and chide me. She then said 'Wretch, you hindered the true and right form of my worship through the uncleanliness of your soul. You did not so long worship me with this maid's blood owing to your ulterior evil purpose. So through this girl, the merits of your previous good acts will be destroyed. I shall never more accept any offerings from you.

'Then I sobbed aloud and rolled at the feet of the Mother who was then pleased to say, "Gentleborn, I prescribe the only means of atonement for you. I want you to sacrifice that Kapalkundala before me. Worship me not till you have fulfilled your mission."

'It is unnecessary to narrate here, how and when I recovered. But, no sooner had I become a convalescent than I set about to carry out the orders of Bhowani. Then, I found that I had not a baby's strength left in my arms and that my labours can never fructify with a pair of powerless hands. So I must needs have a helpmate. But the work of religious merits is not the forte of the average people, now-a-days, the more so, in this iron age, when men do not make it their worth while to come of any service to the working out of a noble mission for fear of punishment as their acts are calculated to be judged prejudicially by the biased minds of authorities. After a prolonged search, I have discovered this wretch's habitation. But due to no strength in my arms, I could not fulfil the words of Bhowani. I am in the habit of performing my rites according to Tantrick rules in order to attain my ends. Last night, when I kept alight the sacrificial fire, I saw with my own eyes Kapalkundala, with love warm upon her, in flirtation with a young Brahmin. This evening, too, is she going out to see him. If you have a mind to look on at the scene, you can come off with me and I will show you over the place. My son, Kapalkundala is worth sacrificing. I will slay her in obedience to Bhowani's call. She has, besides, proved faithless to you, so she is punishable with death before your eyes. Give me the necessary help by seizing this miscreant and conducting her to the sacrificial ground. Slay her, therefore, with your own hand and this will wash the sin you committed before God and men. By this, you will earn religious merits of a far-reaching character—the girl accused of her marriage infidelity shall meet with her condign punishment—and, lastly, it will furnish a fitting denouement to a work of noble revenge.'

The Kapalik finished his speech but Nabokumar made no reply. The Kapalik watched this muteness in Nabokumar and urged 'My son, do you wish to see, now, what I promised to show you over?'

Reeking in perspiration, Nabokumar followed the Kapalik.

7

GREETING WITH CO-WIFE

Kapalkundala, coming out of the house, entered the wood. First, she went inside the ruined house where she had met the Brahmin boy. If it would have been daylight, she could have seen the pallor on his face. The made-up Brahmin said faintly to Kapalkundala, 'As the Kapalik might turn up here, we should not have any talk at this place. So, let us go somewhere else.'

Amidst the greenery, was some clean space with trees on all sides and a track issuing out of it. The youth in Brahmin's attire took Kapalkundala there and, both having seated, said, 'Let me open my own story first. This will enable you to judge how far my words are faithfully correct. When, in company of your husband, you were coming from the Hijli side, you met with a Javan woman on the way. Do you remember that?'

Kapalkundala—'She who gave me ornaments?'

'Yes, I am she.'

Kapalkundala was much astonished. Luthfunnisha marked her astonishment and said, 'There is reason of a greater wonder—I am your husband's co-wife.' Kapalkundala was lost in wonder and cried 'How is it?'

Luthfunnisha, then, recounted the full chapter of her past career, incident by incident. She spoke everything—marriage—ostracism—divorce by husband—Dacca—Agra—Jehangir—Meherunnisha—quitting of Agra—living in Saptagram—meeting with Nabokumar—Nabokumar's treatment—last night's incognito visit to the wood—and chance acquaintance with the sacrificial Brahmin. Now Kapalkundala asked, 'With what object did you wish to visit our house?'

'To separate you from your husband.'

Kapalkundala fell into a thoughtful air and enquired, 'How could you gain your end?'

'At present, I would have engrafted a doubt on your husband's mind as to your fidelity. But truce to such a talk as I have forsaken that path. Now, if you follow my advice, then, through you alone I may attain my object, while at the same time, you will be benefitted.'

'What name did you hear issue from the sacrificial Brahmin's throat?'

'It is yours. I bowed to him and sat down to divine his motive, good or bad, in kindling the sacrificial fire. When the ceremony ended, I asked him by trick of words, why he offered sacrifices in your name. A few minute's conversation convinced me that to harm you was the object of his sacrifice. I was, also, similarly disposed and I let him know this. Immediately, we struck up an agreement for mutual help and co-operation. Then he conducted me inside the broken house for special instruction where he expressed his real motive. Your death is his object but I shall reap no benefit from it. I have committed dark deeds all my life but I have not so far advanced on that sinful path as to cause death of a guileless innocent girl without any ground whatsoever. So I did not fall in with his view. At this moment you came on the spot and, might be, you heard some thing.'

'I heard some discussion of that sort.'

'That man took me for a fool and offered me some advice. I placed you in hiding in the forest in order to know the trend of the whole thing and give you proper intimation.'

'But why did you not come back again?'

'He said manythings and so it delayed me to hear his detailed story. You are sure to know him perfectly well. Can you guess who he might be?'

'My former patron, the Kapalik.'

'My faith! He it is.

'He gave me a detailed account of how he obtained you on the seaside—your upbringing there—Nabokumar's appearance—and your flight with him. Besides, he told me what happened after you had fled with Nabokumar. You don't know what it is all this but I will tell you everything in detail.' After this, Luthfunnisha told her every thing—the Kapalik's fall from the hill-top—his fracture of arms—and the dream. Kapalkundala was electrified to hear the dream and a galvinistic shock ran through her heart.

Lutfunnisha continued. 'The Kapalik is bent upon carrying out the orders of Bhowani. But, without strength in his arms, he stands in need of a second man's help. He knew me for a Brahmin boy and so he told me everything. I never had been a party to his evil motive though I can not believe my tempestuous mind. I can dare say I shall never agree to his proposal. On the other hand, I shall make every endeavour to thwart his purpose. I proposed this meeting in order to let you know everything, though I have not done this from a selfless pious motive. You must do something for me in return for the life I give you back.'

'What can I do for you?' answered Kapalkundada.

'Save me—forsake your husband.'

Kapalkundala did not speak for a length of time.

Then, she added, 'Where shall I go by renouncing my husband?'

'Into an unknown country—far away. I shall give you palace—wealth—servants—and servantmaids and you will spend your days like a princess.'

Kapalkundala again set about thinking. Her mind's eye swept all over the wide wide world but could not see any familiar face there. She looked into her heart but, strange! she could not find Nabokumar there. Then why on earth should she be a thorn in the path of Luthfunnisha's happiness?

So she said to Luthfunnisha, 'I can't realise now whether you have bestowed any benefit upon me. I don't care for your palace—wealth—land—servants and servant-maids. But why should I stand in the way of your happiness? God speed you success! From tomorrow, you shall hear no more of this wrong-doer. A forest-wanderer had I been and a forest-wanderer shall I be.'

Luthfunnisha was struck to hear this as she never looked for such a prompt assent. Charmed with the reply, she began, 'Sister, live long!—you have given me a new life. But I shall never allow you to go away in a helpless condition. Go forth with a trusty clever servant whom I shall send you tomorrow morning. There is a lady friend of mine who holds a high position in Burdwan. She will supply your every want and necessity.'

Luthfunuisha and Kapalkundala were so deep in conversation that they could not look there were breakers ahead. Neither of them could see that Nabokumar and the Kapalik, standing by the pathway that ran from the sheltering place, were darting fierce glances at them.

Nabokumar and the Kapalik simply looked on at them as, unfortunately, due to distance, they could not hear a word of the conversation. If men's ears could hear as much as men's eyes can see, who knows whether the load of human misery would have become all the more light or heavy! This earth is God's strange handiwork.

Nabokumar saw that Kapalkundala's untied hair fell across her back in profusion. She used to never braid her hair only when she was on her own. Besides, he saw her mass of hair, sweeping off the back of the Brahmin youth, intermingled with his side locks. At this, his knees involuntarily bent together and, slowly and gradually, he sat himself down on the earth.

When the Kapalik noticed it, he took out a coconut shell that was fastened on his girdle and said 'My son, you are losing strength. Drink this heroic medicine which is Bhowani's offering as this will restore your strength.'

The Kapalik held up the vessel near Nabokumar's lips whereupon he drank off the contents at a draught and thus quenched his thirst. He knew not that the sweet drink was brewed by the Kapalik's own hands and so was a wine of terrible strength. The stimulant gave him power.

On the otherhand, Luthfunnisha softly said to Kapalkundala, 'Sister, it is not in my power to requite the good you have done me. But I will think it a happiness if I get a niche in your heart. I have heard the ornaments, I made you a present of, you have given to the poor. I have nothing valuable on my person now. I have brought a ring concealed under the hair of my head with some ulterior object for tomorrow's use. But, God willing, I am spared the ill-use of it. Keep this ring—treat it as a souvenir—and remember your Javan sister afterwards. If husband questions you, today, about this ring tell him you have received it from Luthfunnisha, So saying, Luthfunnisha took out a costly ring from her finger and handed it to Kapalkundala. Nabokumar saw all this and, though under the firm grip of the Kapalik, he trembled from head to foot. The Kapalik gave him another dose of that strong new wine which directly went up to his head. The wine killed all his best instincts and put out the little spark of humanity left in him.

Kapalkundala took leave of Luthfunnisha and went homeward. Subsequently, Nabokumar and the Kapalik followed her along an alley, unobserved by Luthfunnisha.

8

HOMEWARD

Slowly and wearily Kapalkundala turned her steps homeward. Slowly and wearily she plodded her way back. The reason was she had been wrapt up in deep thought and meditation. The news of Luthfunnisha wrought a change in the stream of her thoughts. She was ready for self-sacrifice. Self-sacrifice for whom?—for Luthfunnisha?—oh, No!

Kapalkundala was by nature endowed with a Tantrick's instincts. As the Tantrick always feels remorseless in sacrificing other's lives to earn the good graces of the Kalika, so Kapalkundala was ever ready to lay down her own life for the same purpose. It was not like the Kapalik that her whole existence was treated as a mere abstraction for the attainment of divine favour. But the perception of the practice of piety and devotion to the Divine Energy as manifest in Kalika with her own eyes and ears, by night and day, as well as her habitual religious observances inspired in her a considerable portion of her reverential feelings towards the deity. She conceived the idea of Kali as the ruler of the creation and the bestower of salvation. Imbued with soft tender feelings, she could not bear to see the altar of the goddes dyed red in human blood. But, in no other particulars, would she permit of any breach of observance. That goddess—the ruler of the universe—the dispenser of joys and sorrows—and the giver of final beatitude—now bade her in a dream to sacrifice her own life. Why would she not carry out her behest?

You or I do not court death. We are happy despite what we say to the contrary in a fit of petulance. We move in grooves and spin in this world in quest of happiness and not of sorrow. If ever the consequences of our action defeat our expectations we bawl out life is a misery. Then the conclusion is that sorrow is an exception and not the rule. You and I enjoy happiness and that happiness binds us to the world and makes us loth to leave it. Love is the strongest bond of life. But Kapalkundala had not that binding—in fact she had no binding at all. What else was there, then, to hold her back?

That thing is irresistible in its course which knows no check. When a stream leaps down from the mountain side who is there to stem its flow? Once the air is set in motion who can prevent its blowing. When Kapalkundala lost the equanimity of her mind who would restore its equilibrium? When once the young tusker gets infuriated who can quiet it down?

Kapalkundala questioned her heart, 'Why should I not consecrate this fleshy body at the feet of the Goddess? What shall I do with this gross mass made up of five elements?' She put the question but could not receive any clear reply. Our body has a tie of its own even when life loses all its bindings.

Kapalkundala moved onward, her heart heavy with gloomy thoughts. When human mind is under the sway of some powerful emotion that blots out the sense-perception of the outer world, then preternatural things sometime visualise before the eyes. Such was the case with Kapalkundala.

She seemed to hear a voice from above: 'My child, let me show the way.'

Kapalkundala startled and cast her eyes heavenward. She seemed to see a figure in the sky of the colour of newly-formed clouds. Drops of blood were seen dribbling from the human heads strung round the neck—human hands dangling from the waist—a human skull in the left hand—blood streaming down the body—forehead beaming with an ineffable lustre—and a young moon shining at the corner of the brilliant eyes—as if the goddess Bhairobi was beckoning Kapalkundala by raising her right hand. Kapalkundala proceeded with her face turned upward towards the apparition that were the complexion of new clouds and sped along the sky in front of her.

That vision set off with a garland of human skulls sometimes hid under clouds and at other times sprang to her eyes.

This was seen neither by Nabokumar nor the Kapalik. Nabokumar under the influence of wine that aroused his passion grew impatient at the slow step of Kapalkundala and broke forth 'Kapalik!'

'Anything the matter?' asked the Kapalik.

'Give me more drink,' said Nabokumar.

The Kapalik again administered him some wine.

'Is there any more delay?' asked Nabokumar again.

'What is the use of any more delay?' chimed in the Kapalik.

'Kapalkundala,' issued the thundering voice of Nabokumar.

Kapalkundala started at the sound. Of late, no body called her by that name. She turned sharply round and stood facing him at which Nabokumar and the Kapalik came before her. She could not recognise, at first, any of them and said, 'What are you? Are you the messengers of death?'

But the next moment she recognised them and uttered, 'No—No! Father. Have you come to sacrifice me?'

Nabokumar caught hold of Kapalkundala with a firm grasp. But the Kapalik in a tender trembling voice said, 'My child, follow us.'

So saying, he led off the party in the direction of the burning ground. Kapalkundala raised her face skyward and looked up where she had seen that frightful form speeding along the sky. Here she saw again that apparition in female form drunk with war-passion and mad for affray, a peal of laughter breaking from her lips, and with along trident directing her on to the pathway followed by the Kapalik. Kapalkundala, as one infatuated by destiny, silently went behind the Kapalik. Nabokumar, as before, held her fast by her hand and went along.

9

WHERE LAST RITES ARE PAID TO THE DEPARTED HUMANITY

The moon went down leaving the world to darkness. The Kapalik conducted Kapalkundala to the place of worship on a sand-bank bordering on the Ganges. In front of it lay another sand ridge of a bigger size where stood the burning ground.

Very little water enterd into the deep ravine between the two ridges at flood time so much so that it was left, high and dry, when the stream flowed back. Now there was no water in it. The side of the burning ground facing the Ganges was high and precipitious so that any one trying to land into the river risked a fall into the deep water below. Besides, these sand banks gradually worn away at the base by the wind-swept waves, breaking against their sides, sometimes, gave way and slipped down into the river depth. There was no light on the place of worship where a little fire was glowing on a piece of wood and the faint glimmer of that light only intensified the horrors of the dimly seen burning ground. Near by, was every arrangement for worship, sacrifice and sacrificial fire. The broad expanse of the Ganges spread out like a vast sheet through the darkness. The summer (Chaitra) wind swept over its breast with violence and the waves, leaping into fury, dashed against the bank, breaking in sheets of spray that leaping down ran past murmering thousand songs. Carrion beasts of various description sent up their loud wails across the burning ground disturbing the voices of the calm night.

Kapalik made Nabokumar and Kapalkundala sit on mats of sacrificial grass in the appointed places and set about his worship according to Tantrick rites. At the right moment, the Kapalik ordered Nabokumar to fetch Kapalkundala after giving her a dip in the Ganges. So he led Kapalkundala by her hand across the burning ground for a bath. Human bones lying about whitened in the sand pricked into their feet. A pail full of water broke against the feet of Nabokumar and water bursting from it ran down the plane. A dead body lay close by as the wretch had beed denied his last rites. The legs of both as they approached came in contact with it—Kapalkundala went past while Nabokumar trampled it. Carrion-beasts collected round it—some made at them, on their encroachment, while the rest kicked up a noise and fled. Kapalkundala felt Nabokumar's hand tremble on her as she was, herself, without a tinge of fear or tremor.

'Are you afraid?' asked she.

The fumes of wine were gradually working off in Nabokumar's brain and he gravely replied, 'Afraid, Mrinmonyee?—far from it.'

'Why do you tremble, then?'

The question was framed in a voice that can only proceed from a woman's throat—that tone can only issue out from a woman's lips when her heart flows out in tender passions at the sight of other's sufferings. Who knew such a voice would come up the throat of Kapalkundala at the last hour on the burning ground? 'Not in fear—I tremble in rage because I can not weep', said Nabokumar.

'Why do you weep?'

The voice had the same tremolo in it.

'Why do I weep?—how would you know it, Mrinmoyee?' returned Nabokumar, 'Had you ever upon you the infatuation of the glamour of a charming beauty?'

As he spoke, his voice was stifled with agony.

'Did you ever come to the burning ground,' went on he again, 'to pluck out your heart and fling it into fire?' So saying, he wept aloud and broke down at the feet of Kapalkundala.

'Mrinmoyee—Kapalkundala?—just save me. I roll at your feet—tell me once you are true to your love—tell me that and I will carry you home on my breast.'

Kapalkundala raised Nabokumar by his hand and in a soft voice enquired, 'Why did you not ask me that before?'

The moment, these words were said, they stepped upon the brink of the precipice. Kapalkundala stood in the front with her back upon the river that flowed only one step behind. The tide had set in now and she stood on the top of a sand mound and spoke 'You never asked me that?'

Nabokumar, like a maniac, cried out, 'I have lost my senses. How could I ask you?—speak—Mrinmoyee!—speak—speak—speak—save me—and let us go home.'

'I shall answer what you asked me,' said Kapalkundala. 'She whom you saw tonight is Padmabati. I never became faithless. What I tell you is a perfect truth. But I shall never return home. I have come to offer my body as sacrifice at the feet of Bhowani—and do it I must. Go home—I must die—and do not weep for me.'

'No—Mrinmoyee—No'—ejaculated Nabokumar as he held forth his powerful arms to clasp her to his bosom but he missed her on this side of the grave. A big wave driven by a gust of the summer wind came tumbling on at the foot of the bank where Kapalkundala stood and, struck by it, the top came down with a crash and fell into the river dragging Kapalkundala with it. The noise of the land slip met the ear of Nabokumar who also saw Kapalkundala disappear under water. Quick as a flash, Nabokumar plunged into the water. He was not a bad swimmer so he swam long and hard in search of Kapalkundala. He could not find her, so he himself never rose.

Tossed, up and down, by a high summer wind that blew across the river, the bodies of Kapalkundala and Nabokumar floated down the stream of the ever-flowing Ganges—where who can say?

Made in the USA
Monee, IL
03 May 2026

49438755R00305